PowerPivot for Business Intelligence Using Excel and SharePoint

Barry Ralston

Apress®

PowerPivot for Business Intelligence Using Excel and SharePoint

ISBN-13 (pbk): 978-1-4302-3380-0

ISBN-13 (electronic): 978-1-4302-3381-7

President and Publisher: Paul Manning
Lead Editor: Jonathan Gennick
Technical Reviewer: Vidya Vrat Agarwal and Rodney Landrum
Editorial Board: Steve Anglin, Mark Beckner, Ewan Buckingham, Gary Cornell, Jonathan Gennick, Jonathan Hassell, Michelle Lowman, Matthew Moodie, Jeff Olson, Jeffrey Pepper, Frank Pohlmann, Douglas Pundick, Ben Renow-Clarke, Dominic Shakeshaft, Matt Wade, Tom Welsh
Coordinating Editor: Anita Castro
Copy Editor: Mary Ann Fugate and Heather Lang
Compositor: Richard Ables
Indexer: BIM Indexing & Proofreading Services
Cover Designer: Anna Ishchenko

Distributed to the book trade worldwide by Springer Science+Business Media, LLC., 233 Spring Street, 6th Floor, New York, NY 10013. Phone 1-800-SPRINGER, fax (201) 348-4505, e-mail orders-ny@springer-sbm.com, or visit www.springeronline.com.

For information on translations, please e-mail rights@apress.com, or visit www.apress.com.

Apress and friends of ED books may be purchased in bulk for academic, corporate, or promotional use. eBook versions and licenses are also available for most titles. For more information, reference our Special Bulk Sales–eBook Licensing web page at www.apress.com/info/bulksales.

The source code for this book is available to readers at www.apress.com. You will need to answer questions pertaining to this book in order to successfully download the code.

Thank you to my precious and wonderful wife, Kim. You are the love of my life, and all that I have done was because you have loved me and supported my dreams. To my son, Trent, you have been my greatest blessing. I love you and hope you see this book as proof that no barrier exists to fulfilling your own desires in life. To my parents, Beth and Fred, thank you for instilling in me the ambition to achieve, the knowledge that nothing worthwhile comes easily, and the self-confidence to do the work required. Thanks to my brother, Jeff—know that every day you are an inspiration to me. Finally, to my niece, Hayden, and my nephews, Hudson and Sullivan—playtime is back! Uncle Barry has finished his first book.

—Barry Ralston

Contents at a Glance

Contents

About the Author

Barry Ralston is the national practice manager for business intelligence at ComFrame, a division of Waltham-based NWN. Barry is also Microsoft's virtual technical specialist (VTS) for BI, responsible for assisting in Alabama, Mississippi, and northwest Florida in sales efforts, including customer meetings, software demonstrations, and proof-of-concept efforts.

About the Technical Reviewer

 **Rodney Landrum** has been architecting solutions for SQL Server for over 12 years. He has worked with and written about many SQL Server technologies, including DTS, Integration Services, Analysis Services, and Reporting Services. He has authored three books on Reporting Services. He is a regular contributor to *SQL Server Magazine*, sqlservercentral.com, and Simple-talk.com. His articles in *SQL Server Magazine* on building a DBA repository with SSIS and SSRS have been well received and implemented widely by DBAs around the world. Rodney also speaks regularly on SQL topics.

 **Vidya Vrat Agarwal**, is a Microsoft .NET Purist and an MCT, MCPD, MCTS, MCSD.NET, MCAD.NET, and MCSD and a lifetime member of the Computer Society of India (CSI). Vidya started working on Microsoft .NET with its 1ˢᵗ beta release and has been involved in software development, evangelism, consultation, corporate training, and T3 programs on Microsoft .NET for various employers and corporate clients. He is a published author for Apress titles *Beginning C# 2008 Databases: From Novice to Professional*, *Beginning VB 2008 Databases: From Novice to Professional*, and *Pro ASP.NET 3.5 in VB 2008: Includes Silverlight 2* as well as a technical reviewer of many books published by Apress.

Vidya lives with his beloved wife, Rupali, and lovely daughter, Vamika ("Pearly") and believes that nothing will turn into a reality without them. He is the follower of the concept No Pain, No Gain and believes that his wife is his greatest strength. He is a bibliophile and blogs at http://dotnetpassion.blogspot.com. You can reach him via email at Vidya_mct@yahoo.com.

Acknowledgments

I would like to thank Jonathan Gennick of Apress for shepherding an aspiring, rookie technical author through his first book, from idea to proposal to this final product. I would like to express my gratitude to Anita Castro of Apress for suffering with me through the final weeks of production. Rodney Landrum, your comments and experience as technical editor resulted in a better product than I could have possibly made without you. Finally, thanks to Doug Slay, Bill Craig, and Alyson Boyd, and the team at ComFrame for working to move the business intelligence practice to the next level.

Thank you, too, Donald Farmer, Jamie MacLennan, Bryan Smith, Bob Gilmore, Phil Sleboda, Bert Crump, Brad Allen, and Jonathan Brogdon.

■ ■ ■

CHAPTER 1

Getting Started with PowerPivot for Excel

A journey of a thousand miles begins with a single step.

—Lao-tzu

When I began working in business intelligence almost 18 years ago, the overarching goal was to create a subject-oriented data store that could be used by an ordinary business worker without SQL skills to answer questions and confirm hypothesis. Great work was done by my teammates and I to move data from data storage structures designed for transaction capture into dimensional models designed from the start for processing analytical queries. The analytical data store, in the form of a data mart, data warehouse, or otherwise will maintain a vital purpose in business decision-making.

However, there is more to supplying data to the business decision-making process than simply creating a central data store for analysis. Because of the time lag required to design, construct, and test, the data in one of these formal structures, sanctioned by an information technology department, will always lag behind the needs of users. Your organization's information workers, people for whom a part of their job is making decisions based on data they gather and format, are already finding ways to work around this lag and get their jobs done, via massive Microsoft Excel spreadsheets or Microsoft Access databases. Fortunate organizations have someone filling this gap, combining the data from the sanctioned, corporate database with other data to make informed decisions.

Because of the explosion of data available (cash register scans, weather trends, etc.), the job of information workers is becoming increasingly difficult. The information worker may be the CEO of a small business trying to forecast demand for their products to justify expansion or an accounting clerk trying to slice the monthly TPS report in a new way to understand software delivery issues.

Filling the Gap with PowerPivot for Excel

PowerPivot for Excel takes advantage of technologies that are a part of SQL Server 2008 R2, to enable an information worker to manipulate, filter, and sort millions of data rows on a commodity PC. Because of this, PowerPivot for Excel is uniquely positioned to fill the gap between the corporate data store and other related data, which is required for a complete decision picture. Data can be combined from any of the sources below into a single PowerPivot for Excel solution, for analysis without knowledge of Structured Query Language (SQL) or Multidimensional Expressions (MDX).

- SQL Server relational database

- Microsoft Access database

- SQL Server Analysis Services

- SQL Server Reporting Services (SQL 2008 R2)

- ATOM data feeds

- Text files

- Microsoft SQL Azure

- Oracle

- Teradata

- Sybase

- Informix

- IBM DB2

- Object Linking and Embedding Database/Open Database Connectivity (OLEDB/ODBC) sources

- Microsoft Excel

This variety of connections from PowerPivot for Excel to data sources means data that has not yet been included (or may never be included) in the corporate data store is no longer an obstacle for Information Worker analysis. Data from a corporate data mart hosted in SQL Server, can be combined with a text file from a supplier and a spreadsheet maintained by the accounting department. The only limitation on the Information Worker is the ability to relate the disparate sources; otherwise PowerPivot for Excel will connect to the sources and transport data into the PowerPivot data store.

What You Will Need

To begin working with PowerPivot for Excel, you first need to establish a development environment. Fortunately, the installation of PowerPivot for Excel is self-contained. The primary requirement for using the PowerPivot add-in is having Microsoft Office Excel 2010 installed. A wide spectrum of computers, from commodity desktops to high-end workstations can effectively run both Excel 2010 and the PowerPivot add-in. This makes a compelling argument for PowerPivot for Excel as a tool for business users who are not always on the leading edge of hardware acquisition. One of the most compelling demonstrations for PowerPivot for Excel is executing a sort on a 100-million row dataset deployed on an otherwise off-the-shelf Intel Atom-based netbook with 2 GB of RAM installed.

■ **Note**   Unfortunately, at the time of this writing, there is no way to leverage PowerPivot for Excel within versions of Microsoft Excel from version 2007 and earlier.

Other than having Microsoft Office 2010 installed, other prerequisites may only become an issue depending on which operating system you are using. If you intend to develop PowerPivot for Excel solutions using an operating system other than Windows 7 (or Windows Server 2008 R2), you will need to install the .NET Framework version 3.5, Service Pack 1. If you are running Microsoft Vista or Windows Server 2008, you will be prompted to install a platform update specific to those systems, during the PowerPivot add-in installation process.

Anticipating demand from a population of Excel users who may not readily navigate Microsoft.com to locate the PowerPivot add-in, Microsoft created an additional site for prospective PowerPivot users at www.powerpivot.com.

When you go to download the file, you'll be confronted with a choice: should you use the 32- or 64-bit version?

The 64-bit Decision

The most common reason for a user to install the 64-bit version of Excel, and hence the 64-bit version of PowerPivot, is to gain processing speed and capacity to work with large datasets within a worksheet. Because PowerPivot for Excel uses the in-memory SQL Server Analysis Services (SSAS) engine for data storage, the 32-bit version of Excel may allow users to work with the required data volumes, obviating the need for the 64-bit installation. The examples in this book were all created and tested using 32-bit version of Office. However, there may be reasons for using the 64-bit version of Excel in your specific situation. If that is the case, the 64-bit PowerPivot add-in will accommodate all the examples in this book.

▪ **Note**   The PowerPivot add-in for Excel that you will need is specific to the version of Excel you have installed. Microsoft Office Excel 64-bit must use the 64-bit add-in, and the 32-bit version of Excel must use the 32-bit add-in.

Installing the Add-In

At the time of this writing, www.powerpivot.com/download.aspx will render a document containing links to any prerequisites, as well as the 32-bit and 64-bit versions of the PowerPivot for Excel add-in. Choose the appropriate installer for your Microsoft Office version, and save the installer to a location on your PC. After the download completes, you may execute the installer by double-clicking it from Windows Explorer. The installer will prompt you for consent to the licensing terms and for a user and company name, before finally installing the software. You will know the installer has completed when presented with a dialog similar to Figure 1-1.

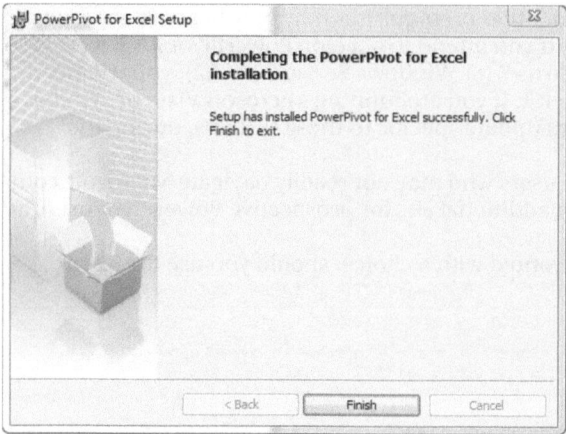

Figure 1-1. *Installation complete*

A Brief Tour of PowerPivot for Excel

With the PowerPivot add-in for Excel successfully installed, we can begin a guided tour of some of the new menus from within Excel. This section will help you verify PowerPivot is installed and working properly.

Your first indication that PowerPivot is available will happen very quickly during the Excel startup process. As you start Excel, add-ins configured to load during the Excel startup will appear in the Excel splash screen, though reading them may be difficult depending on your PC's speed.

The second and more easily spotted indication of a successful install will be a new menu item in the Excel ribbon. A new item, PowerPivot, should appear in the far right of the ribbon. If you have other add-ins installed, your placement may vary, but you should see an Office Excel 2010 ribbon similar to the one shown in Figure 1-2.

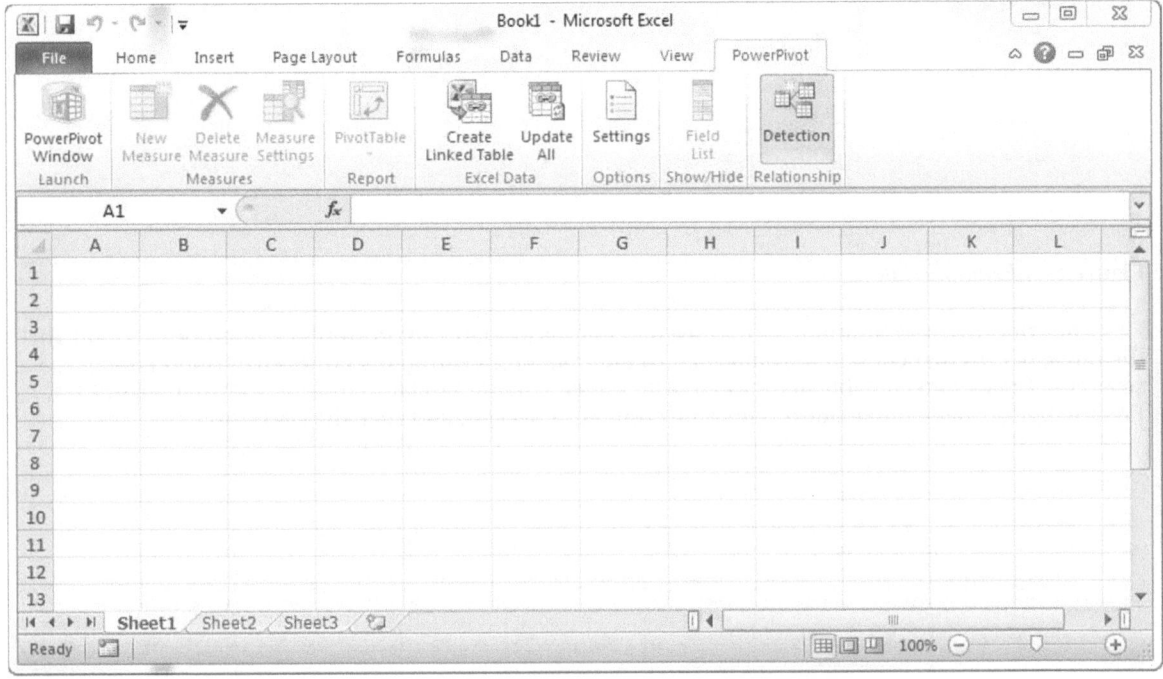

Figure 1-2. *Office Excel ribbon with PowerPivot*

A Trivial Test Case

Now that you have installed the PowerPivot add-in and seen the new feature from within Excel, we will create a very simple test set to ensure the software is working and to prepare you for the next chapter.

With Excel open and with a blank worksheet similar to Figure 1-2, type the following into the first four rows of column A: **Product**, **Widgets**, **Sprockets**, **Jigs**. Likewise, type the following values into the first four rows of column B: **Quantity**, **100**, **200**, **300**. Your finished spreadsheet should look similar to Figure 1-3.

.

	A	B	C
1	Product	Quantity	
2	Widgets	100	
3	Sprockets	200	
4	Jigs	300	
5			

Figure 1-3. *Example data*

Click the PowerPivot ribbon item to see the options available for PowerPivot operations. Highlight the range of cells that contain the data you just entered. From within the PowerPivot ribbon menu, select the Create Linked Table item, which will render a dialog similar to the one shown in Figure 1-4. Ensure the "My table has headers" check box remains checked, and click the OK button.

Figure 1-4. *Create Linked Table dialog*

If the installation of PowerPivot was successful, Excel will quickly load a new window, specifically created for constructing PowerPivot data structures. Figure 1-5 shows that new window. The Excel worksheet window is still open, but the focus for now will be on our data, now in PowerPivot. You are now moments away from creating your first, trivial PowerPivot solution using this linked table data.

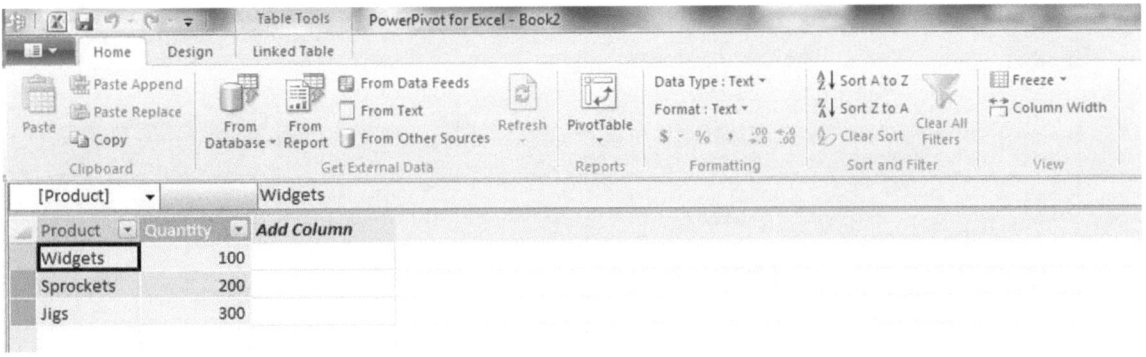

Figure 1-5. *PowerPivot window*

The primary purpose of this new PowerPivot interface is to create data tables and relate them for the purpose of analysis and creating custom calculations. To do any reporting and analysis of our trivial PowerPivot dataset, we will need to navigate back to the Excel worksheet. Returning to Excel from within PowerPivot is accomplished by clicking the tiny Excel icon in the upper left-hand corner of the PowerPivot window. While there are other methods, including cycling through windows using the Alt+Tab keystroke, using the Excel icon is sufficient for our test.

The Test Report

Now, from within Excel, our first test report from PowerPivot can be constructed. Select the PowerPivot ribbon item to show the PowerPivot-specific Excel operations. From the Report section of the PowerPivot ribbon, select the PivotTable drop-down and the PivotChart item. This operation is illustrated in Figure 1-6.

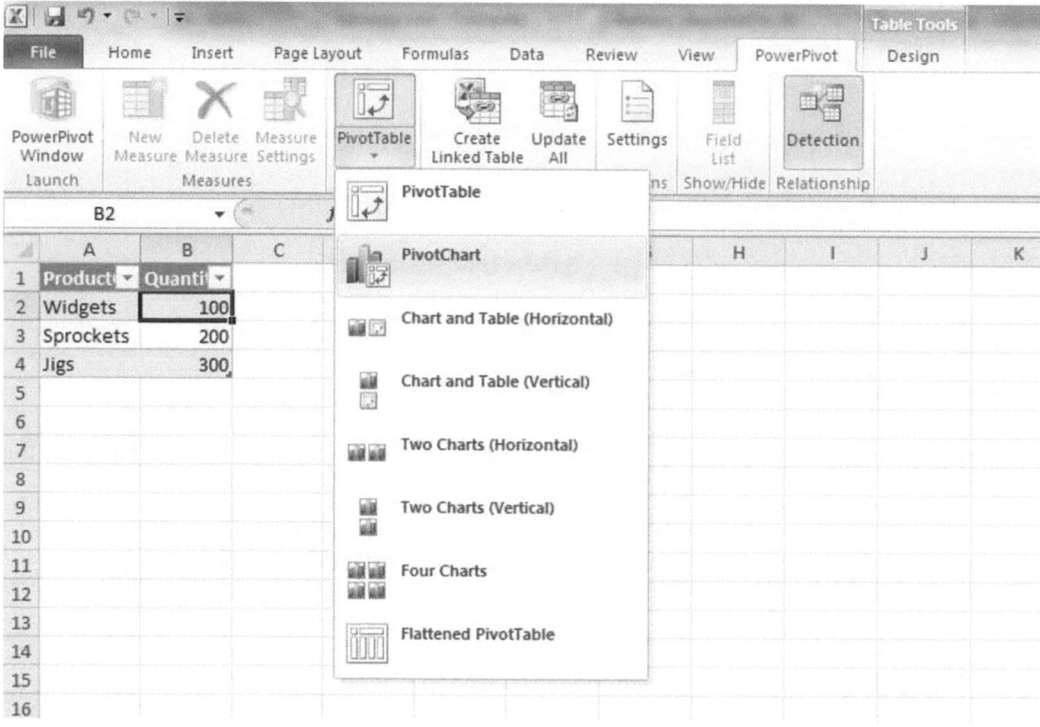

Figure 1-6. *Inserting a PivotChart*

From the ensuing dialog, select New Worksheet as the destination. This will render the PowerPivot Field List on the right-hand side of the worksheet. From the field list, drag Product into the area in the lower left-hand corner of the PowerPivot field list, which is labeled Axis Fields. Similarly, drag the Quantity item into the lower right-hand area of the PowerPivot field list, labeled Values. If the software is installed correctly and the instructions followed precisely, you should have a chart similar to Figure 1-7.

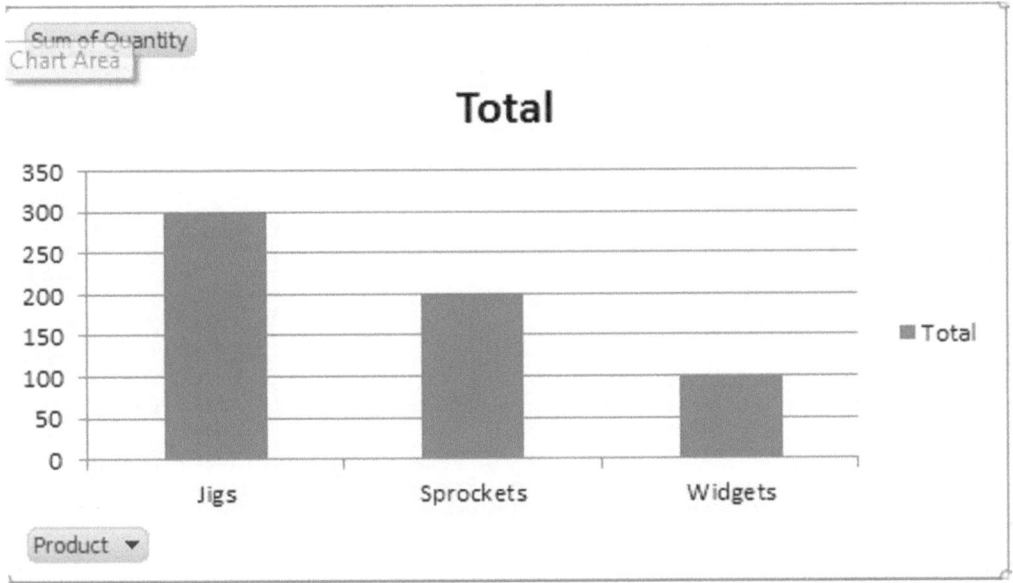

Figure 1-7. *Sample report*

Summary

This first chapter introduced you to the PowerPivot for Excel add-in and covered the following details:

- PowerPivot for Excel allows for the combination of related data from a variety of sources.

- PowerPivot for Excel is available in two distinct versions, 32-bit and 64-bit. The version you need depends on your version of Office, not on your operating system.

- There is no way to author solutions in PowerPivot for Excel without Microsoft Office Excel 2010.

Two distinct user interfaces, Excel and PowerPivot, are used to create PowerPivot solutions.

CHAPTER 2

■ ■ ■

Hello World, PowerPivot Style

The only source of knowledge is experience.

—Albert Einstein

From the publication of the first books on modern computer programming, the "Hello World" example has been used to show the fundamental, bare necessities of a language in the simplest possible manner. This chapter is intended to walk you through your first PowerPivot solution in the simplest possible scenario.

For this chapter's example, you will need access to a SQL Server 2008 R2 database, including the sample databases. Fortunately, SQL Server 2008 R2 Trial edition will be sufficient for the purpose of these exercises and is available for download at `www.microsoft.com/sqlserver/2008/en/us/try-it.aspx`.

Additionally, you will need the sample databases, which are not delivered as part of the SQL Server installation program. To install the sample databases, specifically the `AdventureWorksDW2008R2` database, you can download the installer from Codeplex.com at `http://msftdbprodsamples.codeplex.com/releases/view/45907`.

The Business Scenario

The reason for using SQL Server's built-in example databases in this chapter is to keep the example simple. The preferred use-case for PowerPivot is combining data from multiple, related data sources. However, to begin understanding the relationship between Excel, PowerPivot, and the data, this chapter's example will focus on data from a single database table.

Suppose you are sitting at your desk in the worldwide headquarters of AdventureWorks when you receive an urgent request to create a report of all-time sales for the top ten products by sales volume sold via the Internet sales channel. Fortunately, you have available a database (`AdventureWorksDW2008R2`) containing a table (`FactInternetSales`) that stores just such information for AdventureWorks' Internet sales. With PowerPivot for Excel, you can create the required report, with minimal impact on the database server and no knowledge of query languages (SQL, Multidimensional Expressions [MDX], etc.).

Assembling the Solution

Our solution will take advantage of PowerPivot for Excel's ability to load data from a SQL Server database to the SQL Server Analysis Services database installed by the PowerPivot add-in for Excel. After defining a connection to SQL Server, specifically to the `AdventureWorksDW2008R2` database, we will construct a table of Internet sales, summarized by product key. Finally, we will apply a sort and a value filter to get the top ten products, ranked by all-time Internet sales.

SQL Server As a PowerPivot Data Source

One of the easier data sources to set up for use by PowerPivot is a SQL Server database. After installing the sample databases, your SQL Server 2008 R2 instance should contain a database named AdventureWorksDW2008R2. In this section, we will configure the connection between PowerPivot for Excel and the AdventureWorks corporate data warehouse in SQL Server.

To begin, from a new Excel worksheet, select the PowerPivot Window ribbon element to open the PowerPivot user interface. From within PowerPivot, select the From Database item contained in the Get External Data set of ribbon items, as illustrated in Figure 2-1. Finally, launch the Table Import Wizard by selecting the "From SQL Server database" option.

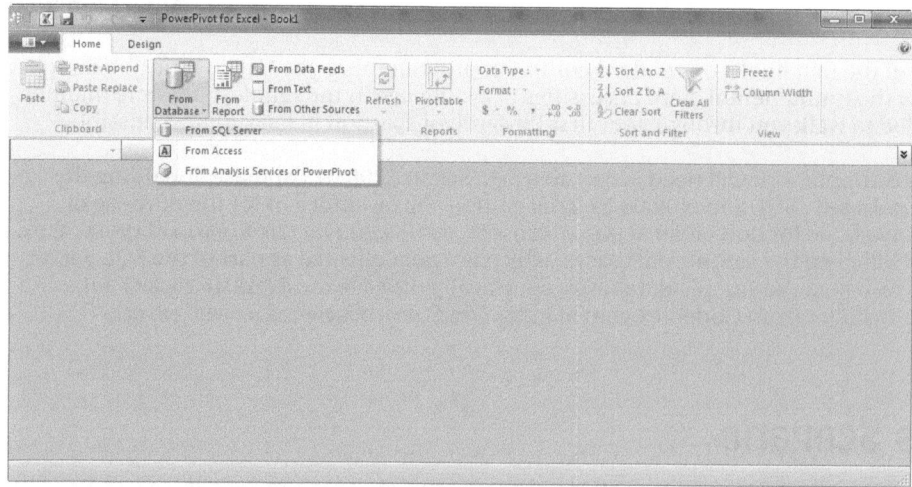

Figure 2-1. *Importing from SQL Server*

Starting the Table Import Wizard

The Table Import Wizard begins your guided path through the process of getting data from the SQL Server database table into PowerPivot's SSAS datastore. The first step is to configure the database server and other parameters to establish the connection between PowerPivot and SQL Server. To complete this first dialog, you need only enter **localhost** for the Server name, leave the default Use Windows Authentication radio selection, and choose AdventureWorksDW2008R2 for the "Database name". If you are utilizing a SQL Server database that does not reside on your local machine, you will substitute the server name and authentication mode that applies to your environment. Figure 2-2 shows these choices.

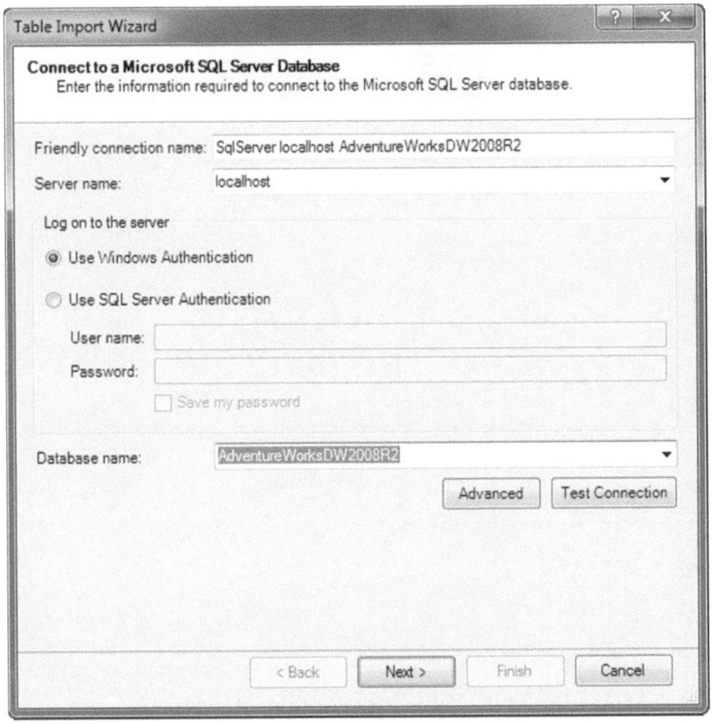

Figure 2-2. *Table import connection dialog*

When your Table Import Wizard connection dialog looks similar to Figure 2-2, click the Test Connection button to ensure you can connect to SQL Server and access the AdventureWorksDW2008R2 database. If you see anything but a "connection succeeded" message, verify your SQL Server Developer Edition and SQL Server 2008 R2 Sample Databases installations. If your connection succeeds, click the Next button to continue the Table Import Wizard.

Wrong data import dialog? If the data import dialog box has the title Data Connection Wizard, as in Figure 2-3, you have attempted to create a connection from Excel, not from the PowerPivot for Excel window. Click the PowerPivot menu from within Excel to reveal a ribbon of PowerPivot selections. Choose PowerPivot Window to get back the PowerPivot for Excel window.

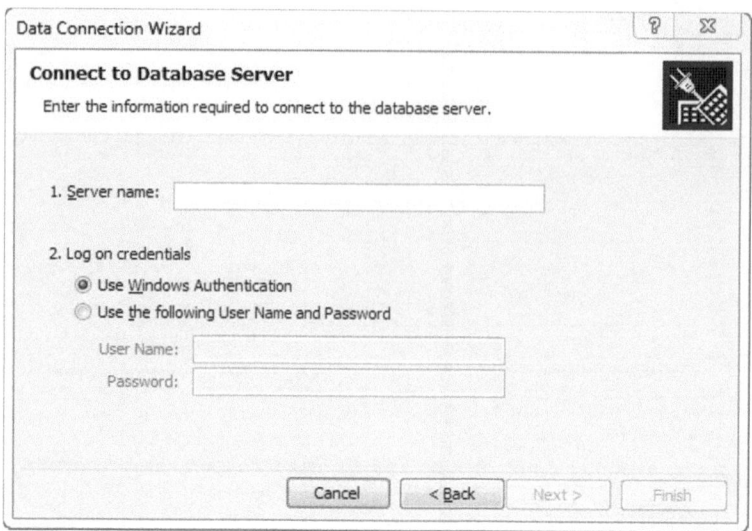

Figure 2-3. *Excel's Data Connection Wizard*

Selecting the Table

The next step in the Table Import Wizard is the selection of the table that contains the data we want to manipulate in PowerPivot. The default radio button at the next step, "Select from a list of tables and views to choose the data to import," will accommodate this perfectly. Alternatively, if you possess skills and experience with SQL, the other radio selection could be used to write a query as the source of the PowerPivot import.

At this point, a list of the tables contained in the AdventureWorksDW2008R2 database is presented in a dialog box similar to the one shown in Figure 2-4. Select the FactInternetSales table by clicking the check box as shown. The PowerPivot Table Import Wizard will generate a friendly name for the table, placing it in the Friendly Name column of the selection list. In your own solutions, you may want to alter the table name prior to import by overwriting this value. Clicking the Finish button will begin the import process; PowerPivot will load data from the table into the PowerPivot for Excel SSAS database for you to work with locally.

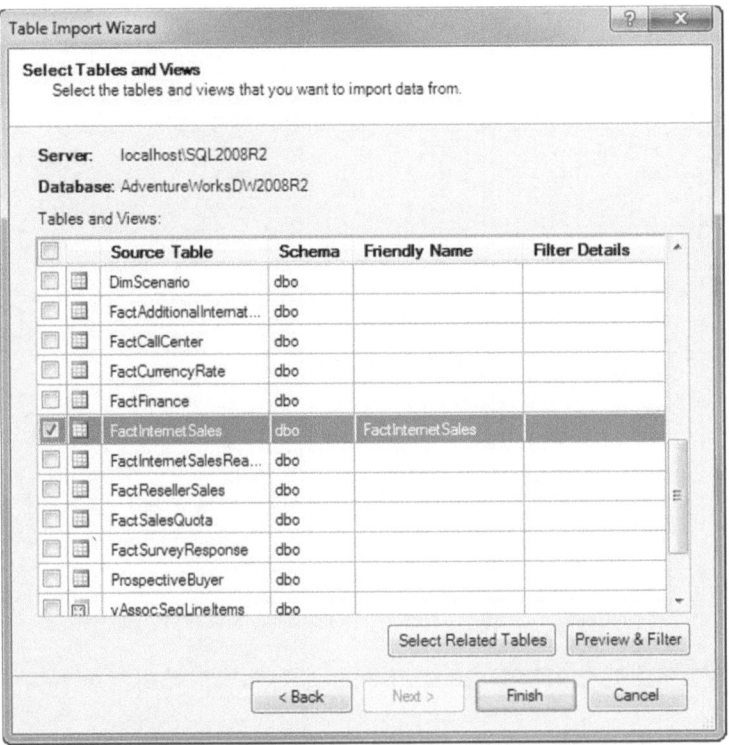

Figure 2-4. *Table selection list*

Monitoring the Import

The next sign of data import work being performed by PowerPivot will be a view of the import process, similar to Figure 2-5. When you begin working with other data sources, the Message area may indicate information related to any import errors that occur. However, for our sample dataset, you should see all 60,398 records successfully loaded.

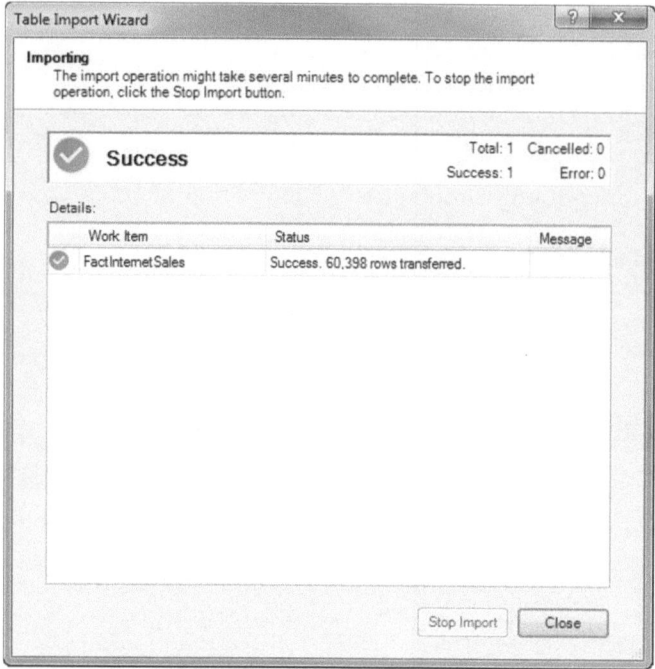

Figure 2-5. *Table import success*

Reviewing the Results

The PowerPivot interface will display all columns and rows for our imported data. The bottom scroll bar can be used to bring columns in the far right of the FactInternetSales table into view. Similarly, the right-hand scroll bar can be used to move additional rows into view. Alternatively, the record count in the bottom left-hand corner of the PowerPivot window can be used to navigate to the first, last, or a specific record number in the active PowerPivot table. The example FactInternetSales PowerPivot data table is illustrated in Figure 2-6.

In addition to importing the data into the in-memory SQL Analysis Services database, PowerPivot has also added metadata (column and table names) to the PowerPivot data table. With a SQL Server database as the data source, the column names for our PowerPivot table are identical to the column names in the source database. For instance, the first column of the FactInternetSales table in the SQL Server database is named ProductKey. Likewise, the first column in our destination PowerPivot table is named ProductKey. Additionally, the source table from which we imported the Internet sales data was named FactInternetSales. Therefore, PowerPivot's Table Import Wizard has named the resulting PowerPivot table FactInternetSales.

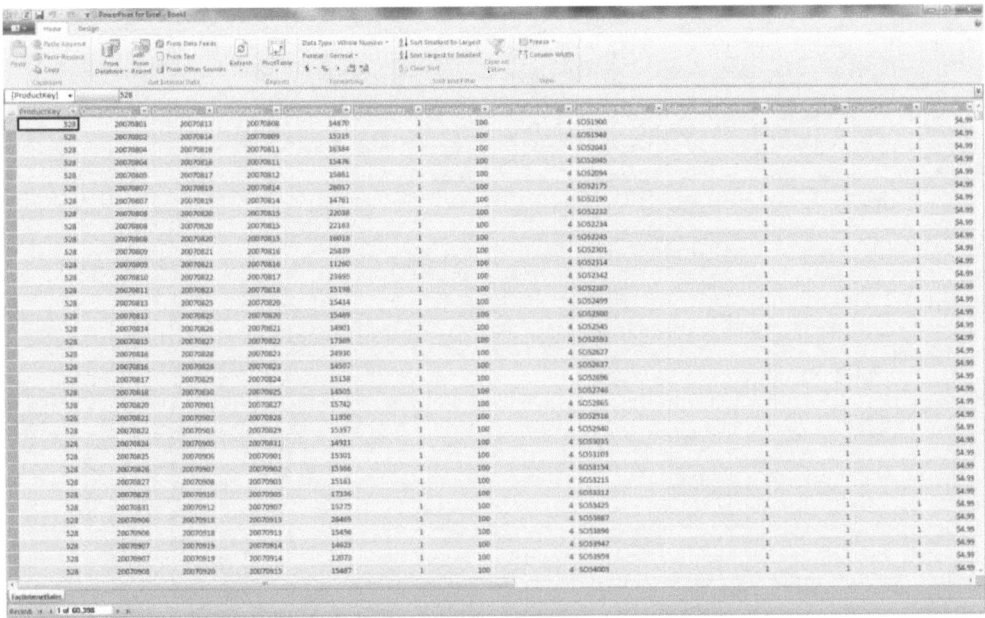

Figure 2-6. *Import complete*

Data Refresh

Because a connection to SQL Server was defined, this PowerPivot solution will have the ability to refresh the PowerPivot FactInternetSales table from the SQL Server database. This can be done within the PowerPivot for Excel interface, via the Refresh selection in the Get External Data area of the PowerPivot ribbon. Additionally, using PowerPivot for SharePoint's scheduled workbook refresh feature can import new data into a PowerPivot solution in an unattended, scheduled scenario (see Chapter 7).

Creating the Report

With the data from FactInternetSales successfully imported into PowerPivot, the report of top ten products, by Internet sales, can be swiftly created. Since the PowerPivot window is for interacting with the content and structure of data, and the Excel window contains the feature set for assembling reports and charts, we will need to be in the Excel window. The Excel icon in the upper left-hand corner of the PowerPivot window will bring the Excel workbook back to the forefront, allowing the creation of our PowerPivot report.

Within the Excel Workbook view, select the PowerPivot ribbon. From the PowerPivot ribbon, insert a PivotTable into the current worksheet using the menu selection shown in Figure 2-7. Next, place the cursor in the PivotTable; this will cause the PowerPivot Field List to appear in the right-hand side of the Excel window.

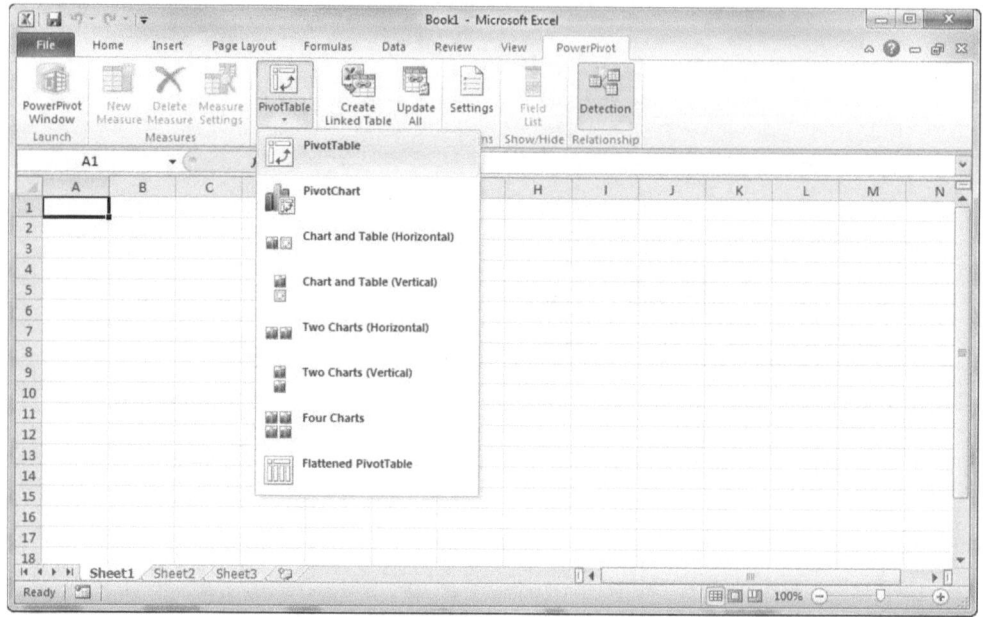

Figure 2-7. *Inserting a PivotTable*

If you have used Excel PivotTables, the PowerPivot Field List may be familiar. The PowerPivot Field List is the primary interface for placing data into tables (PivotTables) and charts (PivotCharts) within the Excel workbook. Moving data from a row to a column of a PivotTable is accomplished by dragging a field from the top window of the field list into one of the Row, Column, or Values windows within the PowerPivot Field List interface.

The PowerPivot Field List also contains features for the unique slicer feature of PowerPivot. A PowerPivot slicer is a user interface component that implements a data-aware means of selecting sets of data for analysis. Slicers will be described in greater detail and employed in Chapter 3.

Additionally, the PowerPivot Field List contains features for creating custom calculations using Data Analysis Expressions (DAX). Data Analysis Expressions and the related included functions comprise the language for programming PowerPivot calculations from both the data source in the PowerPivot window and the workbook via the PowerPivot Field List.

To continue the AdventureWorks Top Ten Sales report, drag the ProductKey from the top window in the PowerPivot Field List to the Row Labels area. This will rather quickly place a row for each of AdventureWorks' 158 products, with a row in the FactInternetSales table, into the PivotTable located in the worksheet. Similarly, drag SalesAmount from the field list to the Values window in the bottom right-hand area of the PowerPivot Field List. PowerPivot will respond by adding a column titled Sum of SalesAmount to the PivotTable in the worksheet. At this point, we have the unique identifier (ProductKey) for every product AdventureWorks has sold via the Internet channel and the total sales for each.

■ **Tip** Where did the PowerPivot Field List go? The PowerPivot Field List is visible only when a cell in a PivotTable or PivotChart is selected. To compound the confusion for new users, an option exists in the PowerPivot Ribbon to hide or show the PowerPivot Field List. This menu item influences PowerPivot Field List visibility subject only to a cell in a PivotTable or PivotChart being selected. If you have lost your PowerPivot Field List, first click any cell of the PivotTable or PivotChart you are working with. If the PowerPivot Field List still does not appear, verify that the PowerPivot ribbon selection for showing (and hiding) the PowerPivot Field List is set appropriately.

Narrowing to the Top Ten

As our task was to create a table of the top ten products by all-time sales through the Internet channel, we are only halfway to our goal. We have the ProductKeys, which for our "Hello World" exercise, we will assume are well known throughout the organization. Relating a key value to get a description is something we will cover in Chapter 4. We could, rather inelegantly, sort the table in descending order by the Sum of Sales Amount column, print the resulting worksheet, and draw a line to indicate the top ten. But this is PowerPivot, and we have more graceful means of accomplishing our goal.

Narrowing our list of all products to the top ten items by sales is a simple as applying existing PowerPivot functionality. Clicking the context menu drop-down to the right of the Row Labels text in the PivotTable will reveal a sort and filter context menu similar to the one shown in Figure 2-8. Selecting Value Filters and then Top 10 will predictably generate a dialog box prompting for parameters by which to determine the Top 10 in our PivotTable. PowerPivot, in its infinite wisdom, will determine by default how to sort the column, and the default values for the remaining settings will be fine for our "Hello World" example. In truth, PowerPivot will use any measure in the PivotTable as the basis of the sort. Because our PivotTable has only one measure, we are assured of using the correct measure. Clicking OK at the sort options dialog will narrow our product table to the top ten by Sum of SalesAmount.

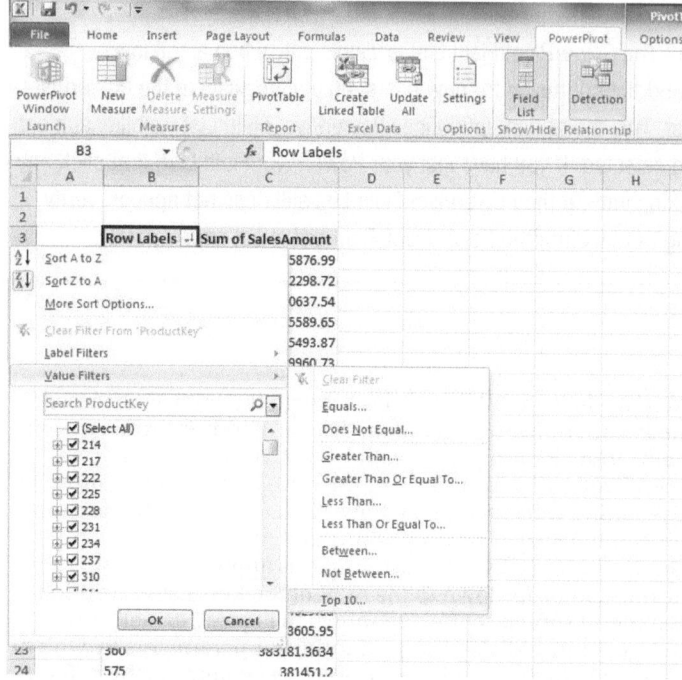

Figure 2-8. *The Row Labels menu*

At this point, you should have a PivotTable that looks similar to the one shown in Figure 2-9. Because this is still Excel, we can apply formatting to our values and change the column headers to make a more professional-looking report. In Figure 2-9, a number format has been applied to the Sum of SalesAmount column. Additionally, the column headers have been renamed by simply typing over the values to rename the first column to Product Key and the second to Total Sales.

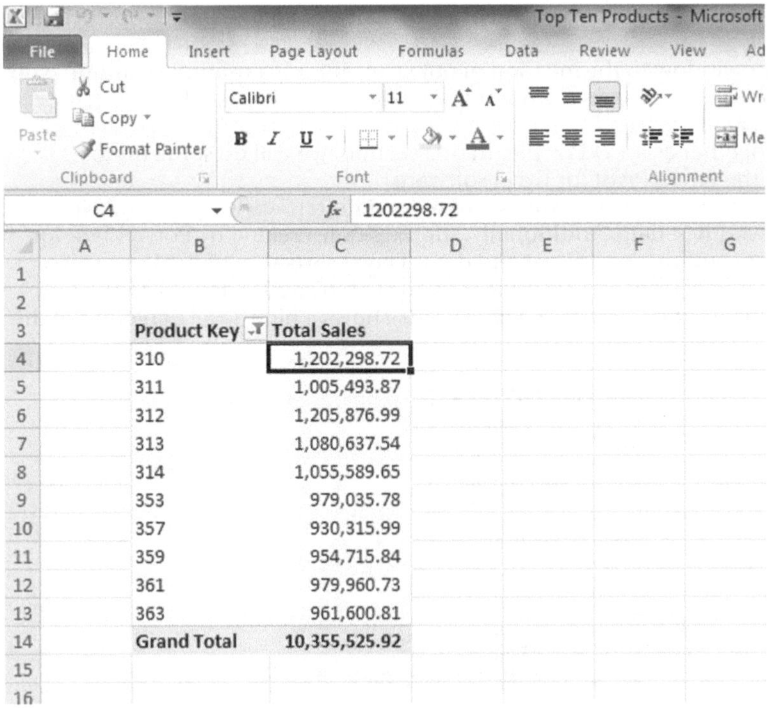

Figure 2-9. *Final top ten products table*

At this point, the PowerPivot for Excel solution can be saved just like any Excel file, choosing any file name within the existing limits of the Operating System and Excel. I have named the example Chapter2.xlsx, in my local My Documents folder. If you choose a different filename or location, make note so you will be able to follow along in the exploration of what PowerPivot for Excel is doing in the next section.

Behind the Scenes in PowerPivot for Excel

It has helped my clients to remember the Excel interface is primarily used to control and influence the presentation of data. Features for formatting values, as well as tasks to save, print, and share the solution, are included in the Excel interface. The existing Excel user community and the familiarity of these features to experienced spreadsheet users contribute to PowerPivot's ease of adoption.

On the other hand, PowerPivot for Excel is a tool for integrating and manipulating large volumes of data. Nothing short of a revolution in database software would be required to create a user-friendly tool for organizing (sorting, filtering, and calculating) datasets that could contain millions of rows, using readily available, commodity, personal computer hardware. The key to solving this problem is the in-memory runtime for SQL Server Analysis Services. This database engine is known as SQL Server Analysis Services, Vertipaq mode. In essence, as you installed the PowerPivot add-in for Excel, you created a specific type of SQL Server Analysis Services instance on your personal computer. The PowerPivot user interface is your window into your local, in-memory version of SQL Analysis Services and the principal data engine for PowerPivot for Excel.

By opening a Windows Explorer window to the location of our Chapter2.xlsx example solution, you should see an ordinary Excel worksheet file as far as the operating system is concerned. However, PowerPivot for Excel has actually created both an Excel worksheet and a SQL Server Analysis Services (SSAS) database file, storing them together as an .xlsx file. In this section, we will do some minor hacking to pull back the curtain on the PowerPivot for Excel software.

As a foundation, recall that PowerPivot for Excel consists of two user interface windows, one for the Excel workbook and one for the PowerPivot data. Additionally, the .xlsx file created by PowerPivot for Excel contains structures to store the required worksheet and data. The xl directory of the PowerPivot for Excel file contains a number of folders. However, worksheets and customData tie directly to the two roles of PowerPivot for Excel: worksheets and SSAS data. Figure 2-10 shows a high-level depiction of the xl folder structures.

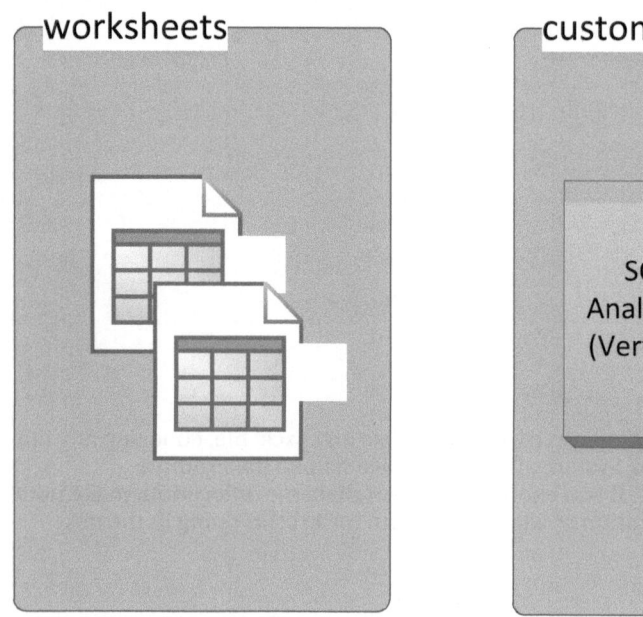

Figure 2-10. *High-level PowerPivot for Excel file structure*

To begin the exploration of the PowerPivot for Excel file structure, navigate to the folder in which the solution is saved. Copy the original file to a .zip archive, as the .xlsx format is really a compressed folder. In the case of our example, Chapter2.xlsx will become Chapter2.zip, and from within Windows Explorer, Chapter2.zip will be treated as a compressed folder. Opening the compressed folder and navigating to the xl\customData folder should produce a list similar to the one shown Figure 2-11.

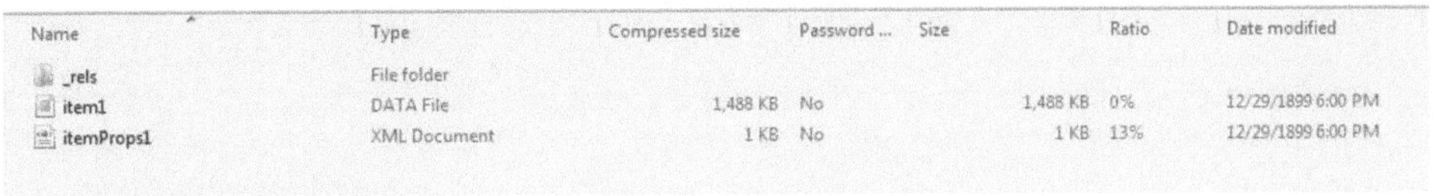

Figure 2-11. *A SQL Analysis Services folder*

The item1.DATA file is in actuality a SQL Server Analysis Services backup (.abf) file. However, because of the in-memory (Vertipaq) mode used by PowerPivot, this file can be restored only to an SSAS instance running in SharePoint integrated mode. Copying this file from the compressed folder into the backup folder for the local SSAS instance, renaming it to item1.abf, and attempting restoration will fail with an error message indicating the destination for the backup is inconsistent with the SSAS mode of the backup file.

These .DATA (also known as Analysis Services backup or .abf) files will be more useful as we progress into PowerPivot for SharePoint examples and establish the required development environment for working with SharePoint. For now, the goal is just to unwrap some of the packaging of the Excel Workbook and PowerPivot for Excel data that exists in the .xlsx files you will create.

Summary

In this chapter, examples of using PowerPivot to access and analyze data from a SQL Server database were explored. Included in this chapter were details on the following:

- Using the Table Import Wizard to quickly establish a connection between PowerPivot and SQL Server

- Navigating the PowerPivot Field List to create a PivotTable or PivotChart

- Using PowerPivot to accomplish complex sorting and filtering without using Structured Query Language (SQL) or Multidimensional Expressions (MDX)

PowerPivot for Excel solution (.xlsx) files are compressed folders containing spreadsheet definition and formatting as well as data definitions and connections.

■ ■ ■

CHAPTER 3

Combining Data Sources

Good judgment is the result of experience. Experience is the result of bad judgment.

—Fred Brooks

The principal reason for utilizing PowerPivot for Excel as an ad hoc reporting and analytics solution is its unique capability to combine large volumes of related data from disparate sources. The goal of this chapter is to give you the skills to connect to different data sources, relate the information from those sources, and reuse the solution over time by refreshing the data.

The taxonomy of corporate data can be organized a number of ways—for example, structured data, organized into strictly defined fields of rigid data types, vs. unstructured data in the form of Microsoft Word documents. Another way of classifying the data used in everyday decision-making is the idea of governed data in corporate transactional databases, data marts, or data warehouse structures. These governed data sources are generally managed by a corporate information technology resource and have established access and change control policies. At the opposite end of this spectrum would be ad hoc or ungoverned data. This is data required by an information worker for the decision-making process, but it has not yet met the threshold for inclusion as an element of a governed data source. From information workers' perspective, this ungoverned last mile of data represents the majority of their efforts to generate required information or insight. In my consulting career, I have seen incalculable numbers of ad hoc solutions put together by information workers to relate the governed to the ungoverned, from Microsoft Access databases containing exports of data (long since out of sync) with their governed sources to Microsoft Excel spreadsheets pressing the very limits of the software and hardware with data volumes. Fortunately, relating governed to ungoverned data in large volumes to analyze and report is PowerPivot for Excel's primary function.

In this chapter, I will present an illustration of combining ungoverned and governed data and techniques for combining data stored in a Microsoft Excel spreadsheet with data from a SQL Server database.

The Business Scenario

A new business day begins at the worldwide headquarters of AdventureWorks. You are just settling in with your first cup of coffee and beginning an initial scan of your e-mail inbox. Of particular notice is a message from your supervisor with a Microsoft Excel spreadsheet file attached. The spreadsheet contains 20 of your competitor's products that directly compete with AdventureWorks' products. A third-party service has supplied the estimated level of sales for the competing products. The accompanying e-mail message details your supervisor's need for a comparative analysis of AdventureWorks' sales with the sales of the market as a whole. The request goes on to elaborate that the creation of this analysis will be required on a weekly basis.

You know from previous experience that AdventureWorks sales information is readily available from your corporate data warehouse. However, how can you quickly and reliably produce this report on a weekly basis? You know there is no appropriate place to store the competitor products and sales data.

Configuring Excel As a Data Source

Our solution will take advantage of two PowerPivot for Excel techniques. First, we will use native Excel data as a source for a PowerPivot table containing competitor products and sales estimates. Next, we will use the existing data warehouse as a data source for a PowerPivot table containing AdventureWorks sales. Once the data is in PowerPivot, we can relate the sales data to the product names. Finally, the resulting PowerPivot relationships will be used to create a compelling sales analysis using a PivotTable and PivotChart.

To create our reporting solution, our first task is to create a PowerPivot data source using the Excel data provided by the supervisor. For our example, we have received a spreadsheet similar in format to Figure 3-1. For each of our competitor's top ten products, the table contains the AdventureWorks product ID, forecast sales date, the competitor product description, and the estimated sales.

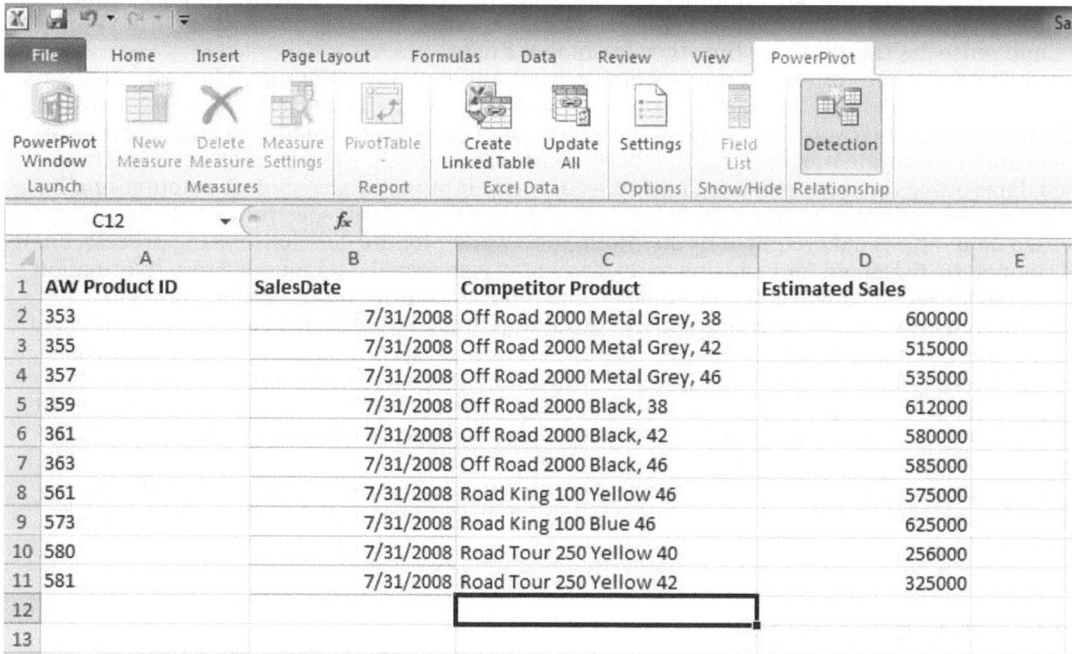

Figure 3-1. *Competitor sales estimates*

Creating a PowerPivot data table from data within Excel is a straightforward process. Here's what to do:

1. Open the supplied data file from the examples\Chapter3\Sales Estimates.xlsx worksheet in Excel.

2. Select the PowerPivot ribbon.

3. Ensure the active Excel cell (cursor) is within the table of values.

4. Click Create Linked Table from the PowerPivot ribbon.

5. If the cursor was within the table of data, PowerPivot automatically enters the range address of the entire table. If the range $A$1:$D$11 is not indicated, enter it in the "Where is the data for your table?" text box of the Create Table dialog.

6. Ensure the check box indicating "My table has headers" is checked.

7. Click the OK button.

PowerPivot will respond by creating a PowerPivot table containing the sales estimates data and changing the active window to the PowerPivot for Excel (data) interface. The new data table will be displayed, similar to Figure 3-2.

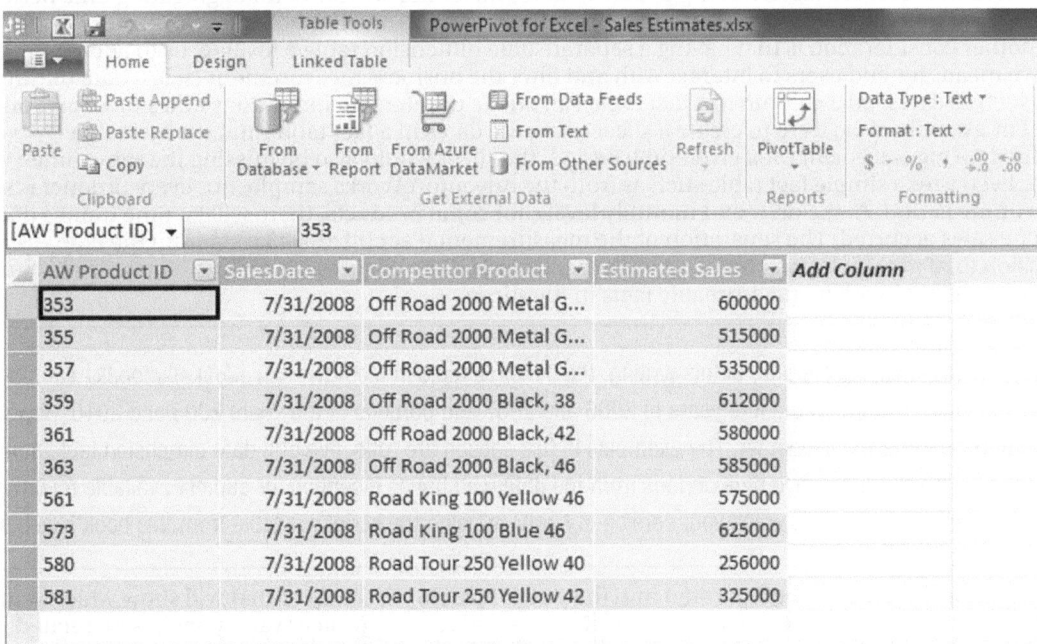

Figure 3-2. *Sales Estimates PowerPivot table*

PowerPivot for Excel has named the column headers with the names supplied in the header row of the source table. However, because we had an address of cells as the source, PowerPivot for Excel is unable to infer a table name. The default name for our table is TableN, where N is the number of linked tables created. This naming convention results in our PowerPivot data table being named a very unhelpful Table1. Additionally, in the table name tab in the lower left, a chain-link icon appears before the table name, indicating this table is sourced from a linked Microsoft Excel worksheet table. Right-clicking the tab in the lower-left corner of the PowerPivot for Excel data window will activate the context menu and access to Delete, Rename, and Move features. Rename the new table Sales Estimates.

Venturing into the Date Dimension

Since one of our requirements is to refresh this report on a weekly basis, it is reasonable to put in place some means of filtering the data by the date of sales order. If you completed the exercise in Chapter 2, you have already created a PowerPivot for Excel workbook that uses one of our data sources. This exercise will be very similar. For the sake of simplicity, the Chapter 2 example did not use multiple tables from our AdventureWorks data warehouse. In this example, we will use both the FactInternetSales and the DimDate tables.tables.

Understanding the Design

Why do we need a separate date (DimDate) table? The answer lies in the need, or at least the desire, to make the port execute efficiently. In our example dataset, there are over 60,000 sales orders represented in the FactInternetSales table. Adding a table of dates including attributes for aggregating time periods (months, quarters, and semesters) will allow PowerPivot to more efficiently access the data.

Another consideration is that having a separate date dimension table will allow us to add an intuitive means for end users to interact with and filter the business measurement (sales) data. Basing a slicer, such as dates, on a column in a fact table can create unintended limitations and side effects on the slicer. For example, if we were to create a slicer using the dates in a fact table, and the fact table contained no measurement for a given time period, the slicer would also be missing the same time period. Even with a simple fact table such as from the AdventureWorks sample, not every product is sold in every time period. At the daily and monthly levels, for some products, there will be time frames during which no sales occurred. The separation of the measurement (FactInternetSales) from the date dimension (DimDate) tables and building our slicer from DimDate ensures the ability to include all date periods, even those with no measureable facts in the slicers.

■ **Note**   Unfortunately, at the time of this writing, the DimDate table in the AdventureWorksDW2008R2 sample database, contains rows for the entire years of 2006 and 2007 and portions of the years 2008 and 2010. Rows for the year 2009 are missing altogether. The examples in this section are reflective of a date dimension table that would typically cover consecutive time periods from the data warehouse inception (or earliest available record) to the most current data. You may patch your version of DimDate using the script available from this book's web site.

Instead, a visual cue is incorporated into the PowerPivot for Excel slicer that will show which years (or other time periods) have no associated FactInternetSales data. A slicer value that has no related measures in an underlying fact table can be "dimmed" to indicate their selection would result in no related data. Additionally, slicer values with no related measurements can be moved to the bottom of the slicer list. These visual cues are illustrated in Figure 3-3. Both 2009 and 2010, because there are no related data rows for these values, have been moved to the end of the CalendarYear slicer, and their visual appearance is dimmed.

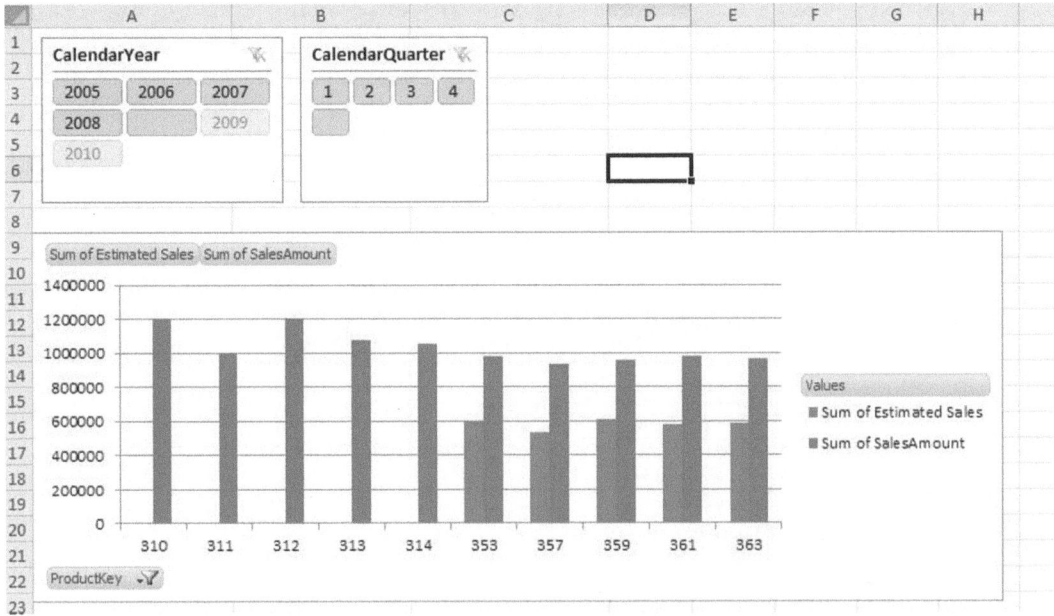

Figure 3-3. *Visual slicer cues|*

These slicer visual cues can be toggled on or off from the Slicer Settings panel. This dialog can be accessed from the Slicer Tools ribbon, which appears as the mouse is moved into a slicer. Additionally, right-clicking while in a slicer produces a context menu that includes the launch of the slicer settings panel. The Slicer Settings dialog is pictured in Figure 3-4.

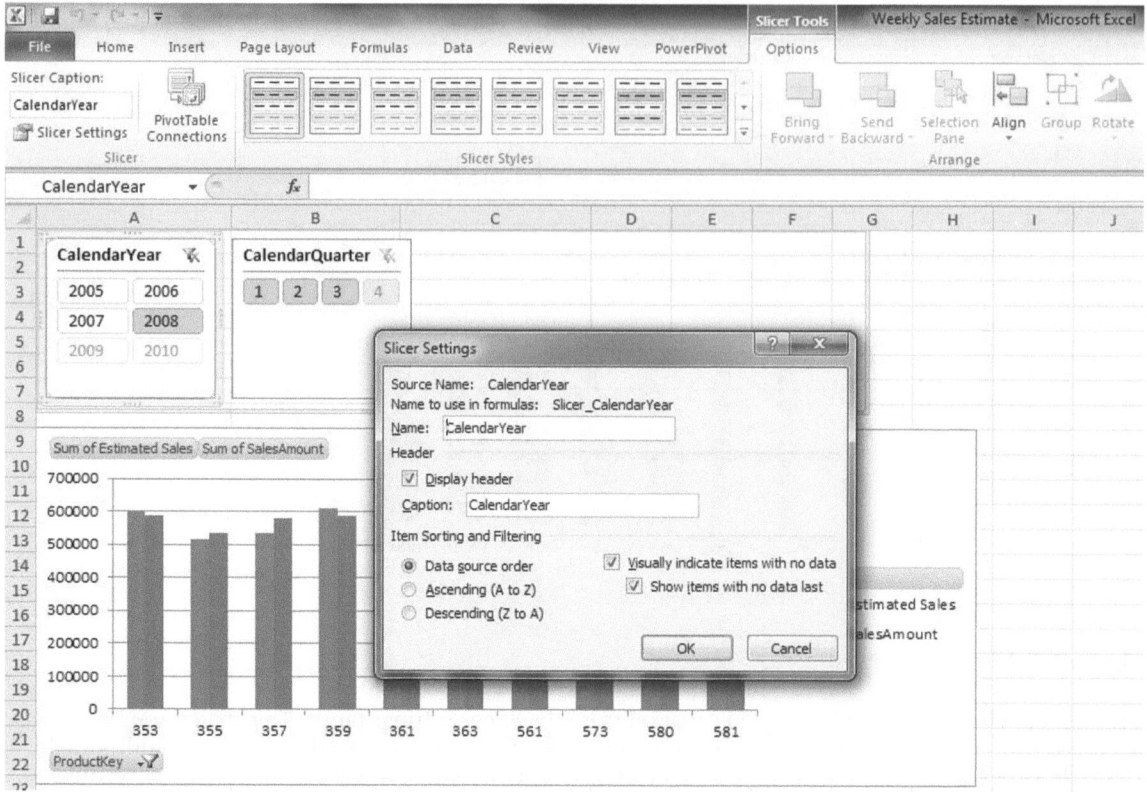

Figure 3-4. *Slicer Settings dialog*

The PowerPivot benefits from a single date dimension aside, a single version of the corporate calendar, expressed in the DimDate table. It ensures a consistent view of activity, across all time periods. In other words, by using the DimDate table, we have eliminated any chance that Fiscal Quarter 3 in the PowerPivot for Excel solution would be defined differently than any other report sourced from the corporate data warehouse.

Good Relationships

At this point, we have the estimated sales data in PowerPivot for Excel. You know from the Chapter 2 example that we will need the FactInternetSales table to have the actual AdventureWorks sales data. To complete our ability to analyze by product, we will also need the DimProduct table. If you recall, aside from actually having access to the data, the only other requirement for using data in a PowerPivot solution is the existence of a logical relationship between data sources. Because we have two sources, the corporate data warehouse and the Excel worksheet, we can be reasonably certain there are logical relationships between FactInternetSales and the dimension tables, DimDate and DimProduct. Because the sales estimate data is described by product and date, we will also require a logical relationship between the sales estimates data and both of the corporate data warehouse tables. Because the estimated sales data contains the AdventureWorks product key for each of the competitive items, we will use the product key to create a relationship from the governed data within the corporate data warehouse and the ungoverned estimated sales data. We will also create a relationship between the estimated sales data and the DimDate table.

To create PowerPivot for Excel data tables from the corporate data warehouse, complete the following steps from the PowerPivot data window:

1. Start the Table Import Wizard. Detailed steps are in Chapter 2.

2. From the "Select Tables and View" dialog, ensure check boxes are checked next to DimDate, DimProduct, and FactInternetSales.

3. Click Finish to complete the Table Import Wizard and populate PowerPivot for Excel tables with the corporate data warehouse data.

After the Table Import Wizard finishes, you may notice the word "Details" as hyperlink text in the Message section of the Table Import Wizard, as depicted in Figure 3-5.

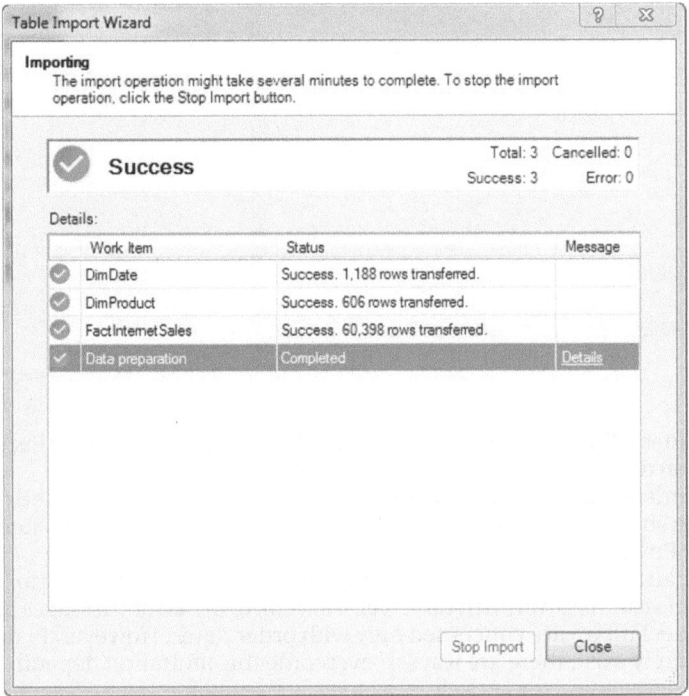

Figure 3-5. *Table import complete*

Clicking this link will activate another dialog containing an itemized list of issues with the Table Import Wizard. The dialog box you see should look similar to Figure 3-6. Of interest in this dialog are the two lines regarding relationships with dbo.FactInternetSales. Specifically, the messages indicate there was no error creating a relationship between FactInternetSales and the DimDate table using

OrderDateKey and DateKey respectively. However, relationships between these same tables using FactInternetSales, DueDateKey, and ShipDateKey failed.

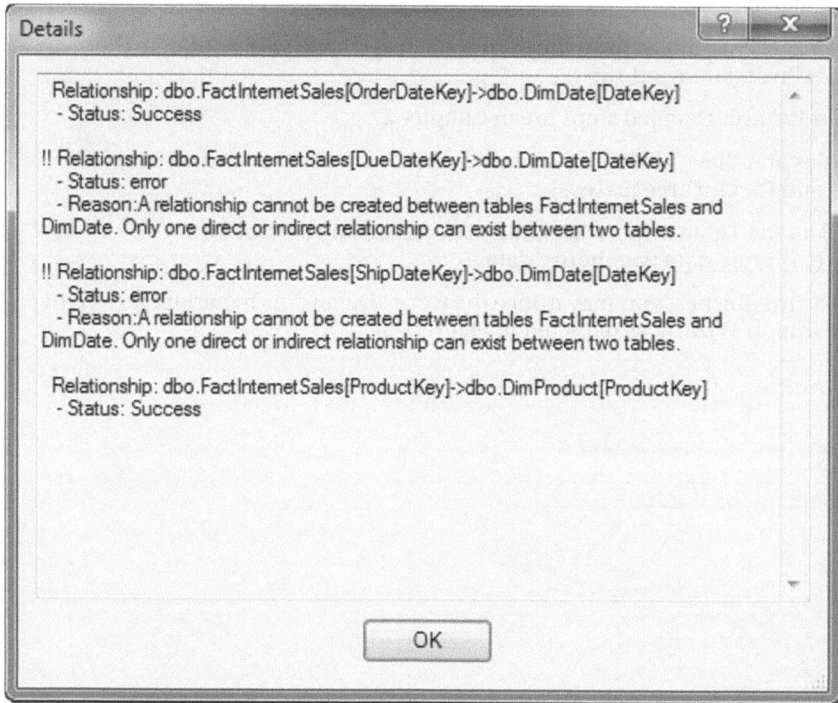

Figure 3-6. *Table import details*

This set of messages actually outlines a limitation in the inaugural release of PowerPivot for Excel. Only one relationship can exist between any two tables. The DimDate table in the corporate data warehouse is actually a role-playing dimension in FactInternetSales. That is, the date can play the role of the order date, the due date, and the ship date. In the data warehouse, DimDate is gracefully related to FactInternetSales three times. As the PowerPivot for Excel Table Import Wizard imports FactInternetSalesFactIntenetSales, it attempts to implement all three relationships but cannot violate the single direct relationship constraint within PowerPivot for Excel. Therefore, the error messages are created. In our case, we could simply declare we are concerned only with order dates. However, in the real world, where such magic wands rarely exist, there are ways to overcome this limitation depending on the source of the data.

As we are dealing with a SQL Server data source, the most direct approach is to import DimDate again, but with a separate PowerPivot for Excel table name. Again, we can leverage the Table Import Wizard to do the data lifting. Follow these steps:

1. From the Table Import Wizard, choose AdventureWorksDW2008R2 as the database.

2. From the select how to import the data, choose "Write a query that will specify the data to import".

3. Within the Specify a SQL Query dialog, enter **DueDate** (or **DimDueDate**) as the Friendly Query Name. This will become the PowerPivot table name. Enter **select * from DimDate** in the SQL Statement text box. Use Figure 3-7 as a guide to ensuring your Table Import Wizard is correct.

4. Click Finish.

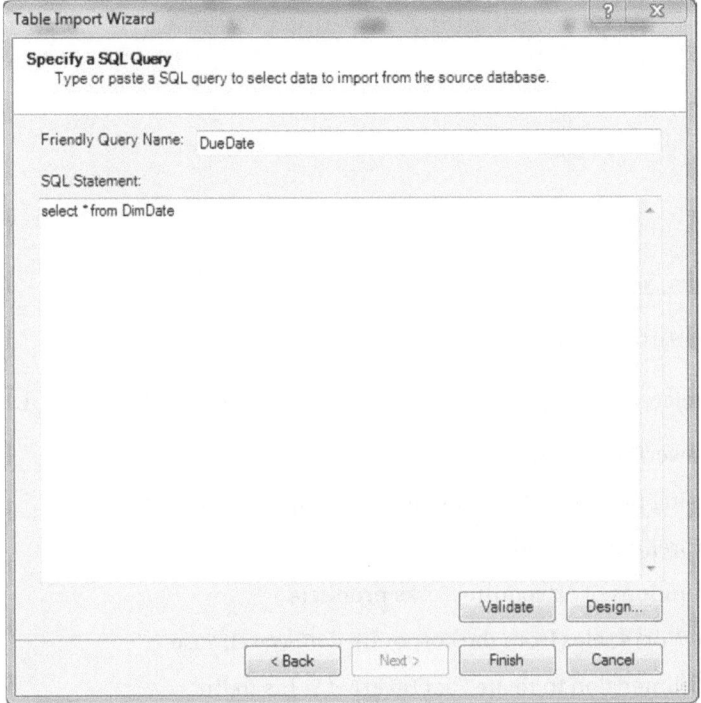

Figure 3-7. *Importing DimDate as DueDate*

We just created a new table, identical to DimDate but named DueDate, but no relationship was established with FactInternetSales. To use the new DueDate dimension within PowerPivot, we will have to establish that relationship.

As with most things software, there are multiple ways to accomplish a given task. As far as creating the relationship between FactInternetSales and DueDate, we will begin in the PowerPivot for Excel data window and then follow these steps to establish the relationship between the two tables:

1. Select the FactInternetSales table.

2. From the PowerPivot Design ribbon, select the Create Relationship item.

3. Complete the fields in the Create Relationship dialog as shown in Figure 3-8.

4. Click the Create button.

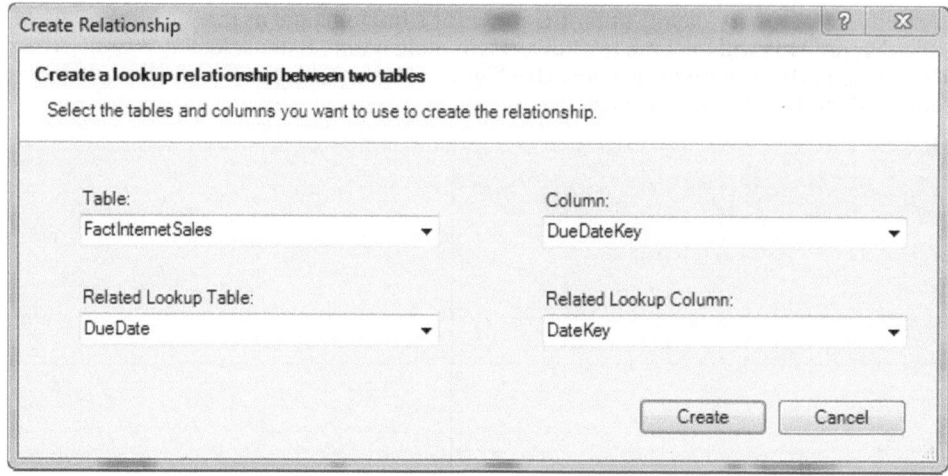

Figure 3-8. *Creating a relationship with DueDate*

The FactInternetSales table is now related to a copy of the DimDate table, implemented by our SQL statement in the Table Import Wizard.

At this point, we have five tables in PowerPivot for Excel:

- *Sales Estimates*: Data containing product sales estimates for competing products

- *DimDate*: The corporate data warehouse calendar

- *DimProduct*: The corporate definitions of AdventureWorks products

- *FactInternetSales*: AdventureWorks sales from the corporate data warehouse

- *DueDate*: A copy of the DimDate dimension to relate FactInternetSales to the corporate calendar by DueDate

However, not all of the PowerPivot tables are related to one another. In the next tasks, you will see how PowerPivot will strive to ensure correct relationships are put in place even as PivotCharts and PivotTables are created.

PivotTables and PivotCharts

The goal, the reason for putting together the data to this point is to create a compelling analysis that can be shared. PowerPivot for Excel exposes three major interfaces for surfacing data from our PowerPivot data tables. PivotTables are row and column cross-tabulations of PowerPivot data, based on existing Microsoft Excel spreadsheet formatting capabilities. PivotCharts are graphical views of PowerPivot data, based on existing Microsoft Excel charting features. Finally, a new element has been added for interaction with PowerPivot data known as slicers. This example will utilize both a PivotTable and a PivotChart. To begin, ensure you have navigated to the Excel Worksheet view, and not the PowerPivot data window. Then do the following:

1. From Excel, choose the PowerPivot ribbon.

2. From the Report set, choose the PivotTable pull-down, and choose "Chart and Table (Horizontal)".

3. Accept the default of New Worksheet from the "Create PivotChart and PivotTable (Horizontal)" dialog, and click OK. The result should be a view similar to Figure 3-9.

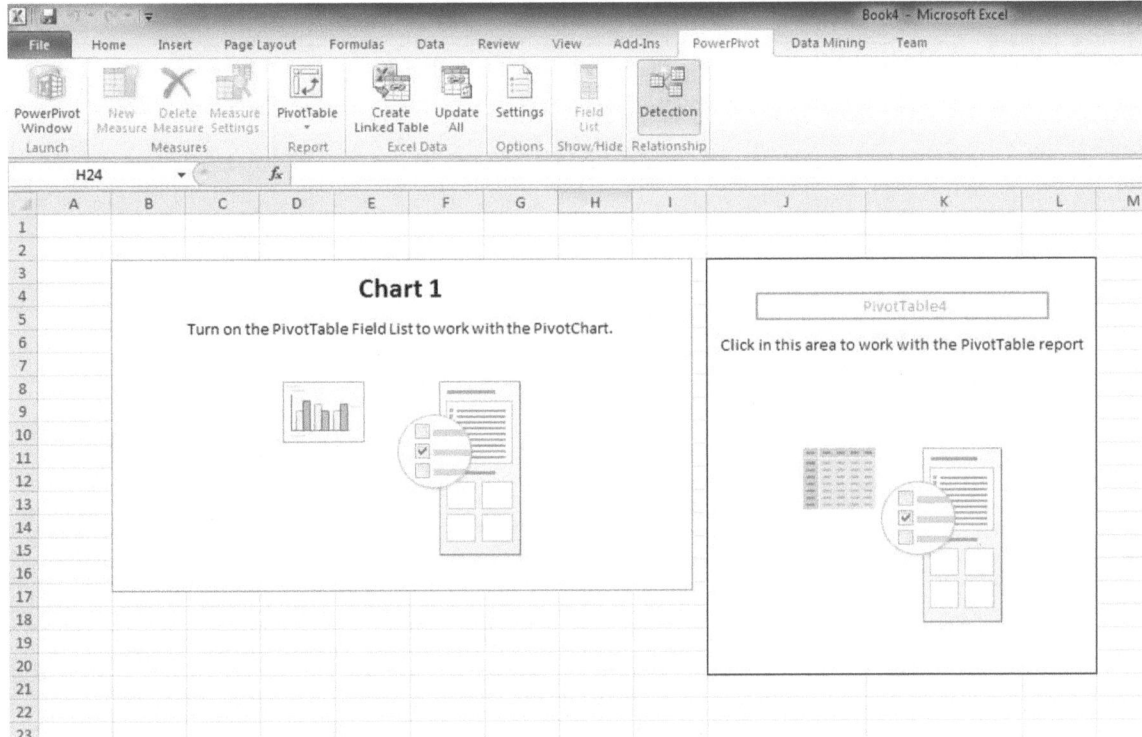

Figure 3-9. *Initial PivotTable PivotChart creation*

If the Excel cursor is not within the range of cells occupied by either the PivotChart or the PivotTable, the PowerPivot field list will be hidden. To begin exposing data in graphical form on our PivotChart, place the cursor within the PivotChart range of cells.

1. Because of the limited space in the PivotChart, we will use the ProductKey as the labels for the x axis of the chart. Drag the ProductKey field of the DimProduct table from the PowerPivot Field List to the Axis Fields in the lower left-hand area of the PowerPivot Field List.

2. Similarly, drag the SalesAmount column from the FactInternetSales table to the Values area of the PowerPivot Field List. This will default to a sum of SalesAmount.

3. At this point, a dizzying number of products are represented in the PivotChart. Reduce this to the top ten products by clicking the ProductKey context menu within the PivotChart. Select Value Filters from the context menu; then select Top 10. Accept the defaults to limit the chart to the top ten products.

4. Since the goal was to compare the AdventureWorks sales to the competing products, drag the Estimated Sales column from the Sales Estimates table. This should result in both a bizarre graph and a warning message from PowerPivot in the PowerPivot Field List; see Figure 3-10.

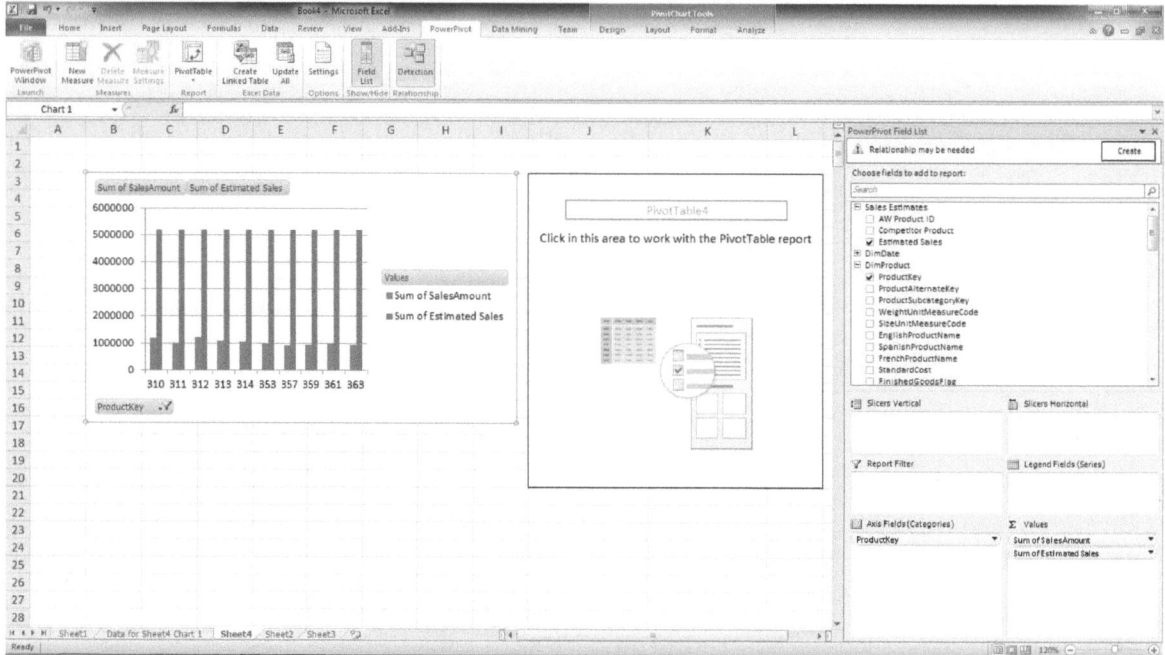

Figure 3-10. *"Relationship needed" warning*

Two things have occurred. First, PowerPivot has satisfied the query implied by the selections in the PowerPivot Field List. Because there is no relationship between the Sales Estimates PowerPivot table and any of the other tables, PowerPivot has responded with the total of all Estimated Sales columns, for all rows in the table. Essentially, a cross-join has been performed. Second, because PowerPivot recognized the absence of a relationship, we have been prompted to create one by the message in the PowerPivot Field List. To ensure we create the desired relationship, return to the PowerPivot data window, and do the following:

1. Select the Sales Estimates table within the PowerPivot data window.

2. Right-click the AW Product ID column header, and choose Create Relationship

3. Complete the Create Relationship dialog by using DimProduct as the Related Lookup Table and ProductKey as the Related Lookup Column.

4. Click the Excel icon in the upper left-hand corner of the PowerPivot window to return to the Excel worksheet.

5. The warning message in the upper portion of the PowerPivot Field List should now read "PowerPivot data was modified". Click the Refresh button. The PivotChart should look similar to Figure 3-11.

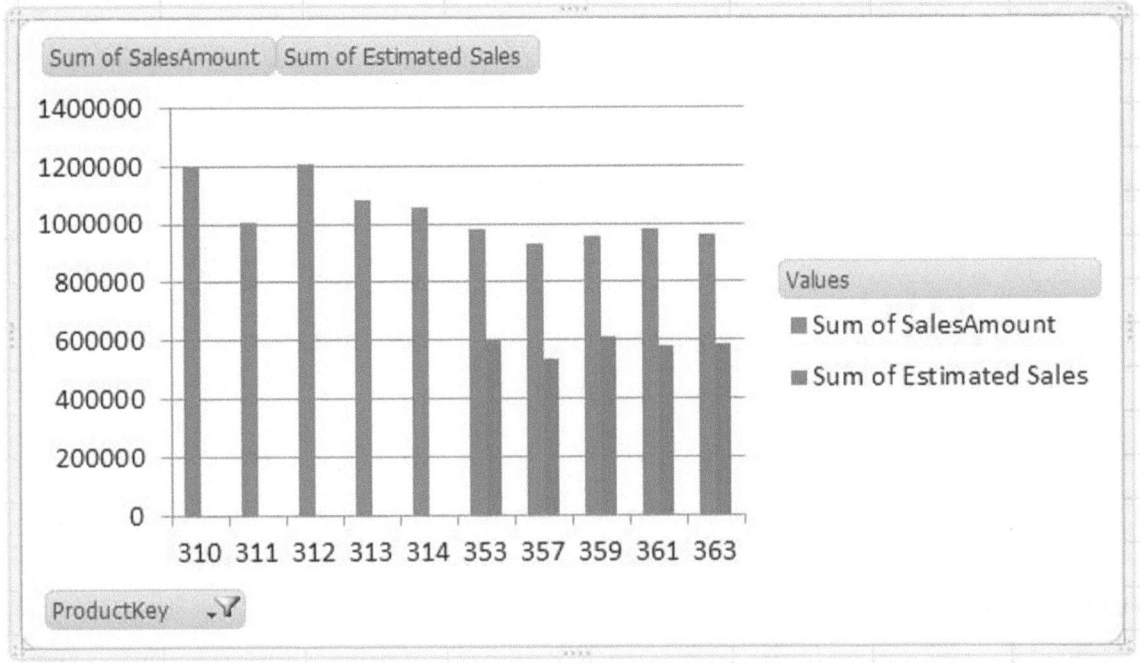

Figure 3-11. *PivotChart after creating a relationship with Estimated Sales*

Slicers

One of the problems with our PivotChart to this point is it includes all data in the AdventureWorks FactInternetSales table. We can both limit the data and greatly increase the reusability of our PowerPivot solution with the addition of slicers.

Slicers utilize data from a PowerPivot data table to create a reporting filter. Because, under the hood, PowerPivot for Excel is SQL Server Analysis Services, the underlying database engine can very efficiently create distinct lists of elements to populate a slicer, as well as rapidly enforce the filtering created by a slicer. To explore the functions of a slicer, we will add Slicers to our current example. Adding a Year and Calendar Quarter slicer is accomplished by the following steps:

1. From the Excel window, drag the CalendarYear column from the DimDate table to the Slicers Horizontal area of the PowerPivot Field List.

2. A list of all of the years in the database 2005 to 2010 will be placed as buttons above the PivotChart. Click the 2008 button.

3.   Similarly, drag the CalendarQuarter column of the DimDate table to the Slicers
     Horizontal Area of the PowerPivot Field List. It should be directly below
     CalendarYear. The PivotChart should look similar to Figure 3-12.

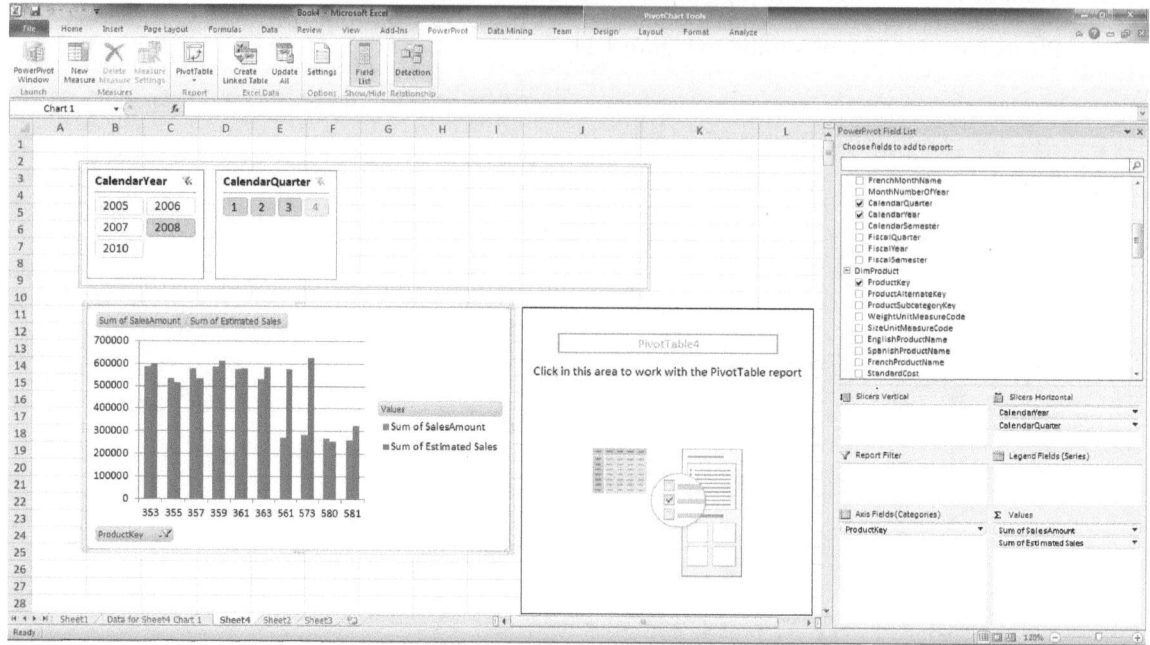

Figure 3-12. *Date slicers*

Slicers are related to one another through the underlying data. For example, because the underlying
database contains data only for the first three quarters of 2008, the CalendarQuarter Slicer reflects
Quarter 4 as grayed out and ineligible for selection. This behavior was outlined earlier in this chapter.
Additionally, slicers interact with the data as they are manipulated. If you were to click the Remove Filter
icon to the right of the CalendarYear Slicer label, the PivotChart would immediately return to the
previous state with all years of data in FactInternetSales being reported.

Slicers respond to usual mouse and keyboard interactions. Ctrl-click to select (or deselect) a single
slicer value. Shift-click to select an inclusive range of slicer values. As previously illustrated, once a slicer
is limiting data, the filtering can be completely removed by clicking the Remove Filter icon to the right of
the slicer name.

At this point, we have combined SQL Server and Excel data, added relationships to ensure accurate
reporting, and implemented a PivotChart and a pair of slicers to filter the report. What remains is to
embellish the analysis with a PivotTable and implement a method of refreshing the data without re-
creating the report each week, month, and quarter.

As we already have a PivotTable in the Excel worksheet, return to the Excel window to begin adding
data. Here are the steps to follow:

1.   Since the slicers affect the connected PivotTables and PivotCharts immediately,
     ensure the slicers have 2008 and all CalendarQuarters selected.

2.   Place the cursor in a cell within the range of the PivotTable.

3. Drag the EnglishProductName column from the DimProduct table to the RowLabels area in the PowerPivot field list.

4. Drag the SalesAmount column from the FactInternetSales table to the Values area of the PowerPivot field list.

5. Drag the Estimated Sales column from the Sales Estimates table to the Values area of the PowerPivot field list.

6. Limit the Products in the PivotTable by using the Row Labels context menu to report the Top 10 products by Sum of Sales Amount.

7. Highlight the Sum of Sales Amount and Sum of Estimated Sales columns to format with a comma and two decimal places. Your PowerPivot report should look similar to Figure 3-13.

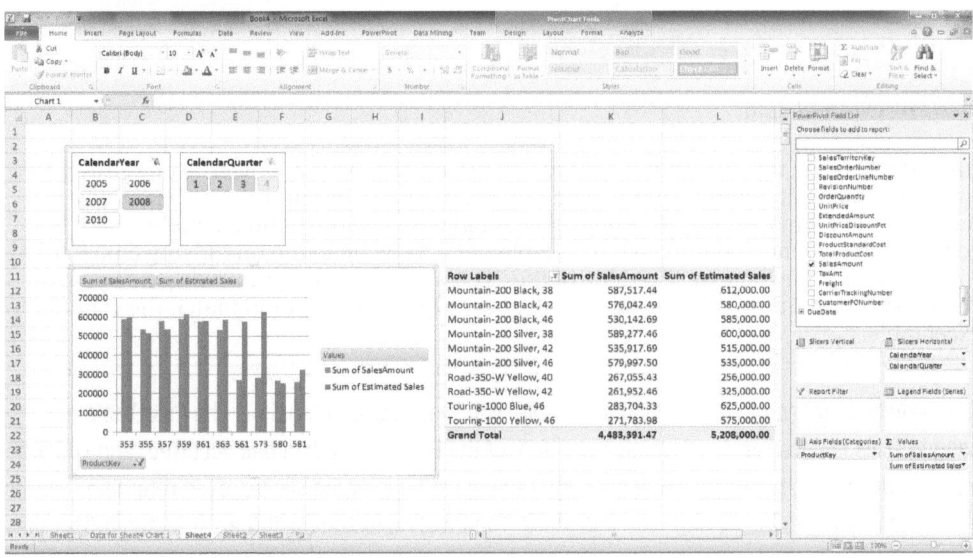

Figure 3-13. *Completed analysis*

Take a moment to interact with the slicers, making note of how the contents of the PivotChart and PivotTable change. Slicers, by automatically reflecting the underlying data, create a filtering mechanism containing values that are synchronized with the PowerPivot data.

Refreshing the Data

To this point, our example solution has imported data from two data sources and related the information for reporting. A report has been developed, and slicers were used to add interactivity. However, we still lack the means to refresh this data on a regular basis. As we have two data sources, Excel and SQL Server, the method by which data is refreshed is twofold.

First, the SQL Server data sources can be updated easily from within the PowerPivot data window. As illustrated in Figure 3-14, from the Home ribbon's "get external data" set of elements, the Refresh pull-down is used to refresh the data from a specific table or from all external (in this case SQL Server) tables at once.

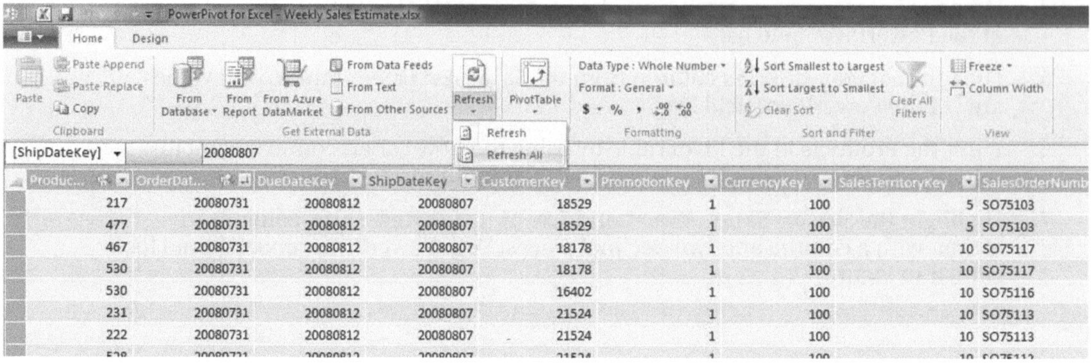

Figure 3-14. *Refreshing external data*

For the estimated sales data that was implemented as a linked table within PowerPivot, refreshing the data is dead simple. The default update mode for a linked table is set to Automatic. That is, any change in the underlying Excel table is immediately reflected in the PowerPivot linked table.

To experiment with automatic updating of linked table data, navigate to the underlying data in the Excel window. Pick a product, and change the value of the Estimated Sales column. Navigate back to PowerPivot, and the Estimated Sales column value in the PowerPivot table should match the value entered in the Excel table.

■ **Note** After successfully updating the PowerPivot data table, you may notice that neither the PivotTable nor PivotChart has changed. This is because no interaction or query of the PowerPivot data has occurred, and you are viewing a stale image of the data in the Excel worksheet. Interacting with any of the slicers, even returning them to original values, will cause a query to the PowerPivot data store. The PivotTable and PivotChart will then reflect the new value of the Estimated Sales column.

As a practical matter, depending on the volume of data involved, you may want to manually enter information into an Excel linked table. As our example deals only with the top ten selling products, we could easily maintain the competitor information in the Excel linked table over time, being assured current data from the corporate data warehouse was being used for each new weekly, monthly, or quarterly report.

Summary

The ability for Excel users to combine multiple, related datasets and create compelling, insightful analytics is the principal feature of PowerPivot for Excel. After completing this chapter and related examples, you should understand the following:

- The principal use-case for PowerPivot for Excel is combining data from structured sources (data warehouses, data marts, or transactional databases) with data that lies outside the administration of the enterprise.

- PowerPivot for Excel can utilize data from a number of sources, including data at very high volumes. The only requirement is a logical relationship between the data.

CHAPTER 4

■ ■ ■

Data Analysis Expressions

If you have built castles in the air, your work need not be lost; that is where they should be. Now put foundations under them.

—Henry David Thoreau

PowerPivot is uniquely suited as a business intelligence development tool in the ability to combine large volumes of disparate yet related data. To this point, our examples have steered clear of an issue that will occur in all but the most trivial business intelligence solutions: the need to create custom measures, or calculated columns, based on the source data. Recognizing this, Microsoft has included a set of functions, known as Data Analysis Expressions (DAX), capable of creating calculations that may not be present in the original source data.

The first case for utilizing DAX is to create a calculated column within a PowerPivot table. When PowerPivot data is retrieved from a relational database, a view or query can be used with PowerPivot for Excel to add a calculated column within the source database. However, PowerPivot for Excel can utilize many nonrelational data sources where creating a query or view workaround for a calculation would not be possible or practical. A trivial example of these row-level calculations would be deriving a month or day calculated column from a source column containing dates.

The other principal use of DAX is to create a measure from two (or more) separate data sources for the purpose of analyzing a business process. Because PowerPivot for Excel is serving as the datastore for separate but related datasets, neither of the inbound sets is capable of performing the required calculation.

As a real example that you can use in your own PowerPivot training efforts, consider data currently available from the Bureau of Transportation Statistics (BTS). BTS is a component of the United States Department of Transportation and maintains an exhaustive web site containing data for multiple modes of transport into and throughout the United States. For a frequent airline passenger for business, the air transport measurements available include two separate datasets of interest. The first is a set of data that details the number of passenger seats available between any two airports. If you want to know the number of seats that were historically available on Mondays in a given month, the bureau's site has a table with the source data. The second dataset represents the on-time performance for every airline representing more than 1 percent of all airline passenger fares for a given reporting month. As the examples in this chapter will show, this can be an interesting dataset to understand on-time performance among cities and airlines. More to the point of using DAX to create new measures from related datasets, there is no way to represent from either of these datasets how many seats were delayed for a given time period. Additionally, neither dataset in isolation of the other has the capability to answer questions around the load factors along a given route. This concept is illustrated in Figure 4-1 below.

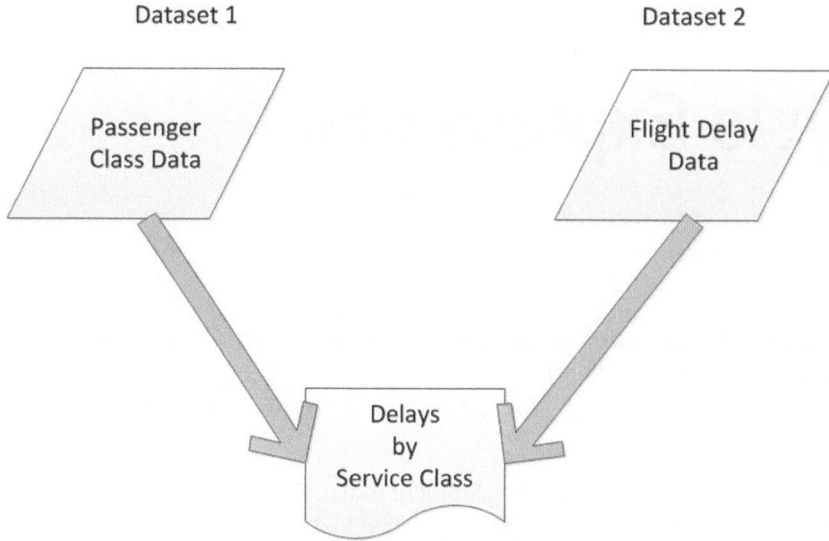

Figure 4-1. *Using multiple datasets for a calculation*

Fundamentals of DAX

DAX uses a syntax structure with similarities to Excel. A vital difference is that DAX functions operate on table columns. It is not possible to reference a cell address, as the building blocks of PowerPivot are data tables and columns; within the PowerPivot data interface, there is no concept of a cell address.

The second fundamental of DAX is the language syntax. Column arguments for DAX functions can either be qualified with a table name in the form TableName[ColumnName] or unqualified as simply [ColumnName]. When creating a DAX formula from within a single table, an unqualified reference can be used. If the expression uses columns from two different tables, as would be the case in creating a measure derived from two data sources, qualification of the column names with a table name is necessary.

Finally, calculations using DAX operate within a filter context. That is, as slicer values are applied to a PivotTable or PivotChart, DAX functions can leverage the context to create a calculation flexibility not easily achieved with Excel formulas.

Calculated Columns

Using the data from the BTS site, you can create a calculated column using DAX. To begin, download the data files from the BTS site at the following URL:

`http://www.transtats.bts.gov/DL_SelectFields.asp?Table_ID=236&DB_Short_Name=On-Time`

Figure 4-2 shows the download page.

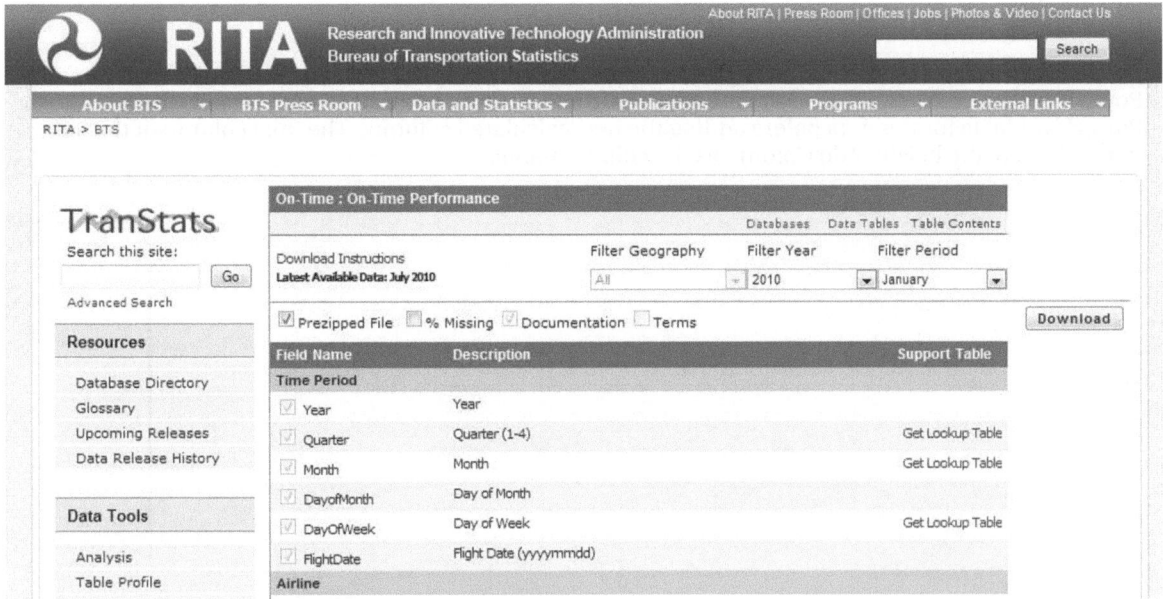

Figure 4-2. *BTS download site*

From the BTS download site, ensure you choose the Prezipped option, and download the file to your development computer. Uncompressing the file will result in a file in the name form On_Time_On_Time_Performance_YYYY_MM.csv, where YYYY is the year of the data and MM is the month number. Import this file into PowerPivot for Excel, noting the column names are in the first row of the dataset. Figure 4-3 below is an example of the On_Time_Performance_2010_07.csv file.

```
 1  "Year","Quarter","Month","DayofMonth","DayOfWeek","FlightDate","UniqueCarrier","AirlineID","Carrier","TailNum","FlightNum","Origin","OriginCityName","OriginState",
 2  2010,3,7,3,6,2010-07-03,"WN",19393,"WN","N664WN","2328","DAL","Dallas, TX","TX","48","Texas",74,"TUL","Tulsa, OK","OK","40","Oklahoma",73,"1940","1948",8.00,8.00,0
 3  2010,3,7,3,6,2010-07-03,"WN",19393,"WN","N608SW","3029","DAL","Dallas, TX","TX","48","Texas",74,"TUL","Tulsa, OK","OK","40","Oklahoma",73,"0755","0757",2.00,2.00,0
 4  2010,3,7,3,6,2010-07-03,"WN",19393,"WN","N729SW","1265","DEN","Denver, CO","CO","08","Colorado",82,"ABQ","Albuquerque, NM","NM","35","New Mexico",86,"0755","0754",
 5  2010,3,7,3,6,2010-07-03,"WN",19393,"WN","N789SW","2695","DEN","Denver, CO","CO","08","Colorado",82,"ABQ","Albuquerque, NM","NM","35","New Mexico",86,"1645","1700",
 6  2010,3,7,3,6,2010-07-03,"WN",19393,"WN","N628SW","1066","DEN","Denver, CO","CO","08","Colorado",82,"AMA","Amarillo, TX","TX","48","Texas",74,"1820","1904",44.00,44
 7  2010,3,7,3,6,2010-07-03,"WN",19393,"WN","N349SW","1448","DEN","Denver, CO","CO","08","Colorado",82,"AMA","Amarillo, TX","TX","48","Texas",74,"1110","1112",2.00,2.0
 8  2010,3,7,3,6,2010-07-03,"WN",19393,"WN","N361SW","1422","DEN","Denver, CO","CO","08","Colorado",82,"AUS","Austin, TX","TX","48","Texas",74,"0830","0827",-3.00,0.00
 9  2010,3,7,3,6,2010-07-03,"WN",19393,"WN","N246LV","3921","DEN","Denver, CO","CO","08","Colorado",82,"AUS","Austin, TX","TX","48","Texas",74,"1830","1829",-1.00,0.00
10  2010,3,7,3,6,2010-07-03,"WN",19393,"WN","N914WN","21","DEN","Denver, CO","CO","08","Colorado",82,"BDL","Hartford, CT","CT","09","Connecticut",11,"1020","1026",6.00
```

Figure 4-3. *On-time performance file example*

■ **Note**   While not strictly necessary for this example, you can also download additional months of data from the BTS site, concatenating all the files into one using the following command within a DOS Command Window, assuming the current directory context is the folder containing your On Time Performance downloads from BTS:

copy On_Time_On_Time_Performance_2010_*.csv On_Time_Performance_2010.csv

---

Creating a Calculated Column

To create the calculated column, navigate to the PowerPivot window, and move to the last column of the PowerPivot for Excel data table containing the on-time performance data. Figure 4-4 illustrates the PowerPivot table for this data before adding the new calculated column. The final column of the data table will have the header Add Column as the column name.

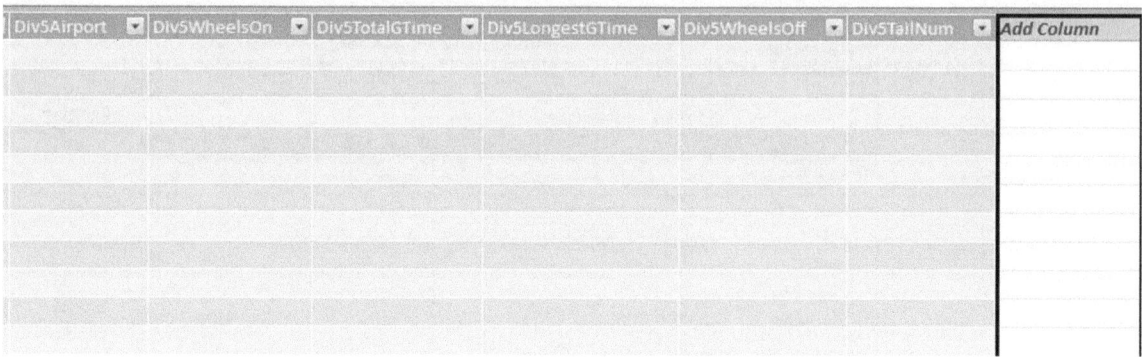

Figure 4-4. *On-time performance table, before adding the calculated column*

Navigate to the first row of this new column, and enter the following:

```
=MONTH(On_Time_On_Time_Performance_2010[FlightDate])
```

The preceding formula can be entered in its entirety from the keyboard, but the PowerPivot formula editor can assist in finding the correct object names for function arguments. As illustrated in Figure 4-5, typing **MONTH(ON** in the formula editor will create a pull-down list of potential PowerPivot table columns, in fully qualified table (column) form, beginning with the letters "ON."

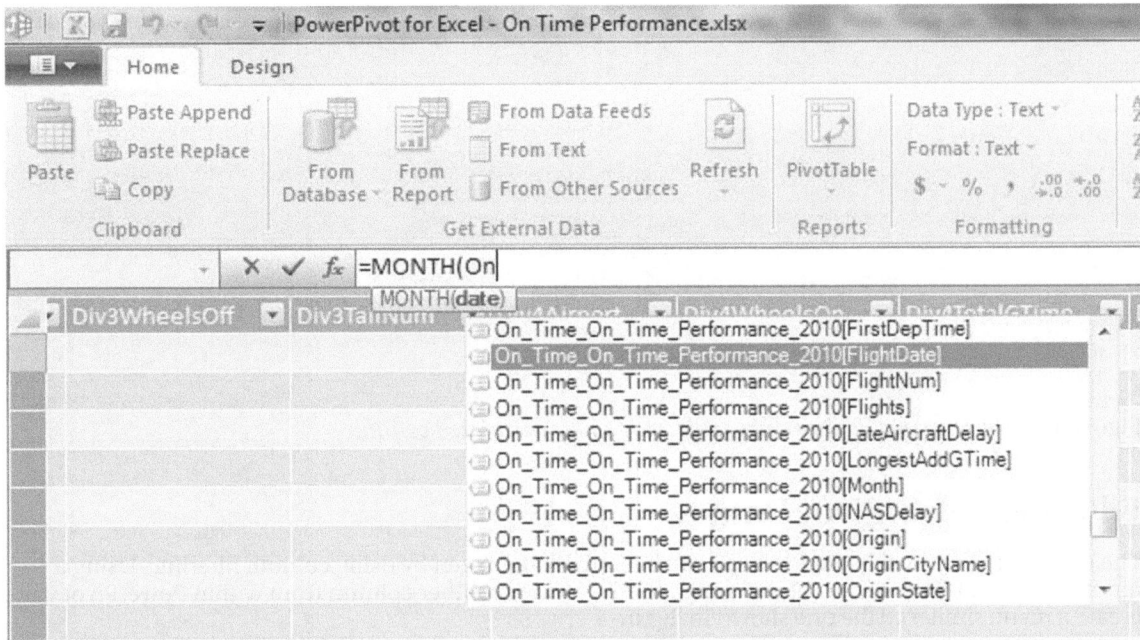

Figure 4-5. *Formula editor object name pull-down*

Regardless of the method of DAX formula entry, at the completion of the formula, PowerPivot will populate the entire table with the new calculated data and add a new heading to the column with the default name of CalculatedColumn1. Create a new name for the column by right-clicking the column header and selecting the Rename option from the context menu. Use MonthNumber to have a more meaningful name for the new column.

Of particular importance to note here is that in PowerPivot, DAX formulas operate on entire tables. Even though we are working within Excel, the concept of a cell address does not exist within DAX. This is a vital concept to keep in mind as you design and develop your own PowerPivot solutions leveraging DAX. The data for each calculated column is stored at the point in time data is loaded from the source. Because all of the data has been loaded, our MonthNumber column has been populated for the entire table. Moving the record cursor to the end of the table will reveal a value in the MonthNumber column for the final row. Figure 4-6 below contains an excerpt of the On Time Performance table, including the new calculated column MonthNumber.

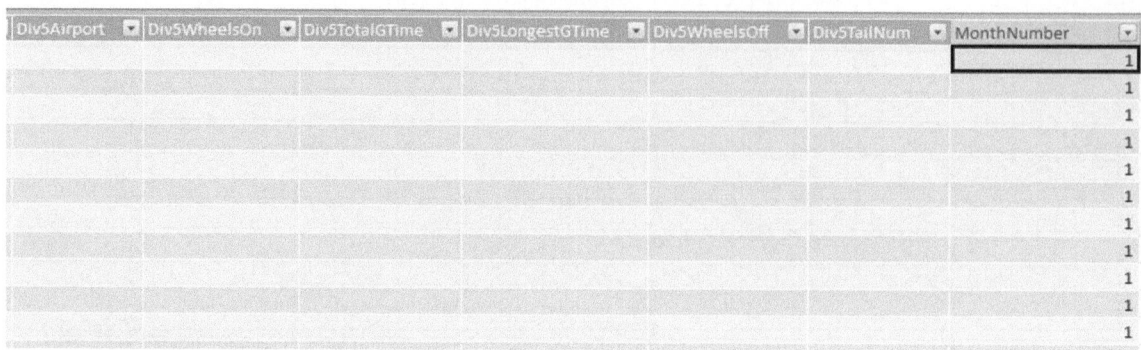

Figure 4-6. *The On Time Performance table with a new calculated column*

Filtering PowerPivot Data

The effect of the new calculated column can be immediately seen by using column filtering. Using a mouse-click to pull down the column menu for the MonthNumber column from within PowerPivot will create a menu similar to the one shown in Figure 4-7.

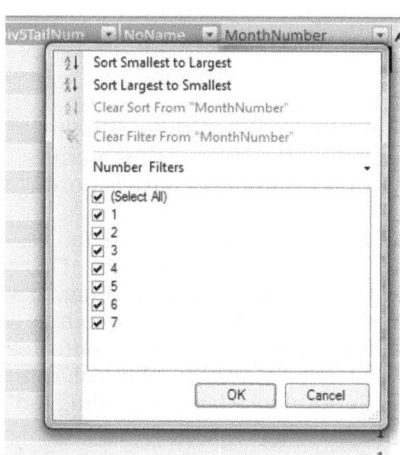

Figure 4-7. *Column Menu*

The contents of the menu will vary based on the actual data contained in the PowerPivot table. In the example screenshot, the underlying table contains data for the first seven months of 2010. If you downloaded a single month of on-time performance data, \ your filter dialog will contain a single row representing the month for which data was available.

Spotting Calculated Columns in the PowerPivot Field List

Calculated columns are available for use anywhere columns from the original source data can be used. The PowerPivot Field List renders the calculated column, just as any other column within the source table grouping area. As depicted in Figure 4-8, the new calculated column appears at the bottom (highlighted) of the fields available from the table from which it is calculated.

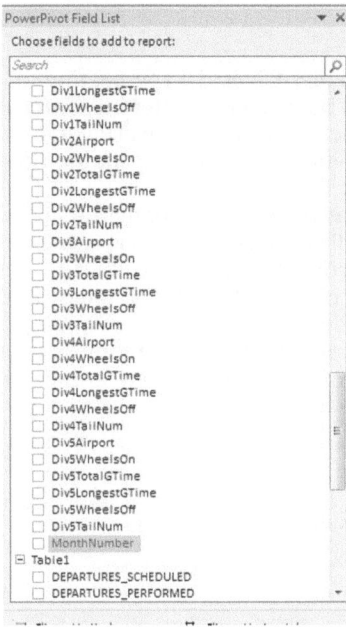

Figure 4-8. *PowerPivot Field List with the calculated column*

Table Relationships

One of PowerPivot for Excel's current limitations is that there is no direct means of creating relationships between tables based on multiple columns. You can use DAX expressions as a way of crafting a workaround.

Understanding the Problem

One of the limitations in the initial release of PowerPivot for Excel concerns relationships between tables. At this time, PowerPivot for Excel only supports one-to-one and one-to-many relationships between tables.

A one-to-one relationship exists where a given row in one table is related to at most one row in a lookup table. Figure 4-9 illustrates a one-to-one relationship between a table of employees and a table of spouses. Each employee row would have at most one related row in the spouse table.

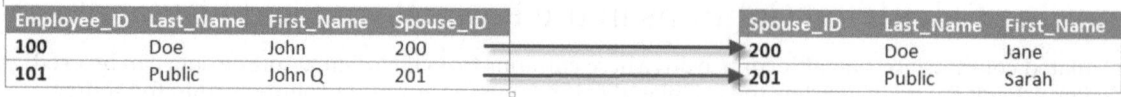

Employee_ID	Last_Name	First_Name	Spouse_ID		Spouse_ID	Last_Name	First_Name
100	Doe	John	200		200	Doe	Jane
101	Public	John Q	201		201	Public	Sarah

Figure 4-9. *One-to-one relationship*

Usually, these one-to-one relationships become columns in the original table. Given the aggregating nature of PowerPivot, it is possible to have a one-to-one relationship exist between two different sources of data, and combining the attributes into a single table may not be practical. However, PowerPivot for Excel supports one to one relationships both in table definitions, through inclusion of the attributes into a single table and in the creation of PowerPivot Table relationships.

A one-to-many relationship exists where a row in the lookup table may be related to many rows in the Primary Table. The context from which the lookup is occurring is vitally important. PowerPivot for Excel supports one-to-many relationships between tables. For example, consider a primary table of product-level retail sales records and a lookup table containing the entire catalog of products sold by the company. Each row in the sales table would be related to exactly one product row. However, as most products have many sales transactions associated with them, a product would be related to many sales rows. This is illustrated in Figure 4-10. Several rows in the Sales Transaction Table contain a reference to a single row of the Product Table, for Product ID = 100, as indicated by the arrows.

Sales Transaction Table   Product Table

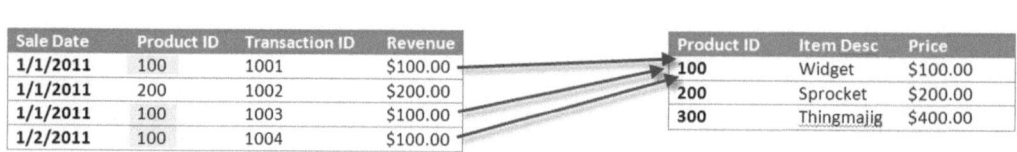

Sale Date	Product ID	Transaction ID	Revenue		Product ID	Item Desc	Price
1/1/2011	100	1001	$100.00		100	Widget	$100.00
1/1/2011	200	1002	$200.00		200	Sprocket	$200.00
1/1/2011	100	1003	$100.00		300	Thingmajig	$400.00
1/2/2011	100	1004	$100.00				

Figure 4-10. *One to Many Relationship of Sales and Product*

Another common example of the one-to-many relationships can occur in databases that store address information. Given a table of customers with addresses including a two-character state abbreviation and a lookup table containing the same abbreviation and the long state name, it is possible to construct a similar one-to-many relationship. Each customer address would be related to exactly one state, yet each state may have many customers.

■ **Note**   The existence of an Excel Vlookup in your existing Excel solutions is an indicator of a one-to-many relationship.

A many-to-many relationship exists where a row in the primary table is related to many rows in the lookup table. Additionally, the lookup table is related to many rows in the primary table. An example to consider for this relationship type is in banking, specifically the relationships between customers and accounts. An account may have many owners, via marriage or business partnership. Additionally, a customer may have many accounts. This release of PowerPivot for Excel cannot directly support many-to-many relationships. However, your organization may already have databases, both operational and analytical data stores, that directly support and account for this relationship type.

Illustrating Relationships with Football

Yes, you read that correctly. I had the good fortune to spend my youth in the southeastern United States. For a young man who enjoys sports, that means there are only two seasons, college football and college football recruiting. This example is intended to convey, with real data, the use of a DAX calculated column to relate PowerPivot tables and uses data readily available from the National Collegiate Athletics Association (NCAA) web site.

The NCAA provides updated statistics (at http://web1.ncaa.org/mfb/download.jsp) for players, including the offensive and defensive game-level statistics for each player's performance. The relevant files, as of the end of the 2010 regular season games, are available from this book's example download as NCAA.xlsx. This example is intended to illustrate how DAX is used to create columns to relate the Roster and Offense tables. As you will see in Figure 4-11, there is a Player ID column in the Roster table. This would seem to be an ideal column to relate the offensive statistics to a player in the Roster table. However, the Player ID column does not exist in the Offense table shown in Figure 4-12. As will often be the case with related data, a number of columns must be used to relate a row in the Offense table to a row in the Player table. The multiple columns would not be an issue except, PowerPivot for Excel, in the initial release does not support multiple column keys for relationships.

Institution ID	Institution	Uniform Number	Last Name	First Name	Position	Year	Player ID
5	Akron	63	Pachuta	Joe	OL	FR	271675
5	Akron	76	Pughsley	Jarrod	OL	FR	271677
5	Akron	78	Lio	Micah	OL	FR	371362
8	Alabama	59	Kouandjio	Arie	OL	FR	360765
8	Alabama	61	Steen	Anthony	OL	FR	271953
8	Alabama	63	Williams	Kellen	OL	FR	360745
8	Alabama	76	Fluker	D.J.	OL	FR	271933
8	Alabama	78	Lindsay	Chad	OL	FR	360747

Figure 4-11. *Roster table*

InstitutionID	Institution	GameDate	UniformNumber	LastName	FirstName	Rushes
721	Air Force	10/30/10	82	DEMERATH	CHAZ	
721	Air Force	10/09/10	81	FREEMAN	JOSHUA	
721	Air Force	10/16/10	81	FREEMAN	JOSHUA	
721	Air Force	10/23/10	81	FREEMAN	JOSHUA	
721	Air Force	10/30/10	81	FREEMAN	JOSHUA	
721	Air Force	09/18/10	80	HIRNEISE	BRANDON	
721	Air Force	10/16/10	80	HIRNEISE	BRANDON	
721	Air Force	09/04/10	85	KAUTH	ZACH	
5	Akron	09/04/10	40	BAILEY	AUSTIN	
5	Akron	09/11/10	40	BAILEY	AUSTIN	
5	Akron	09/25/10	40	BAILEY	AUSTIN	

Figure 4-12. *Offense table*

Relating Tables with DAX

The solution to this relationship issue is easily accomplished with a little DAX. Because both tables contain Institution ID, Uniform Number, and Last Name columns, we can manufacture a key column to relate Offense to Roster.

First, from the PowerPivot window, move to the empty row immediately below the Add Column column header in the Roster table. Enter the following in the formula entry area directly below the Office Ribbon:

```
=[Institution ID]&"-"&[Uniform Number]&"-"&[Last Name]
```

When you're finished, your formula edit area should look similar to Figure 4-13.

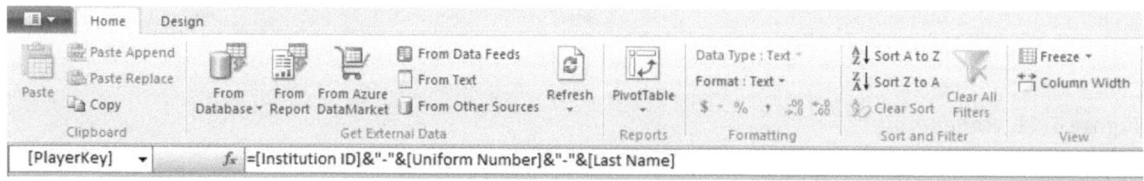

Figure 4-13. *Roster PlayerID DAX*

What we have used the concatenation operator (the ampersand) and literals (the dashes inside quotation marks) to build a single-column unique key from the three columns required to uniquely identify a row in the Roster table. It is important to delimit the data values within the new compound key column to ensure an unintended relationship is not formed. For example, what would happen if the data contained an institution ID of 100 and a uniform number of 2 for a last name of Smith and another row with an institution ID of 10 and player ID of 02 (these are text data types, not integers) and a last name of Smith? The two keys would be the same. This example is illustrated in Table 4-1. As a matter of housekeeping, we prefer to rename calculated columns from the PowerPivot generated name to a meaningful name. In this case, we will use PlayerKey.

Table 4-1. *Duplicate Key Creation*

Institution ID	Uniform Number	Last Name	Without Delimiter	With Delimiter
100	2	Smith	1002Smith	100-2-Smith
10	02	Smith	1002Smith	10-02-Smith

To relate the Roster and Offense tables, we will duplicate the calculation of the player key, using the column names in the Offense table. It is unnecessary to name the columns that comprise the key identically. It is necessary for the player key DAX formula to employ the same column order. To create the same key value calculation in the Offense table, do the following:

1. In the PowerPivot window, move to the column of the Offense table named Add Column. In the formula editor, enter the same formula used in the Roster table, using the corresponding columns in the Offense table. Recall the original Player Key formula was =[Institution ID]&"-"&[Uniform Number]&"-"&[Last Name].

2. Rename the new column in the Offense table to PlayerKey by right-clicking the column heading and choosing the Rename Column option.

3. The final step in this solution is to create a relationship from the Offense table to the Roster table. The important concept to keep in mind here is the uniqueness of the two tables. Although PowerPivot for Excel supports one-to-many relationships, it is critical to build the relationship correctly. That is from the table with many rows, to the table containing a single, distinct row for each PlayerKey (the one side of the relationship). In this example, the Offense table contains many rows for each PlayerKey, because it is a summary, by game date, of the offensive performance of a PlayerKey. Conversely, there is one row for each distinct player in the Roster table. A PlayerKey uniquely identifies a single row in the Roster table. Figure 4-14 illustrates the correct formation of the Offense to Roster tables' relationship.

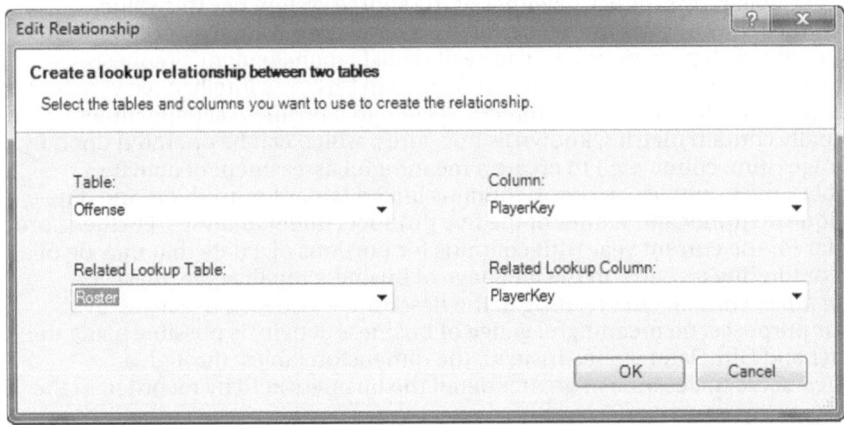

Figure 4-14. *Offense-to-Roster relationship*

Note that if both tables for which a relationship is being created contain multiple records for each key, PowerPivot for Excel will not allow the relationship to be created. Instead, PowerPivot for Excel will respond with an error dialog similar to the one shown in Figure 4-15.

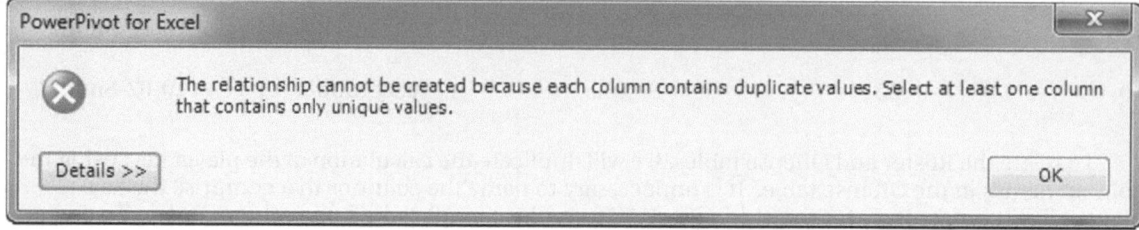

Figure 4-15. *Duplicate key values*

Calculated Measures from Multiple Data Sources

Another reason to employ a DAX calculation is in the creation of a new measure from multiple data sources. From the example download, Chatper04\DAX Measures.xlsx is a sample workbook containing a trivial amount of data from a fictional Internet retailer. The workbook contains data for both product sales (SalesFacts) and page views from the company web site (PageViewFacts).

The Business Problem

While the example workbook contains data for both sales and web activity, as is often the case in real work, both datasets are needed for the calculation of a value not stored in either source. For example, one of the management team for a fictitious web retailer believes understanding how many page views occur for every dollar of sales, by product, will aid the decision-making process. You have been asked to combine information from the sales system and the web activity logs to generate just such an analysis, highlighting page views per sales dollar, by product. Neither of the source system has this value, because neither contains all of the required data for the calculation. However, using PowerPivot to combine the measures for sales and web page views, we can easily satisfy management's request.

The two tables containing sales and page view activity are known in business intelligence vernacular as fact tables. *Fact tables* as a general rule contain data directly related to a business activity under analysis. A Fact Table will usually contain metrics, known as measures, which can be operated upon by an aggregating function (average, sum, count, etc.) to create a meaningful assessment of activity.

In addition to the fact tables, the example workbook contains linked tables for products and dates. DimProduct contains the unique identifier and names of the five products under analysis. Furthermore, DimDate contains the calendar for the current year with columns for portions of a date that may be of interest for sorting, grouping or filtering activity. In the language of business intelligence, these are dimension tables. *Dimension tables* contain data relating to the description of a fact, usually with a historical perspective. For our purposes, no meaningful gauge of business activity is possible using the dimension tables (DimProduct and DimDate) alone. Instead, the dimension tables, through a relationship with the fact tables, serve to describe in greater detail the business activity recorded in the fact table.

Separation of Facts and Dimensions

If dimension tables only serve to describe activity in the fact tables, why not have one big table containing columns from both the fact and dimension tables? My initial response will be familiar to any parent, "Because I said so". Actually, the better answer lies in research and methodologies developed long before I began working in this field. However, I may be able to illustrate the best reason to strive for this design using the PowerPivot solution at hand.

The example workbook contains a set of four tables, two fact tables and two dimension tables. The tables have been related using PowerPivot relationships in the following manner:

- SalesFacts is related to both Product and DimDate

- VisitorFacts is related to both Product and DimDate.

These relationships are depicted in the lines connecting each table's representation in Figure 4-16 .

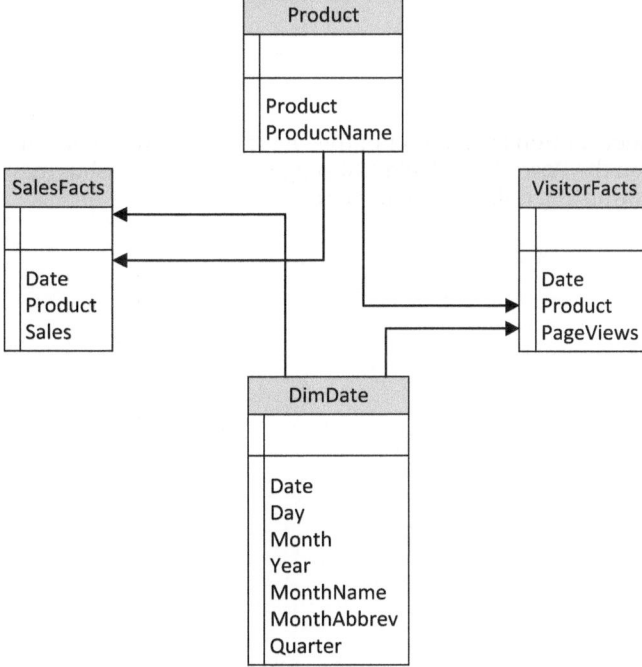

Figure 4-16. *Example fact and dimension relationships*

If we create a very simple pivot table containing the measures for each of the fact tables, Sum of Sales and Sum of PageViews, a table like Figure 4-17 is produced.

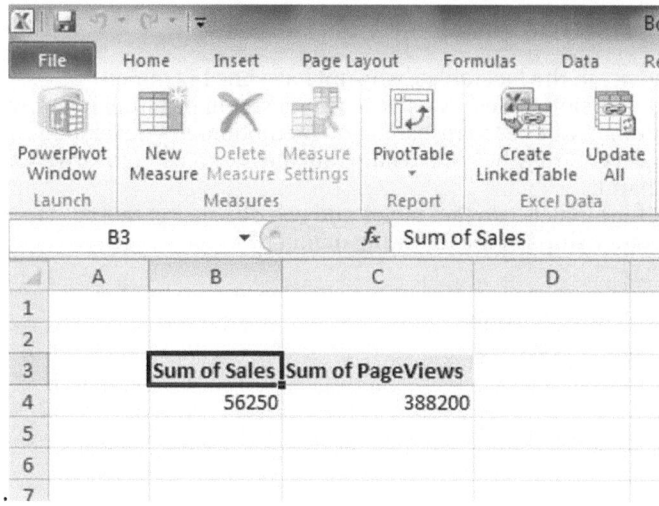

Figure 4-17. *Facts from separate tables*

However, if we then attempt to include a Product column from either of the fact tables, PowerPivot will respond with both an odd result, and an error in the PowerPivot Field List suggesting a relationship may be needed. The "Relationship may be needed: warning is illustrated in Figure 4-18.

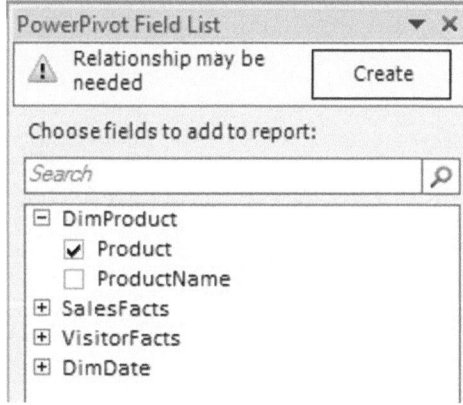

Figure 4-18. *Relationship warning message*

If the Product column from VisitorFacts is used as a row label, PowerPivot uses the grand total of all SalesFacts as the Sum of Sales for each Product. This behavior is illustrated in Figure 4-19. Conversely, if the Product column from SalesFacts is used as a row label, PowerPivot uses the grand total of all VisitorFacts as the Sum of PageViews for each Product. This behavior is illustrated in Figure 4-20. If you recall the earlier relationship diagram for our four-table solution, the reason for the behavior will be evident.

	A	B	C	D	E
1					
2					
3		Row Labels ▾	Sum of Sales	Sum of PageViews	
4		100	56250	30000	
5		200	56250	15000	
6		300	56250	900	
7		400	56250	4800	
8		500	56250	337500	
9		Grand Total	56250	388200	
10					
11					
12					

Figure 4-19. *VistorFacts product as a row label*

	A	B	C	D	E
1					
2					
3		Row Labels ▾	Sum of Sales	Sum of PageViews	
4		100	3750	388200	
5		200	7500	388200	
6		300	11250	388200	
7		400	15000	388200	
8		500	18750	388200	
9		Grand Total	56250	388200	
10					
11					
12					

Figure 4-20. *SalesFacts product as a row label*

The reason for this seeming inconsistency is in Figure 4-16. There are no relationships between each of the fact tables, SalesFacts and VistorFacts. They are only related to each other via their separate relationships with the DimProduct and DimDate tables. PowerPivot has no means by which to resolve the request to assign Product as a row label to a PivotTable containing measures from two separate fact tables when the row label is a column in only one of the fact tables. However, each of our fact tables has a relationship with the Product column in the DimProduct table (DimProduct[Product]). Further complicating the issue is the values being computed into the PivotTable by PowerPivot. But the explanation is the same. Because there is no relationship between SalesFacts and PageViewFacts, PowerPivot has no choice but to use an implied value to constrain the query that supplies the Sum from the unrelated fact table. This is why the values for each Product row label are consistently the grand total for the measure in the unrelated table. SQL Server Analysis Server users recognize PowerPivot is supplying the default member, in the absence of a relationship.

If we substitute the column from the dimension table for the row label sourced from a fact table, will that solve the problem at hand? Absolutely, but wait there is more.

1. First, remove the value from the Row Label area of the PowerPivot Field List.

2. Drag the Product column from the DimProduct table to the Row Labels area of the PowerPivot Field List.

3. Ensure the Values area of the PowerPivot Field List contains the measures from the two fact tables: Sales and PageViews. The resulting PivotTable should resemble Figure 4-21.

	A	B	C	D		E
1						
2						
3		Row Labels ▾	Sum of Sales	Sum of PageViews		
4		100	3750	30000		
5		200	7500	15000		
6		300	11250	900		
7		400	15000	4800		
8		500	18750	337500		
9		**Grand Total**	**56250**	**388200**		
10						
11						

Figure 4-21. *Using Dimension Table Columns*

Because the PivotTable now uses a column related to *both* fact tables, the row label, product-level totals for each measure are accurately reported.

New Measures

Begin adding a new measure with DAX to our example PowerPivot solution by opening the Excel window. From the PowerPivot Field List, right-click the VisitorFacts table, and select Add New Measure from the context menu. Alternatively, the same dialog can be reached via the PowerPivot Ribbon New Measure selection.

Using Figure 4-22 as an example, enter data in the Measure Name, Custom Name, and Formula fields. Notice we are using the SUMX function to ensure we calculate the sum of PageViews for all rows in the table. SUMX is also used to evaluate sales for all rows in the table. This will ensure accurate calculations if new fields from the PowerPivot data tables are added to the PivotTable.

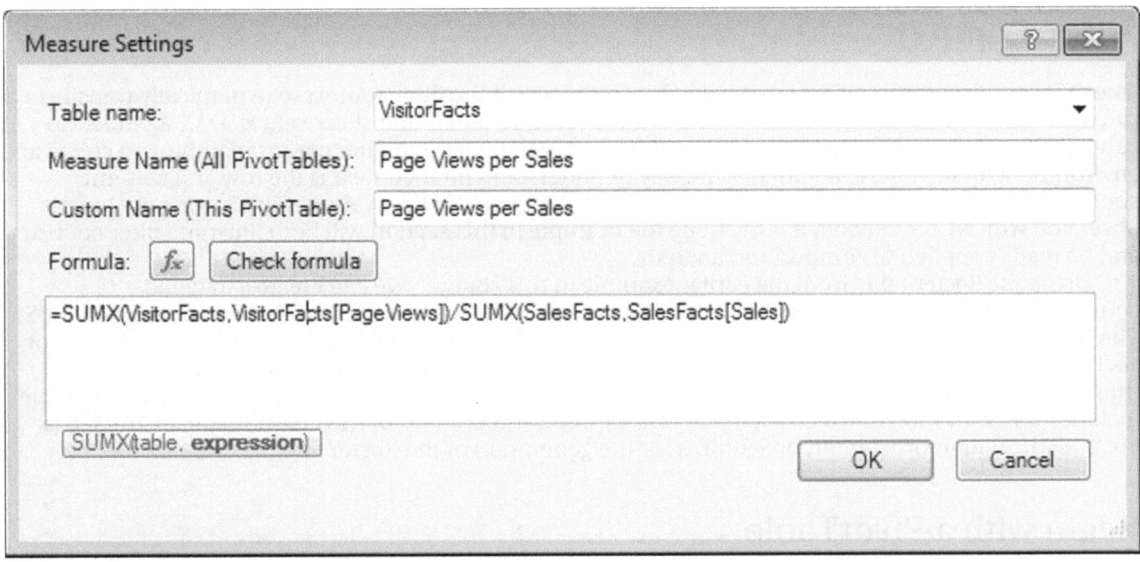

Figure 4-22. *The Measure Settings dialog*

PowerPivot will add the new measure as a selection in the Values area of the PowerPivot Field List. When completed, your worksheet should resemble Figure 4-23.

	A	B	C	D	E
1					
2					
3		Row Labels ▼	Sum of Sales	Sum of PageViews	Page Views per Sales
4		100	3750	30000	8
5		200	7500	15000	2
6		300	11250	900	0.08
7		400	15000	4800	0.32
8		500	18750	337500	18
9		Grand Total	56250	388200	6.901333333
10					

Figure 4-23. *New Measure Added to PivotTable*

■ **Note**   Unlike their cousin SQL Server Analysis Services's concept of a calculated measure, PowerPivot calculated measures must be related to a table in the PowerPivot solution.

Filter Context

One of PowerPivot for Excel's unique behaviors is the use of the filter context to dynamically transform a calculation to take advantage of additional row (or column) labels and slicer values. DAX includes no concept of cell addressing. Instead, relationships between tables and filter context combine to create an environment for formula evaluation. One way to understand filter context is the row and column context created by both data labels in addition to any applicable slicer values. Considering my fanatic obsession with NCAA football, it is my hope the example in this section will both illustrate filter context and be readily applied to composition analysis.

Using the Roster table from the earlier example in this chapter, we can create a detailed composition analysis of the personnel available to each of the teams in Football Bowl Subdivision (FBS). The Roster table includes some interesting attributes to help you understand the relative experience of each team's players. In the simplest of terms, each player is granted the ability to play four years, roughly aligning with the time period required to complete a four-year college degree. The Roster table includes the institution in which each player is enrolled and the year of their enrollment, expressed as Freshman, Sophomore, Junior, or Senior, as of the generation of the Roster file.

Begin with a PivotTable

To understand the data, start with a PivotTable using Institution as the row label and Year as the column label. Placing PlayerKey in the values area of the PivotTable Field List (from the earlier example in this chapter) will cause a unique behavior by PowerPivot for Excel. Because the PlayerKey is a text column, there is only one operation that can be applied to the data: Count. The other aggregating functions for measures (Min, Max, Average, and Sum) do not apply and will generate an error. This example will actually take advantage of this behavior, as you need to understand the relative composition of the four classes, by institution. Your PivotTable should resemble Figure 4-24.

	A	B	C	D	E	F	G	H
1	Count of PlayerKey	Column Labels						
2	Row Labels		FR	JR	NA	SO	SR	Grand Total
3	Air Force		8	9	28	22	19	86
4	Akron		1	33	20	15	18	87
5	Alabama		2	44	29	27	16	118
6	Arizona		1	21	26	9	22	79
7	Arizona St.		1	44	35	19	13	112
8	Arkansas		1	47	23	31	22	124
9	Arkansas St.		1	32	24	20	22	99
10	Army		3	8	24	38	25	98
11	Auburn		1	37	22	19	24	103
12	Ball St.		1	22	18	23	24	88
13	Baylor		1	50	20	27	18	116
14	Boise St.		1	34	28	26	18	107
15	Boston College		1	44	15	23	19	102
16	Bowling Green		10	20	10	24	21	85

Figure 4-24 *Count by Instition and Class*

At this point, we have some data, but there are at least two problems with this table format. First, the order of the column labels does not follow the normal progression from Freshman to Senior; it's alphabetical. Second, there are additional Year values representing an empty string and NA.

For the first problem, we can craft a DAX expression that will sort our Roster[Year] column labels in a meaningful order. To most efficiently implement the sort, first we will implement a new table and relationship and then a new DAX expression

Since the meaningful sort order of Freshman, Sophomore, Junior, Senior, NA does not exist in the source data, we can implement the sort using a linked table. In a new sheet, enter the data as it appears in Figure 4-25 . The first column is the key for a Year value in the Roster table. The second column, SortYear, represents a string the PivotTable (and perhaps a slicer) will use to sort the Year values in a meaningful way.

	A	B
1	Year	SortYear
2	FR	01-Fresh
3	SO	02-Soph
4	JR	03-Junior
5	SR	04-Senior
6	NA	05-NA

Figure 4-25. *SortYear linked table data*

After entering the data, create a Linked Table using the Create Linked Table selection from the PowerPivot Ribbon. If you check the "My table has headers" option, the new table will contain two columns named Year and SortYear. Additionally, as a matter of personal preference, you can rename the new table from the default TableN+1. My solution uses SortYear as the new table name. Create a relationship from the Year column of the Roster table to the Year column of the new SortYear (or whatever name you chose) table.

Now, it is time to sling a little DAX. Since there is now a relationship between the Roster[Year] and SortYear[Year], we can employ the RELATED() DAX function. The RELATED() function puts a column from another table, into the current table, via an existing relationship between the two tables. As there is already a relationship between Roster and SortYear (via the Year column in both tables), this is a potential solution to the SortYear problem. To implement, enter the following in the formula entry area for a new column:

```
=RELATED(SortYear[SortYear])
```

This use of the RELATED() function will add a new column to the Roster table, named predictably enough in the form CalculatedColumnN+1. Rename the column to something more recognizable (maybe SortYear). Return to the Excel window to further edit the PivotTable to enjoy the benefits of your work in DAX.

The PowerPivot Field List should display the "PowerPivot data was modified" warning. You will need to press the Refresh button to actually see the new table and column that have been implemented. Replace the Year column with the new Roster[SortYear] column in the Column Labels area. Your results should look something like Figure 4-26.

	A	B	C	D	E	F	G	H
1	**Count of PlayerKey**	**Column Labels** ▼						
2	**Row Labels** ▼		**01-Fresh**	**02-Soph**	**03-Junior**	**04-Senior**	**05-NA**	**Grand Total**
3	Air Force		8	9	22	28	19	86
4	Akron		1	33	15	20	18	87
5	Alabama		2	44	27	29	16	118
6	Arizona		1	21	9	26	22	79
7	Arizona St.		1	44	19	35	13	112
8	Arkansas		1	47	31	23	22	124
9	Arkansas St.		1	32	20	24	22	99
10	Army		3	8	38	24	25	98
11	Auburn		1	37	19	22	24	103
12	Ball St.		1	22	23	18	24	88
13	Baylor		1	50	27	20	18	116

Figure 4-26. *SortYear in PivotTable*

Note that the values of Year in the column labels are now sorted in a meaningful order, based on the prefix assigned to each when the data was entered (01, 02, etc.). Additionally, you may wonder why the Blank Year values would appear when there is no corresponding row in the SortYear table. This is actually an intended consequence to ensure no accidental misrepresentation of the underlying data occurs. To remove the Blank Year column headers, you would have to filter the with a slicer (or filter at the data source description).

To explicitly eliminate the Blank Year column, add a horizontal (or vertical) slicer to the solution. Select the values of SortYear other than the blank values, and the PivotTable removes the Blank column header. However, the absence of the data from the report is self-evident by the presence of the SortYear slicer (and the deselection of the Blank SortYear).

Compute Percent of Whole

To illustrate filter context, add an additional horizontal slicer to the solution representing the Conference column from the Teams table. Additionally, replace Institution with Conference as the Row Label. Your PivotTable should look something like Figure 4-27.

SortYear								
	01-FR							
02-SO	03-JR							
04-SR								

Conference								
ACC		Big East		Big12		BigTen		
Conf USA		Ind		Mid-American		Mountain West		
Pac10		SEC		Sun Belt		WAC		

Count of Player ID	Column Labels				
Row Labels	01-FR	02-SO	03-JR	04-SR	Grand Total
ACC	481	299	254	197	1231
Big East	253	173	171	146	743
Big12	464	278	267	227	1236
BigTen	487	289	226	201	1203
Conf USA	382	311	291	223	1207
Ind	92	95	95	81	363
Mid-American	495	279	288	206	1268
Mountain West	316	223	196	166	901
Pac10	339	246	244	168	997
SEC	467	275	297	223	1262
Sun Belt	354	200	196	171	921
WAC	337	196	228	154	915
Grand Total	4467	2864	2753	2163	12247

Figure 4-27. *PivotTable by Conference*

The Filter Context applied to each cell in the PivotTable is comprised of the selections made by the slicers and the Column and Row labels. The slicers, in this case, only determine which values of Conference and SortYear will appear as Row and Column labels respectively. However, as we add more layers to this illustration, you should see Labels (row or column) that are not directly tied to a slicer. The calculation for the number of Freshman (01-FR) players in the ACC is based on filtering the Roster data for Conference and SortYear.

To add another layer to the example, add Institution as a Row Label after Conference. Subtotaling of the conference-level data is achieved by PowerPivot using Filter Context, which, depending on the row label, may be at the conference or team level. While this is valuable data manipulation, the slicing of the table is not unique to PowerPivot for Excel.

To further understand the usefulness of Filter Context, right-click any of the measures in the PivotTable to reveal the context menu. Select "Show Values as" from the context menu, and select "% of Row Total" from the subsequent menu. Because PowerPivot evaluates each cell based on the implied constraints of the slicers and row and column labels, converting the absolute count of players by year into a percentage for each row total is efficient.

Finally, to dress up the visually unappealing PivotTable, select a single conference from the Conference slicer. Highlight the cells for each of the years, for all teams, avoiding the Conference and

Grand Total rows and the Grand Total Column. From the Excel 2010 home ribbon, choose the Conditional Formatting drop-down. Choose Color Scales, and then the three-color pattern. Apply the pattern to the table of percentages, and your solution should look similar to Figure 4-28.

	A	B	C	D	E	F	G	H	I
1									
2									
3		**SortYear**		**Conference**					
4				ACC	Big East	Big12		BigTen	
5		01-FR							
6		02-SO	03-JR	Conf USA	Ind	Mid-American		Mountain West	
7		04-SR		Pac10	SEC	Sun Belt		WAC	
8									
9									
10									
11		**Count of Player ID**	**Column Labels**						
12		**Row Labels**	**01-FR**		**02-SO**	**03-JR**	**04-SR**	**Grand Total**	
13		⊟SEC	37.00%		21.79%	23.53%	17.67%	100.00%	
14		Alabama	32.69%		25.96%	19.23%	22.12%	100.00%	
15		Arkansas	39.64%		21.62%	25.23%	13.51%	100.00%	
16		Auburn	37.50%		24.11%	27.68%	10.71%	100.00%	
17		Florida	18.75%		24.11%	33.93%	23.21%	100.00%	
18		Georgia	31.68%		23.76%	25.74%	18.81%	100.00%	
19		Kentucky	34.31%		27.45%	19.61%	18.63%	100.00%	
20		LSU	42.55%		23.40%	13.83%	20.21%	100.00%	
21		Mississippi	46.03%		12.70%	19.05%	22.22%	100.00%	
22		Mississippi St.	41.58%		16.83%	27.72%	13.86%	100.00%	
23		South Carolina	42.59%		21.30%	27.78%	8.33%	100.00%	
24		Tennessee	32.95%		20.45%	26.14%	20.45%	100.00%	
25		Vanderbilt	42.72%		21.36%	15.53%	20.39%	100.00%	
26		**Grand Total**	37.00%		21.79%	23.53%	17.67%	100.00%	
27									

Figure 4-28. *Percent of whole, with conditional formatting*

Summary

Data Analysis Expressions (DAX) is a set of functions and language elements that adds a robust calculation feature to PowerPivot for Excel. DAX is intended to be familiar to anyone that has created Excel formulas. The two principal uses of DAX are to create calculated columns within a data table and to create custom measures within the PowerPivot field list. In our introduction to DAX, these are the important points:

- DAX is a calculation language for PowerPivot based on an Excel-like function set.

- DAX can be used to create calculated columns or custom measures.

DAX formulas cannot reference a cell address, all function data is at the table and column levels.

CHAPTER 5

■ ■ ■

A Method to the Madness

A fool with a plan can beat a genius with no plan.

—Boone Pickens

The goal of this chapter is to take the skills you developed in the previous chapters and build on them to create the beginnings of a methodology for success with your PowerPivot for Excel solutions. Much like students of architecture begin not by designing a structure but by learning how to measure, cut, and fasten building materials together with basic tools, you have acquired the essential basics of PowerPivot. The basic carpentry skills of PowerPivot for Excel include

- Installing the software

- Loading data from text files, spreadhseets, and databases

- Creating relationships between disparate data sources

- Bending the data to our will using Data Analysis Expressions (DAX)

What follows in this chapter is a suggested recipe for successfully building extendable, reusable PowerPivot solutions, based on hundreds of hours of PowerPivot development. It is my sincere hope this chapter assists you in quickly creating success in your enterprise using insight revealed by your PowerPivot solution. Can you create successful solutions and analytics without this method? Of course you can. But my reason for sharing the method in this chapter is twofold. First to ensure you gain the benefit of my experience and in doing so will find a place for PowerPivot in your organization. Secondly, I contend that by making some of the difficult features in PowerPivot easy to use, the overall body of knowledge for the product will expand.

Justification for a Method

I believe that PowerPivot for Excel (and PowerPivot for SharePoint) will disrupt the business intelligence market much as Microsoft Access did for relational database solutions development. The barrier for entry, the threshold of effort required to implement a business intelligence solution has been dramatically lowered. Elimination of this barrier to entry will increase the number of business intelligence solutions created.

Compare what we have done in the initial examples with the some of the tasks required to create a subject oriented data mart. A database platform, ETL tool set, and ad hoc reporting software all have to be acquired and installed before development on the data mart can begin. As an alternative to efforts led by the IT department, PowerPivot for Excel is intended to be installed by Microsoft Excel users. Included with PowerPivot for Excel is a data store, an extraction tool, and report development platform.

With this great power comes much responsibility, and *the* goal of this chapter is to ensure users of your PowerPivot solutions find them easy to use and enhance. Even if the entire, expected user community of your solutions is reading these very words. I have organized this as a set of principals and practices that should set your PowerPivot for Excel efforts on a tried and true course toward success.

Principles

Every good method is founded on some underlying principles that guide the decisions you make in implementing the method. They also guide the practices that the method espouses. Principles glue your practices together into a unified and coherent whole.

Embrace Failure

Failure is inherent to software development, and not exclusive to business intelligence solutions. Don't be afraid to try something with PowerPivot for Excel that would have been impossible with just Excel. For example, you can put far more data into PowerPivot for Excel than Excel alone could ever handle. I have loaded tens of millions of rows, on the same local network as the source database server, in a matter of minutes. For the vast majority of users, little you do with PowerPivot that can result in losing anything more than the Excel worksheet (.xlsx) file in which you are building a PowerPivot solution.

Additionally, be willing to delete a solution and start over. In a traditional business intelligence project, the decision to scrap a database, population system, and reports would be difficult if not impossible to make. Execution of the decision could take considerable time and effort. To do so with a PowerPivot for Excel solution involves a single file. The database, population system, and reporting are all rolled up into your .xlsx file. Don't be so attached to an approach that you don't take the time to clear the decks and start over. Almost without exception, version 2.0 of every piece of software is better than its predecessor.

Think Dimensionally, Act Locally

Dimensional modeling is a technique for organizing data in a manner that is efficient for satisfying queries with an analytical purpose. This is opposed to databases that are organized for efficiency and accuracy in transaction capture. I was first exposed to the idea of dimensional modeling in Ralph Kimball's *The Data Warehouse Toolkit* (Wiley 2002).

Transactional vs. Analytical Data Stores

To make clear the differences between transaction and analytical data stores, you can hardly do better than to look at retail sales. Filling the car with gasoline, buying tickets to a concert of movie, even purchasing groceries, usually involves a transaction processing software application and database.

Imagine, for example, what has to occur with every beep of the cash register scanner at your grocery store. The bar code is read to determine the item's identifier (also known as the stock keeping unit or SKU). The price for that SKU must be determined; inventory may be relieved of the quantity of products sold; and discounts for quantities sold (or time of sale) may be applied. All of these operations are more or less transactional in nature. The cash register system is keeping a running journal of the business activity. However, the main goal of the cash register system is to quickly and accurately determine the total amount due from a customer and process the receipt of the payment due.

To accomplish the goal of quickly and accurately determining the amount due, the data structures behind the cash register system are organized using a technique known as *normalization*. In the example cash register system, it would not be uncommon for the design to encompass multiple tables for individual business entities the system needs in order to function. Normalization works in the transaction capture role, because even though a grocery megastore may serve thousands of customers a day, each transaction involved only a fraction of the entire catalog of items stocked for sale (and stored in the database). Storing the data in structures optimized for transaction capture allows the system to service the volume, because individual business transactions cause very little change activity to the data store.

However, in a business intelligence setting, it is not uncommon for a single query to operate on millions of records in the underlying datastore. For example, a query to find the correlation between the sales of beer and pretzels might find every transaction that had both an item from the beer category and the pretzel category. Such a query may involve the database software examining all transactions involving beer and pretzels and filtering out certain dates, times, or geographic locations. However, the query would be very unlikely to actually create new transactional data; instead, it would only read the vast quantity of available transactional data.

Without creating an entire treatment of dimensional modeling, this chapter contains a primer to direct your PowerPivot development efforts. Since the data store behind PowerPivot for Excel (and PowerPivot for SharePoint) is SQL Server Analysis Services (SSAS), it would stand to reason a dimensional approach to modeling your PowerPivot data would be useful. In fact, a dimensional approach may be the only way to create correct answers to some problems.

Measures, Dimensions, and Hierarchies

To embrace the idea of a business process context to analytical data, dimensional models organize information into three main structures:

- Measures

- Dimensions

- Hierarchies

A *measure* is a generally numeric value that is related to activity for a given process. If you can apply an aggregating function (sum, min, max, count, average) to a value and create a meaningful result, you likely are dealing with a measure. Returning to our cash register example, if the sum of units sold was 1,000 for a given register, 1,000 items left the store today via that register. That aggregate value has meaning. On the other hand, if we were to total the value for the SKU's, or even average the SKU numbers, there would likely be little meaning in the value, because the SKU really only serves to describe the measure (units sold). In fact, knowing the total number of units sold grouped by SKU is a valuable piece of information for a retailer.

In dimensional modeling, the role of a *dimension* is to further describe a measure. Much as our cash register data would likely contain the time and date of the sale, the store in which the sale occurred and perhaps even a customer identity using a bar-code-based affinity program. Because each of these dimensions are known for each sale, our model for cash register's sales can answer any number of interesting questions combining criteria for a dimension, without any need to reorganize the data to quickly service each new query.

The final primary dimensional modeling structure is a *hierarchy*, which is simply a relationship among dimensions that serves to organize or classify values for a dimension. The simplest example of a hierarchy is in a date dimension. Revisiting the cash register system, we can organize the date dimension to provide interesting summarization of the measures related to a date, because each sale occurs on a given calendar date. For example, knowing the date of a sale was January 5, 2010, a calendar hierarchy in our date dimension could be used to determine the month in which that date is contained: January. Additionally, because we know the month of the sale is January, the date hierarchy could determine the sale was in the first quarter of the year 2010. Finally, because we know which quarter the sale occurred in, we know the year (2010). Hierarchies give both PowerPivot and traditional BI tools the ability to slice and dice the data, drilling down from a total to a specific value of interest.

Practices

The habits and actions that are executed routinely as part of every project are the practices of the method described in this chapter. Practices are the activities of execution that produce working, reusable PowerPivot solutions. The practices that follow include activities that are part of all modern software development, such as using revision control. The majority of these practices, however, pertain specifically to PowerPivot development, such as object naming and basics of dimensional modeling.

Take Advantage of Revision Control

Usually, when I am using a revision control system on my projects, it is Team Foundation Server. However, because of the compact unit of distribution, the Microsoft Excel .xlsx file, for distributing PowerPivot for Excel solutions your revision control system need not be so complex. In writing this book, I worked on multiple devices (two laptops, a desktop computer, an Atom-based netbook, an iPhone, and an Android phone), and I used DropBox (www.dropbox.com) to maintain a single version of my manuscripts, images, examples and notes. I can attest to DropBox's ability to maintain a history of revisions for a given .xlsx file, even across multiple devices.

You could also accomplish the same thing with Microsoft's LiveMesh. However, at the time of this writing, the LiveMesh Beta was ending, and Windows Live Essentials 2011 was not yet released.

Finally, and saving the best for last, if your company uses SharePoint, save your PowerPivot for Excel work there. Even if PowerPivot for SharePoint is not available on your company SharePoint install, your .xlsx files can be stored (and with document library revision history set on) and history maintained.

Contrast any of these free or low-cost solutions for maintaining your PowerPivot for Excel solutions with losing your work. The integration with Windows for all three is nearly seamless, and it just doesn't make sense to leave preservation of your efforts to chance.

Rename Early to Keep DAX Formulas Sane

PowerPivot for Excel performs a dizzying array of functions on behalf of the solution developer. Management of table and column names is one area where you can either save extra work by taking time to name (or rename) structures early. As shown in previous examples, when a dataset is added to PowerPivot by means of the Linked Table option, by default PowerPivot assigns a name in the form of TableN, where N is the number of previously created linked tables plus one. So the first Linked Table would be Table1, the second Table2, and so on. Hardly a meaningful way of naming the data, but PowerPivot will then work with DAX formulas in the form Table1[ColumnName]. As soon as you decide to give Table1 a more meaningful name, say DimDate, DimProduct, or SalesFacts, your existing formulas referring to Table1 now return #ERROR. However, PowerPivot Relationships are handled differently.

Creating a Relationship

As an example, begin with a clean Excel worksheet. In the first four rows of the first sheet, enter the data as depicted in Figure 5-1. Create a PowerPivot linked table from this data; PowerPivot should name the new table Table1. Leave the name as the default.

⟋	A	B	C	D
1	Product	Date	Quantity	
2	a	1/1/2010	1	
3	b	2/1/2010	2	
4	c	3/1/2010	3	
5				

Figure 5-1. *Our fact table*

In the next tab of the current sheet, enter the data shown in Figure 5-2. This will be the basis of a trivial product dimension table for our example on the effects of renaming on PowerPivot relationships. Create a linked table from this data; PowerPivot should name this recent table Table2. Do not rename the new PowerPivot table.

⟋	A	B	C
1	Product	Grade	
2	a	Best	
3	b	Better	
4	c	Good	
5			

Figure 5-2. *Product dimension data*

Create a relationship from Table1 to Table2, as depicted in Figure 5-3.

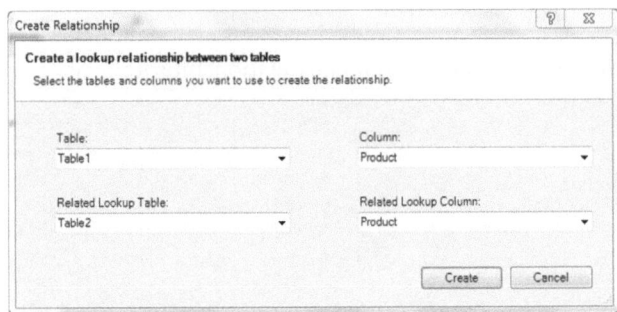

Figure 5-3. *Creating an initial relationship*

We now have two PowerPivot tables related to each other by a single column. If PowerPivot relationships behave like formulas, a rename of a table or column, on either side of the relationship should break the relationship.

Renaming an Object in a Relationship

From the PowerPivot window, select Table2 (the product data) and rename the PowerPivot table to DimProduct. From the table name tab, right-click and select the Rename option, as illustrated in Figure 5-4.

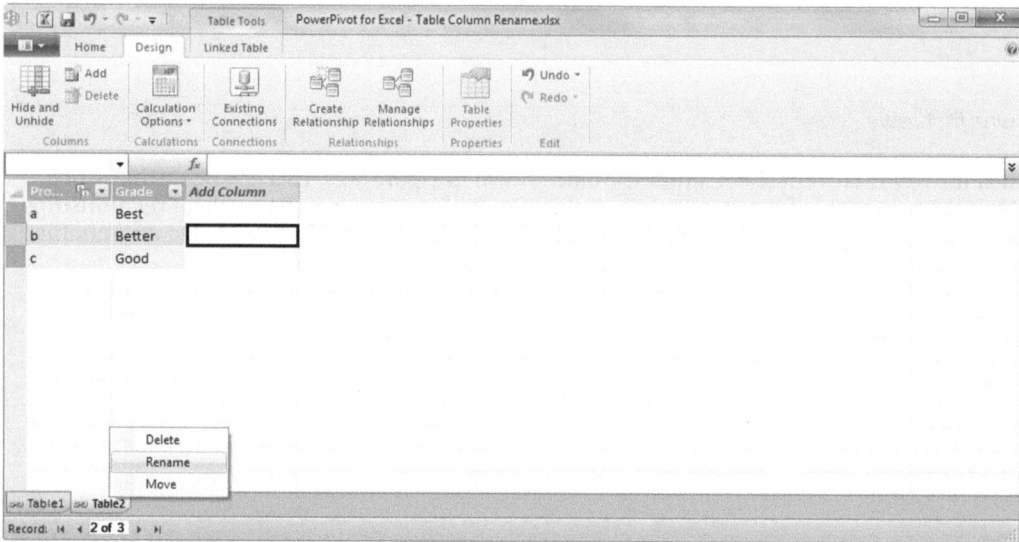

Figure 5-4. *Renaming a table in PowerPivot*

Examining the Result

From the PowerPivot window, select the Design ribbon and then the Manage Relationships item, as pictured in Figure 5-5.

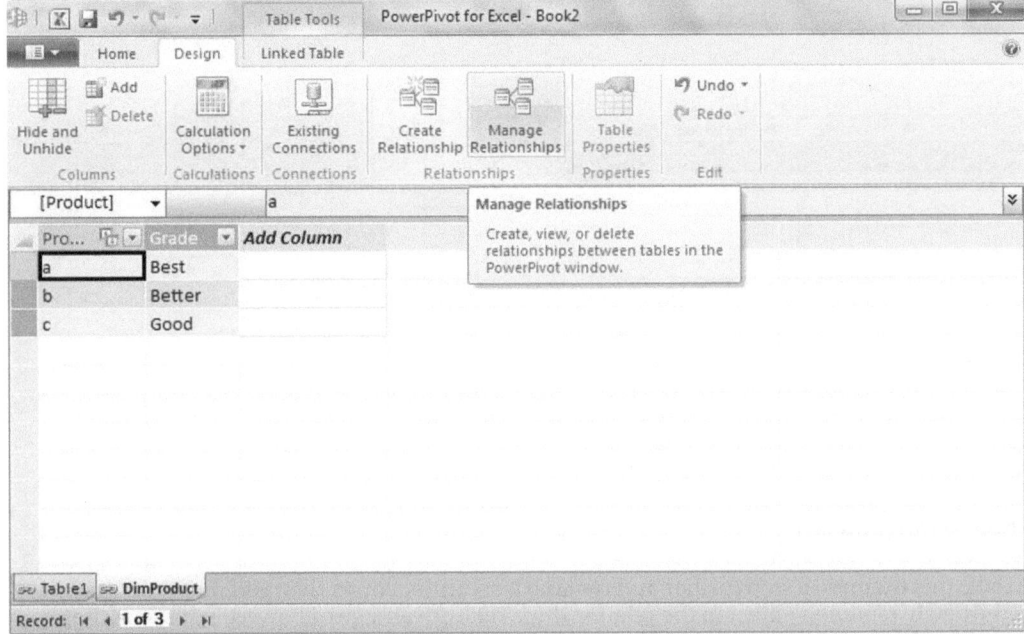

Figure 5-5 *Design and manage relationships*

From the ensuing dialog, you will notice a list of relationships. Because of the trivial nature of our PowerPivot solution to demonstrate the resiliency of PowerPivot relationships, there is only one relationship, as shown in Figure 5-6. However, PowerPivot has propagated the table name change to the relationship on our behalf. The relationship that existed between Table1[Product] and Table2[Product] now exists between Table1[Product] and DimProduct[Product].

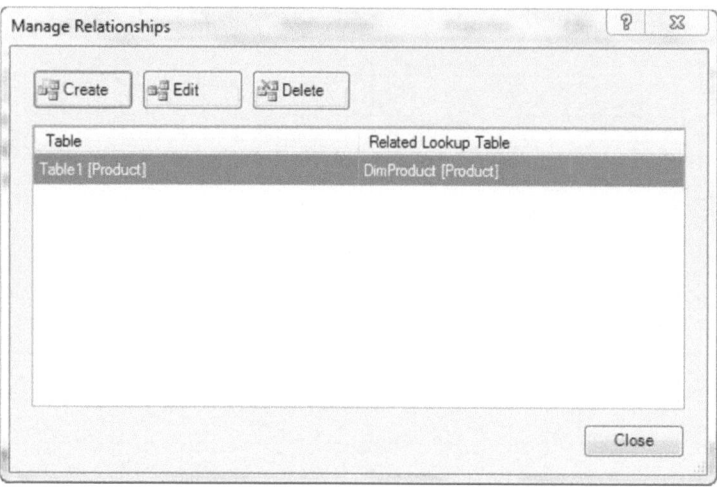

Figure 5-6. *Relationship changed*

You can take this example a step further and rename a column. PowerPivot will maintain the reference to the newly renamed object in the relationship. Take advantage of PowerPivot's work here on your behalf, and don't be afraid to rename tables and columns as a way of making your formulas more readable.

Choose Online Datasources When Possible

As you will soon find in the PowerPivot for SharePoint chapters, not all datasources are treated equally within PowerPivot. Your primary use of PowerPivot may be to combine data that exists only in a spreadsheet or text file with data stored in an online data store. Whenever possible, choose an online datasource over data that only exists on a single machine. You should prefer online data sources because data that exists as only a copy-and-paste from a source into a Microsoft Excel table has no connection information by which to regularly refresh the data. Even a text file, once it is made available as a PowerPivot for Excel data source, can be regularly refreshed.

For example, the data for the airline on-time performance example in Chapter 4 is readily available via the Internet, and you can download the data for the most recent month at http://www.transtats.bts.gov/DL_SelectFields.asp?Table_ID=236&DB_Short_Name=On-Time in comma separated variable (CSV) format. Import the data into PowerPivot for Excel, using the location of to which you have saved the data from the BTS web site. While PowerPivot for Excel imports the data, note the record count. After a successful import, open the original data file in a text editor, deleting either the first or last data row (or any nonheader rows) noting the record count before *and* after the row deletions. Save the data file (with fewer records) to the same location originally specified to PowerPivot. Open the PowerPivot for Excel window, and use the Refresh option from the PowerPivot ribbon's Get External Data section, as pictured in Figure 5-7.

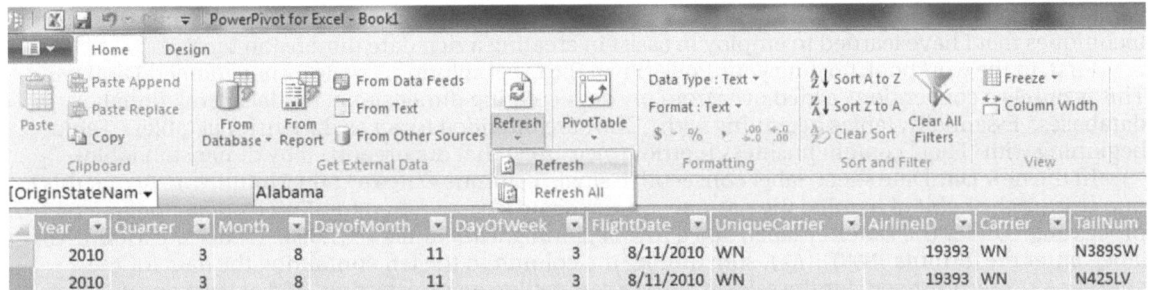

Figure 5-7. *Refreshing your connections*

The record count for the refreshed table should contain the same record count as the data file from which rows were deleted. In other words, PowerPivot for Excel can maintain a connection to a text file. This can be a valuable tool to refresh PowerPivot for Excel from a regularly updated, yet nonrelational source of data.

The large difference here is in having to manipulate data from the clipboard and into an Excel worksheet, as we may have done to incorporate text data into a PowerPivot for Excel solution. First, the data file does not have to be opened by a user in order to refresh PowerPivot with the new data. This is not the case with copy and paste data. Second, PowerPivot for Excel can actually make use of more rows (or records) of data using a text file than with a copy and paste data source. This is because a copy and paste (or linked table) datasource is limited by Microsoft Excel's maximum rows in a worksheet. These limits don't apply with text file datasources, because the data is read from the inbound file and stored in the SSAS (Vertipaq mode) in-memory runtime on the PC.

Relate Fact Sets Through a Dimension Table

In Chapter 4, I discussed the problems with relating two fact sets directly, without a related dimension table. That example outlined the issues with relating a fact set (sales) with another (page views) without a dimension table. If nothing else, strive to involve a date dimension between fact tables. Take a second look at your design should you find the need to join two fact tables together.

Create a Separate Date Dimension

Rules were made to be broken, but if you work with PowerPivot for Excel to develop analytic solutions, you will soon see the value in creating a date dimension separate from your business fact (that is, measure) tables. The two principle uses of a date dimension center around relating facts sets to each other and ensuring a common set of to-date calendar periods are observed. But first, how do you quickly create a rich date dimension?

Shortcut to a Rich Date Dimension

The first choice for populating a date dimension table for your PowerPivot for Excel solutions will usually be the time (or date or calendar) tables used in an existing data source. Data mart and data warehouse databases usually contain a single version of the enterprise calendar accounting for year-to-year variances such as holidays. In case using such a table is not an option, I will share with you a few techniques that I have learned to employ to assist in creating a rich date dimension table.

First, in the workbook hosting your PowerPivot for Excel solution, create a sheet named DimDate. This is purely a convention carried over from my days creating dimensional models in relational databases. Essentially, tables beginning with "Dim" are intended to act as dimensional tables. Table beginning with "Fact" contain business metrics (measures) that are organized by dimension tables.

In the new DimDate sheet, label consecutive single columns DateKey and MonthNbr. Again, this is purely from the habit of naming the natural and surrogate keys required for dimensional update processing. Under the DateKey label, add a row beginning with January 1, 2009. Under the MonthNbr label, enter the formula =MONTH(A2), substituting the column to the left containing the date for the address A2. I recommend, for the sake of a more compelling demonstration, add at least two years of dates to both columns. From this table, create a linked PowerPivot table via PowerPivot's Create Linked Table ribbon selection.

You will notice that PowerPivot has not named the new linked table DimDate, but instead Table1 (assuming this is the first linked table). Rename the PowerPivot table now, as the balance of this technique uses DAX formulas.

Return to the Excel Worksheet window, and add a new sheet named Calendar Lookups. In this worksheet, you will enter the calendar specifics for your organization, similar to Figure 5-8.

	A	B	C	D	E
1	MonthNbr	MonthName	MonthAbbr	Quarter	FiscalQtr
2	1	January	Jan	1	2
3	2	February	Feb	1	2
4	3	March	Mar	1	2
5	4	April	Apr	2	3
6	5	May	May	2	3
7	6	June	Jun	2	3
8	7	July	Jul	3	4
9	8	August	Aug	3	4
10	9	September	Sep	3	4
11	10	October	Oct	4	1
12	11	November	Nov	4	1
13	12	December	Dec	4	1

Figure 5-8. *Calendar Lookups linked table*

In this table, enter both the long form and abbreviated names for each month. Microsoft Excel will handle this series for you after you enter and then select January and the Jan cells and drag the series selection to the final row. The final two columns relate to which quarter a month is associated. For our example, we have a both a calendar quarter and a fiscal quarter to represent a fiscal new year of October 1 of each year. After the data entry is complete, create a linked table from this data named CalendarLookup. Ensure you rename the PowerPivot table; otherwise, you will have "Table2" propogated in your DAX formulas.

From the PowerPivot window, create a relationship between DimDate[MonthNbr] and CalendarLookup[MonthNbr]. This is the basis for the rest of the solution. Next, add a column named Year, populated by the following DAX formula: =YEAR(DimDate[DateKey]). This will ensure we know the year for slicer purposes. Next, add a column to the DimDate table named Quarter. In the formula area, use the following DAX to populate Quarter with the correct quarter number entered from Figure 5-7, =RELATED(CalendarLookup[Quarter]). Repeat this operation for a column named FiscalQuarter that returns the FiscalQtr column from CalendarLookup. At this point, your DimDate table should resemble Figure 5-9.

Date	Month	Year	Quarter	FiscalQuarter
1/1/2009	1	2009	1	2
1/2/2009	1	2009	1	2
1/3/2009	1	2009	1	2
1/4/2009	1	2009	1	2
1/5/2009	1	2009	1	2
1/6/2009	1	2009	1	2
1/7/2009	1	2009	1	2
1/8/2009	1	2009	1	2
1/9/2009	1	2009	1	2
1/10/2009	1	2009	1	2
1/11/2009	1	2009	1	2
1/12/2009	1	2009	1	2
1/13/2009	1	2009	1	2
1/14/2009	1	2009	1	2

Figure 5-9. *The DimDate table*

At this point, you may be asking wondering why we did not just copy everything in Microsoft Excel? Creating a single DimDate linked table in Microsoft Excel is certainly an option. However, one of the greatest advantages to this technique is being able to quickly create DAX formulas for date attributes, such as Quarter Number, plus being able to quickly and reliably change them. While it is not a frequent occurrence to have the Fiscal Year change, if the Fiscal Year end was moved to November 1, we could quickly implement by changing the Calendar Lookups table and refreshing the PowerPivot linked table. Additionally, this technique requires very little data to actually be stored in Excel. Most of the date attributes are implemented via DAX and stored in the PowerPivot SSAS instance.

Handling Moving Holidays

What about special dates? How could the previous technique accommodate 'moving' holidays such as Thanksgiving in the United States? One way to accommodate these yearly moving holidays is via a lookup table. Creating a table similar to below would allow for quick identification within PowerPivot for Excel as a holiday. Simply create the linked table, relate Holiday[Date] to DimDate[Date], and use Related() to populate an IsHoliday_YN column in DimDate.

■ **Note** When populating a date dimension, ensure you have rows in the date table for each day of the year. PowerPivot time intelligence functions rely on a fully populated date dimension when building sets of dates for year-to-date and similar calculations.

Leverage Built-In Measures

PowerPivot for Excel includes out-of-the-box features for a vast set of calculations available to report, based on measures within a PivotTable or PivotChart. The underlying SSAS database (the in-memory data store) that is part of PowerPivot for Excel establishes a platform from which percent-of-whole and other variations of composition analysis can be quickly calculated. Taking advantage of these calculations in your solutions can give a new insight to your existing data.

Revisiting the NCAA Football roster example from Chapter 4, we can illustrate several ways of reporting different measures using the same data. Using a PivotChart with a column label of SortYear and row labels of Conference and Team, as illustrated in Figure 5-10, choose Count of Player ID as the sole Values element.

Conference			
ACC	Big East	Big12	BigTen
Conf USA	Ind	Mid-American	Mountain West
Pac10	SEC	Sun Belt	WAC

Count of Player ID	Column Labels ▼					
Row Labels ⬚		01-FR	02-SO	03-JR	04-SR	Grand Total
⊟ SEC	16	467	275	297	223	1278
Alabama	1	34	27	20	23	105
Arkansas	2	44	24	28	15	113
Auburn	1	42	27	31	12	113
Florida	2	21	27	38	26	114
Georgia	1	32	24	26	19	102
Kentucky	2	35	28	20	19	104
LSU	1	40	22	13	19	95
Mississippi	1	58	16	24	28	127
Mississippi St.	1	42	17	28	14	102
South Carolina	1	46	23	30	9	109
Tennessee	2	29	18	23	18	90
Vanderbilt	1	44	22	16	21	104
Grand Total	16	467	275	297	223	1278

Figure 5-10. *Count of players by year (and team)*

PowerPivot for Excel provides a group of ratios that can be calculated based on the filter context of the PivotTable. Access the alternative calculations by right-clicking a measure within the PivotTable and selecting Show Values As from the context menu. The context menu will look similar to Figure 5-11.

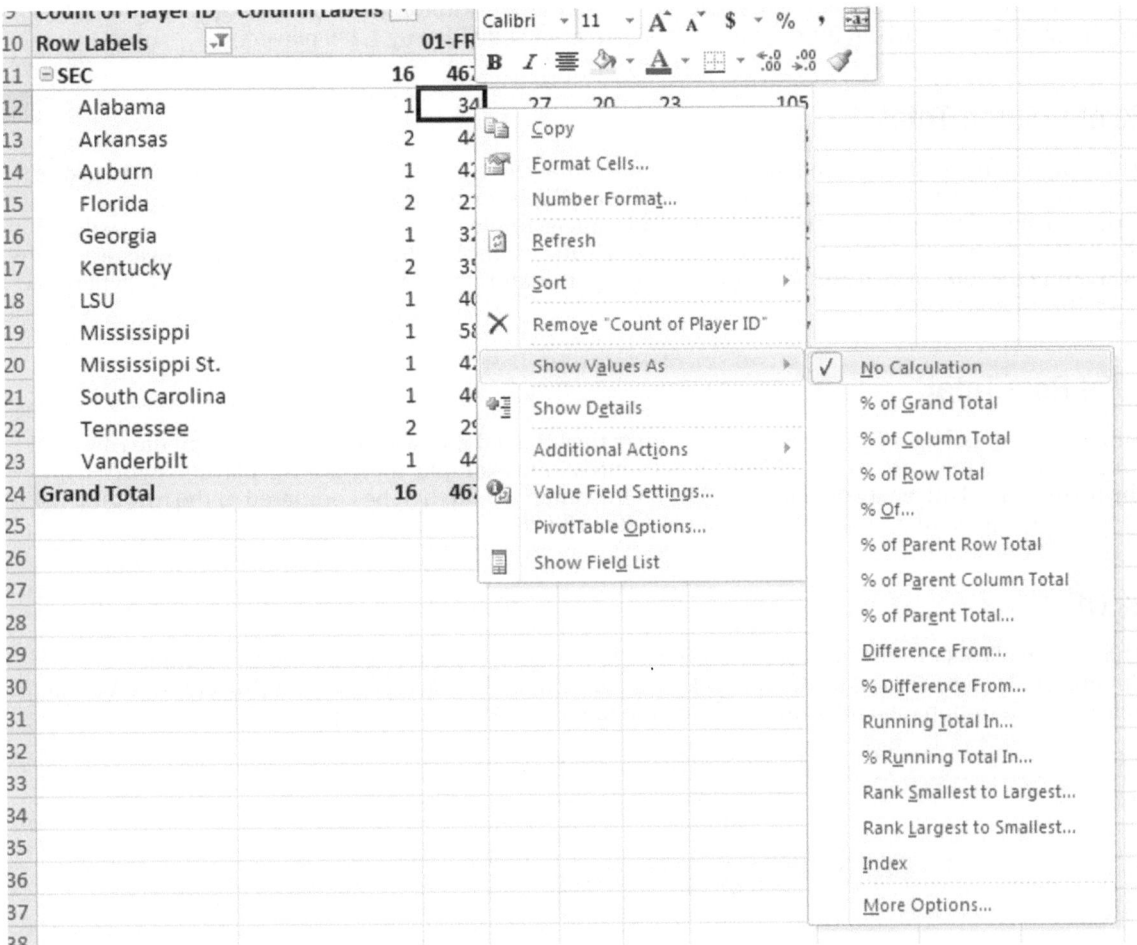

Figure 5-11. *Show Values As menu*

No Calculation

This option renders the measure as placed in the Values section of the PowerPivot Field List. No aggregate comparison calculation is applied.

% of Grand Total

This option renders the selected measure as a percentage of the grand total value for the measure. In the NCAA Class Composition example, there are 1,278 players reported in the grand total. The University of Alabama reported 34 freshmen in the dataset. When the % of Grand Total option is applied, the value for the Alabama and '01-FR intersection is 2.66 percent (34 divided by 1,278 players).

% of Column Total

This option renders the selected measure as a percentage of the column total for the selected measure. In the NCAA Class Composition example, there are 467 players reported across all selected (Southeastern Conference) institutions. To maintain example consistency where possible, we will use the 34 freshman year players from the % of Grand Total example. However, because the measure is now evaluating the total of all freshman (467) as the denominator, the percentage value used is 7.28 percent (34 / 467 = 7.28).

% of Row Total

Similar to % of Column Total, this option renders the selected measure as a percentage of the row total for the selected measure. In the NCAA Class Composition example, there are 105 players reported on the roster of the University of Alabama. The 34 freshman would then be compared to the row total (105) to render the percentage of 32.38 percent (34 / 105 = 32.28).

% Of

This option allows the PowerPivot for Excel user to baseline a measure organized by multiple dimensional values (Team) by the values for a single dimension (in our case, the University of Alabama). Selecting this option for a measure produces the dialog box depicted in Figure 5-12.

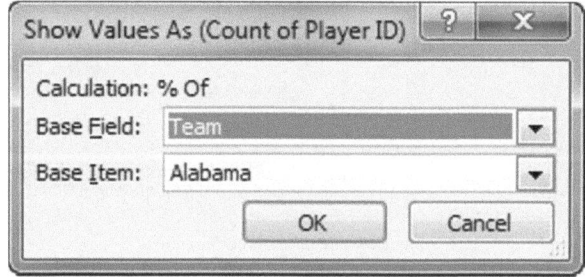

Figure 5-12. *% Of baseline dialog*

The dialog allows the selection of a base field and an item within the field by which to gauge the values of all other elements in the chosen field. In our case, we are comparing the other eleven teams in the Southeastern Conference with the University of Alabama. Pressing OK in the Show Values As dialog will render a PivotTable similar to Figure 5-13.

PlayerCount	Column Labels ⊤				
Row Labels ⊤	01-FR	02-SO	03-JR	04-SR	Grand Total
⊟ SEC					
Alabama	100.00%	100.00%	100.00%	100.00%	100.00%
Arkansas	129.41%	88.89%	140.00%	65.22%	106.73%
Auburn	123.53%	100.00%	155.00%	52.17%	107.69%
Florida	61.76%	100.00%	190.00%	113.04%	107.69%
Georgia	94.12%	88.89%	130.00%	82.61%	97.12%
Kentucky	102.94%	103.70%	100.00%	82.61%	98.08%
LSU	117.65%	81.48%	65.00%	82.61%	90.38%
Mississippi	170.59%	59.26%	120.00%	121.74%	121.15%
Mississippi St.	123.53%	62.96%	140.00%	60.87%	97.12%
South Carolina	135.29%	85.19%	150.00%	39.13%	103.85%
Tennessee	85.29%	66.67%	115.00%	78.26%	84.62%
Vanderbilt	129.41%	81.48%	80.00%	91.30%	99.04%
Grand Total					

Figure 5-13. *The percentage of a baseline*

As Figure 5-13 illustrates, the values for the baseline instance are all 100.00 percent, because the numerator and denominator are the same value: the baseline is the value. However, the real use in this out-of-the-box calculation is in baselining data to a known dimensional value.

% of Parent Row Total

To create a meaningful illustration of the % of Parent Row Total, a new subtotaling level will have to be added to the example. Dragging Division into the Row Labels area of the PowerPivot Field List, so that it appears between Conference and Team, will create a new subtotal at the Division level. The results should be similar to Figure 5-14.

Count of Player ID	Column Labels ⊤				
Row Labels ⊤	01-FR	02-SO	03-JR	04-SR	Grand Total
⊟SEC	467	275	297	223	1262
⊟East	207	142	153	112	614
Florida	21	27	38	26	112
Georgia	32	24	26	19	101
Kentucky	35	28	20	19	102
South Carolina	46	23	30	9	108
Tennessee	29	18	23	18	88
Vanderbilt	44	22	16	21	103
⊟West	260	133	144	111	648
Alabama	34	27	20	23	104
Arkansas	44	24	28	15	111
Auburn	42	27	31	12	112
LSU	40	22	13	19	94
Mississippi	58	16	24	28	126
Mississippi St.	42	17	28	14	101
Grand Total	467	275	297	223	1262

Figure 5-14. *Subtotal by division*

Choosing % of Parent Row Total will then render the selected measures evaluated over the parent level (in this case subtotaled by division). To continue with the University of Alabama freshmen, the 34 members of this class would be evaluated as a percentage of the 260 freshmen in the entirety of the Western division (34/260=13.08 percent). However, the % of Parent Row continues. The 260 Western Division freshmen are evaluated against to total of all freshmen in the conference (467). The Western Division freshmen total is reported as 55.67 percent (260 / 467 = 55.67).

This can be a very powerful tool for decomposing measures across and up a hierarchy.

% of Parent Column Total

This selection renders the selected measure in a manner identical to the % of Parent Row, except by levels used in the Column Labels area of the PowerPivot Field List. For example, in the example PivotTable, add Position to the Column Labels area of the PowerPivot field list. This should result in a PivotTable similar to below.

Adding the breakdown shows three of Alabama's 34 freshman (the parent column total) play the defensive back position. Therefore the reported % of Parent Column Total is 8.82 % (3 / 34 = 8.82).

% of Parent Total

This selection renders the selected measure similar to % of Parent Row and % of Parent Column but allows the solution author to choose the base field for comparison.

Difference From

This selection renders the selected measure, as compared to a baseline selected by the PowerPivot solution author. To continue with the current example, after selecting Difference From on the Show Measures As context menu, a dialog similar to Figure 5-15 will be produced.

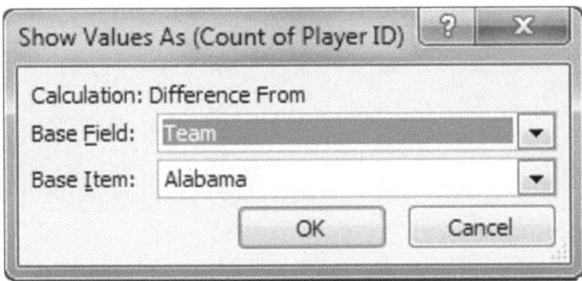

Figure 5-15. *Show Values as a difference*

This dialog allows the solution author to select which base field and which item in the field as the basis for comparison of the other values. To continue with our example, selecting the options as depicted in Figure 5-12 will produce a PivotTable comparing all other teams in the SEC to the University of Alabama.

The end result of the comparison will resemble Figure 5-16. As you will note the values for Alabama are all blank, indicating this is the baseline row. Additionally, each of the other eleven teams in the conference has been reduced to the difference between their values for each class year and those reported by the University of Alabama (the baseline). For example, Alabama reported 34 freshmen and the University of Arkansas reported 44. The difference of 10 is rendered by PowerPivot given the baseline selection.

Count of Player ID	Column Labels ▼				
Row Labels ▼	01-FR	02-SO	03-JR	04-SR	Grand Total
⊟ SEC					
Alabama					
Arkansas	10	-3	8	-8	7
Auburn	8	0	11	-11	8
Florida	-13	0	18	3	8
Georgia	-2	-3	6	-4	-3
Kentucky	1	1	0	-4	-2
LSU	6	-5	-7	-4	-10
Mississippi	24	-11	4	5	22
Mississippi St.	8	-10	8	-9	-3
South Carolina	12	-4	10	-14	4
Tennessee	-5	-9	3	-5	-16
Vanderbilt	10	-5	-4	-2	-1
Grand Total					

Figure 5-16. *Difference from baseline*

% Difference From

This selection works similarly to the Difference From selection, except the reported value is the percentage difference from the selected baseline. If the Difference From example in the previous section is extended to use instead % Difference From, the value reported for the 44 Arkansas freshmen, relative to the 34 Alabama freshmen in the baseline would be 29.41 percent ((44-34) / 34 = 29.41).

Running Total In

Occasionally, it is necessary to create an analysis of measures that includes the running total of a measure. For example, which product classes constitute 80 percent of revenue? The Running Total In option renders the selected measure as a sum, over a set of column or row values. To further the current example, selecting SortYear as the base field for this option yields a PivotTable reporting the running total of players, by their SortYear value, as shown in Figure 5-17.

Count of Player ID	Column Labels ⊤				
Row Labels ⊤	01-FR	02-SO	03-JR	04-SR	Grand Total
⊟ SEC	467	742	1039	1262	
Alabama	34	61	81	104	
Arkansas	44	68	96	111	
Auburn	42	69	100	112	
Florida	21	48	86	112	
Georgia	32	56	82	101	
Kentucky	35	63	83	102	
LSU	40	62	75	94	
Mississippi	58	74	98	126	
Mississippi St.	42	59	87	101	
South Carolina	46	69	99	108	
Tennessee	29	47	70	88	
Vanderbilt	44	66	82	103	
Grand Total	467	742	1039	1262	

Figure 5-17. *Running Total In (SortYear)*

Conversely, we could apply the Team as the base field, which would have caused the running totals to run down the table (following the columns).

% Running Total In

Similar to the Running Total In option, the % Running Total In selection creates a percentage based on a running total of a measure value over a base field. Continuing with the existing example, first, reverse the order of SortYear from 04-SR to 01-FR (instead of 01-FR to 04-SR). Second, apply the % Running Total In option using SortYear as the base field yields a PivotTable similar to Figure 5-18.

Count of Player ID	Column Labels ⬇				
Row Labels ⬇	04-SR	03-JR	02-SO	01-FR	Grand Total
⊟ SEC		17.67%	41.20%	63.00%	100.00%
Alabama		22.12%	41.35%	67.31%	100.00%
Arkansas		13.51%	38.74%	60.36%	100.00%
Auburn		10.71%	38.39%	62.50%	100.00%
Florida		23.21%	57.14%	81.25%	100.00%
Georgia		18.81%	44.55%	68.32%	100.00%
Kentucky		18.63%	38.24%	65.69%	100.00%
LSU		20.21%	34.04%	57.45%	100.00%
Mississippi		22.22%	41.27%	53.97%	100.00%
Mississippi St.		13.86%	41.58%	58.42%	100.00%
South Carolina		8.33%	36.11%	57.41%	100.00%
Tennessee		20.45%	46.59%	67.05%	100.00%
Vanderbilt		20.39%	35.92%	57.28%	100.00%
Grand Total		17.67%	41.20%	63.00%	100.00%

Figure 5-18. *% Running Total In by SortYear*

This PivotTable shows the percentage of the Roster for Alabama, at the junior (03-JR) or senior (04-SR) level as 41.35 percent.

"Rank Smallest to Largest" and "Rank Largest to Smallest"

Both of these options rank the values for the selected measures including ties. In other words, the example data includes four institutions that report the same number of freshmen class members (Auburn and Mississippi State at 42, and Arkansas and Vanderbilt at 44). Therefore, the ranks for the twelve teams are from one to ten, with the previously mentioned ties being ranked seventh and eighth respectively.

Conversely, if the Rank Largest to Smallest option is selected, these ties are reported as Arkansas and Vanderbilt tied at number three, and Auburn and Mississippi State tied in the number four position.

Index

The Index option of the Show Values As context menu essentially evaluates as (Value In cell * Grand Total of Grand Totals) / (Grand Row Total * Grand Column Total). This would mean our Alabama Freshmen value would be calculated as (34 * 1262)/ (104 * 467) = 0.883462362.

Customize Your PivotCharts via PivotTables

Beneath every PowerPivot PivotChart is a PivotTable. You may have noticed by now PowerPivot creating an underlying PivotTable for each PivotChart being expressly added by you, the PowerPivot for Excel author. An interesting side-effect to this PowerPivot for Excel feature is the ability to greatly customize a PivotChart, without touching the chart itself. By manipulating the PivotTable using filters, for example, the PivotChart will change to reflect the filtered data in the PivotTable.

For example, Figure 5-19 contains a PivotChart that was inserted into Sheet5 of the current Excel file. This is simply a summary of flights, by carrier, from a given airport. Notice that immediately preceding Sheet5 is an Excel sheet labeled Data for Sheet5 Chart1. This is a sheet inserted by PowerPivot at the time Chart1 was added to Sheet5 to contain the data behind the new PivotChart in Sheet5. If we had inserted additional PivotCharts into Sheet5, PowerPivot would create an additional sheet for each, naming them in the same form Data for Sheet5 ChartN.

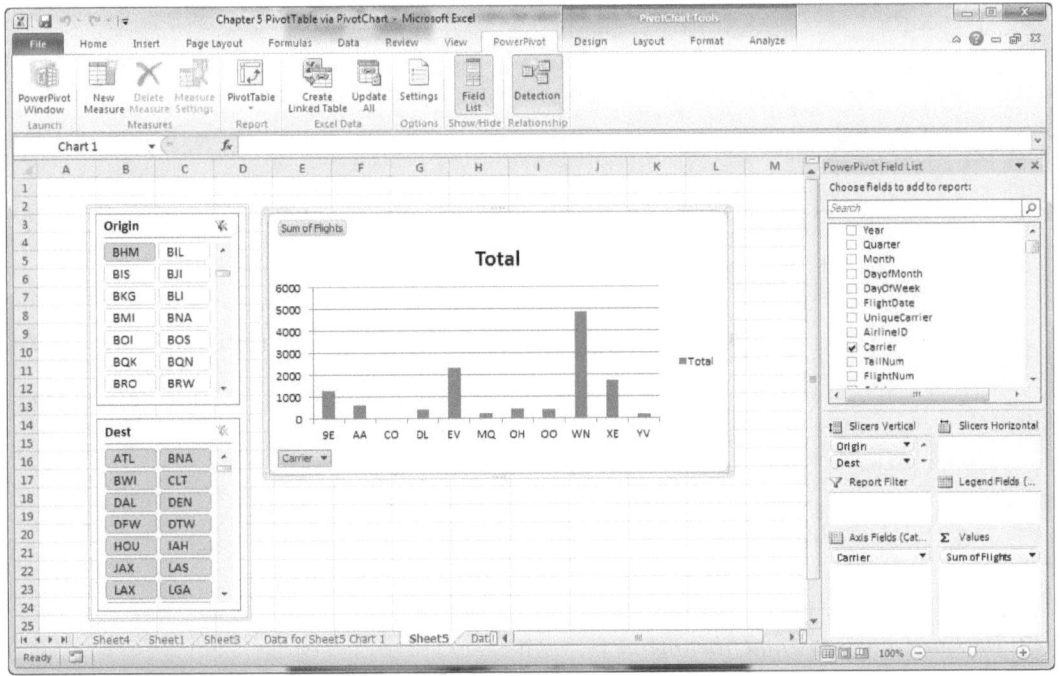

Figure 5-19. *A PivotChart and related data sheet*

Also notice the Carrier button just below the origin of the chart. Within PowerPivot for Excel, this button is called an *axis field button*, and it allows rapid access to the sort and filter context menu, for a particular field, in this case Carrier. Access and expansion of the sort and filter context menu, from the carrier axis button, is illustrated in Figure 5-20.

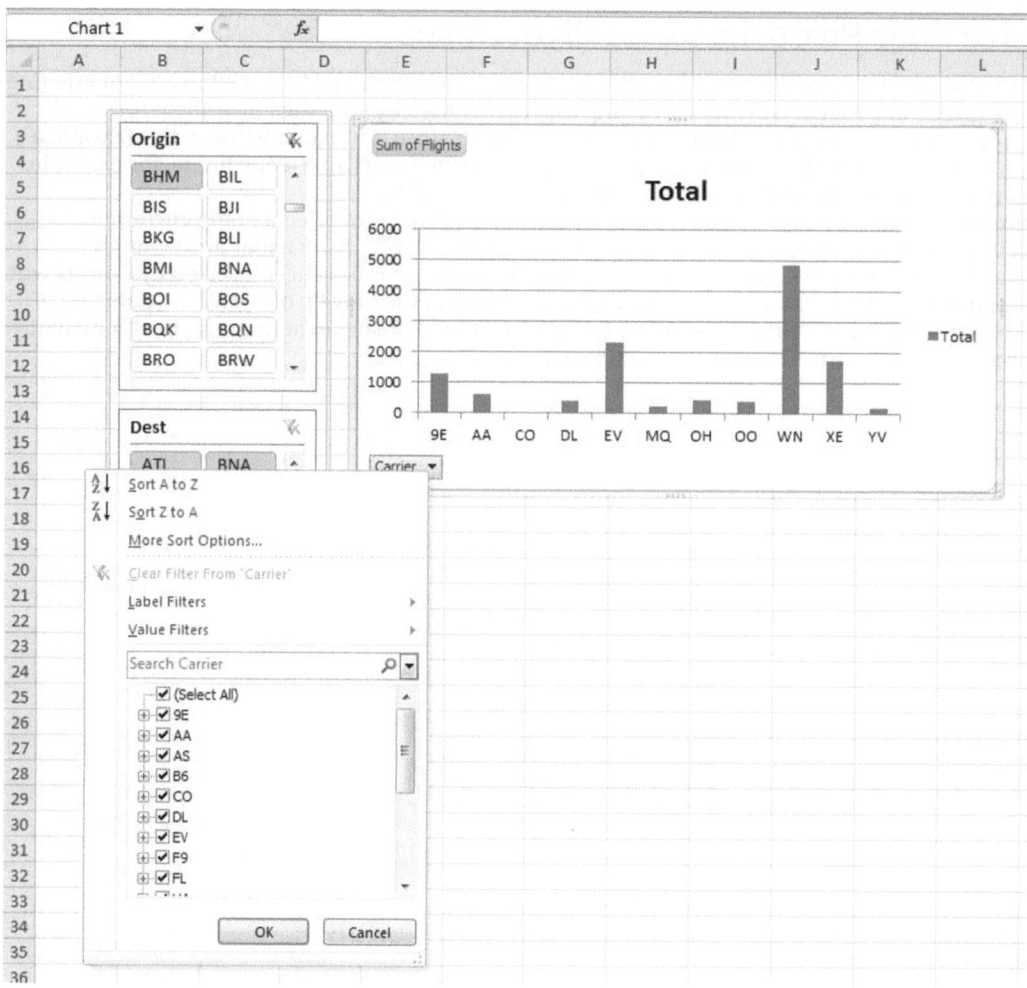

Figure 5-20. *The Carrier axis sort and filter menu*

For the purposes of interactive and ad hoc analytics, the button allows a PowerPivot for Excel developer easy access to features that are also available by selecting a value on the Carrier axis of Chart1. As illustrated in Figure 5-21, right-clicking an axis value will also render the sort and filter menu for values of Carrier.

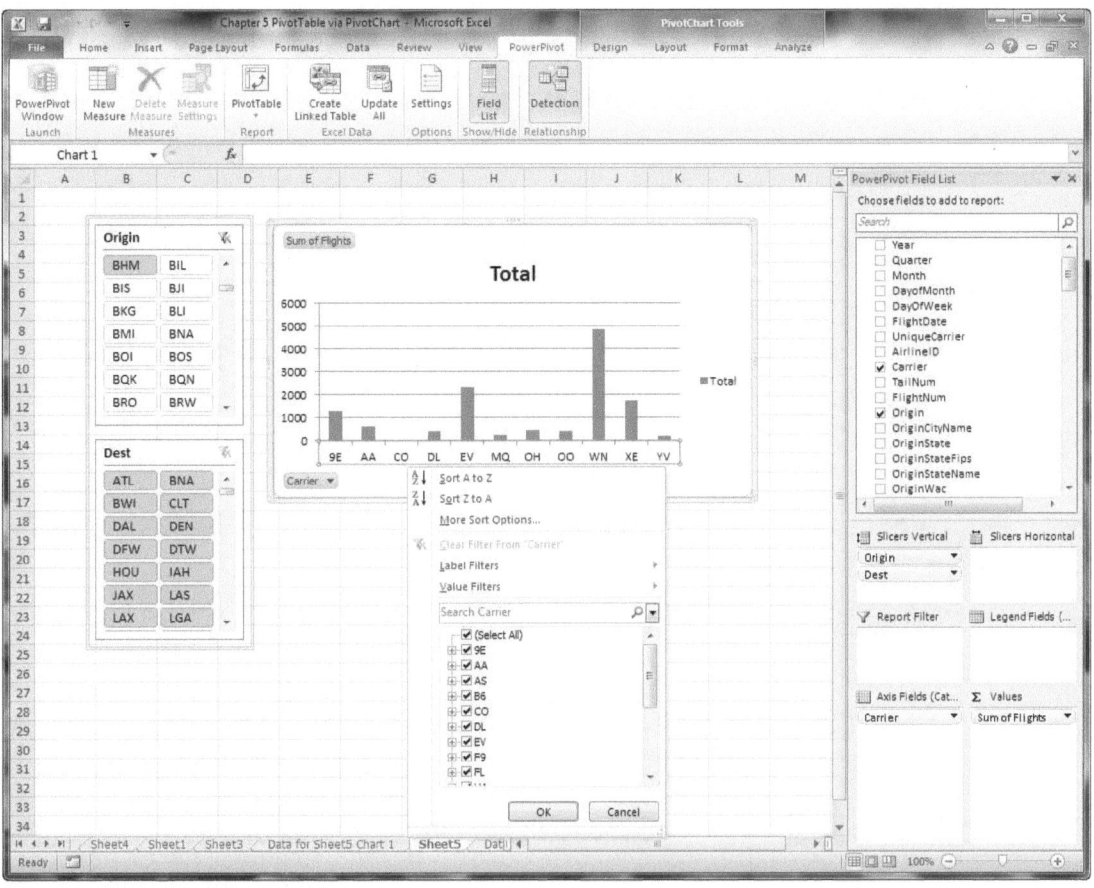

Figure 5-21. *Carrier Axis Sort and Filter Menu*

Perhaps this technique of customizing PivotCharts via the underlying PivotTable is more of a preference than a practice. But in my experience, clients have found the axis buttons confusing and feel that the buttons clutter the chart space. We can remove them altogether and still customize the appearance and data content of the PivotChart. Removal of the axis buttons from a PivotChart is a simple matter of right-clicking the axis field button and selecting Hide Axis Field Buttons on Chart, as illustrated in Figure 5-22. The result is a PivotChart without the Carrier axis field button and more room to display data. Similarly, the Hide All Field Buttons on Chart option removes both the Carrier axis button and the Sum of Flights field button, yielding even more area for the chart data within the chart zone.

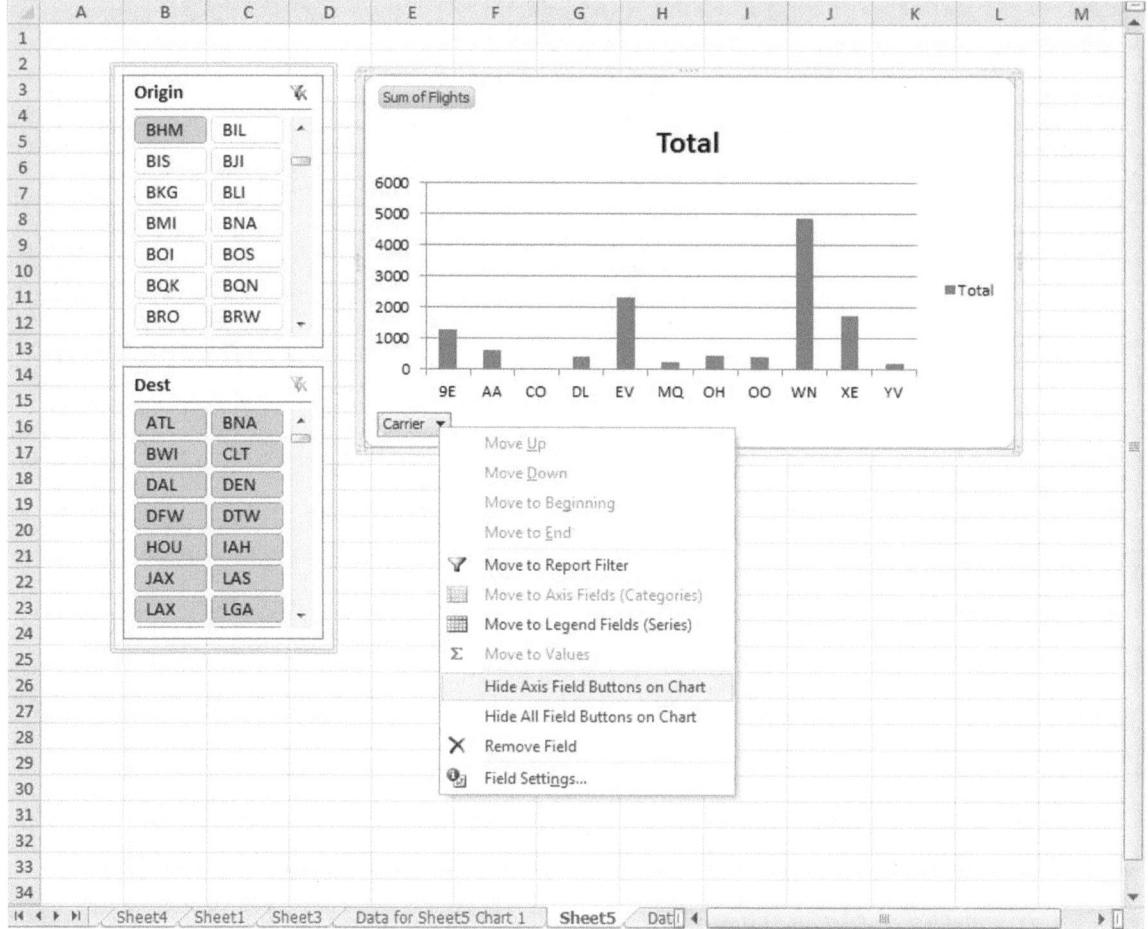

Figure 5-22. *Hiding axis field buttons*

With the axis field buttons removed, Chart1 can still be manipulated using the underlying data contained in the PivotTable within the Data for Sheet5 Chart1 sheet. For example, if we wanted to report on the percentage of flights serviced by each carrier, we can quickly alter the chart without the creation of a new measure. Instead, navigate to the sheet containing the chart data ("Data for Sheet5 Chart1"). Select a measure value, in this case Sum of Flights, and right-click the cell. As illustrated in Figure 5-23, this will produce a context menu, from which we choose Show Values As and then select % of Grand Total. Notice the default selection is No Calculation, but with the highlighted selection, we will show each of the measures as their percentage of the grand total.

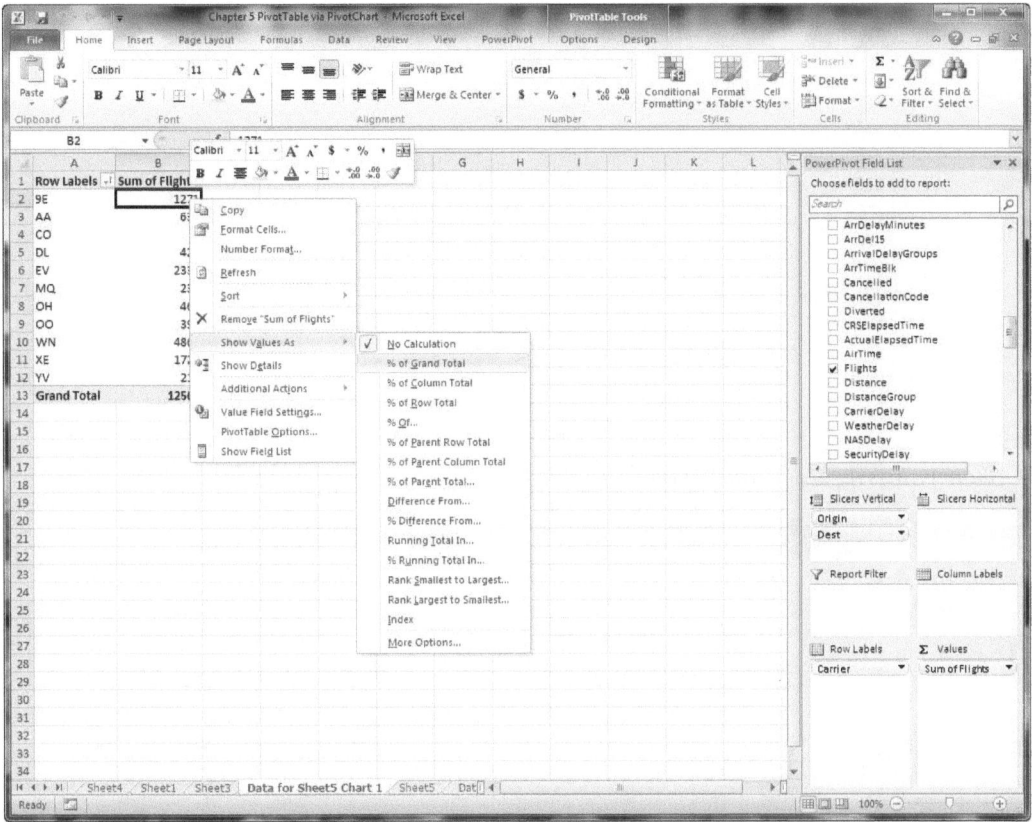

Figure 5-23. *Show Values As menu*

Immediately after applying the % of Grand Total selection, each of the values in the PivotTable are changed to percentages of the grand total, summing to be 100 percent of flights as illustrated in Figure 5-24. However, the valuable effect of this is seen in the original PivotChart. The y axis values are now formatted as percentages, associated with the original data bars illustrated in Figure 5-25.

	A	B
1	Row Labels ⬇	Sum of Flights
2	9E	10.12%
3	AA	5.06%
4	CO	0.02%
5	DL	3.36%
6	EV	18.61%
7	MQ	1.85%
8	OH	3.69%
9	OO	3.17%
10	WN	38.70%
11	XE	13.69%
12	YV	1.74%
13	Grand Total	100.00%
14		

Figure 5-24. *Show Values As % of Grand Total*

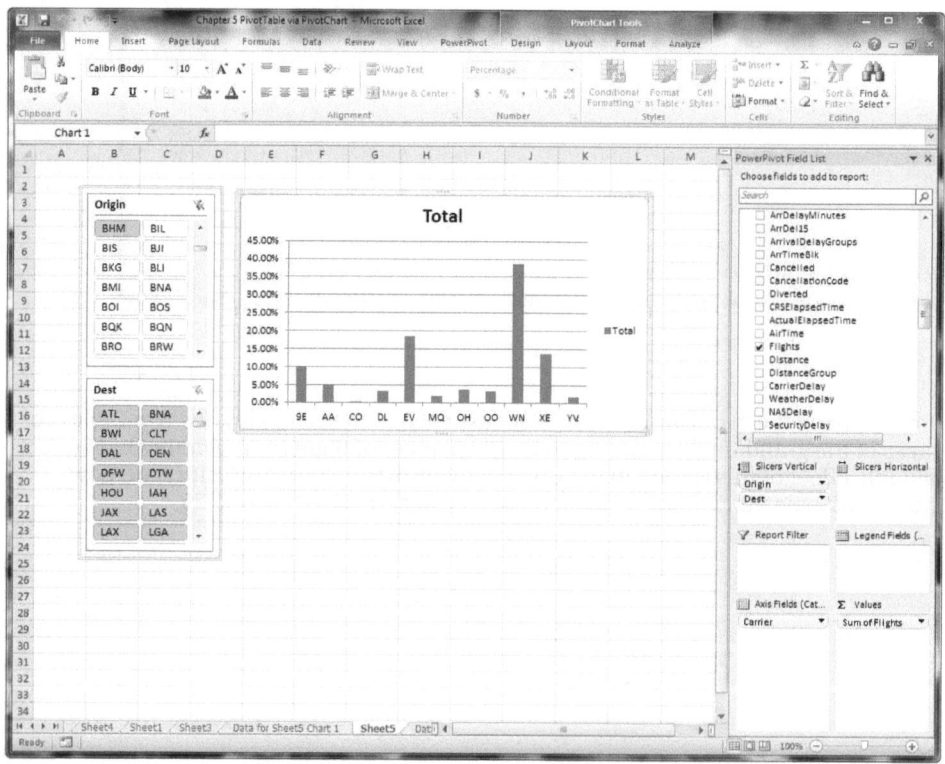

Figure 5-25. *PivotChart using Show Values As % of Grand Total*

Similarly, the Carriers in the PivotChart can be ranked by their percentage of volume by applying a variation of this technique. From the sheet containing the underlying data for the PivotChart ("Data for Sheet5 Chart1"), select a cell a measure value. Our illustration uses the Sum of Flights measure value. From the right-click context menu, select the Sort option and then Sort Largest to Smallest. This will immediately sort the PivotTable and predictably, Carriers in Chart1 will be sorted in order by flight volume, as illustrated in Figure 5-26.

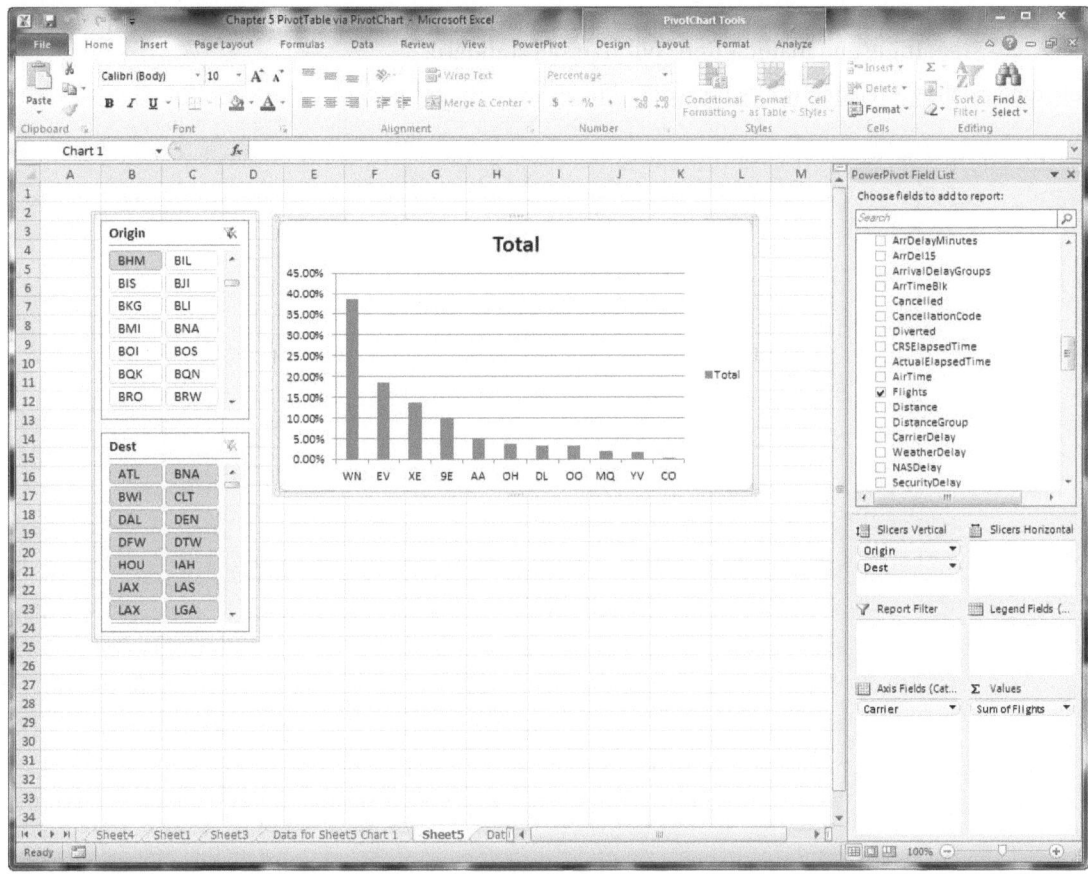

Figure 5-26. *Final PivotChart Sorted by Percentage*

Summary

Strive to use a repeatable method in your PowerPivot development efforts. Over time, this will lead to a robust library of PowerPivot solutions instead of a tangled mess of spreadsheets with little rhyme or reason known as a spreadmart. In addition to creating a durable decision-making tool, you will hopefully avoid a few of the pitfalls of an initial product release. Lastly, keep in mind the following key points from this chapter:

- Embrace failure in your PowerPivot efforts. Given the compact and generally portable nature of PowerPivot for Excel, you will only have one artifact to delete.

- Consider using a dimensional construct for your PowerPivot data models.

- Employ a revision control system. It's always nice to have a global rewind button on your projects.

- Rename names created by PowerPivot early. You won't regret the effort in both renaming and maintaining your naming standard.

Leverage existing Excel features where possible.

CHAPTER 6

■ ■ ■

Installing PowerPivot for SharePoint

If we did all the things we are capable of, we would literally astound ourselves.

—Thomas A. Edison

After reading the preceding chapters, you should have a solid understanding of how PowerPivot for Excel can be used to author Business Intelligence solutions. To this point, all that is needed to utilize PowerPivot features was Microsoft Excel 2010 (32- or 64-bit) and the free PowerPivot add-in. With these tools, you can gather data from disparate, related systems, and generate compelling analysis of the data. Because the unit of work is a single Excel workbook (.xlsx) file, your work can be shared with others via e-mail, flash drive, or other transportation methods. The SSAS in-memory runtime will compress some datasets to create a portable file size.

Eventually, however, a dataset will result in an Excel file that is too unwieldy for transport via e-mail and flash drive. Consumers of your PowerPivot analytics may not actually need all of the data moved to their workstation, but would be completely satisfied with a method by which to view the solution in a browser. With large datasets, data refresh times may expand to a level at which a batch process could be employed to move new data into the PowerPivot solution. Finally, with the increased ability to create and publish PowerPivot solutions, information workers will require a set of features to index, find, and version control PowerPivot solutions.

PowerPivot for SharePoint addresses all of these needs, providing a repository for storing, securing, and sharing PowerPivot solutions. SharePoint Server is the third product comprising Microsoft's Business Intelligence platform. Combined with SQL Server 2008 R2 Enterprise Edition and Microsoft Office Professional Plus, PowerPivot for Excel users can enjoy new data sources with which solutions can be constructed as well as new ways to utilize and share their PowerPivot development.

Getting Started

In order to truly appreciate PowerPivot for SharePoint, you will eventually require an installation of the software. While there are a number of different PowerPivot for SharePoint configurations possible, we are going to concentrate on three. First, assuming you have access to an existing SharePoint 2010 server, we will detail the steps your SharePoint Administrator will have to execute in order for you to begin taking advantage of PowerPivot for SharePoint. Next, the process for establishing a development environment in a single, virtual machine will be detailed. The final configuration will cover the options for installing SharePoint 2010 Server (and PowerPivot for SharePoint) on a single workstation.

Existing SharePoint 2010 Installation

Working with an existing installation is by far the simplest from a solution developer point of view. Coaxing, coercing, or otherwise convincing your SharePoint Administrator to execute the steps described in the following subsections will enable the PowerPivot for SharePoint features and allow publishing of PowerPivot solutions to an existing SharePoint server.

■ **Note** The steps to install PowerPivot into an existing SharePoint installation are already outlined in great detail in Microsoft's MSDN Library at http://msdn.microsoft.com/en-us/library/ee210616(SQL.105).aspx. I have listed the high-level tasks here as a guide to the process.

There are a number of pre-conditions for adding PowerPivot to an existing SharePoint server. First, the SharePoint server must have been installed using the Server Farm setup installation, as the built-in database installed during the stand-alone option is not supported for PowerPivot. The installing user must be a local administrator for the computer to which PowerPivot will be added. Additionally, the user must also be a farm administrator in order to add PowerPivot for SharePoint to the farm. From a SQL Server edition perspective, you must have licensing for Enterprise, Evaluation, or the Data Center editions of SQL 2008 R2.

Finally, the target computer should be joined to a domain. You will need a minimum of two domain accounts, one each for Analysis Services and the PowerPivot service application. For development installations, I go with domain\AnalysisService and domain\PowerPivotService, just to add consistency.

Step One: Install SQL Server PowerPivot for SharePoint

The first task is to add PowerPivot for SharePoint using the SQL Server 2008 R2 installation media. Start the SQL Server 2008 R2 setup.exe program, selecting the new installation option. The key point in this installation is in the Setup Role dialog, illustrated in Figure 6-1. You must choose the SQL Server PowerPivot for SharePoint option, as illustrated in the figure.

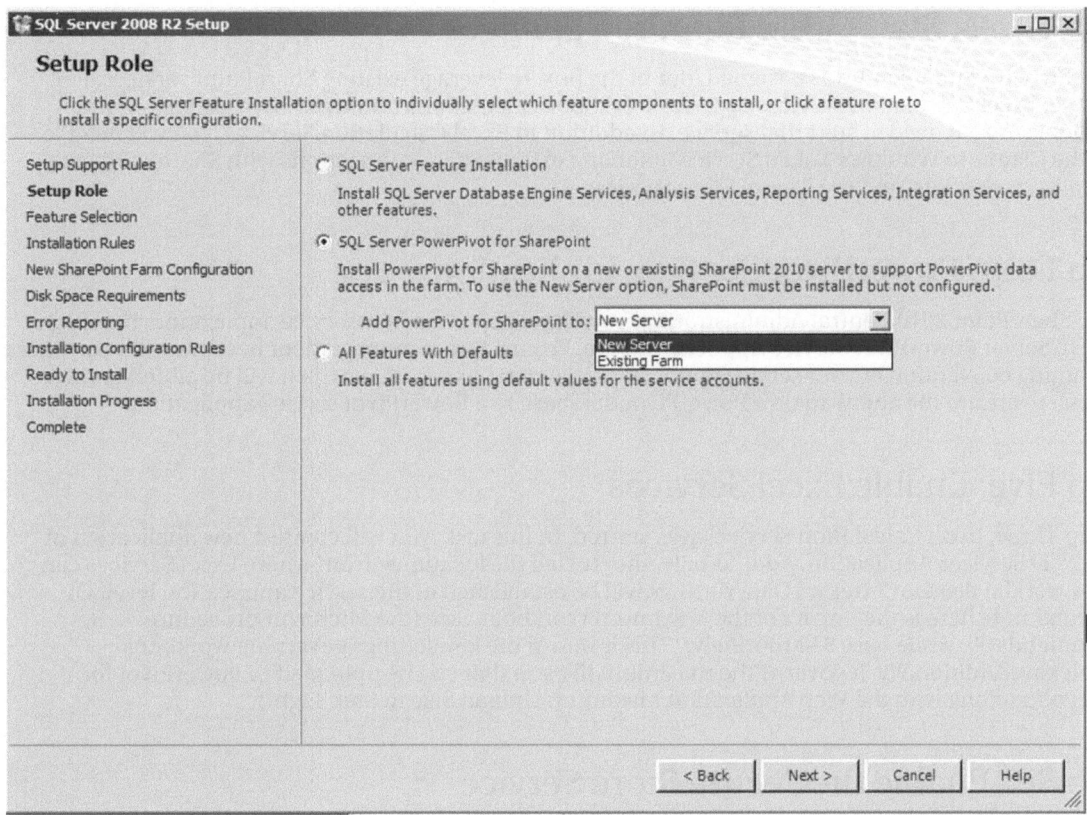

Figure 6-1. *Setup Role selection*

Step Two: Deploy the PowerPivot Solution Package

With the software installed on the farm, the next task is to deploy the PowerPivot solutions
(powerpivotwebapp.wsp) to the farm via SharePoint 2010 Central Administration. The installer deploys
this solution to Central Administration, but your SharePoint Administrator must manually deploy this
solution to each web application that will use PowerPivot for SharePoint features.

The PowerPivot Management Dashboard is the part of Central Administration that monitors usage,
calculation, refresh, and storage of PowerPivot solutions. The dashboard is actually written in
PowerPivot, making deployment of the solution package vital for Central Administration. That's why the
solution package is automatically deployed by the installer. However, additional web applications
hosted on the SharePoint farm will have PowerPivot available only after the solution
(powerpivotwebapp.wsp) is deployed to each.

Step Three: Start Other Required Services

PowerPivot for SharePoint was designed, out of the box, to leverage existing SharePoint services. For example, Excel Calculation Services supplies workbook calculations for PowerPivot for SharePoint workbooks. You'll need to start that service. In addition to Excel Calculation Services, you will need to start the Claims to Windows Token Service (enabling external data connections with SharePoint user's Windows credentials) and the Secure Store Service.

Step Four: PowerPivot Service Application

Using SharePoint 2010 Central Administration, you should create a new service application, based on the SQL Server PowerPivot Service Application type. From a future management best practice, consider the naming convention of your service application and database, both of which will be added in this process, to ensure the ability to tie a PowerPivot database to a PowerPivot service application.

Step Five: Enable Excel Services

In Step Three, Excel Calculation Services was started. In this task, you will create a new application of type Excel Services Application. Additionally, the trusted file locations (from where Excel Services can access workbooks) and External Data settings will be established at the service application level. Of particular note here is the impact of the Maximum Workbook Size (the Microsoft procedure recommends 50, while I use 512 routinely). This is one of the key settings governing workbook complexity. Additionally, it governs the maximum file size that can be uploaded to PowerPivot for SharePoint (along with the Web Application Maximum Upload Size in Step Eight).

Step Six: Enable the Secure Store Service

In order to allow workbook authors to use external data sources, a means of securely storing the credentials for those sources must be deployed. The Secure Store Service supplies this encrypted storage layer for external data credentials. Using SharePoint 2010 Central Administration, the farm administrator will create a new service application, based on the SQL Server PowerPivot Service Application type. From a future management best practice, consider the naming convention of your service application and database, both of which will be added in this process, to ensure the ability to tie a PowerPivot database to a PowerPivot service application.

Step Seven: Enable Usage Data Collection

One of the appealing enterprise architecture features in PowerPivot for SharePoint is the management dashboard. Enabling usage data collection allows the management dashboard to accurately reflect the frequency of calculation, query, and usage of the PowerPivot for SharePoint solutions on this farm.

Step Eight: Maximum File Upload Size

Even with compression from the in-memory SSAS instance, PowerPivot workbooks can be large. SharePoint governs the maximum file upload size in two separate settings. As a best practice, I encourage you to keep these values the same. The first place this value is set is the Excel Service

Maximum Workbook Size (from Step Five). The second related value is the Maximum File Upload size for the SharePoint web application.

Step Nine: Activate PowerPivot at the Site Collection Level

At this point, PowerPivot for SharePoint is installed and configured on your SharePoint farm, and activated as a feature for a SharePoint web application. However, before a user can actually publish a PowerPivot workbook to SharePoint, the features must be activated for at least one site collection. At this point, your administrator may want to activate online as well for the PowerPivot feature.

Step Ten: Verify the Configuration Changes Work

Verifying that PowerPivot for SharePoint is as easy as opening the web application into which PowerPivot for SharePoint was installed and using the Site Actions menu to ensure there is a PowerPivot Gallery available. Additionally, uploading one of your PowerPivot solutions from an earlier chapter into a PowerPivot Gallery document library should allow a preview similar to Figure 6-2.

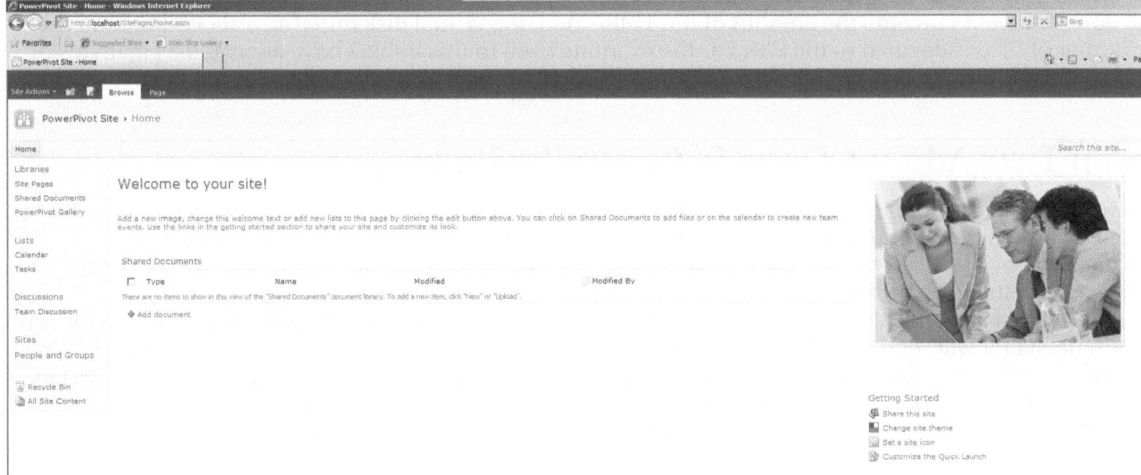

Figure 6-2. *PowerPivot Gallery*

Virtual Success

Given the issues with running a server environment as the operating system for my laptop, it was inevitable that I would experiment with virtualization for a PowerPivot for SharePoint development environment. I have used virtualization technologies (VirtualBox, Hyper-V, and VMware) to create a "virtual" server environment that is as portable as an additional hard disk for my laptop. On the plus side, I can copy a virtual hard disk and share it with team members (assuming licensing of the underlying software is in place). The ability to revision an entire project by using a base image plus client-specific "differencing disk images" is another advantage of the virtualization approach.

In this section, I will describe the steps required to build a complete installation of PowerPivot for SharePoint. I'll cover some technical considerations and obstacles that you might encounter. The examples used here were constructed with VMware Workstation version 7.1.3, but the instructions are intended to be independent of the specific virtualization technology.

The overall road map for this installation is to complete the following tasks:

1. Create a Virtual Machine (VM) and Install Windows Server 2008 R2 on the VM.

2. Add the Domain Controller Role to the VM.

3. Use DCPROMO to create a new domain, domain controller, and Active Directory forest.

4. Install SharePoint Server 2010.

5. Install PowerPivot for SharePoint via the SQL Server 2008 R2 installer.

Step One: Create a New Virtual Machine

Create a new virtual machine using your choice of virtualization technology. Some basic specifications to consider would include the amount of RAM allocated, the virtual disk initial size allocation, and the number of CPUs allocated to the VM. For the example used in this book, I have allocated 5 gigabytes of RAM, two physical processors, and 120 gigabytes of disk storage.

Step Two: Add the Domain Controller Role

PowerPivot for SharePoint requires domain (not local machine) accounts for service accounts used with the PowerPivot for SharePoint Analysis Services instance. Because we are creating a complete installation of all required components on a single VM, our target machine must perform the Active Directory Domain Controller role as well as normal PowerPivot for SharePoint duties.

The Domain Controller role can be accessed via Server Manager. Selecting the Roles item in the left-hand navigator will render the Roles Summary, as depicted in **Error! Reference source not found.** 6-3. Select the Add Roles link in the main window, and check the Active Directory Domain Services roles in the list of available roles. At the conclusion of the Active Directory Domain Controller binaries installation, proceed to using DCPROMO to actually add the server to the domain.

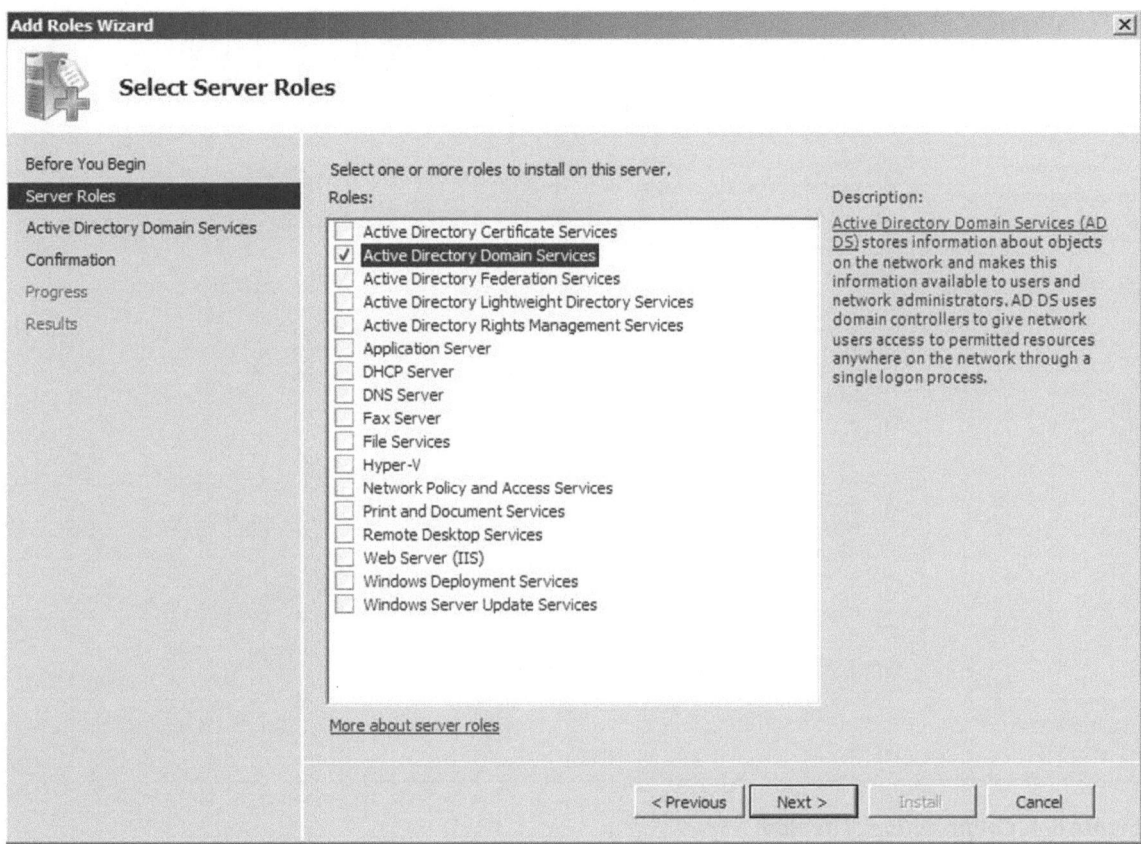

Figure 6-3. *Adding Domain Controller role*

Step Three: Add the Server to Your Domain

First, ensure your local Administrator account has a strong password, as your local Administrator account will immediately become the domain Administrator account. Then from a command prompt, enter the command DCPROMO. This will launch a graphical dialog in which you will enter the fully qualified domain name, the forest type, and a recovery password for the Directory Services Restore Mode administrator. At the conclusion of a lengthy process, the program will request a machine restart. The restart can be largely automated by checking "Reboot on completion" in the final dialog window.

When the VM restart is completed, log in with domain credentials for your new environment. Open the Computer properties and verify the new full computer name for your VM. You should have something similar to Figure 6-4.

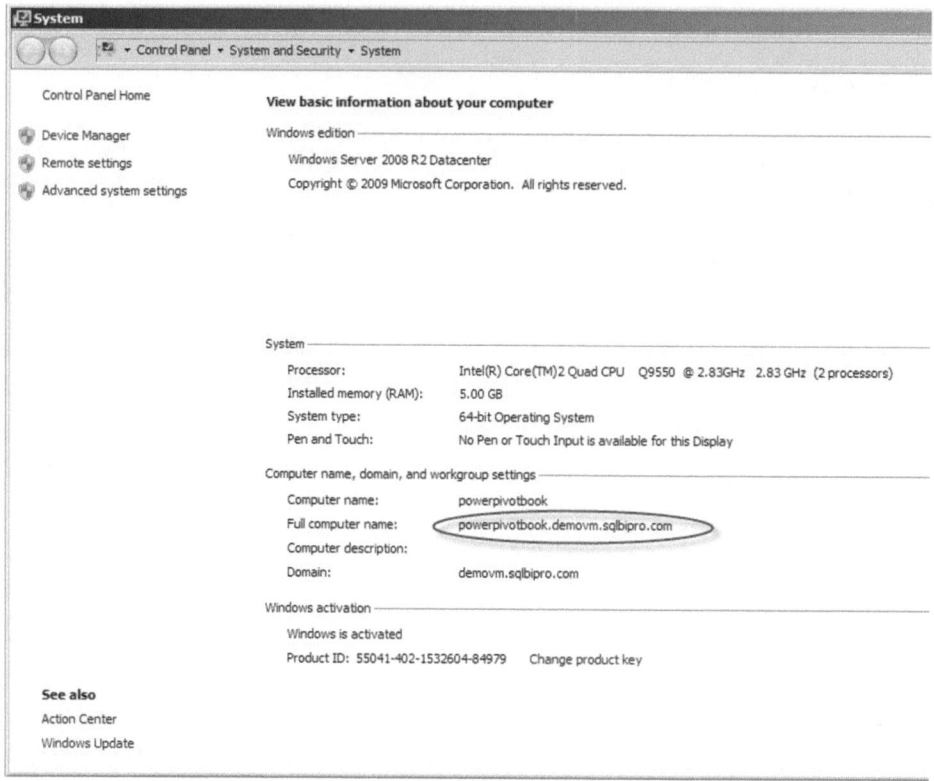

Figure 6-4. *Confirmation of domain*

Step Four: Install SharePoint 2010 Server

As you will see in the section on running SharePoint 2010 Server on Windows 7, there are a healthy number of patches (hotfixes) and other prerequisite software components. The first step in the installation for SharePoint 2010 Server is to execute the installation of these components. Execute the Prerequisite installer from the installation CD, as shown in **Error! Reference source not found.** 6-5.

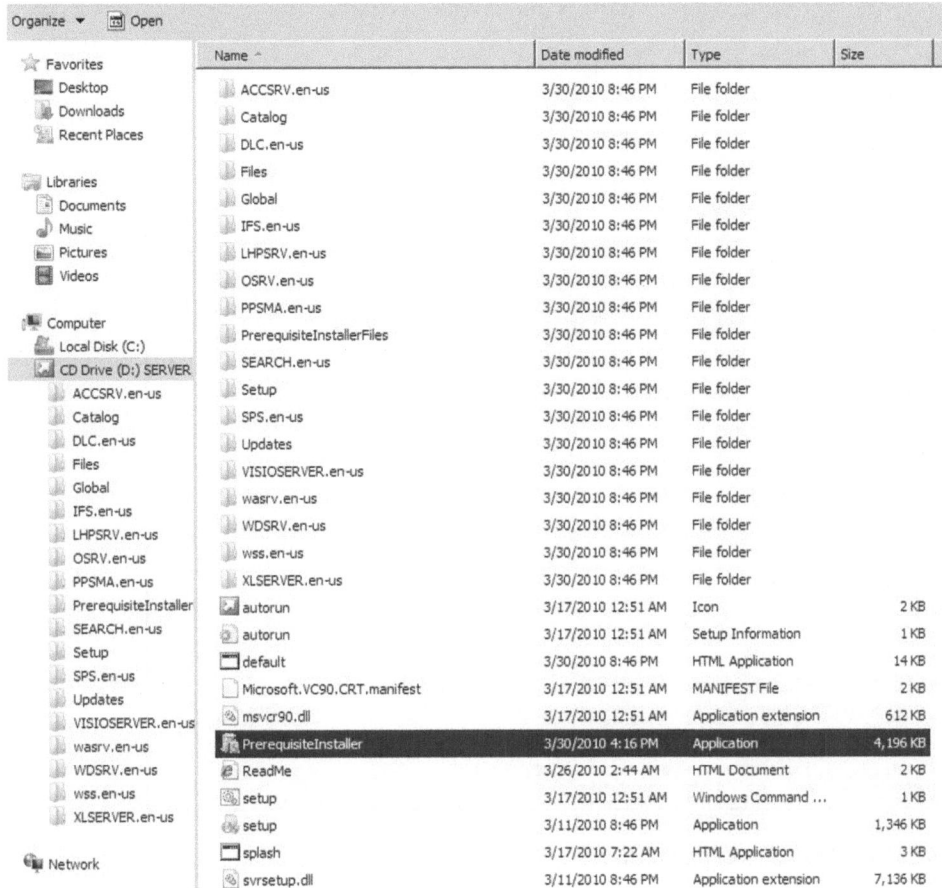

Figure 6-5. *Prerequisite installer*

The Prerequisite installer will download the correct versions of all the required components and eventually complete; then you can move on to the SharePoint 2010 Server installer (setup.exe). Because we are installing on a Domain Controller, the only options are a Farm and Complete server type. Therefore those dialogs are omitted from the install. However, the most important aspect of this step is to uncheck the "Run the SharePoint Products Configuration Wizard now" check box on the dialog pictured in Figure 6-6. The SQL Server 2008 R2 installer will handle SharePoint configuration for us.

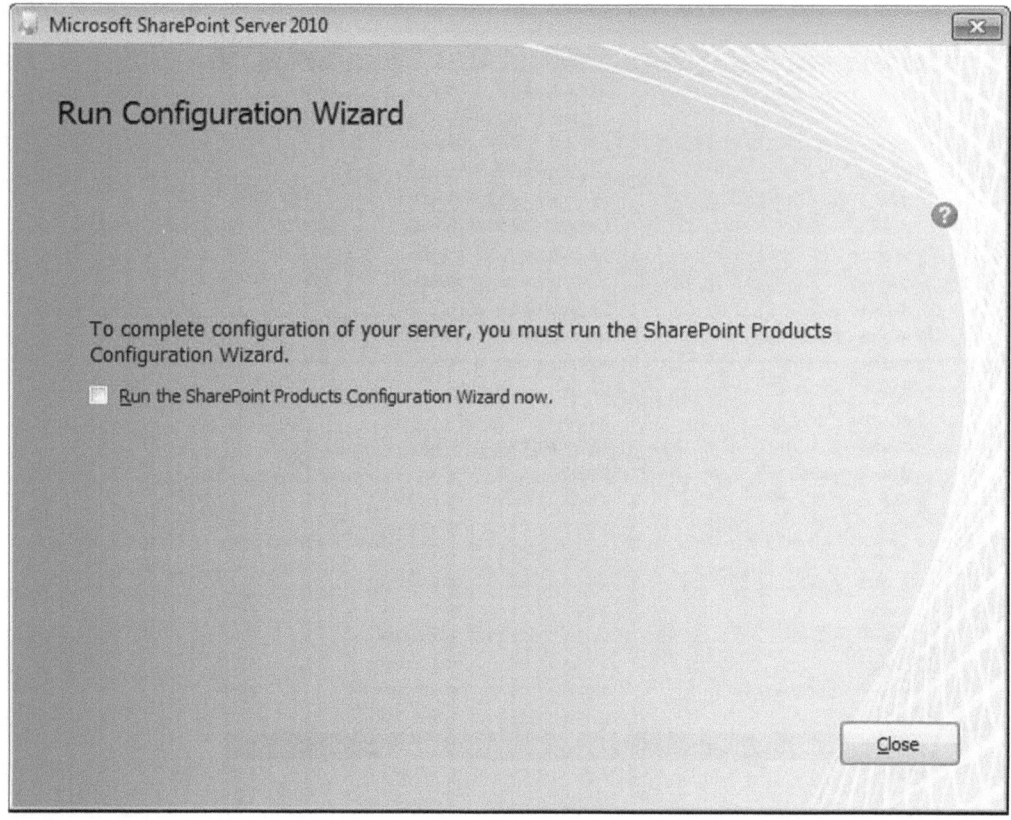

Figure 6-6. *End of the SharePoint Server installation*

Step Five: Install SQL Server 2008 R2 and PowerPivot

The final step in the VM installation is to add SQL Server 2008 R2. This installation will accomplish three things. First, the installer will create a relational datastore for the SharePoint farm. Second, an Analysis Services installation, specifically for SharePoint Integrated mode to service PowerPivot for SharePoint queries, will be installed. Finally, the entire SharePoint farm, including PowerPivot features and underlying services, will be configured.

To begin the installation processes, execute the Setup.exe program from the root directory of the SQL Server 2008 R2 installation media. Choose new installation and proceed through the dialogs. Of particular importance is the dialog in Figure 6-7. Your answer to the dialog determines two crucial elements of the installation—first, that you are installing PowerPivot and second, that you are doing so in a new server. If you choose Existing Farm, no underlying relational datastore for the SharePoint farm will be installed. Ensure your Setup Role dialog resembles Figure 6-7.

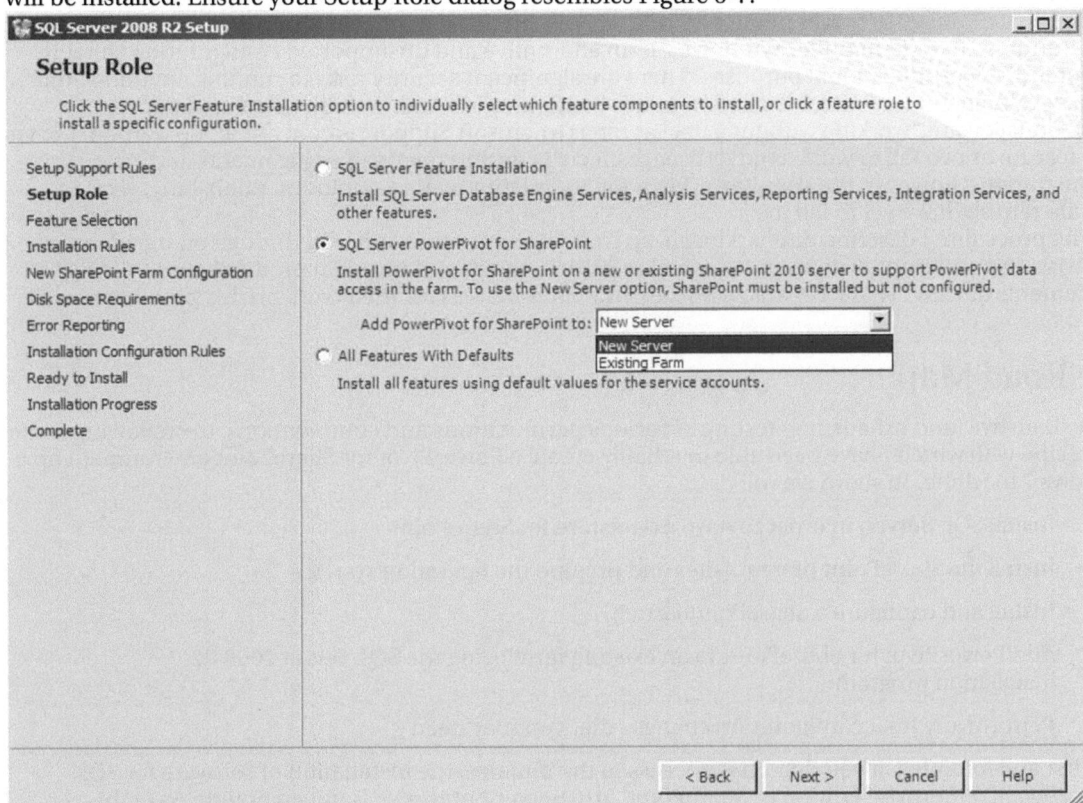

Figure 6-7. *New Server or Existing Farm*

Running PowerPivot for SharePoint on Windows 7

Given the allure of being able to work on PowerPivot for SharePoint solutions on a single workstation, laptop, or personal computer, my first choice in development environments is to run everything on a single machine. However, given Microsoft's decisions around both their virtualization products (Hyper-V and Virtual PC) and the move of the application platform to 64-bit–only versions (SQL Server 2008R2 and Office SharePoint Server), running PowerPivot for SharePoint leaves some significant decisions for the training environment.

As an example of the choices, unless you are prepared to install (or at least dual-boot) a server operating system (Windows Server 2008 R2), then Hyper-V is not really a viable option. The virtualization technology for Windows 7 Microsoft Virtual PC as of this writing does not allow for the hosting of 64-bit operating systems. Therefore, Virtual PC is not an option for hosting a learning installation. Virtualization technologies are on the market that will host the 64-bit operating systems required for your development environment; VirtualBox and VMware come to mind.

While I personally evaluated a number of configurations, what has personally worked best for me is running SharePoint 2010 Server under a Windows 7, 64-bit installation, without using any virtualization at all. Running SharePoint under Windows 7 is an alternative and unsupported configuration suitable only for individual educational purposes. There are significant security risks to running anything other than a developmental training installation in this configuration. Additionally, as an unsupported installation, you are "working without a net" as far as Microsoft Support is concerned. Be warned, I have had a feature or two fail to work as advertised, especially during speaking engagements and demonstrations; however, the core PowerPivot for SharePoint features (solution publishing, security, and data refresh) have yet to fail me.

The procedure I describe next is a mash-up from resources that I poured through on the Web and otherwise, in an attempt to develop a method of getting myself and my team productive on engagements quickly. Thanks to Stacia Misner and Vidas Matelis for their work on this problem as well.

The Road Map

After exhaustive (and exhausting) testing of various permutations and combinations, the following is the only recipe with which I have been able to reliably create a PowerPivot for SharePoint environment on a Windows 7 machine. In short, we will

1. Install SQL Server, in order to have a datastore for SharePoint

2. Install the SharePoint prerequisites and prepare the operating systems

3. Install and configure a SharePoint farm

4. Add PowerPivot for SharePoint to an existing farm using the SQL Server 2008 R2 installation program

5. Perform any final configuration changes that you may need

First and foremost, if you don't have access to the binaries, the installation of software for SQL Server 2008 R2 Enterprise Edition or SharePoint 2010 Server Enterprise is not an option. As of this writing, both are available from Microsoft.com in the form of time-limited (180-day) licenses. Alternatively, the full versions (with time-limits removed) are available via Microsoft's TechNet Plus Direct subscription service (http://technet.microsoft.com). I strongly endorse the TechNet Plus Direct subscription as a tool for anyone learning Microsoft Business Intelligence technologies.

Second, both the PowerPivot for SharePoint Unattended Service account and the SQL Server Analysis Services SharePoint Integrated Mode database will require domain credentials. Local user accounts are simply not supported. Therefore, if the target of your installation is not part of a Windows domain, the following procedure will not work.

Step One: Install SQL Server 2008 R2

From the SQL Server 2008 R2 (Enterprise Edition) media, run the Setup.exe program in the root directory. This will display a dialog similar to Figure 6-8. Select "New installation or add features to an existing installation."

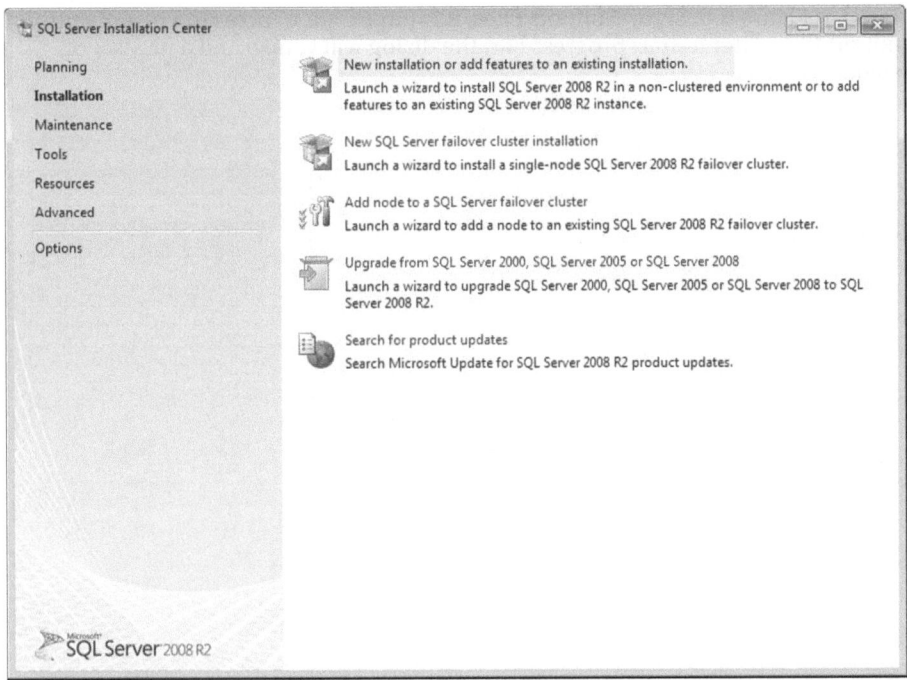

Figure 6-8. *SQL installation: Step One*

From the next dialog, a group of setup support rules will execute. Press OK to continue. The next dialog will require a product key (unless you are installing an evaluation edition). Enter the key if required and proceed by pressing the Next button. Agree to the software license terms in the next dialog, and press the Next button to continue.

In the dialog illustrated in Figure 6-9, Setup Support Files, it is important to press the Install button to actually install the support files. After a short progress bar, the dialog will vanish and a new set of windows will be generated.

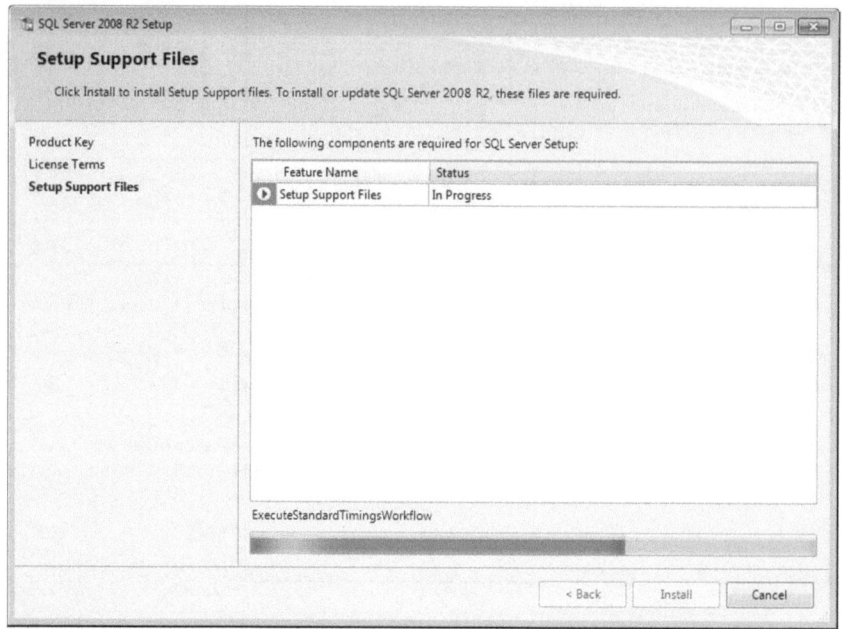

Figure 6-9. *Setup Support Files*

The next set of dialogs will begin with a group of Setup Support Rules being executed. This is a means of ensuring common problems with the particular installation environment are avoided. Assuming no rules require correction, press Next to proceed.

The next dialog, Role Selection, is of great importance to the process. Because we are creating only a SharePoint farm and not a PowerPivot for SharePoint installation, in this step, select SQL Server Feature Installation, as depicted in Figure 6-10.

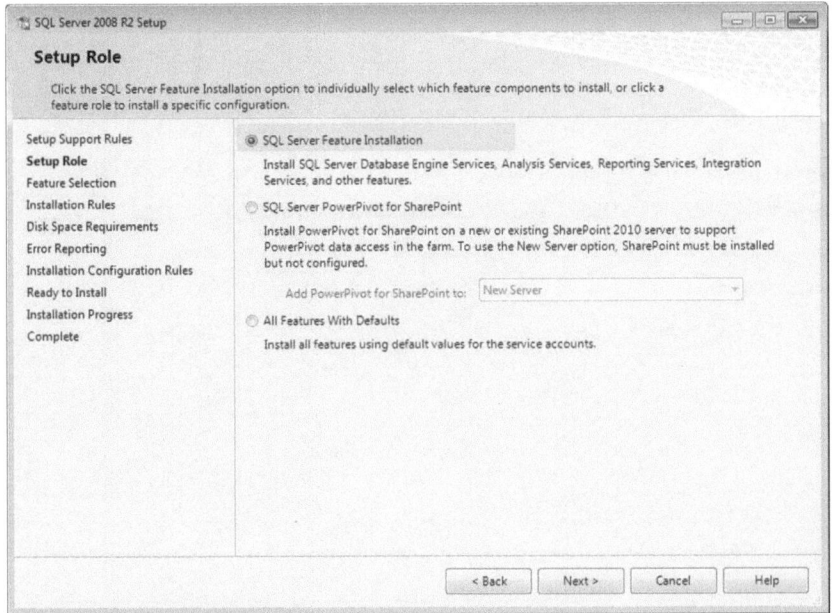

Figure 6-10. *Role Selection*

In the next dialog, Feature Selection, all that is strictly required is the relational database. However, in order to have the client tools, Business Intelligence Developer Studio, etc., I generally use the Select All button and then deselect SQL Server Replication and Full-Text Search features. The remaining dialogs in the installation are of little impact to PowerPivot, though you will want to add the account performing the installation as the administrator for both relational databases and in the event of a Select All installation, the Analysis Services databases. After the pressing the Next button within the Features Selection dialog, the Installation Rules dialog pictured in Figure 6-11 will be shown.

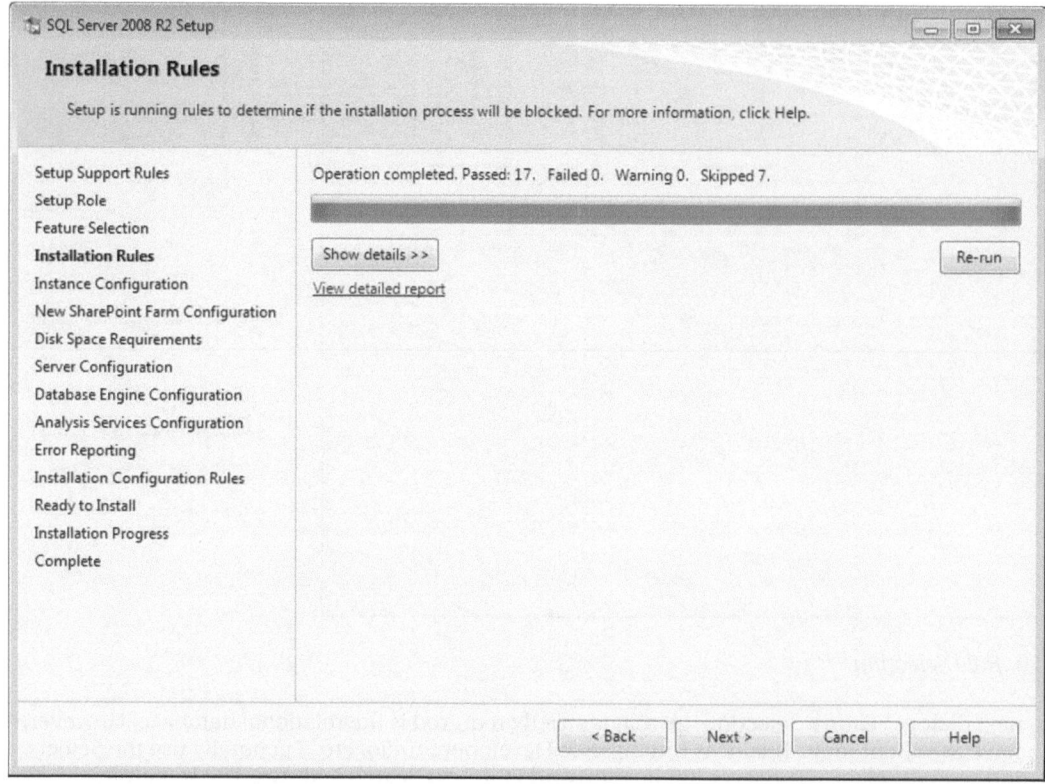

Figure 6-11. *Installation Rules dialog*

Step Two: Install the SharePoint Prerequisites

Because you're doing an unsupported installation, using the normal SharePoint Server installer to check for and load prerequisite software will not be possible. That said, there are a number of components that will have to be installed onto the target machine manually. The first element needed is the Microsoft FilterPack 2.0, which is contained in the SharePoint installation media. Additionally, as we are "hacking" an installation normally not supported on Windows 7, we will have to do some editing of the setup .xml file. To facilitate both of these operations, copy the installation media to a directory on a local drive. In my case, I used a folder named SPInstall off the root of the C: drive.

Edit the Config.xml File

In order to coax Windows 7 into running a setup routine specifically created for a server operating system, the config.xml file will have to be modified. Since I have copied the installation media contents to a directory on my drive, I can find the target .xml file at <Install Files Location>\Files\Setup\config.xml. In my specific case, this is C:\SPInstall\Files\Setup\config.xml. The sole modification of the file is to add the following line inside the </Configuration> tag.

```
<Setting ID="AllowWindowsClientInstall" Value="True"/>
```

The resulting file should look like Figure 6-12. Save this file in the location on the local drive for use later.

```
config - Notepad
File  Edit  Format  View  Help
<Configuration>
        <Package Id="sts">
                <Setting Id="LAUNCHEDFROMSETUPSTS" Value="Yes"/>
        </Package>

        <Package Id="spswfe">
                <Setting Id="SETUPCALLED" Value="1"/>
        </Package>

        <Logging Type="verbose" Path="%temp%" Template="SharePoint Server Setup(*).log"/>
        <!--<PIDKEY Value="Enter Product Key Here" />-->
        <Setting Id="SERVERROLE" Value="SINGLESERVER"/>
        <Setting Id="USINGUIINSTALLMODE" Value="1"/>
        <Setting Id="SETUPTYPE" Value="CLEAN_INSTALL"/>
        <Setting Id="SETUP_REBOOT" Value="Never"/>
        <Setting Id="AllowWindowsClientInstall" Value="True"/>
</Configuration>
```

Figure 6-12. *Completed config.xml edit*

Install Microsoft Filter Pack 2.0

Expanding the installation media to the local directory also affords an easy method of installing one of the prerequisites, the Microsoft FilterPack 2.0. Executing the installer is dead simple. Just run the following command from a command prompt.

```
<Install Files Location>\PrerequisiteInstallerFiles\FilterPack\FilterPack.msi.
```

This command will launch the Microsoft Filter Pack 2.0 Setup Wizard. Proceed through the Wizard, agreeing to the license terms, and the dialog in Figure 6-13 will indicate installation success.

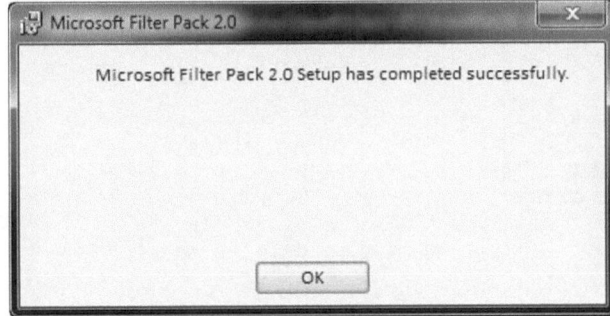

Figure 6-13. *Filter Pack installation complete*

Install WCF Hotfix KB976462

A known issue involving Windows Communication Foundation requires this hotfix to be applied. One of the first symptoms of not having installed it will be an inability to perform PowerPivot slicer operations. The hotfix can be obtained at `http://go.microsoft.com/fwlink/?LinkID=166231`. This URL will result in an installation file to be executed that will apply the update. Download the installation file and execute it.

Install ADO.Net Data Services Update

Another needed hotfix applies to Windows 7 machines using REST data services (which we will). The hotfix can be obtained at `http://go.microsoft.com/fwlink/?LinkId=163524`. Similar to the WCF hotfix, this URL will result in an installation file to be executed that will apply the update. Download and install the update.

Install the Microsoft Sync Framework

Another needed hotfix applies to Windows 7 machines using REST data services (which we will). The hotfix can be obtained at `http://go.microsoft.com/fwlink/?LinkID=141237`. This URL will launch a series of installation dialogs, including a license agreement. The process will conclude with a dialog box similar to Figure 6-14.

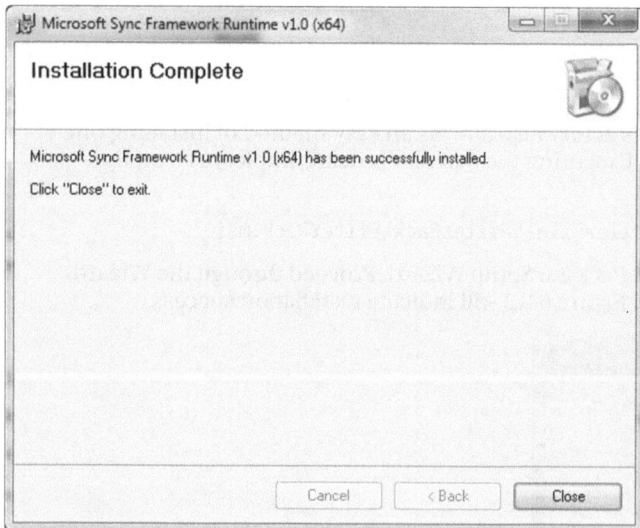

Figure 6-14. *Microsoft Sync Framework complete*

Install SQL Server Native Client

As SharePoint will need to connect to a SQL Server database to store configuration and content data, the SQL Server Native Client would normally be installed as part of the installer, executing on a Windows server. However, as we are hacking the software installation process to use Windows 7, this is an item to be manually installed. The client components can be downloaded from http://go.microsoft.com/fwlink/?LinkId=123718. The only part of this installation that warrants further instruction is in the dialog pictured in Figure 6-15. Only the client components need be installed to use PowerPivot for SharePoint. The SQL Server SDK need not be installed.

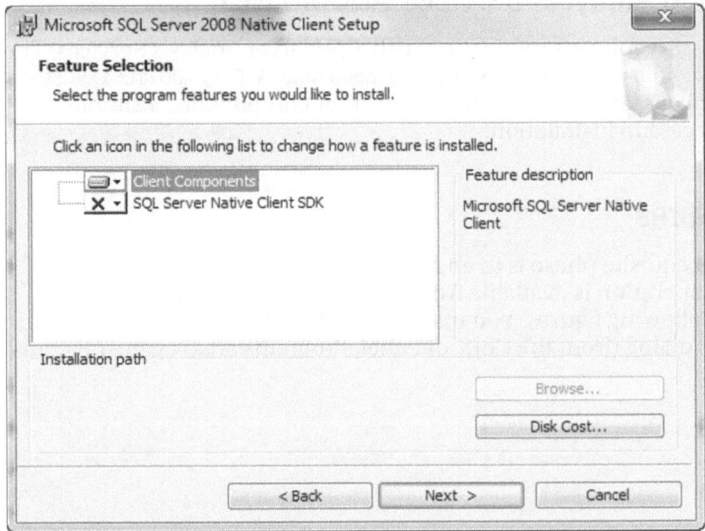

Figure 6-15. *SQL Server Native Client*

Install Windows Identity Foundation

In short, this hotfix is required for certain identity capabilities that may be used in SharePoint solutions. Ensure you install the 6.1 version of the hotfix for 64-bit operating systems. The hotfix can be downloaded from http://support.microsoft.com/kb/974405. As with other hotfix items, the installation is short and sweet after a quick agreement to the software license terms.

Install Chart Controls

The chart controls, another software component the server installation handles well, must be added manually for our Windows 7 platform. The software can be downloaded from http://go.microsoft.com/fwlink/?LinkID=122517. The installation is similar to a hotfix, with yet another license agreement.

Install Microsoft SQL Server 2008 Analysis Services ADOMD.NET

This package contains components necessary for communication with SQL Server Analysis Services. The software is available for download at http://download.microsoft.com/download/A/D/0/AD021EF1-9CBC-4D11-AB51-6A65019D4706/SQLSERVER2008_ASADOMD10.msi. Similar to the other components, a simple license terms agreement will result in successful installation.

Enable Required Windows Features

The final step in this preparation and prerequisite phase is to ensure required Windows features are enabled. A command file to execute this operation is available from the book's web site. However, the entire list of features is contained in the following figures. You may verify the completeness of your work by checking your own Windows Features dialog (from the Control Panel, Programs area) against Figures 6-16 and 6-17.

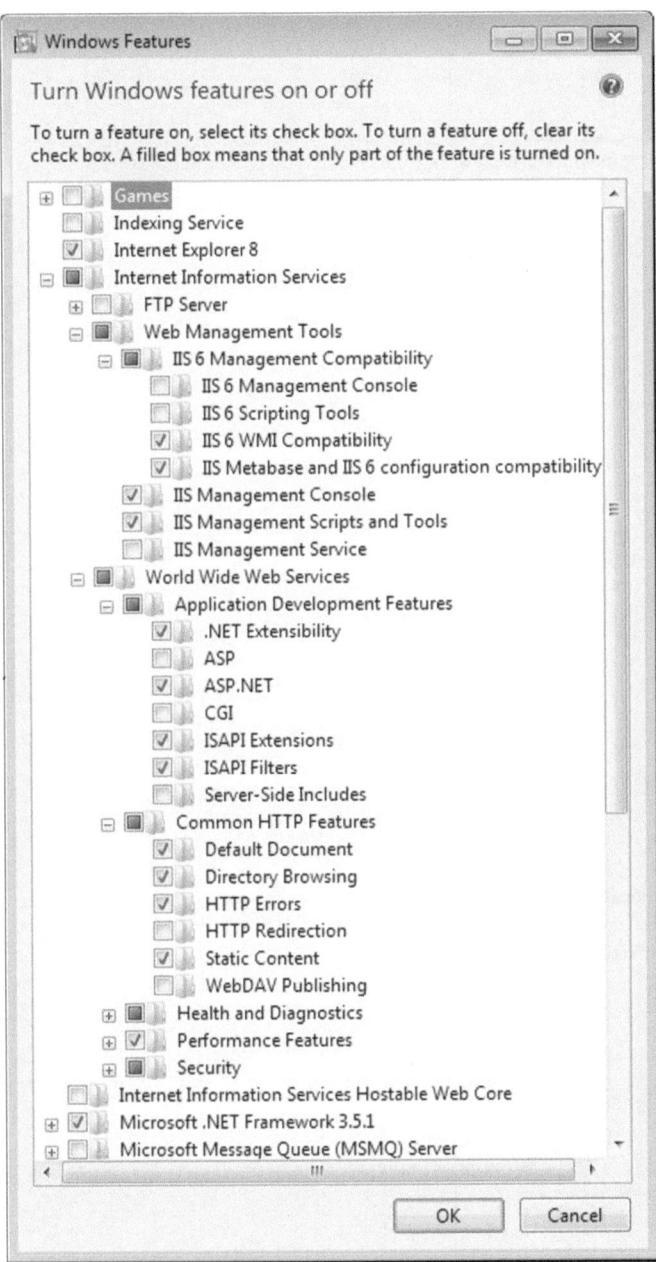

Figure 6-16. *Upper portion of required Windows features*

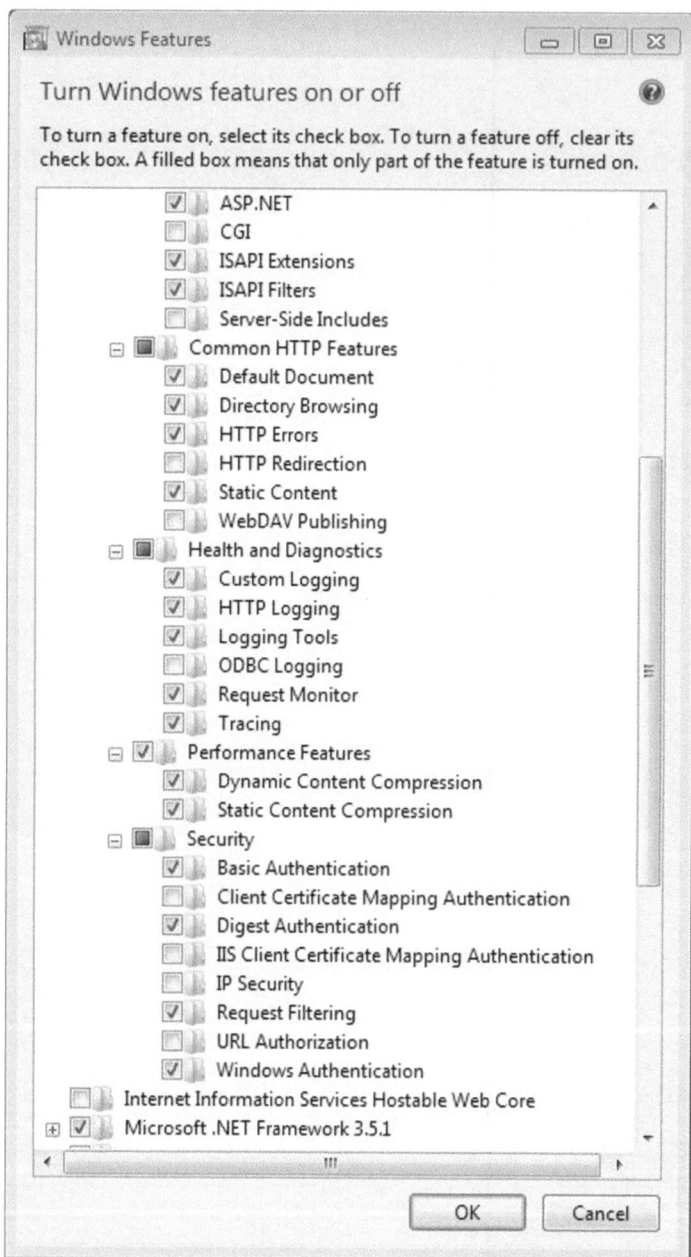

Figure 6-17. *Lower portion of required Windows features*

Step Three: Install SharePoint 2010 Server

With the operating system and other software prerequisites installed, the next step is to install, but not configure, the SharePoint 2010 Server instance. This process will begin with issuing the following command from a Windows command prompt, substituting your specific location for the SharePoint installation files for <Install Files Location>. At the command prompt, issue the command <Install Files Location>\Setup.exe. If the modifications to the config.xml file have been done correctly, the next result should be a dialog requesting a product key, similar to Figure 6-18.

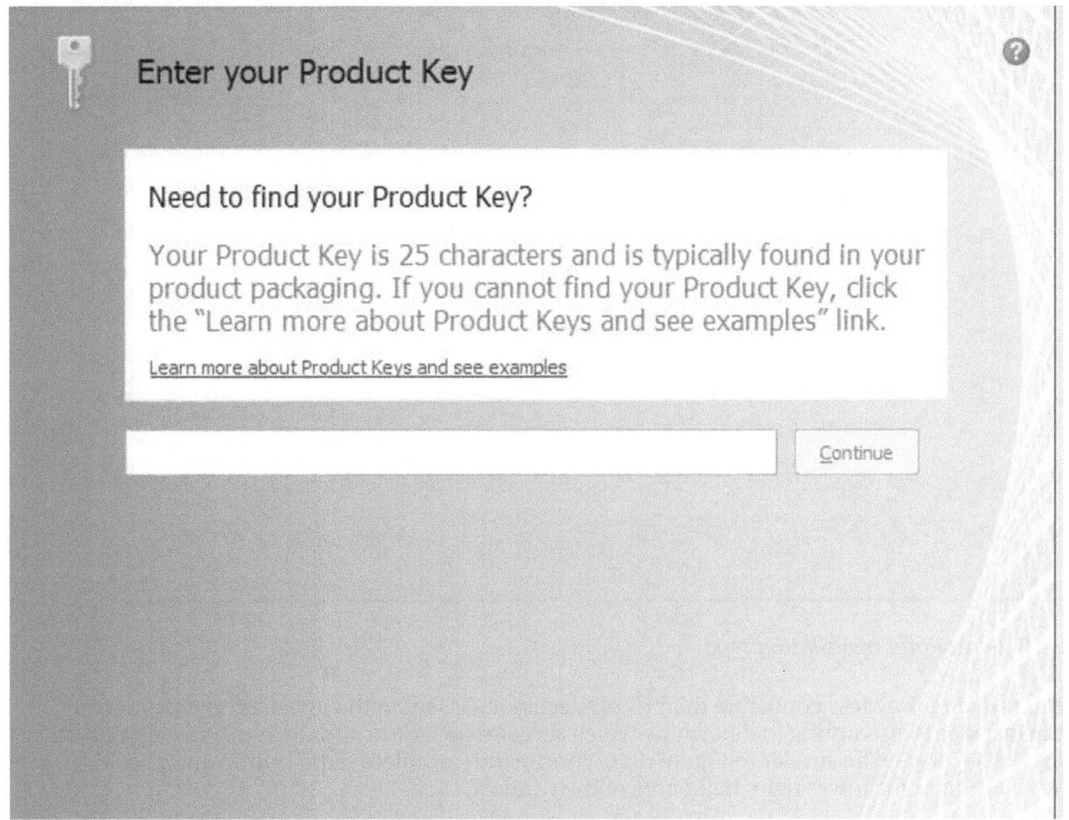

Figure 6-18. *SharePoint product key*

After entering a correct and successfully validated key, read and agree to the Microsoft Software License Terms in the dialog window that follows. After agreeing to the license terms, the Installation Type dialog will appear. PowerPivot for SharePoint requires a farm installation. Although it is a bit confusing, because we are in fact creating an all-in-one (aka stand-alone) installation, the stand-alone option must not be chosen. Click the Server Farm button as indicated by Figure 6-19.

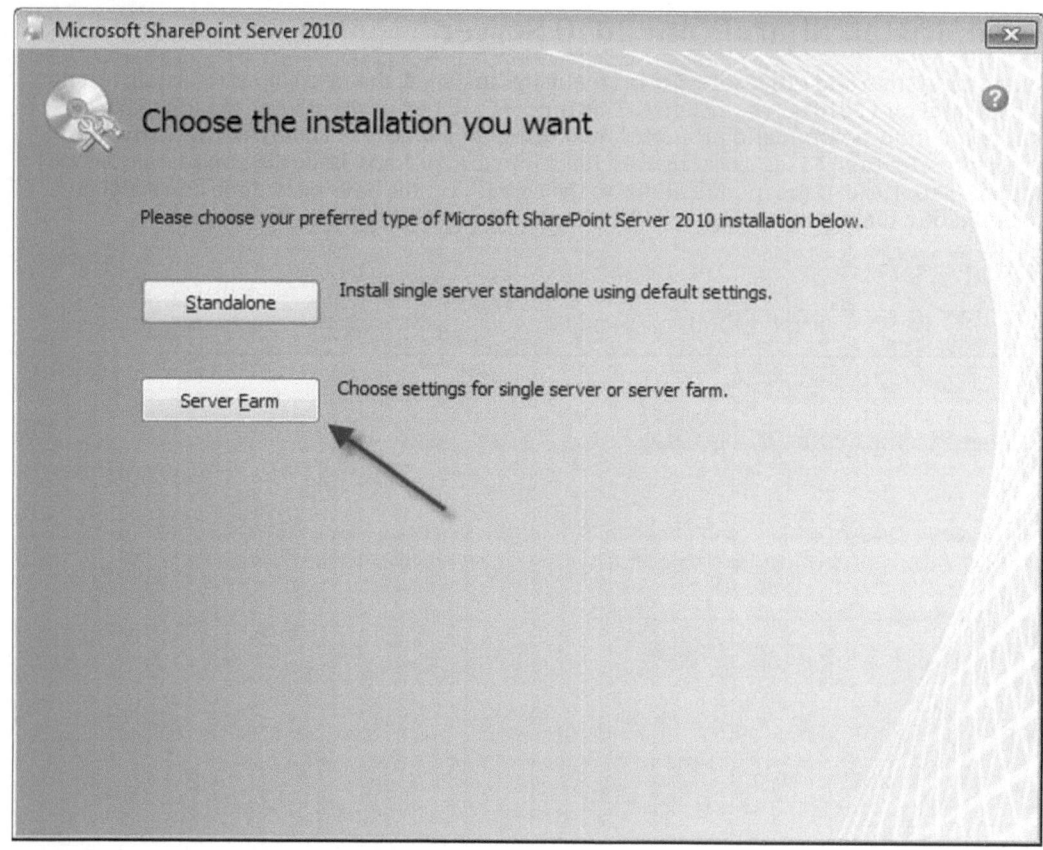

Figure 6-19. *SharePoint installation type*

The next dialog is no less confusing than its predecessor. Based on the installation type (Server Farm), the installer is attempting to determine which server type we are adding in this installation. At this dialog, which should be similar to Figure 6-20, choose the Complete radio button and click the Install Now button in the lower right-hand area of the window.

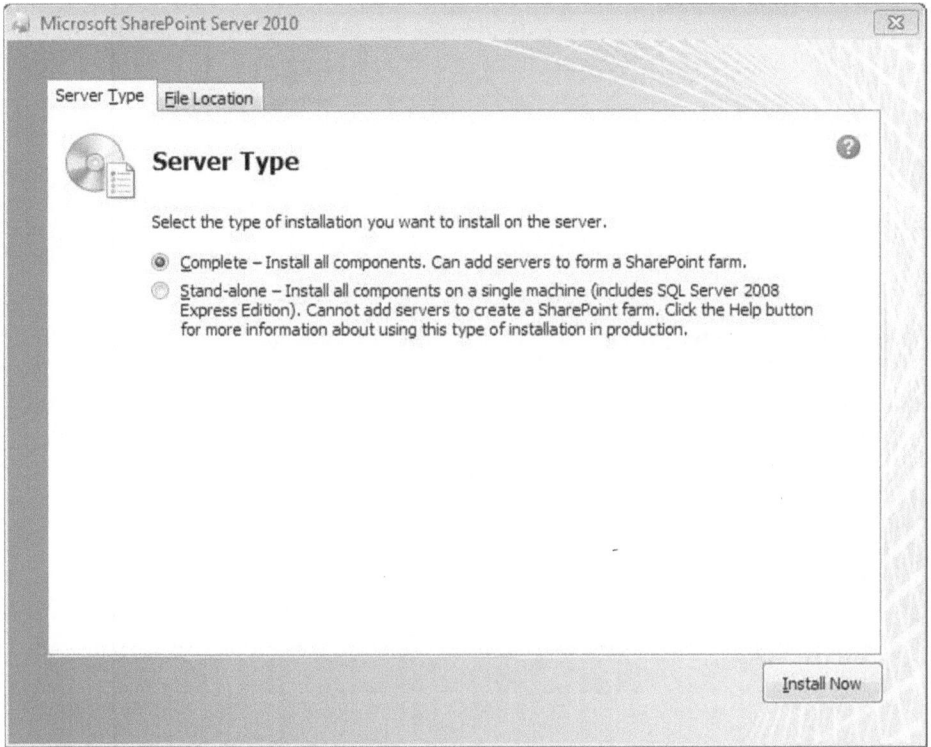

Figure 6-20. *Server type selection*

At this point, take a break; get a cup of coffee or tea. Do something to take your mind off the progress bar indicating Installation Progress. At this point, SharePoint Server 2010 is being installed onto your Windows 7 target machine. When the installation is completed, you will see a dialog similar to Figure 6-21. Before clicking the Close button, ensure the check box to the left of "Run the SharePoint Products Configuration Wizard now" is in an unchecked state. The reason for this is twofold. First, we don't have a database in which to store our SharePoint configuration (and content) at this point. Second, the SQL Server 2008R2 Installer for PowerPivot for SharePoint will take care of that for us.

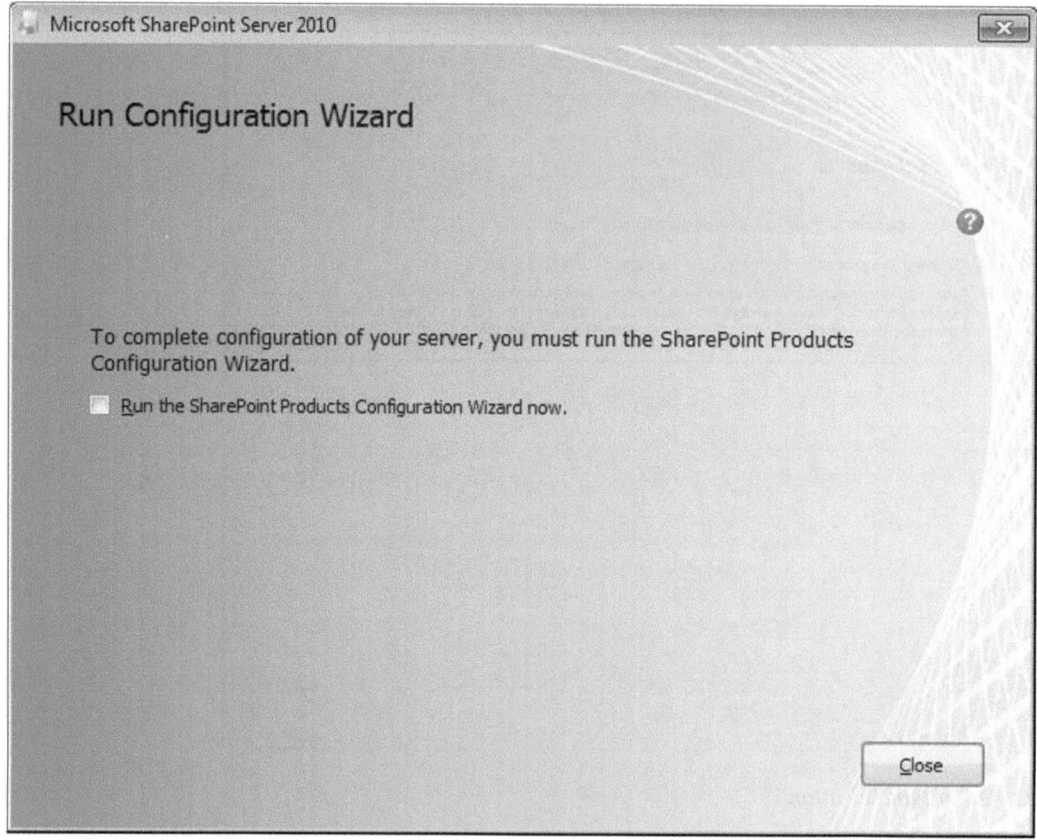

Figure 6-21. *End of the SharePointServer installation*

Step Four: Add PowerPivot for SharePoint Existing Farm

Congratulations, you have installed SharePoint 2010 Server on your Windows 7 machine. However, before you can actually show it off and make use of it, we have to configure SharePoint and install PowerPivot for SharePoint. In order to do that, we execute the SQL Server 2008 R2 installer. Thankfully, no modifications to the SQL Server installation scripts are necessary, as SQL Server has been available on client operating systems for some time.

Instead, consider what will be happening when we install SQL Server. Similar to how the PowerPivot add-in for Excel created an in-memory runtime version of SQL Server Analysis Services, the PowerPivot for SharePoint installer will create the analogous server-hosted Analysis Services instance with which to store the data that comprises our PowerPivot solutions.

To get started with the final, major software installation required to enable our development environment, load the SQL Server 2008 R2 installation program (setup.exe). At the first dialog box, similar to Figure 6-22, choose Installation from the left-hand navigation, then "New installation or add features to an existing installation."

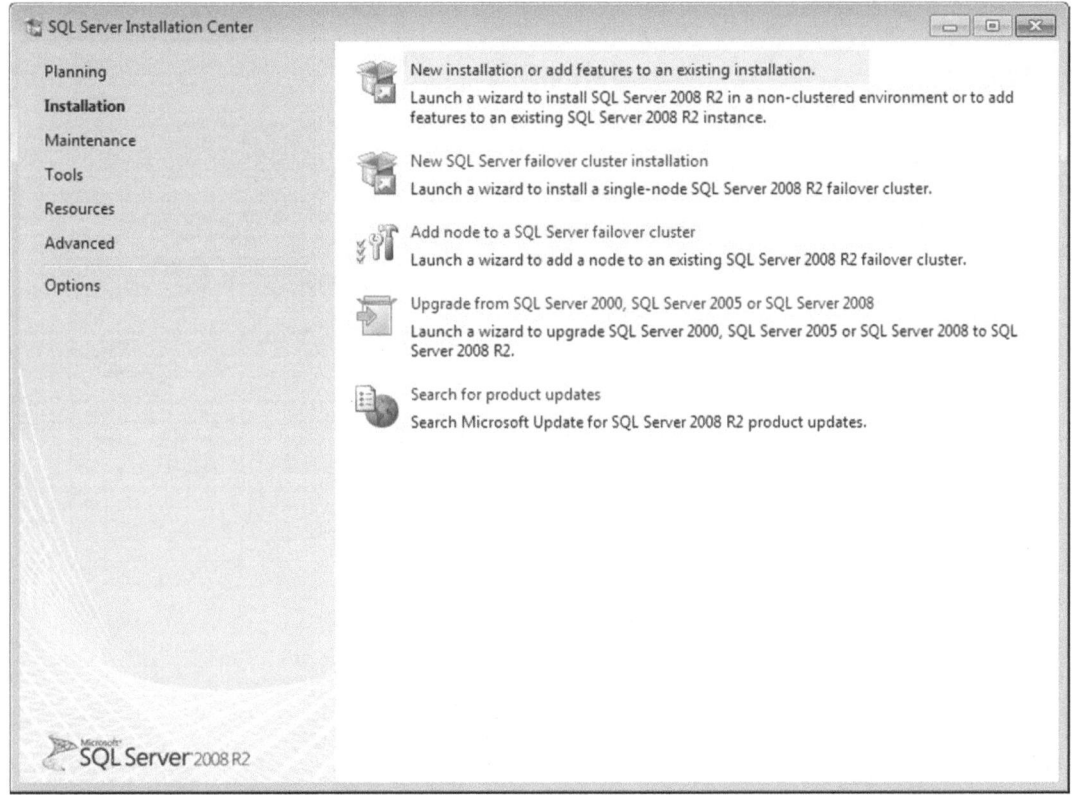

Figure 6-22. *SQL Server Installation Center*

The installer will execute a set of setup rules, and eventually present a dialog for entry of the product key. After entering a valid license key, agree to the license terms, which will render a dialog similar to Figure 6-23. Ensure that you click the Install button at this dialog, as nothing will happen otherwise. Clicking Install will cause the installation program to install the needed Setup Support Files and eventually present a dialog similar to Figure 6-23.

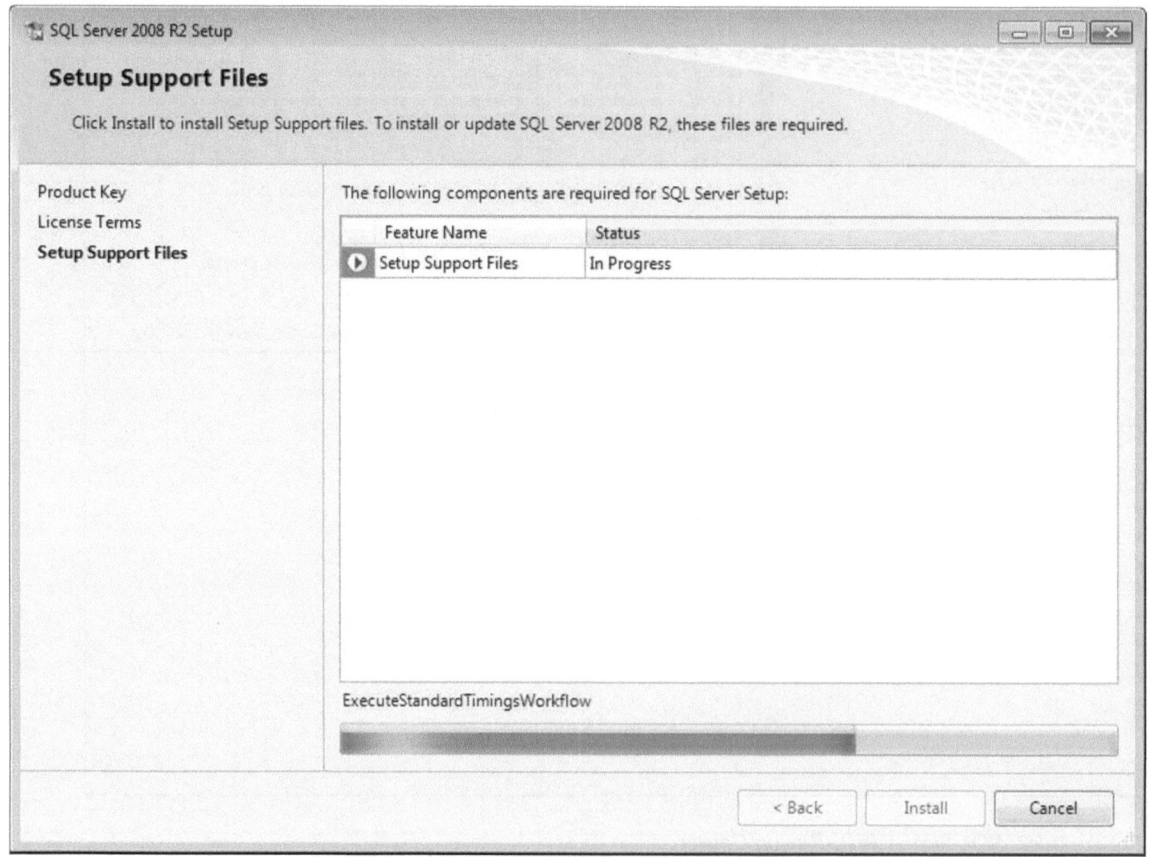

Figure 6-23. *Setup Support Files*

At the conclusion of the Setup Support Files phase, the SQL Server portion of the installation may appear to be finished, as the dialog vanishes without user input. Eventually, you will be presented with a set of setup support rules the installer has completed. If a rule fails, correct the situation (usually as simple as uninstalling software) and return to the installer. Don't be alarmed with a Warning for the Windows Firewall rule—as this is a "stand-alone" machine, we will not have to be too concerned with connections to and from our development instance of SQL Server. Unless your Setup Support Rules dialog looks vastly different than Figure 6-24, you will be able to press the Next button to continue.

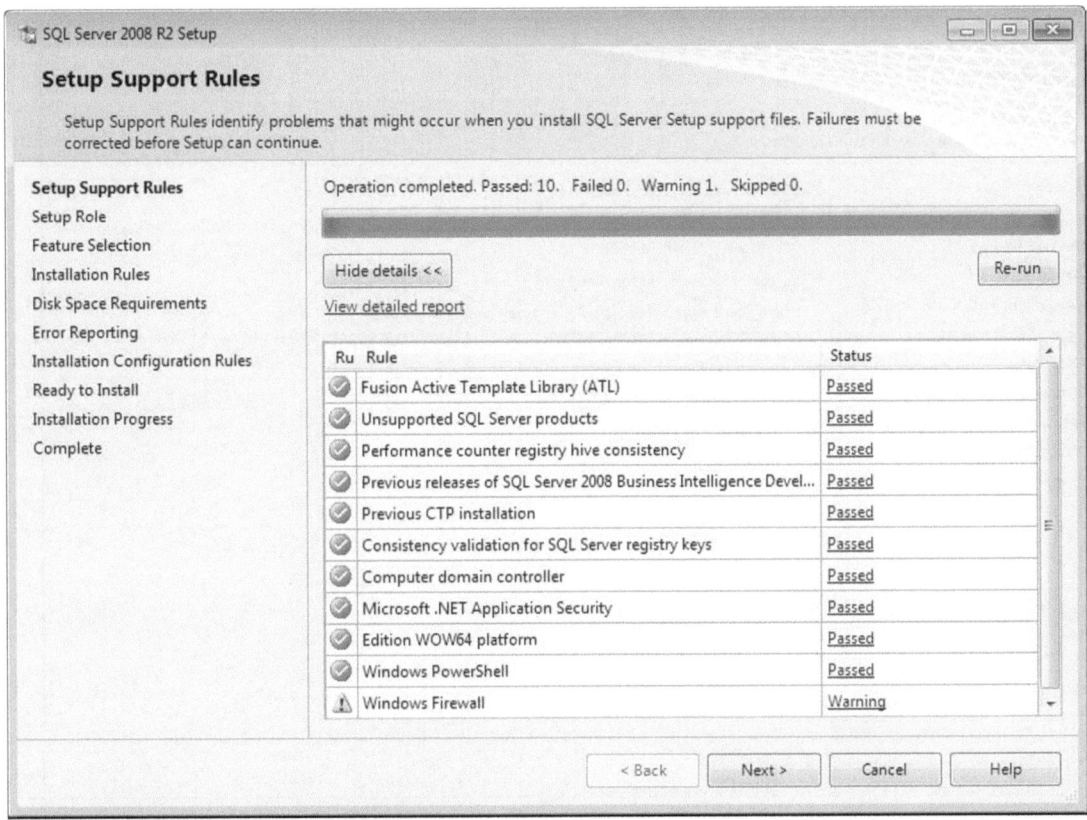

Figure 6-24. *Setup Support Rules*

The next step in the installation is where we can begin to see the PowerPivot wheels begin to turn. In the Setup Role dialog, similar to Figure 6-25, choose the SQL Server PowerPivot for SharePoint radio button. In the "Add PowerPivot for SharePoint to:" pulldown, ensure New Server is selected. At this point, the Setup Role dialog must look like Figure 6-25.

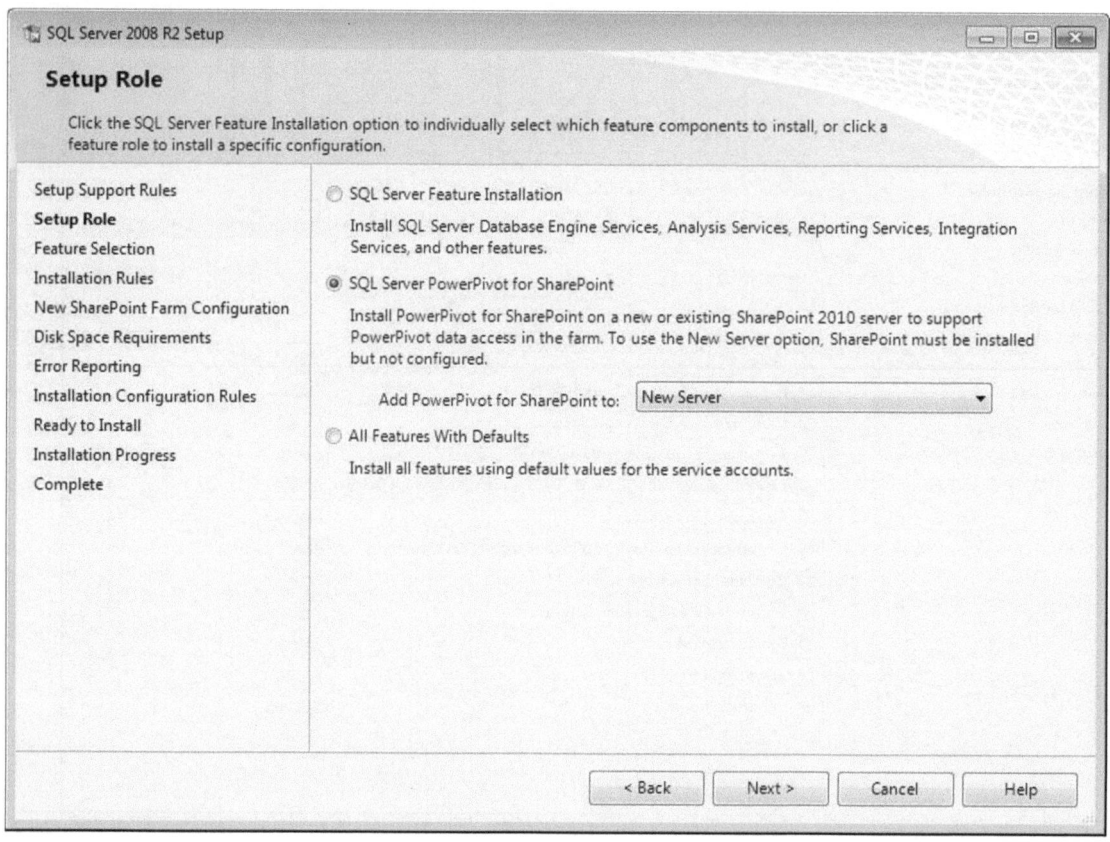

Figure 6-25. *Setup Role*

At this point, things get a little easier, because the PowerPivot for SharePoint installer dictates many of the selections. For example, in the dialog immediately after Setup Role, the features selected and installation directories are predetermined by the installer. Click the Next button to proceed.

Step Five: Final Configuration

The maximum file upload size for PowerPivot for SharePoint solutions is a function of *two* SharePoint settings. First, the web application limit needs to be adjusted. This is accomplished via SharePoint Central Administration. Second, the Excel Services maximum file upload size must also be adjusted upward from the default setting in order to accommodate typical PowerPivot file sizes.

Fun with PowerPivot and SharePoint

Now it's time to have some fun. First, take some time verify that the installation works. You should end up with a pleasant-looking page to welcome you to your PowerPivot site. Next, you can begin to upload your PowerPivot for Excel documents to SharePoint, and there is where the fun really begins.

Verifying That the Installation Works

The first indication that you have successfully installed PowerPivot for SharePoint will be the screen pictured in Figure 6-26. Depending on your installation method, either this screen will be rendered in Internet Explorer at the conclusion of the installation, or you will have to navigate to `http://yourhostname/SitePages/Home.aspx`. To verify everything is working, navigate to the PowerPivot Gallery from the link in the left-hand navigation.

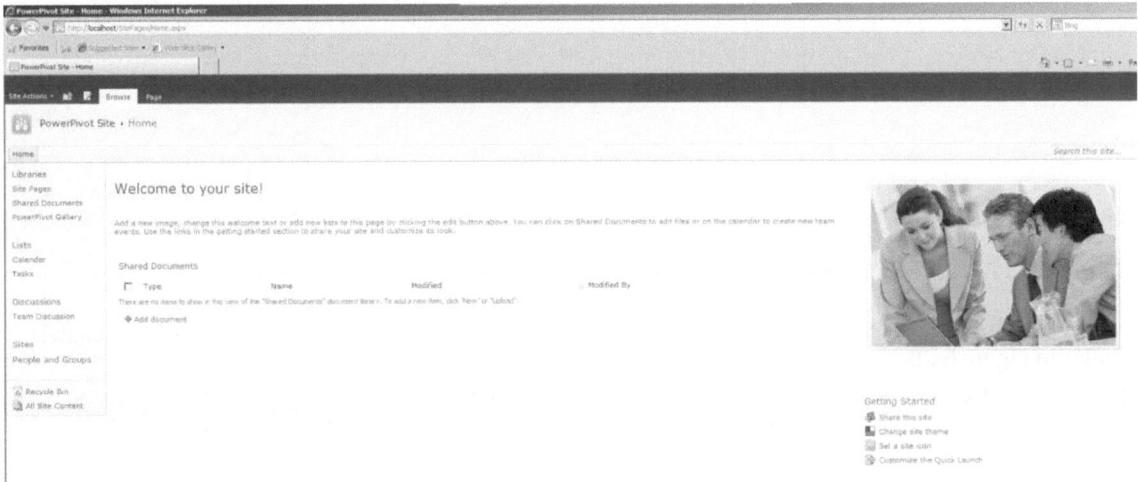

Figure 6-26. *Default home site*

Viewing the PowerPivot Gallery

A document library by any other name, the PowerPivot Gallery is specifically created to showcase, allow users to search for, and utilize PowerPivot for SharePoint solutions. This is where PowerPivot for Excel solutions are deployed to PowerPivot for SharePoint. Select the documents link from the top navigation, as pictured in Figure 6-27. From the resulting ribbon, select the Upload Document menu item and browse for a PowerPivot for Excel file on your workstation.

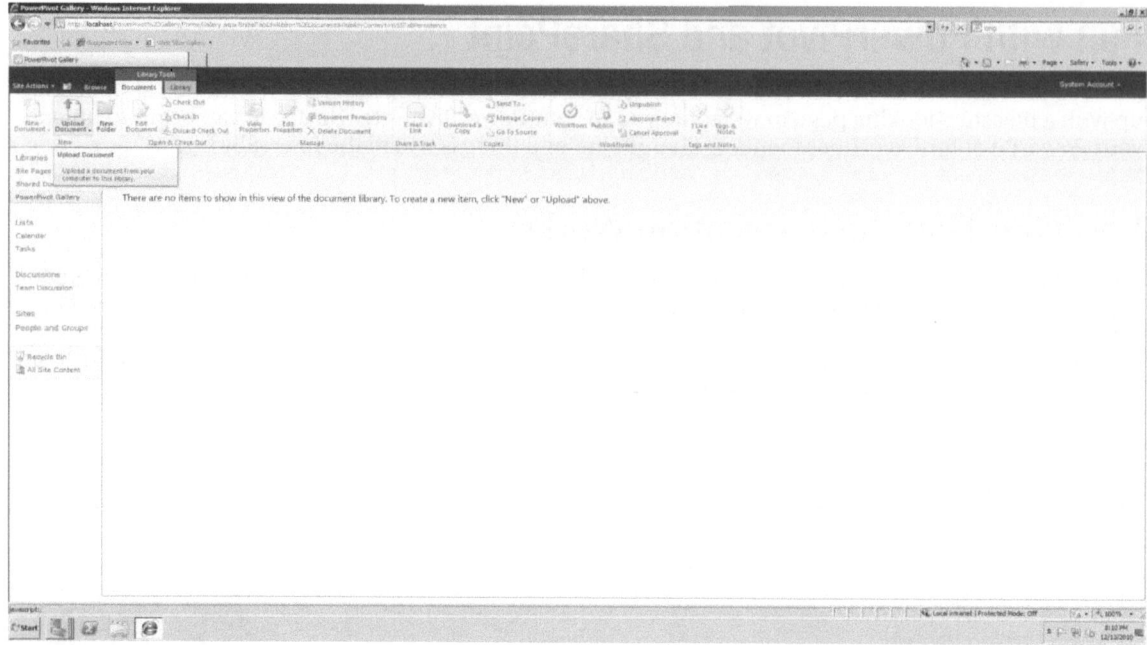

Figure 6-27. *Document library upload*

Uploading a PowerPivot for Excel document will cause it to be displayed in the PowerPivot Gallery, similar to Figure 6-28.

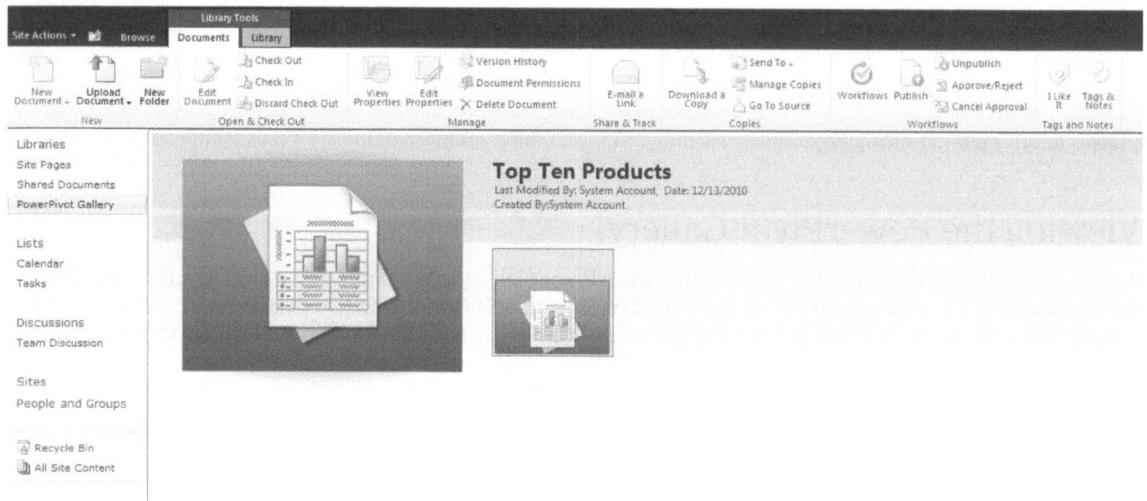

Figure 6-28. *PowerPivot Gallery preview*

Potential Errors

One error message that you might encounter is "Could not load type ReportGalleryView." This error can occur because the installer by default deploys the PowerPivotWebApp.wsp only to Central Administration and not individual SharePoint sites. To correct, log into SharePoint 2010 Central Administration and select System Settings from the left-hand navigation. From the resulting page, select Manage Farm Solutions from the Farm Management section. In the Solution Management page, click the powerpivotwebapp.wsp link. From Solution Properties, select the Deploy Solution link. From the final dialog, choose the web application from the pulldown list and click OK. You should then see results similar to Figure 6-29. In this case, the machine name is THINKPAD.

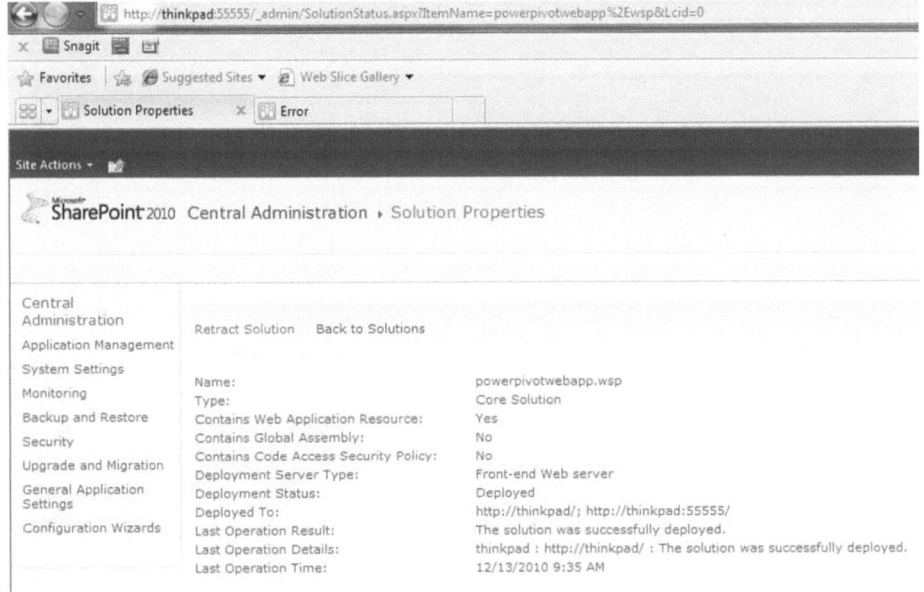

Figure 6-29. *Deployed PowerPivotWebApp.wsp*

Summary

There are many ways to create a PowerPivot for SharePoint development environment. This chapter covered three that have proven useful in real-world work:

- Adding PowerPivot for SharePoint to an existing SharePoint installation

- Creating a virtual machine containing a Domain Controller, SharePoint, and SQL Server components, in an All-Up installation

- Hacking the PowerPivot for SharePoint installation in order to run SharePoint 2010 and PowerPivot for SharePoint on a Windows 7 machine

You should understand the purpose of the PowerPivot Gallery, and how SharePoint document libraries are the underlying SharePoint structure for PowerPivot.

CHAPTER 7

∎∎∎

Collaboration, Version Control, and Management

Books serve to show a man that those original thoughts of his aren't very new at all.

—Abraham Lincoln

In the previous chapter, we discussed the factors and techniques involved in creating a PowerPivot for SharePoint environment. In this chapter, we will discuss in detail the benefits of using SharePoint as the collaboration and sharing platform for your PowerPivot solutions.

As you create solutions involving larger volumes of data, by no coincidence PowerPivot's sweet spot, sharing workbooks via e-mail will no longer be practical. Even with the data compression features of PowerPivot for Excel, solutions with millions of fact rows can quickly outstrip the attachment restriction policies of most corporate e-mail systems. SharePoint is the ideal platform for publishing your PowerPivot solutions.

Sharing Solutions

If PowerPivot solutions consume too much storage for e-mail, keeping multiple copies of a solution is a poor revision control solution. In this chapter, we will cover using SharePoint document library revision control, inherent in the PowerPivot Gallery, as a solution-level rewind button.

In the initial release of PowerPivot, there is no user-level security built into the product. However, using SharePoint and permissions on the storage mechanism, the PowerPivot Gallery, we can implement restrictions on the user's ability to see and open PowerPivot solutions stored in SharePoint.

If SharePoint is the standard deployment platform for PowerPivot solutions, why do we need Excel, or a desktop for that matter, to consume PowerPivot for SharePoint solutions? We will cover interactions with PowerPivot for SharePoint solutions via Excel Services in environments where the Windows desktop is absent. Consider the possibilities for using PowerPivot solutions with smartphones, tablet computers, and other non-traditional computing devices.

PowerPivot differs from other self-service Business Intelligence products in that a path to enterprise migration has existed from inception. PowerPivot for SharePoint includes deep usage gathering and performance monitoring capabilities out of the box. We will examine configuring and using the PowerPivot Management Dashboard as a means to understanding what is happening in our PowerPivot for SharePoint farm, and how solutions should be migrated or combined.

Publishing

Publishing a PowerPivot for Excel solution to SharePoint could hardly be easier. After the environment is established, deploying a PowerPivot solution takes one of two major paths. The first of these is conveniently located within Excel 2010's File option off the ribbon. The second is in SharePoint 2010, as an option of the PowerPivot Gallery's Document ribbon.

Working in Excel, publishing to PowerPivot for SharePoint is a simple matter of using the File menu. From an existing file, open PowerPivot for Excel solutions, as illustrated in Figure 7-1, and choose the "Save & Send" File menu option, which will enable options for Email, Web, and SharePoint. Choosing Save to SharePoint will show the most recent SharePoint servers used, similar to a recent files listing.

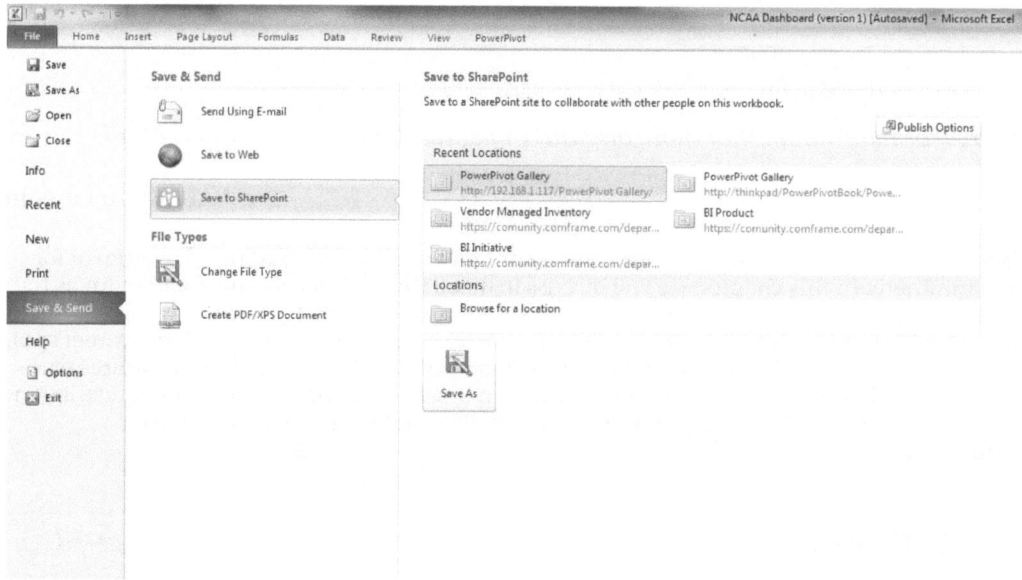

Figure 7-1. *Excel Save & Send menu*

In your development environment, it is unlikely existing servers will be listed. Select the "Browse for a location" option by double-clicking it. Doing so will render what appears to be a typical file location dialog, in which you may enter the URL of the desired SharePoint server. Pressing the right-arrow button immediately following the URL (indicated in Figure 7-2.) may generate a prompt for your credentials. Enter your domain credentials and you will be able to browse to the PowerPivot Gallery, the intended destination for the workbook.

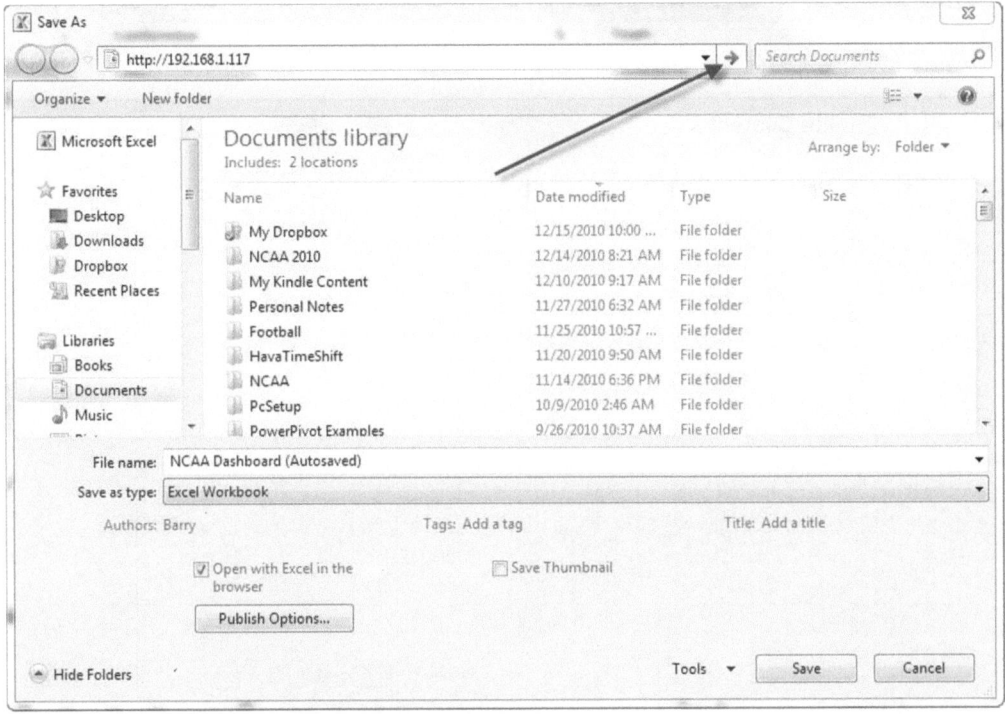

Figure 7-2. *Browse SharePoint server location*

■ **Note**   You will not be prompted if your current logon account is the domain account for your development environment and the development environment is in a Local Intranet Internet Explorer security zone.

Successful validation of your credentials will result in a dialog similar to Figure 7-3. From this window, choose the PowerPivot Gallery, optionally name the file, and click the Save button. After the contents of your worksheet are physically transported up to the SharePoint server, you will have published your first PowerPivot for SharePoint solution.

■ **Note**   If you should experience an error dialog concerning the maximum allowed file size, refer to Chapter 6 instructions on configuring the SharePoint web application (maximum file upload size) and the Excel Services configuration (maximum file size in megabytes).

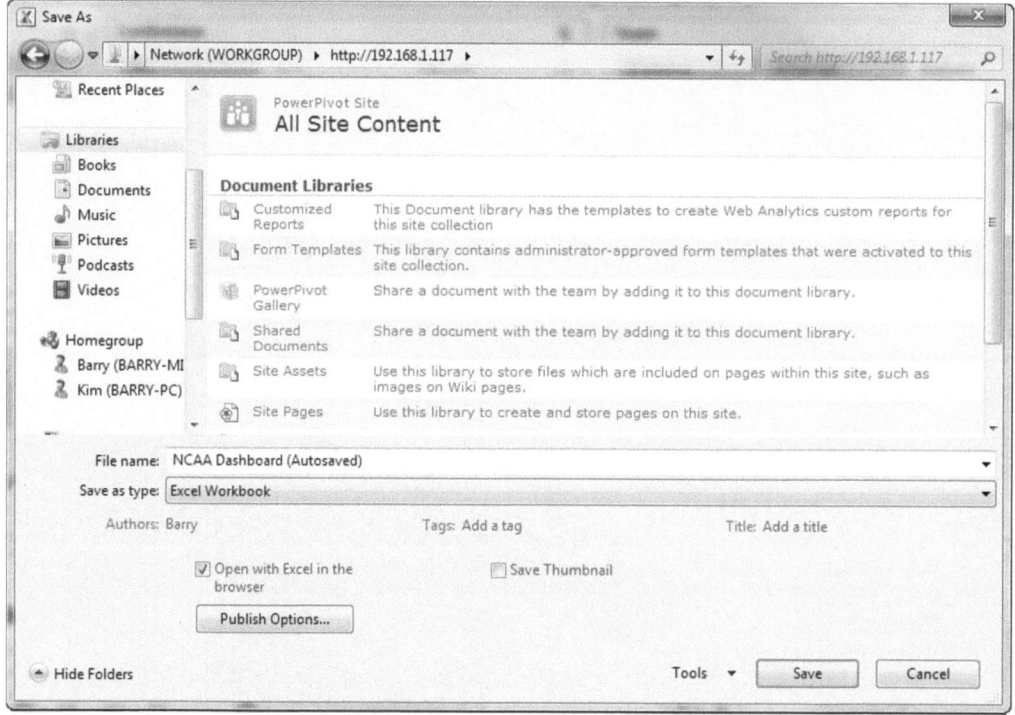

Figure 7-3. *SharePoint browse for location*

This workflow is fine when we are concerned with publishing to SharePoint a single file. However, we have the option, via the SharePoint Documents menu Upload selection, to move multiple files in a single batch upload request.

Publishing a file using the SharePoint Documents ribbon is very similar to the Save & Send operation from Excel. However, as we know the destination of the file (the location from which the Upload Document menu was invoked), we only have to select the file (or files) to upload from the workstation. To begin, navigate to the PowerPivot Gallery of your development environment, choose the Documents menu, and then choose Upload Document from the New section of the ribbon. This navigation is illustrated in Figure 7-4.

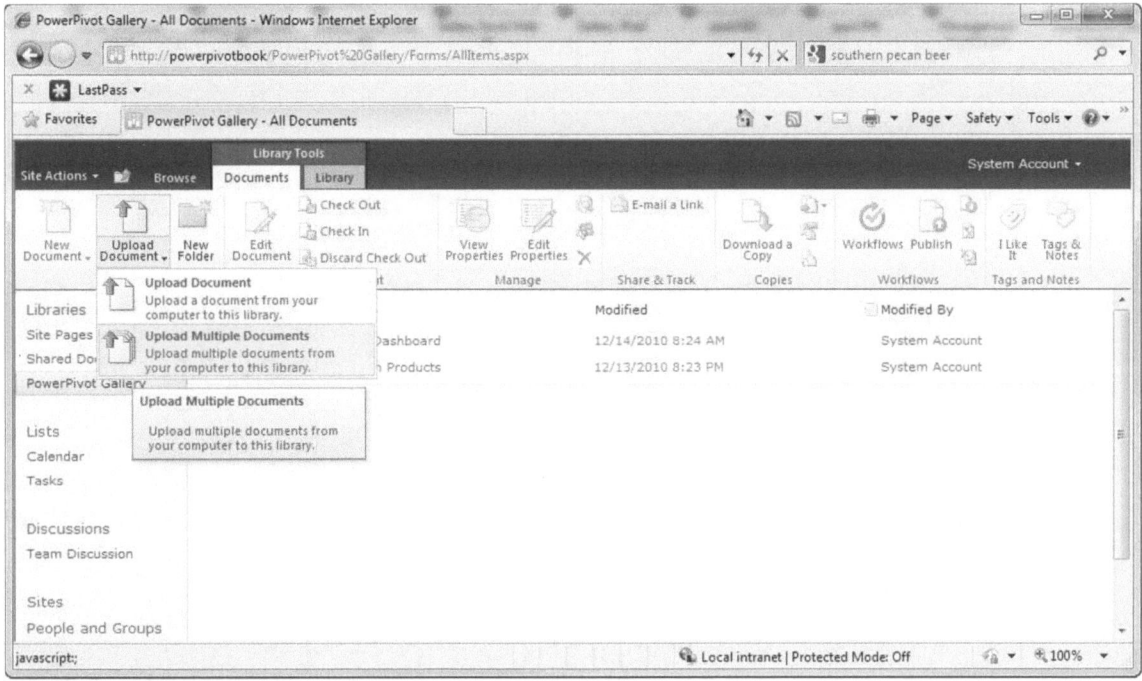

Figure 7-4. *Upload Document menu*

From the menu, there will be options to upload a single document, or multiple documents. The behavior of the single upload is similar to the save to SharePoint, except the user will determine which file (from what location) is uploaded. The really interesting behavior is the Upload Multiple Documents option. Selecting this option will present a dialog similar to Figure 7-5. Simply drag files onto the shaded area of the control (or browse), and press OK when finished. A batch upload of your PowerPivot for SharePoint solutions will begin. Assuming no file size or permissions issues, the dialog will vanish at the conclusion of the upload.

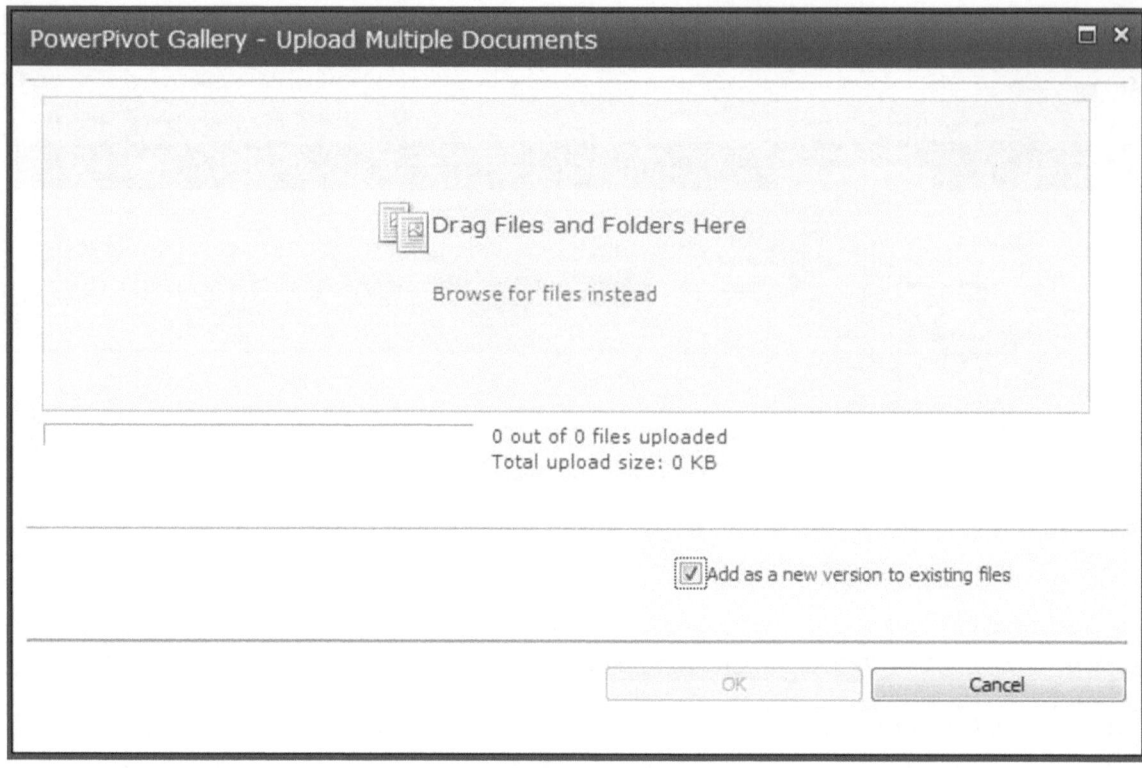

Figure 7-5. *Multiple file upload*

Revision Control

Moving the files from the workstation to a SharePoint server's PowerPivot Gallery is only part of the PowerPivot solution publishing story. Because the ancestry of a PowerPivot Gallery includes the lineage of a SharePoint document library, there are some interesting features available to PowerPivot developers. The greatest of these is the revision control built into SharePoint. As I have mentioned in Chapter 5, the primary unit of work in PowerPivot is an Excel file. Revision control of the Excel file gives you, the developer, a solution-level "undo" in the event of an unanticipated side effect to a workbook change.

Out of the box, revision control is not configured. However, implementing this feature is a simple task for a user with adequate SharePoint permissions. From the PowerPivot Gallery's Library ribbon, choose the Library Settings menu item, as illustrated in *Figure 7-6.*

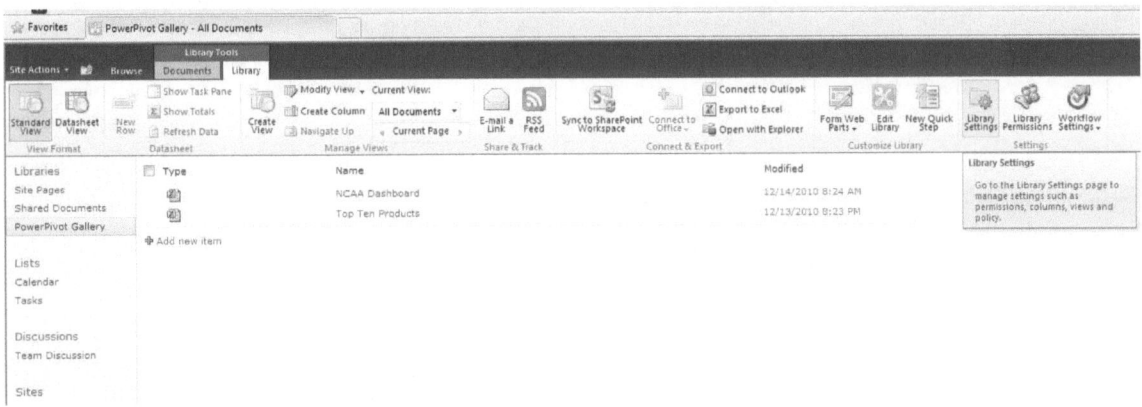

Figure 7-6. *Libary Settings*

The Library Settings page is a feature-rich page showing of all the potential settings related to a document library. In the General Settings area of the Document Library Settings page, choose the "Versioning settings" hyperlink. This will render a page similar to *Figure 7-7.* From there, you can activate version history by selecting either the "Create major versions" or "Create major and minor (draft) versions" radio buttons.

If you are working solo on any of your PowerPivot files, you can safely ignore the Require Check Out option at the bottom of the page. However, if there is any chance two people could be editing a single workbook at the same time, from within PowerPivot for Excel, this is a frustration-reducing feature. In order to save your changes to the Library Settings, press the OK button at the bottom of the page.

Figure 7-7. *Versioning Settings*

The chief difference between the two settings is how drafts (revisions between major, published revisions) are handled. Both methods, though, allow for users to recall other revisions to the file, from the SharePoint user interface. For instance, after implementing version history, and making a change to one of the PowerPivot workbooks on my development environment, there is a "version history" menu selection possible from each file. Selecting this option will render the published versions of the file, in a format similar to Figure 7-8. Each entry will have the modification date, who executed the check-in, and if comments were added during the check-in process. Each revision is then available for restoration (replacing the most recent revision with a historical one), viewing, or deletion.

Version History

Delete All Versions

No. ↓	Modified	Modified By	Size	Comments
2.0	12/17/2010 9:42 AM	System Account	2.1 MB	Added Georgia to Team Slicer
1.0	12/14/2010 8:24 AM	System Account	2 MB	

Figure 7-8. *Version History*

PowerPivot Gallery View Settings

The PowerPivot Gallery includes four different view settings in order to best communicate to your PowerPivot for SharePoint users the content of the library and the PowerPivot solutions. The three graphical representations (Gallery, Theater, and Carousel) require Microsoft Silverlight as part of the presentation tier. As you open a PowerPivot Gallery from within a virtual machine environment, you may be prompted to install Silverlight, in order to use the default view setting of Gallery.

The default view setting can be changed from the Document Library Settings page. Additionally, users have the ability to change their view of a library via the Library Tools, Library, Current View setting.

The overall goal of the graphical library options is to enhance the user's ability to recall and reuse a workbook based on visual memory of the contents. To that end, each of these options presents a preview of the workbook contents in a unique way.

Each of the graphical library view settings has a common set of icons for management of workbook refresh schedules as well as using a PowerPivot for SharePoint workbook as a SQL Server Reporting Services data source.

Gallery

The Gallery view, illustrated in Figure 7-9, contains a row for each workbook in the document library, with a large preview image of the currently selected sheet and smaller preview images of each of the other available sheets within the workbook.

As depicted, there are at least two workbooks in the example PowerPivot Gallery: Top Ten Products and NCAA Dashboard. Each of these workbooks is represented by a row in the Gallery view. The currently selected sheet in NCAA Dashboard is labeled Offense, and an image of the contents is previewed to the left of the workbook name.

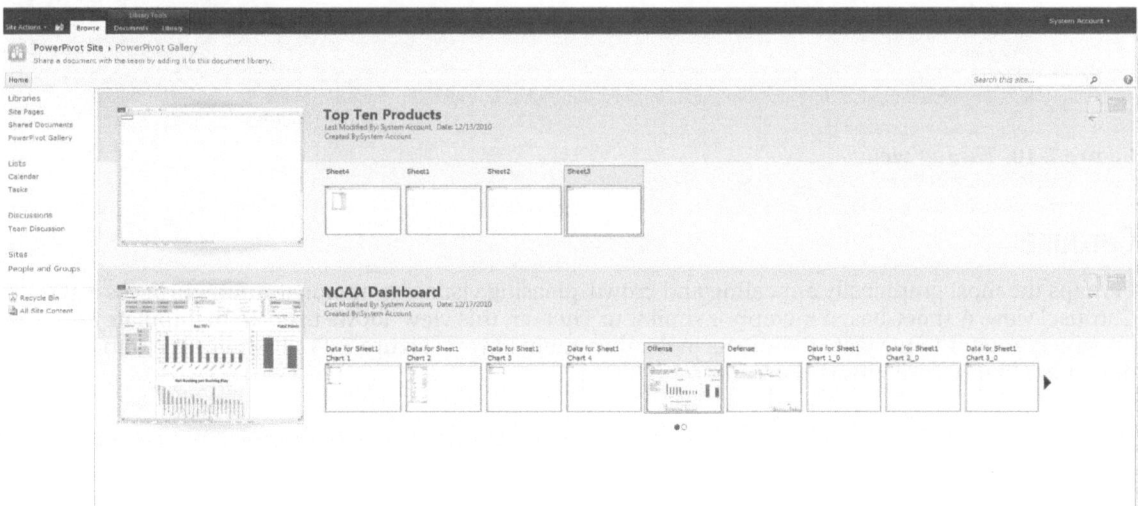

Figure 7-9. *Gallery view*

Theater

The Theater view is a completely different visual metaphor than the Gallery view. Instead of a row per workbook, the Theater view lists all sheets, contained in all workbooks, in the document library across the bottom of the view. Only by the workbook name in the bottom left area of the view does the user know by moving from one sheet to another that workbook boundaries have been crossed. To scroll through the sheets, left and right arrows allow for navigation to sheets not currently on the screen. For comparison, *Figure 7-10.* contains the same worksheets as the foregoing Gallery view.

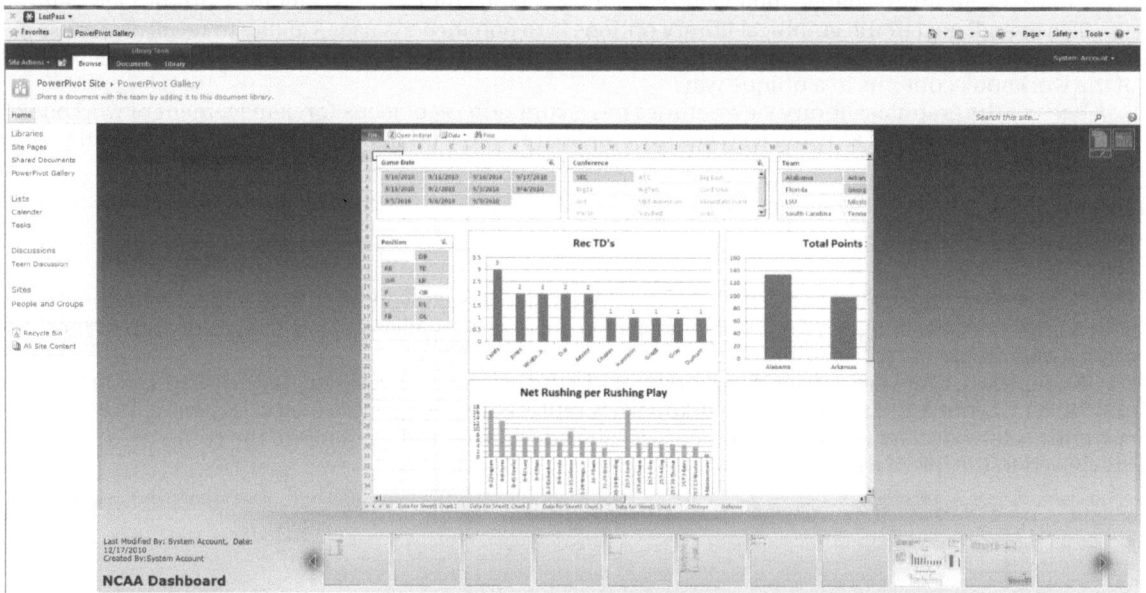

Figure 7-10. *Theater view*

Carousel

Perhaps the most graphically appealing and crowd-pleasing visual for demonstration purposes is the Carousel view. A sheet-based metaphor similar to Theater, this view allows users to manipulate an imaginary rotator to navigate the sheets in the document library. Figure 7-11 illustrates the same document library contents, in the Carousel view.

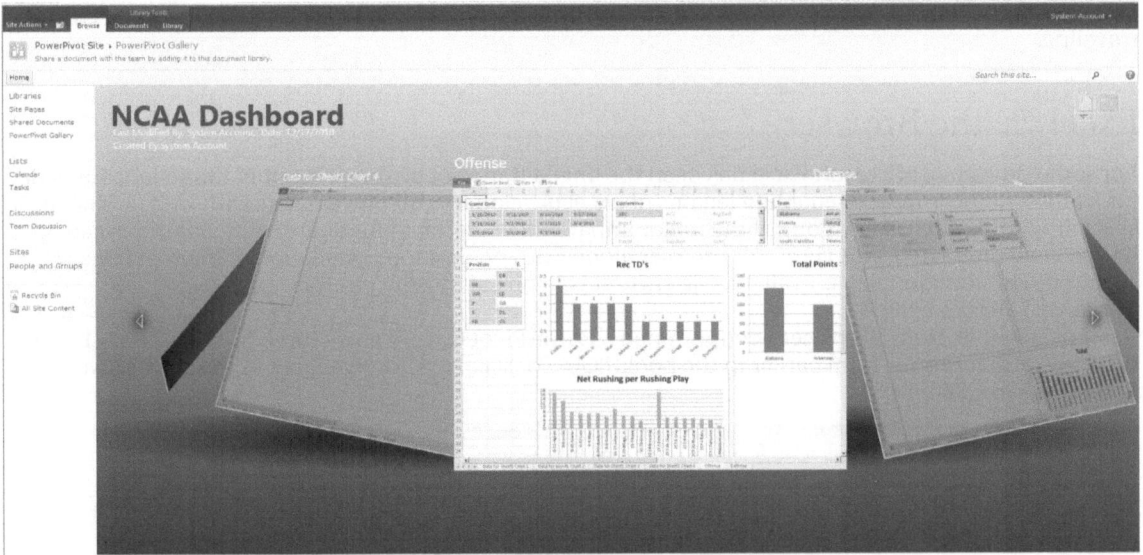

Figure 7-11. *Carousel view*

All Documents

The All Documents view is a plain-text listing of all files (available to the user) in the PowerPivot Gallery. This is a library view feature of all SharePoint document libraries. As you will see later in this chapter, the All Documents view can be very useful in environments without Silverlight.

PowerPivot Gallery Permissions

Just like other documents stored within SharePoint, it is possible to create a set of permissions to restrict use of the PowerPivot solutions. Because the PowerPivot Gallery comprises all of the features of a SharePoint document library, it is possible to create an elaborate governance implementation using permissions at the Site Collection, PowerPivot Gallery, folder (within the Gallery), and the individual file. I mention this here only to make you, the PowerPivot solution developer, aware of the grain at which SharePoint can control access to your solution files. Establishing the SharePoint governance plan for your site is quite outside the scope of this book, though.

Web Usage Scenarios

There are a number of situations in which consumption of a PowerPivot for SharePoint solution via a web browser is advantageous. Deskless workers—those who perform their duties while not tied to a desk—aren't likely to have a dedicated PC, and often benefit from access through a browser on whatever PC they can find. Members of mobile and field service workforces may consume all of their analytics from a browser on a laptop, tablet, or smartphone. Finally, even traditional information workers that enjoy desktops and laptop computers occasionally have the need for browser access to analytics when traveling.

Excel via the Browser

For some time now, Microsoft Excel has been the lingua franca of business number crunchers. Consider for a moment the impact of enabling legions of Excel developers and power users with web publishing skills. Imparting such skills is one of the major impacts of PowerPivot for SharePoint. Solutions can be opened and interacted with via a web browser alone, with no desktop installation of Microsoft Excel required. This functionality is available via current versions of Mozilla Firefox, Apple Safari, and Microsoft Internet Explorer.

For example, from a browser window, open a PowerPivot Gallery as pictured in Figure 7-12. In this case, I have an example from earlier in the book, `NCAA Dashboard.xlsx`, available in this PowerPivot for SharePoint installation.

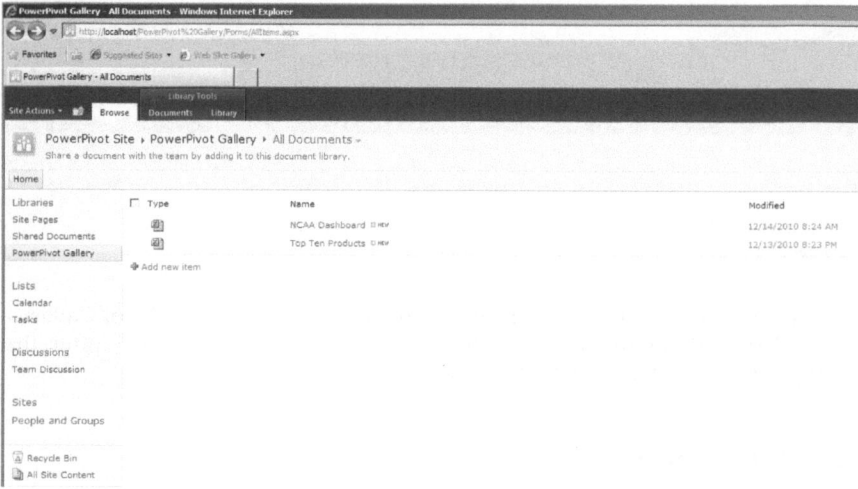

Figure 7-12. *PowerPivot Gallery*

To open the file, single-click the file name in the PowerPivot Gallery. By default, this will open the workbook using Excel Services. The result should be similar to Figure 7-13. Notice the grid-lines and slicers, similar to the presentation in the desktop version of Excel. Additionally, we are simply rendering this inside an Internet Explorer tab. Except for the browser, no desktop software is required to present the worksheet to a user in this mode.

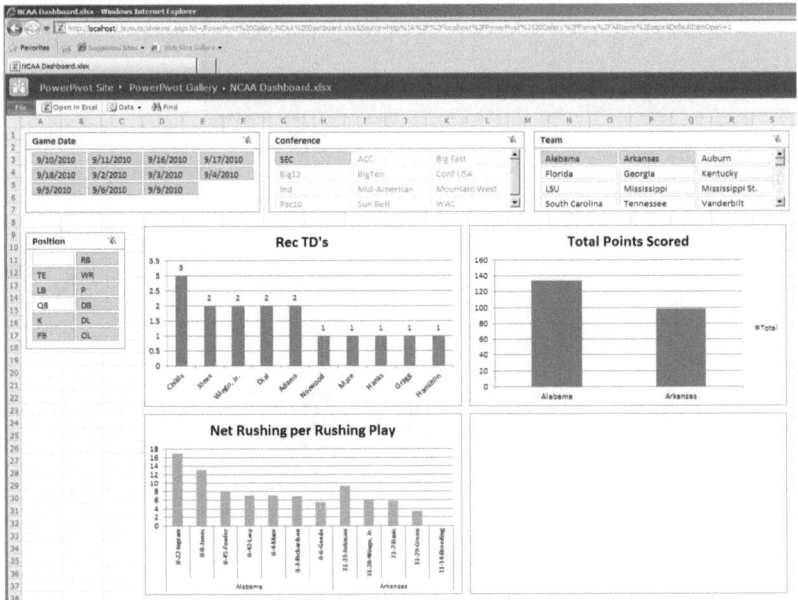

Figure 7-13. *File open in web browser*

While the display of the file may be less than remarkable, there is more. All of the slicer and filter interactions possible in the desktop version of Microsoft Excel are available to the web user via Excel Services. For example, with a Shift-click of the Florida item in the Team slicer, the charts in the dashboard are updated to add data for Florida, as pictured in Figure 7-14.

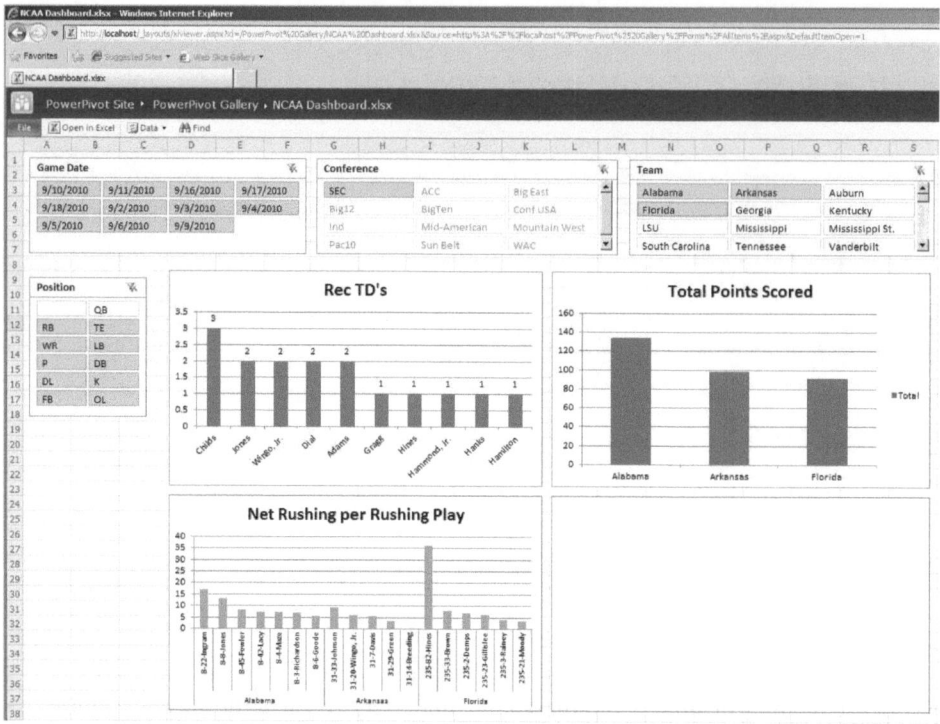

Figure 7-14. *Slicer update in web browser*

However, the web presentation of PowerPivot solutions does carry limitations. No "authoring" capabilities are available for web users. There is no way for a user to change the layout of an existing PivotChart or PivotTable via the web interface. The exception to this would be columns and rows that may be added to (or removed from) a PivotChart or PivotTable (for example, the foregoing Florida data) via a user's interaction with a slicer. However, there is a compelling case to be made for SharePoint as a consumption tier for a group of users making decisions by interacting with but not creating PowerPivot solutions. This limitation can be considered an advantage in that Excel web users cannot change the underlying PowerPivot solution from a data or layout perspective. Instead, we have the ultimate in a "protected" workbook as an ad hoc analytics platform.

PowerPivot from an iPad or Other Tablet

The good news is you can access PowerPivot for SharePoint workbooks from a tablet device—for example, an iPad. The bad news, however, especially on the iPad, is limitations, because Silverlight simply is not available on the iOS. Therefore using the graphical preview PowerPivot Gallery presentation methods (Gallery, Theater, and Carousel) is not possible. This is because each of the gallery views relies on Silverlight as the presentation layer. The All Documents view is a simple list of the PowerPivot Gallery content that will render correctly within a browser without Silverlight (such as Safari on iOS).

Figure 7-15 contains an example of using the All Documents view of the PowerPivot Gallery from an iPad. The solution can be opened on the device, and the primary user interface elements of PowerPivot for SharePoint respond to gestures. These user interface elements include slicers and the filter context menu.

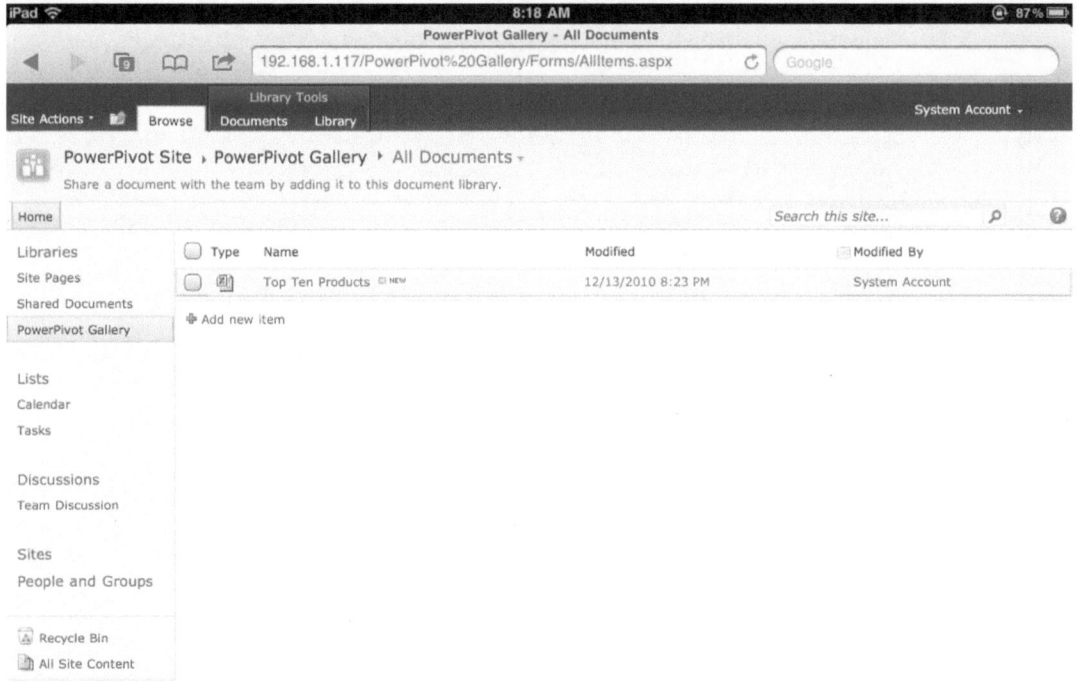

Figure 7-15. *PowerPivot Gallery, All Documents view on iPad*

Figure 7-16 is an example of interaction with a PowerPivot for Excel solution via Safari on the iPad. However, the diagram does not indicate the navigation differences that may become issues in a real project. For example, the ability to Ctrl-click (or Shift-click) to select multiple slicer values is not apparent, if at all possible. Additionally, the usual mouse navigation to move around the worksheet is another unimpressive user experience.

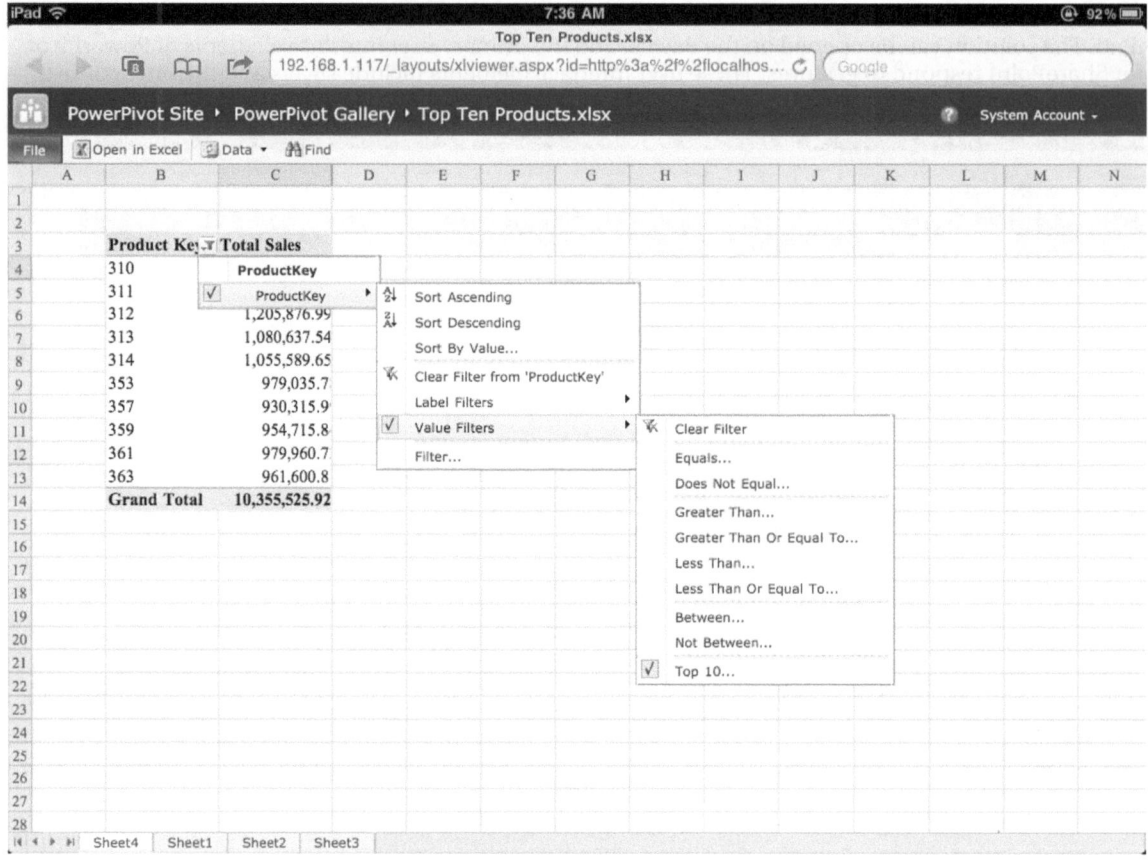

Figure 7-16. *Interaction with filter context on iPad*

PowerPivot Management Dashboard

From its inception, a path to enterprise migration has been a part of PowerPivot. The PowerPivot Management Dashboard is a component of that strategy, ensuring usage monitoring was included as "out-of-the-box" functionality for the PowerPivot for SharePoint installation. For example, the dashboard includes monitoring of query performance over time in a manner very similar to the SQL Server 2008 Performance Data Warehouse feature. This is a monitoring tool for PowerPivot, written in PowerPivot.

Accessing the PowerPivot Management Dashboard

The PowerPivot Management Dashboard is most directly accessed via SharePoint Central Administration. If you are using a dedicated development environment such as that described in Chapter 6, then access to SharePoint Central Administration will be no problem. However, if you are using an enterprise SharePoint farm installation, access may not be forthcoming from your SharePoint Administrator.

In the event you do have access to SharePoint Central Administration, there are at least two methods for accessing the PowerPivot Management Dashboard. First, from SharePoint Central Administration, choose the "Manage service applications" option from the Application Management group of management hyperlinks. When the list of service applications renders on the next screen, click the link for the PowerPivot service application you wish to analyze. For an out-of-the-box installation, this will be Default PowerPivot Service Application. The next screen consists of a number of items to understand and predict the health of your PowerPivot for SharePoint installation.

Using the Management Dashboard

In the upper left-hand corner of the PowerPivot Management Dashboard is a Web Part containing a multipurpose report. This report reveals a number of leading indicators of system performance over time. As depicted, the pulldown control allows the user to select between the following diagnostic reports: Query Response Times, Average Instance CPU, Average Instance Memory, (Workbook) Activity, and (Overall Server) Performance. These reports should be taken as a whole to help you understand and perhaps forecast future PowerPivot for SharePoint performance.

One of the truly great features of the PowerPivot Management Dashboard is the automatic nature of data collection. This is a double-edged sword with respect to development environments. If you are running PowerPivot for SharePoint only occasionally in a virtual machine or a bootable image, the SharePoint timer jobs that would normally gather data will not have actual activity. This can cause the PowerPivot Management Dashboard to be underpopulated with data, and thus the diagnostic reports will be rather unimpressive. I use a virtual machine for the example in this book, and I have made a point to run that virtual machine consistently for a number of days. An alternative to populate your virtual machine–based Management Dashboard would be to open a number of workbooks over time, and ensure the data collection jobs for the Management Dashboard are executed either on schedule or via the Execute Now option within Timer Job Schedule management.

Query Response Times

The Query Response Times report is a graphical representation of the categorization of query workload over time. In Figure 7-17, we have query responses for the past four days, graphically indicating the response time category by color. The installation defaults for these time periods are listed in Table 7-1.

Table 7-1. *Default Query Response Configuration*

Category	Does not Exceed
Trivial	500 milliseconds
Quick	1,000 milliseconds
Expected	3,000 milliseconds
Long	10,000 milliseconds
Exceeded	Greater than 'Long' upper limit

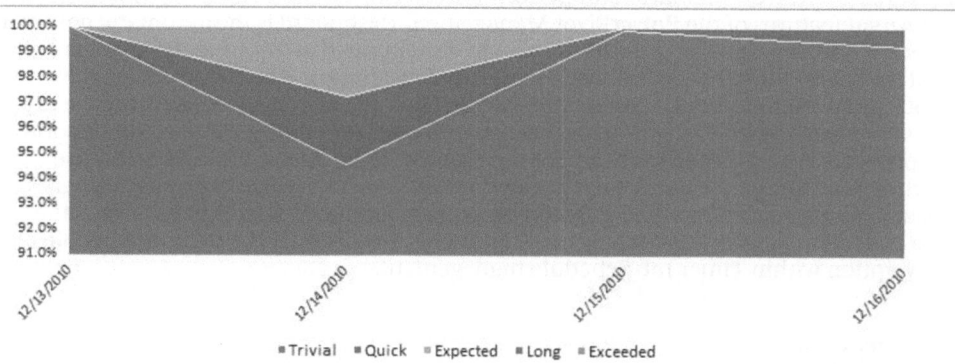

Figure 7-17. *Query Response Times report*

The query response times classification upper bounds are installation-configurable. From the Management Dashboard, in the upper right-hand corner under the "Configure service application settings", link in the Actions section. The resulting page will allow for configuration of Trivial through Long upper bounds. The Exceeded category is not directly configurable. It is the derived category for any query response taking longer than the Long category upper bound.

The occasional "trough" in query response times, that is the occurrence of query responses consistently in greater response time categories, can be an indication of which time periods are contributing to the greatest server workload and may benefit from tuning. Additionally, cross-checking the Query Response Times report with the Workbook Activity Chart will allow precise identification of resource-intensive workbooks.

Average Instance CPU

With the idea that no single diagnostic image from the Management Dashboard should be taken in isolation, the Server Health report also includes a graph of the measured CPU activity percentage over time. The goal of this report is to assist the SharePoint Administrator in assessing overall server under-utilization or alternatively if the server is consistently exceeding capacity. Figure 7-18 is an example showing the utilization for the "life span" of my virtual machine instance for about five days.

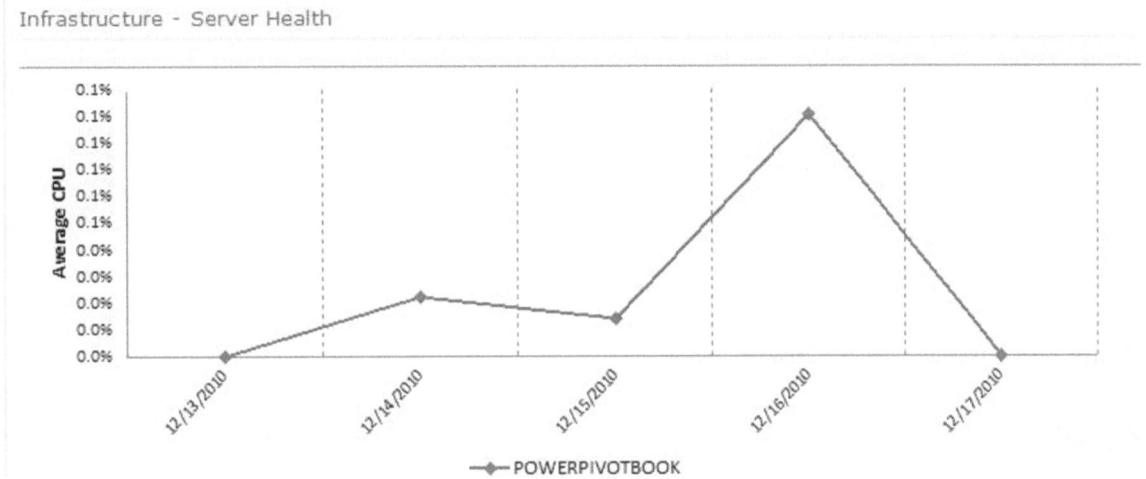

Figure 7-18. *Average Instance CPU report*

Average Instance Memory

Another key indicator of overall server capacity is how much memory is being consistently used by PowerPivot for SharePoint. When the average instance memory is near peak configured memory on a consistent basis, the server is being over-utilized relative to capacity. Figure 7-19 depicts the historical memory utilization for one of the virtual machines used in the production of this book.

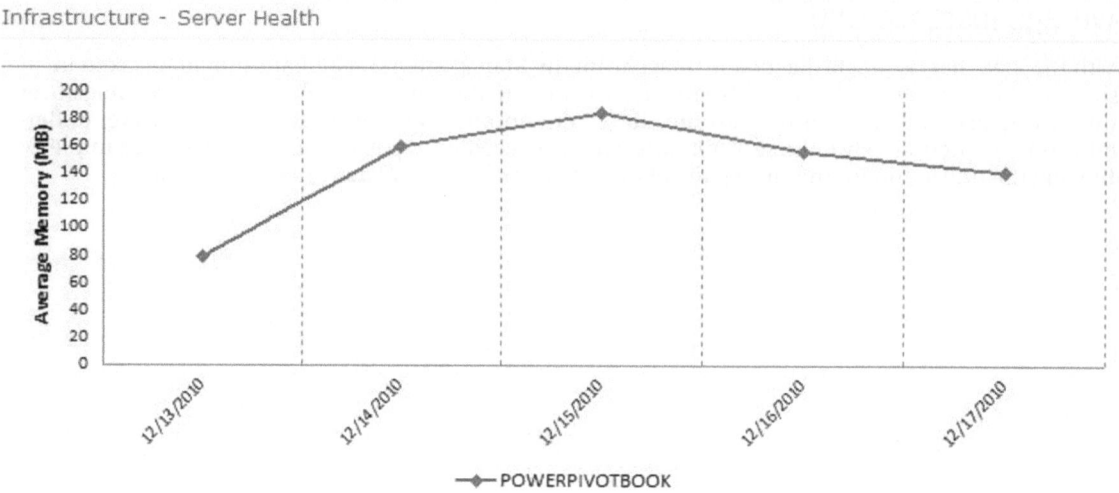

Figure 7-19. *Average Instance Memory report*

Activity

The Activity report differs from the others, because of the interactivity incorporated into it. While the entire PowerPivot Management Dashboard is built on PowerPivot for SharePoint, the Activity report is the first report that is rendered as a PowerPivot workbook. For example, the vertical slicers for Machine, Year, and Month allow for a customized view of the overall server metrics. The number of connections, queries executed, workbooks loaded (and unloaded), and user volume are all charted based on the slicer settings.

The example in Figure 7-20 shows a large volume of queries occurring on December 15, causing the line for that date to be shaded in red. The days before and after appear to be nominal, so the activity on the 15th could have been a one-time anomaly. However, it could have been the result of a monthly operation that will occur again on the 15th of the next month. Both the PowerPivot Management Dashboard operational facts as well as business operations schedule must be evaluated for tuning decisions.

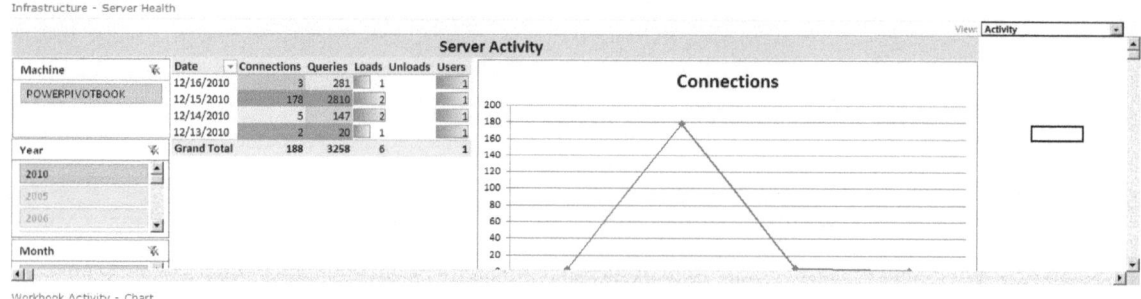

Figure 7-20. *Activity report*

Performance

Similar to the Activity report, the Performance report is an interactive PowerPivot workbook that can be sliced by Machine, Year, and Month. The PivotTable indicates visually relative health by CPU, memory, and query execution classification.

Figure 7-21 contains an example of the Performance report. Red highlighting is used to indicate peak levels of CPU and memory usage. Conversely, the lowest levels of CPU and memory resource utilization are formatted with a green cell background to visually indicate the dip in usage.

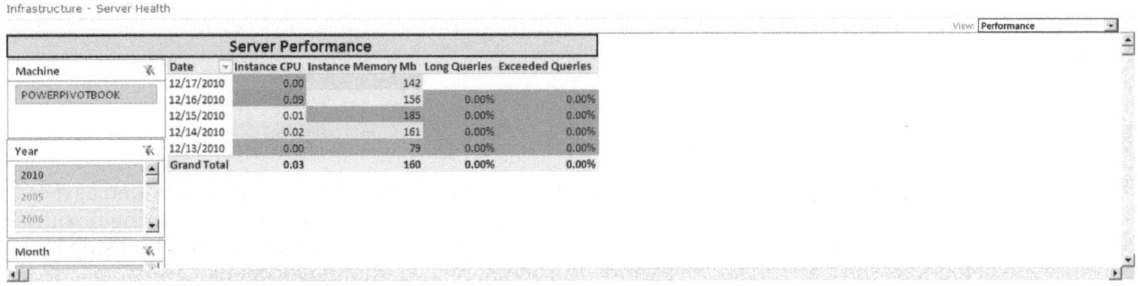

Figure 7-21. *Performance report*

Workbook Activity Chart

The Workbook Activity Chart, illustrated in Figure 7-22, is one of the more visually impressive and interactive tools in the PowerPivot Management Dashboard. This chart is comprised of the workbooks currently on the server, with a bubble representing each. The relative size of the bubble is indicative of the relative size of the workbook. In the case of the example virtual machine, all of the workbooks are of similar size. The vertical axis indicates the average number of users per week. The horizontal axis is the number of queries executed by the workbook to the PowerPivot for SharePoint database engine.

The interactive part of this chart is the slider, just below the horizontal chart axis. This control allows the administrator to travel through time, by week, in order to understand which workbooks are gaining in popularity (user count) and activity (query executions). As the slider is repositioned, each bubble may shift position on both axes and in size (as relative data size changes).

One of the more valuable uses of this chart is to understand when a PowerPivot solution, based on user community and/or query activity, may have outgrown the PowerPivot environment and be a candidate for migration to a SQL Server Analysis Services solution.

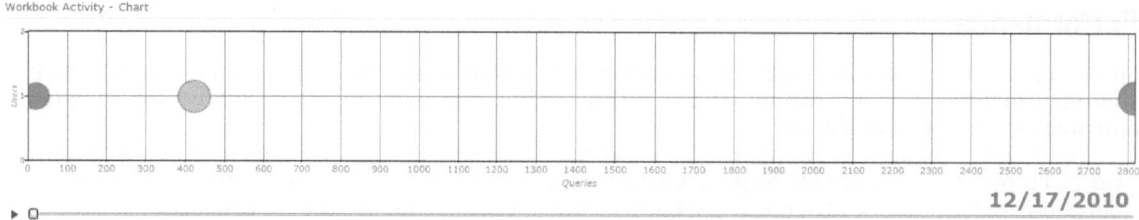

Figure 7-22. *Workbook Activity Chart*

Workbook Activity List

The Workbook Activity List is a list of workbooks on the observed server. The report is provided as a convenience for the SharePoint Administrator. Understanding which workbooks are requiring resources from the other elements of the PowerPivot Management Dashboard is sometimes a good first step in tuning. One of the next steps would be to examine the actual high-demand workbooks.

Figure 7-23 shows the report. You can see that it lists each of the workbooks from the usage data collection period.

■ **Note** The data collection period is the interval of time for which PowerPivot for SharePoint has been gathering query performance metrics. When PowerPivot for SharePoint is installed, a default schedule for SharePoint timer jobs is established. These jobs gather workbook query activity for presentation in the PowerPivot Management Dashboard.

The list includes the name, the number of users and queries, and the overall size for each workbook on the server. The report is sorted by popularity by default, in descending order by Users. However, sorting by one of the other metrics, Query or Size, is a matter of clicking the column header. The sort order can be inverted by clicking the column header of the current sort column.

Workbook Activity - List

Workbook	Users↓	Queries	Size (Mb)
NCAA Dashboard.xlsx	1	422	2.05
Workbook Deleted	1	20	1.50
PowerPivot Management Data.xlsx	1	2816	2.20

Figure 7-23. *Workbook Activity List*

Configuring Usage Data Collection

Upon installation of PowerPivot for SharePoint, default values are used to establish the boundaries between the categories of query performance: Trivial, Quick, Expected, Long, and Exceeded. While an installation default is set, you can also adjust the time threshold for a reported usage event. Finally, the default is for the PowerPivot Management Dashboard to maintain 365 days of usage data. That history interval can be changed as well.

In order to alter the usage data collection parameters, click the link in the Actions section in the upper-right corner of the PowerPivot Management Dashboard, as illustrated in Figure 7-24.

Figure 7-24. *Service application settings*

The resulting page will contain all of the settings for the PowerPivot for SharePoint service application, similar to Figure 7-25. Scrolling to the bottom of the page will navigate to the section labeled Usage Data Collection. You may change the parameters by editing the values in the text box corresponding to each setting. Click the OK button to apply your settings.

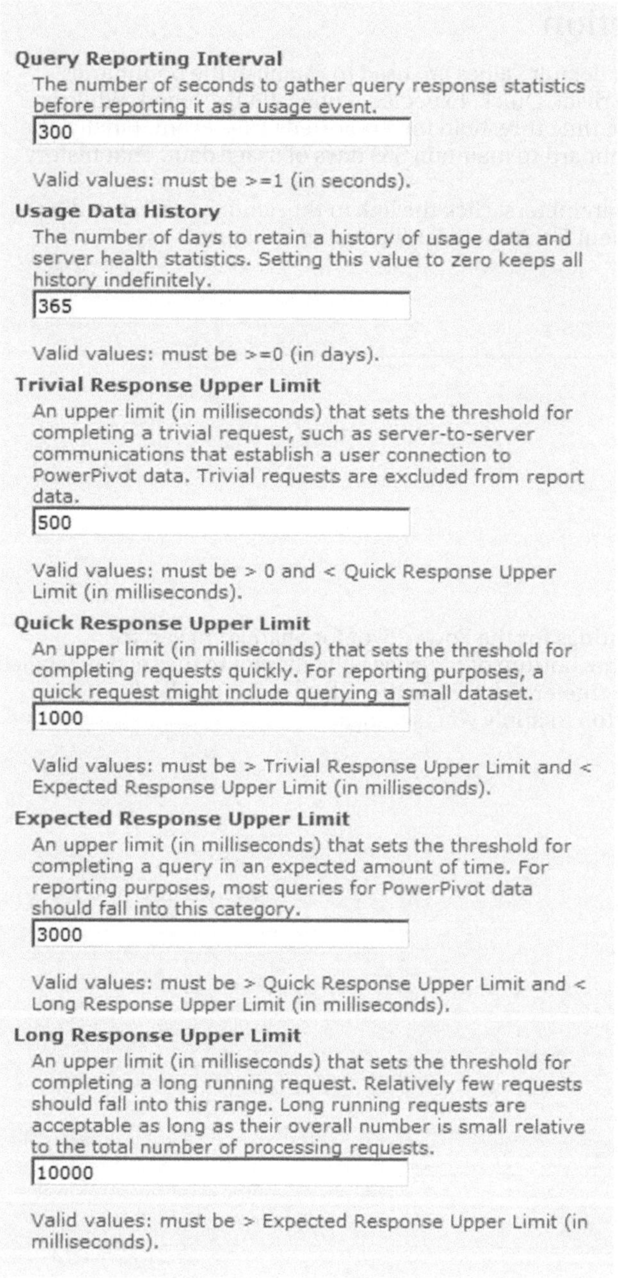

Query Reporting Interval

The number of seconds to gather query response statistics before reporting it as a usage event.

300

Valid values: must be >=1 (in seconds).

Usage Data History

The number of days to retain a history of usage data and server health statistics. Setting this value to zero keeps all history indefinitely.

365

Valid values: must be >=0 (in days).

Trivial Response Upper Limit

An upper limit (in milliseconds) that sets the threshold for completing a trivial request, such as server-to-server communications that establish a user connection to PowerPivot data. Trivial requests are excluded from report data.

500

Valid values: must be > 0 and < Quick Response Upper Limit (in milliseconds).

Quick Response Upper Limit

An upper limit (in milliseconds) that sets the threshold for completing requests quickly. For reporting purposes, a quick request might include querying a small dataset.

1000

Valid values: must be > Trivial Response Upper Limit and < Expected Response Upper Limit (in milliseconds).

Expected Response Upper Limit

An upper limit (in milliseconds) that sets the threshold for completing a query in an expected amount of time. For reporting purposes, most queries for PowerPivot data should fall into this category.

3000

Valid values: must be > Quick Response Upper Limit and < Long Response Upper Limit (in milliseconds).

Long Response Upper Limit

An upper limit (in milliseconds) that sets the threshold for completing a long running request. Relatively few requests should fall into this range. Long running requests are acceptable as long as their overall number is small relative to the total number of processing requests.

10000

Valid values: must be > Expected Response Upper Limit (in milliseconds).

Figure 7-25. *Usage Data Collection settings*

Summary

The following are some of the key points from this chapter's discussion. Keep them in mind as you deploy PowerPivot for SharePoint in our own environment.

- PowerPivot for SharePoint is a platform by which users skilled in Excel can publish browser-enabled analytic solutions.

- Deploying PowerPivot for SharePoint solutions is simply a matter of uploading the Excel file to SharePoint.

- The PowerPivot Gallery is a SharePoint document library specifically created to store, share, and render PowerPivot for SharePoint solutions.

- PowerPivot for SharePoint file permissions should be part of a comprehensive SharePoint governance plan.

- In addition to Internet Explorer, PowerPivot for SharePoint can be accessed by devices using Apple Safari and Mozilla Firefox.

The PowerPivot Management Dashboard provides, out of the box, usage statistics and analytical tools written in PowerPivot to manage PowerPivot.

CHAPTER 8

■■■

PowerPivot As a Data Source

If I have seen further it is only by standing on the shoulders of giants.

—Sir Isaac Newton

At the most basic level, there are three tiers that comprise a business intelligence (BI) solution. The most immediately visible tier is the consumption or user interface tier, which provides a means for user actions to be translated into the information presented in filtering, formatting, or both. Examples of tools and products in this tier would include SQL Server Reporting Services, Excel, and dashboards in SharePoint.

The consumption tier can be thought of as a window into the next tier, the data tier. Source data that is derived from or generated by business activity is stored, in a method optimal for servicing analytic queries in the data tier. Products that execute the role of the data tier include Microsoft SQL Server's relational engine and the SQL Server Analysis Services (SSAS) OLAP engine. Examples of the data tier include the AdventureWorks data warehouse used in earlier examples in this book.

The final BI solution tier is the "Extract, Transform, and Load" (ETL) tier. The primary role of the ETL tier is to transport and transform data from source systems into the format required by the data tier. In earlier releases of SQL Server, this role would typically be fulfilled by SQL Server Integration Services (SSIS).

In the preceding chapters, we have focused on the ability of PowerPivot (both for Excel and SharePoint) to fulfill all three tiers. PowerPivot's in-memory SSAS runtime is the data tier. PowerPivot data connections and DAX combine to create the ETL tier. Finally, Excel PivotTables and PivotCharts comprise the consumption tier. PowerPivot can also serve as a building block for other PowerPivot solutions, leveraging, for example, separate, related solutions to create a unified analytical platform.

PowerPivot As a Data Source for PowerPivot

An existing PowerPivot for SharePoint solution can act as a data source from which related PowerPivot solutions can be created. Figure 8-1 shows an example scenario.

Because a PowerPivot for Excel solution, once deployed to PowerPivot for SharePoint, creates a SQL Server Analysis Services database, the database can be accessed by other PowerPivot solutions. This ability to serve as a data source is limited to PowerPivot for SharePoint, however, as connections to the SSAS instance behind PowerPivot for Excel are not supported in the same manner as PowerPivot for SharePoint.

Consider the following scenario: An enterprise has created two separate PowerPivot for SharePoint solutions, one for analysis of sales and another for analysis of production. Audiences in the sales management and production operations management areas use each PowerPivot solution separately, updating the PowerPivot database with new, fresh data on independent schedules. However, summary-level information from each of the departments, sales and production operations, is of interest to a single analyst reporting directly to the chief operating officer (COO). The COO's analyst could create from scratch a solution to report key sales and operations metrics, or that analyst could leverage the existing solutions as data sources for a third, summary-level PowerPivot solution. As the underlying data in the PowerPivot for SharePoint solutions used by sales and production is updated, the new data would be available to the COO-level solution.

One of the advantages to using one PowerPivot solution as a data source for another is that the technique allows your solutions to steer away from the "spreadmart" chaos of the past. Spreadsheets stored on file shares are replaced with orderly, indexed, and searchable storage in PowerPivot Galleries. Furthermore, PowerPivot's robust, built-in ETL replaces relatively brittle and inelegant cell and range linking within spreadsheet files.

The other, more obvious advantage is the reuse of existing analytical work to create a new perspective. Very similar to the concept of a mash-up application, PowerPivot for SharePoint solutions can be pieced together to create new insight, as illustrated in Figure 8-1.

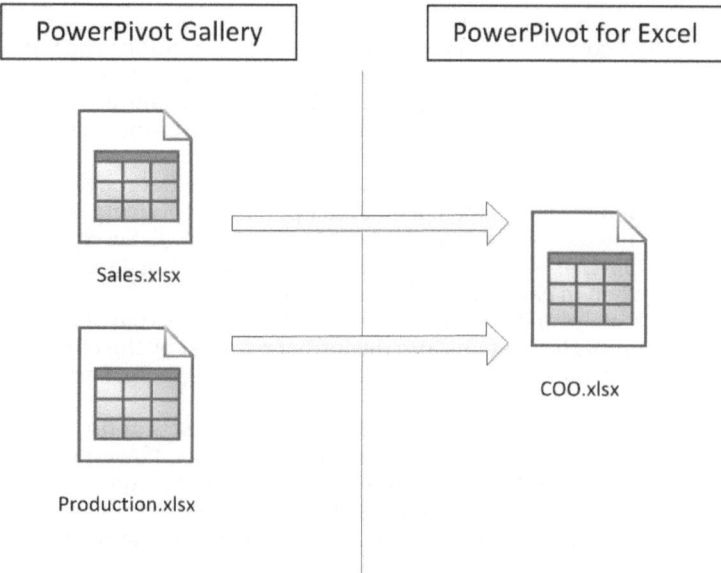

Figure 8-1. *Combining PowerPivot for SharePoint solutions*

To maintain clarity as we discuss the scenario in Figure 8-1, the Sales and Production Operations solutions will be referred to as *primary solutions*. In other words, those solutions connect directly to the primary data sources the transactional systems for sales, manufacturing operations, etc. The *summary solution* uses each of the primary solutions as the data sources, instead of connecting firsthand to the operational data sources.

Verifying the Solution Prerequisites

There are pre-conditions to understand and verify before using the solution in Figure 8-1. First, both the computer on which the PowerPivot for Excel solution will be developed and the PowerPivot for

SharePoint instance should be on the same domain. It is possible to upload both the Sales and Production Operations solutions from a computer not on the domain of the SharePoint server. However, in order to author the PowerPivot solution that uses these (Sales and Production) primary solutions as a data source, both primary solutions must be on the same domain.

Second, it may be necessary to open firewall ports on the PowerPivot for SharePoint server, in order to allow incoming connections from the PowerPivot for Excel development computer. Microsoft Books Online (BOL) describes this as not being the case, as the connection should be from the PowerPivot for Excel computer via port 80 for http (or 443 for https), a port already established for inbound connections.

Finally, the PowerPivot for Excel user developing the derived solution must use a domain account that has farm administrator privileges on the PowerPivot for SharePoint farm. This level of security is generally limited to a small group within an enterprise SharePoint implementation. You may find that your organization is unwilling to give you such access.

Nonetheless, utilizing PowerPivot as a data source is an important technique to understand as there are environments where the solution is useful. Moreover, as PowerPivot for SharePoint matures, the security privilege limitation may be eliminated. Finally, the technical foundation of PowerPivot is the creation of SQL Server Analysis Services databases, in order to facilitate rapid, ad hoc business intelligence. Understanding how the solution in Figure 8-1 is assembled will give you familiarity with accessing multi-dimensional databases (such as non-PowerPivot SSAS databases).

Assembling the Pieces

I have created two primary solutions, named Sales.xlsx and Operations.xlsx, containing sales measurements and operations measurements respectively. To avoid being bogged down in the details of actual data, each solution has two years of data, for two imaginary products: Widgets and Sprockets. Both solutions have been deployed to a PowerPivot Gallery on a SharePoint server, also a member of my demonstration domain. The idea is to illustrate the combination possibilities of PowerPivot for SharePoint, using the underlying data SSAS databases, not to create an exhaustive sales and production operations database.

Begin the summary solution similarly to any PowerPivot for Excel development. On our development computer, we open a new Excel worksheet and use the PowerPivot ribbon command to open a corresponding PowerPivot window. From the PowerPivot window, we can add a new data source, similar to any other source database. From the Get External Data set of the PowerPivot ribbon, choose From Database and then the From Analysis Services or PowerPivot option. This will launch the Table Import Wizard, as illustrated in Figure 8-2.

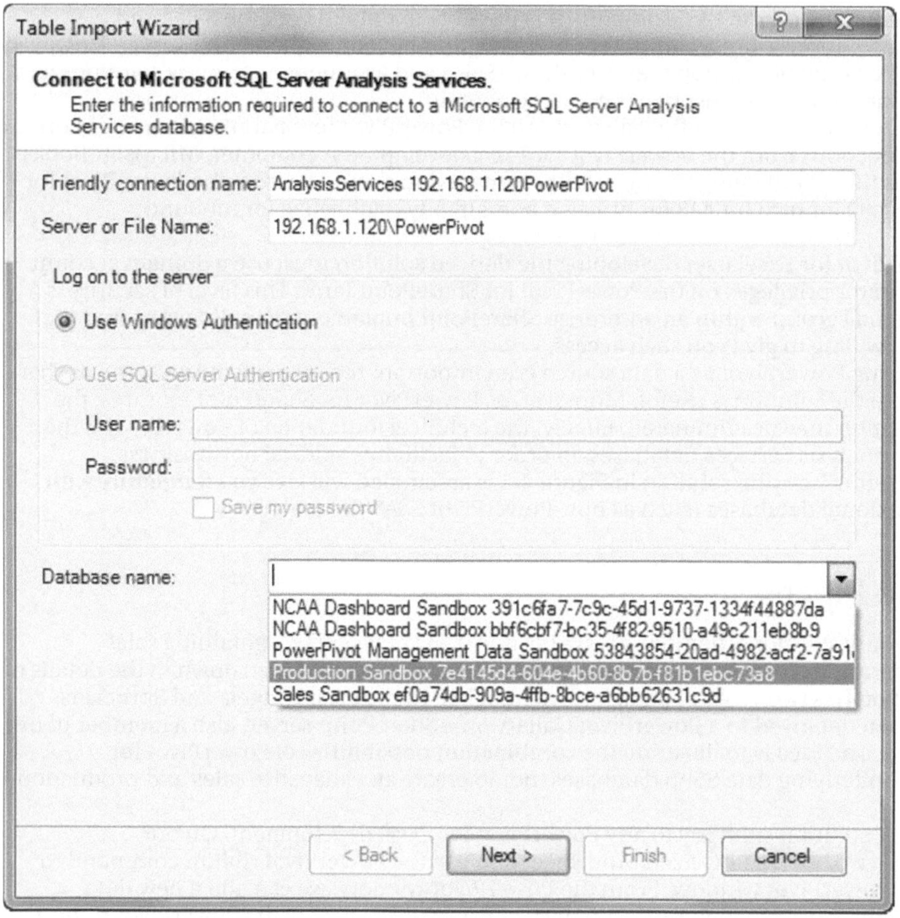

Figure 8-2. *Table Import Wizard for PowerPivot data source*

In the Table Import Wizard, enter information similar to that in Figure 8-2. In the illustration, we are using the Internet Protocol (IP) address 192.168.1.120 in order to access the PowerPivot for SharePoint server on this development domain. Your address or server name will be different. One thing that will be the same is the "\PowerPivot" immediately following the server name or server IP address. The text "\PowerPivot" modifies the connection string for a specific, named instance of SSAS on the target server. If we attempted to connect without this suffix, the connection would be made (or attempted to be made) to the default instance of SSAS on the target server. Recall from Chapter 6 that one of the requirements of the initial release of PowerPivot for SharePoint is the use of a specific, named SSAS instance ("PowerPivot") on the SharePoint server.

After completing the Server Name of the Table Import Wizard, ensure the Use Windows Authentication radio button is checked. Pressing the Test Connection button near the bottom of the dialog will verify the ability to connect from the PowerPivot for Excel development computer to the PowerPivot for SharePoint database.

After establishing the ability to connect to PowerPivot for SharePoint, the next step is creating the queries to fetch data into the derived solution. From the Table Import Wizard, as illustrated in Figure 8-2, use the Database Name pulldown list to select a PowerPivot database. You will notice the names of the solutions in the Table Import Wizard are different from the actual solution (.xlsx file names). For example, a unique ID has been added to all of the PowerPivot for SharePoint solution names. Additionally there are two versions of the NCAA Dashboard solution. This is because of SharePoint document library revision control. There are two revisions of the NCAA Dashboard published on my PowerPivot for SharePoint server; therefore, there are two potential SSAS databases for the Table Import Wizard. The multiple revisions of a given file will reinforce the next point. Use the file name URL in the connection instead of the server+instance (server\PowerPivot) and a database name.

The reason for using a file instead of the server and database name is when a connection request is made to the underlying database, the server+database name connection bypasses PowerPivot for SharePoint web services that will ensure the PowerPivot file is loaded on a server, even if it is currently unloaded. Second, the PowerPivot for SharePoint web service will load the latest, published version of the file, eliminating the need to manage the workbook name and GUID in the database connection strings.

In our example, we will begin by creating the query for the data from the Sales primary solution. The Table Import Wizard defaults to a Mulitdimensional Expressions (MDX) dialog, where an MDX string can be used if you are familiar with both MDX and the source SSAS database. Choose instead the Query Designer option, and you will be presented with a dialog similar to Figure 8-3. This tool will allow creation of a dataset from our PowerPivot for SharePoint SSAS database with no understanding of MDX.

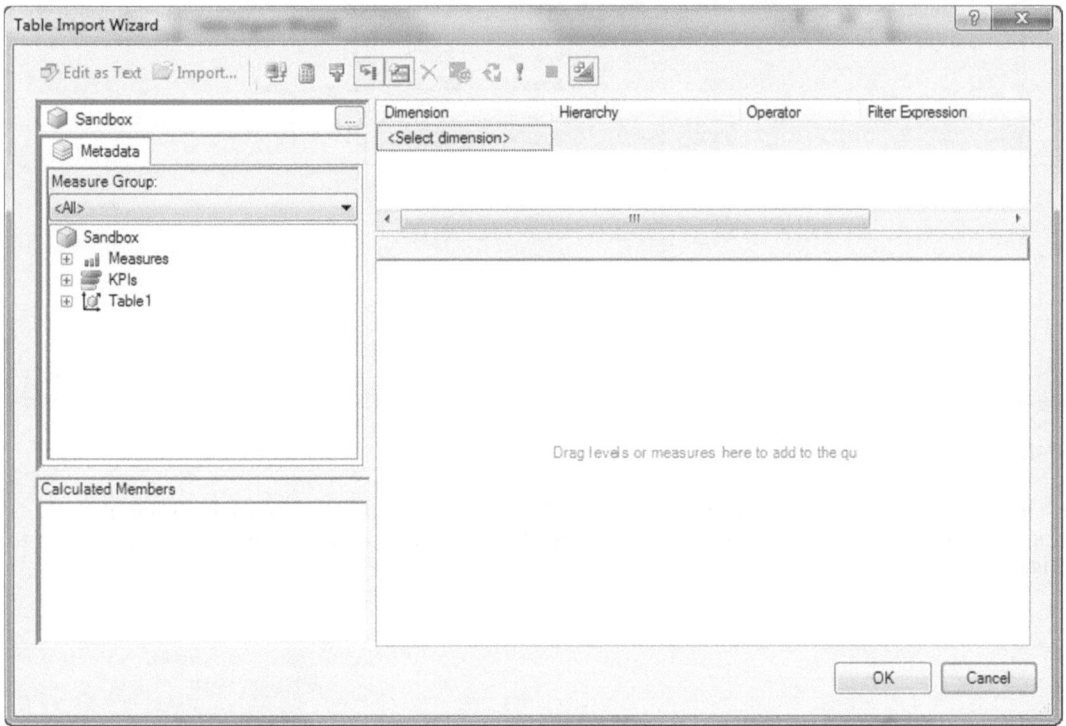

Figure 8-3. *Table Import Wizard Query Designer*

The left-hand explorer-like window allows for navigation of the PowerPivot for SharePoint data structure. Each element from the explorer can be dropped onto the query dataset canvas. If you are using the `Sales.xlsx` solution provided in the book's example download, drag the `Product` and `Sales Dollars` columns onto the canvas. The query designer will respond with two rows in the dataset, one for each of the two products, Widgets and Sprockets. Additionally, the `Sales Dollars` column has been renamed to `Sum of Sales Dollars`. This is by design, as the default aggregation method of the Sales Dollars measure. Complete the query design by adding the `Year` and `SortMonth` columns, as illustrated in Figure 8-4.

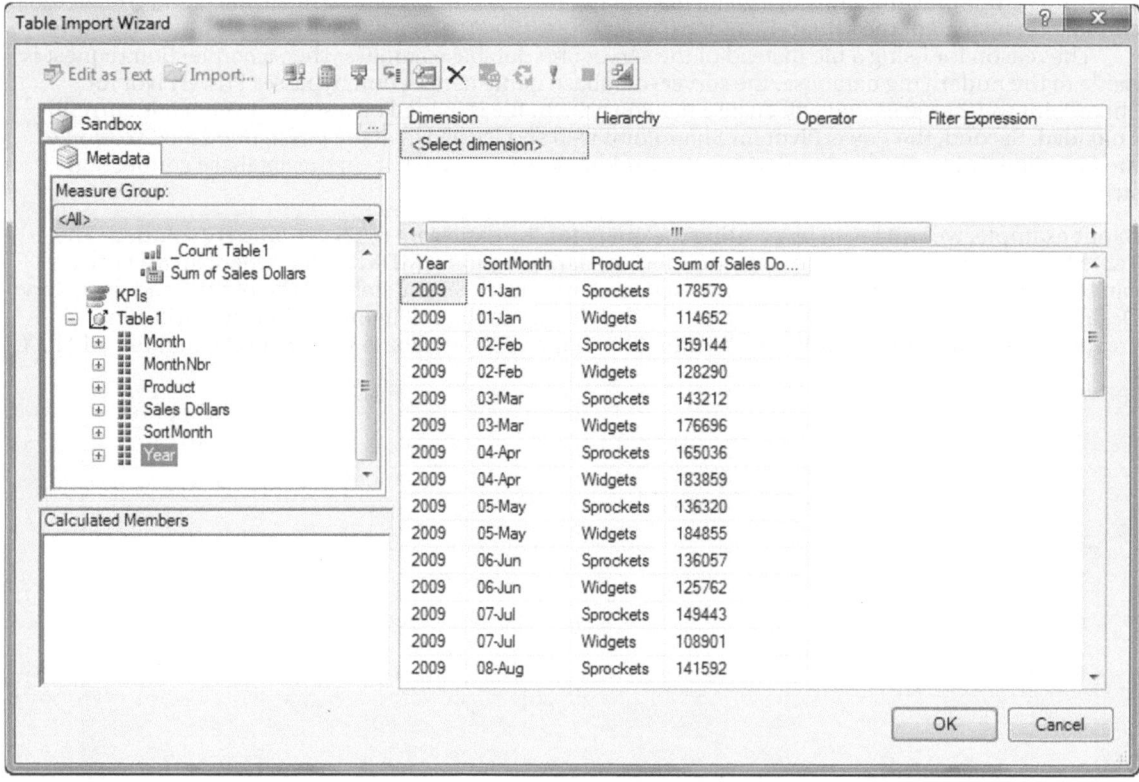

Figure 8-4. *Sales query design complete*

Pressing the OK button at this point will close the Query Designer and return to the original MDX text dialog with the completed query for the Sales dataset. The completed MDX query will look similar to that in Figure 8-5.

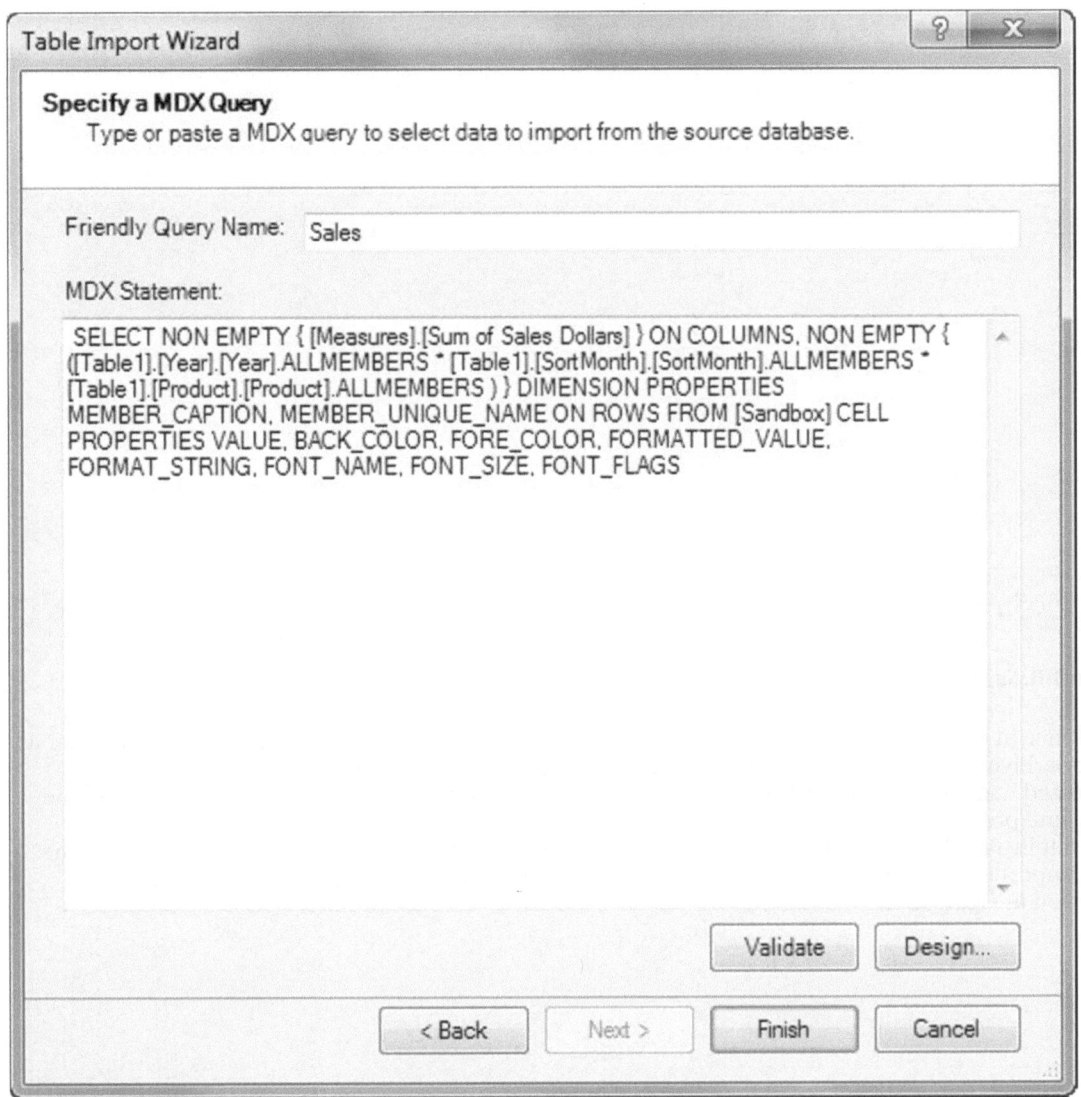

Figure 8-5. *MDX query*

Pressing the OK button from the Specify MDX Query dialog will execute the import of the dataset as reflected earlier in the Query Designer. You should see a familiar Table Import Wizard completion dialog, similar to Figure 8-6. In our case, with two years of monthly data, for two products, we expected to see 48 (2*12*2) rows imported.

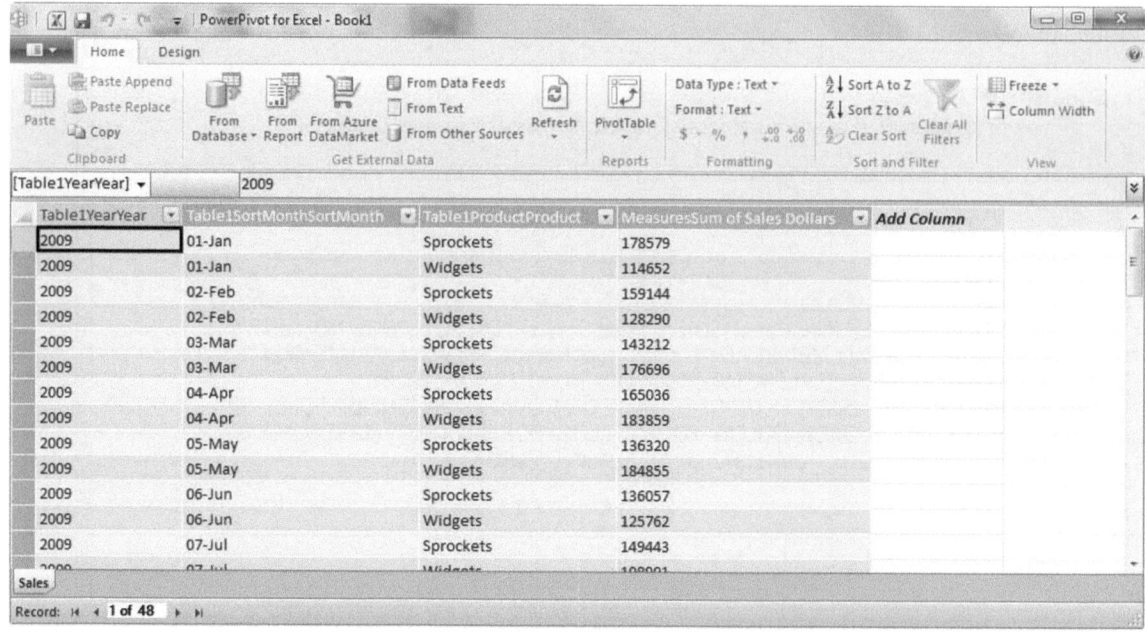

Figure 8-6. *Sales table import complete*

Notice in Figure 8-6 that PowerPivot has used the friendly query name "Sales" from the designer as the PowerPivot table name. However, the column names have not been named with an easily recognized naming convention. We do have the primary measure, sales in dollars, and keys for a time period and product.

Establishing the data connection for the production operations primary solution is similar. In the Table Import Wizard, the Production solution is specified in the database name pulldown list, as illustrated in Figure 8-7.

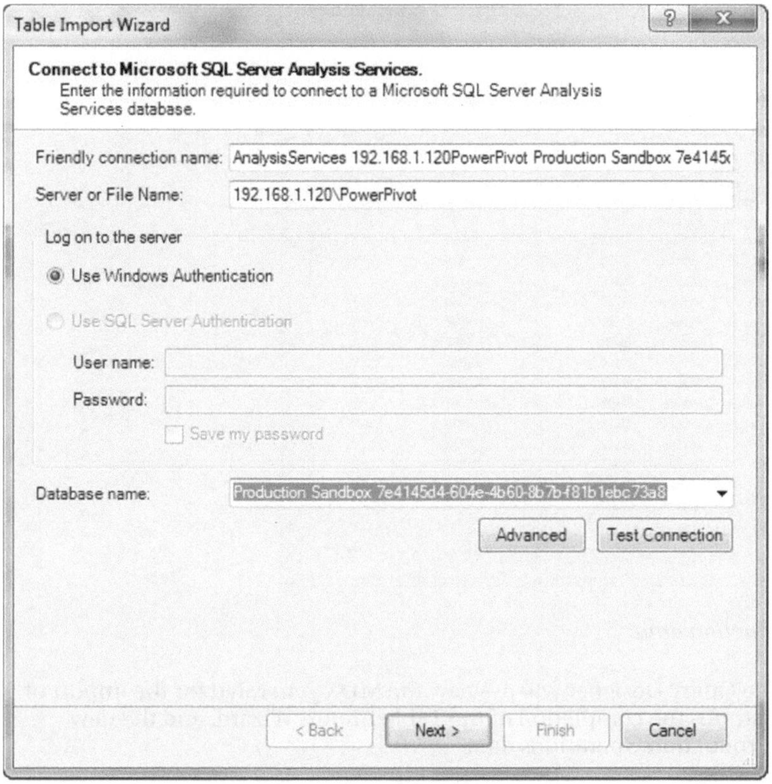

Figure 8-7. *Connection to Production data*

Additionally, in the Table Import Wizard Query Designer, we will select similar dimension key columns, as well as the two measures available in the Production primary solution. Similar to the illustration in Figure 8-8, the Sum of Production Cost and Sum of Production Units will be dropped onto the query design surface. Adding to the query design surface the columns for Year, SortMonth, and Product will generate rows in the dataset that detail the Units and Cost measures by all of the combinations of Year, SortMonth, and Product.

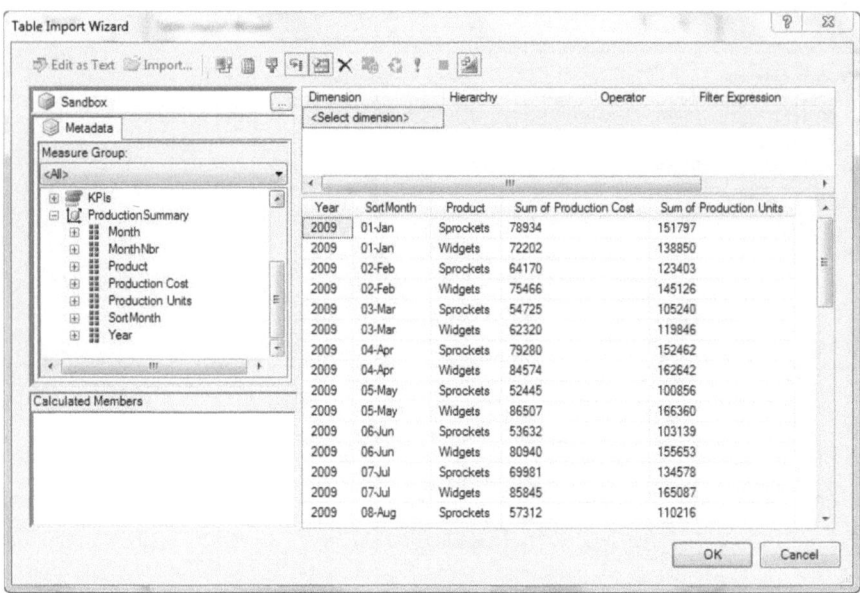

Figure 8-8. *Query Designer for Production data*

Pressing the OK button from the Query Designer will preview the MDX generated for the import of the Production data. Figure 8-9 illustrates the completion of the Table Import Wizard, and the new PowerPivot table created with the Production Operations data.

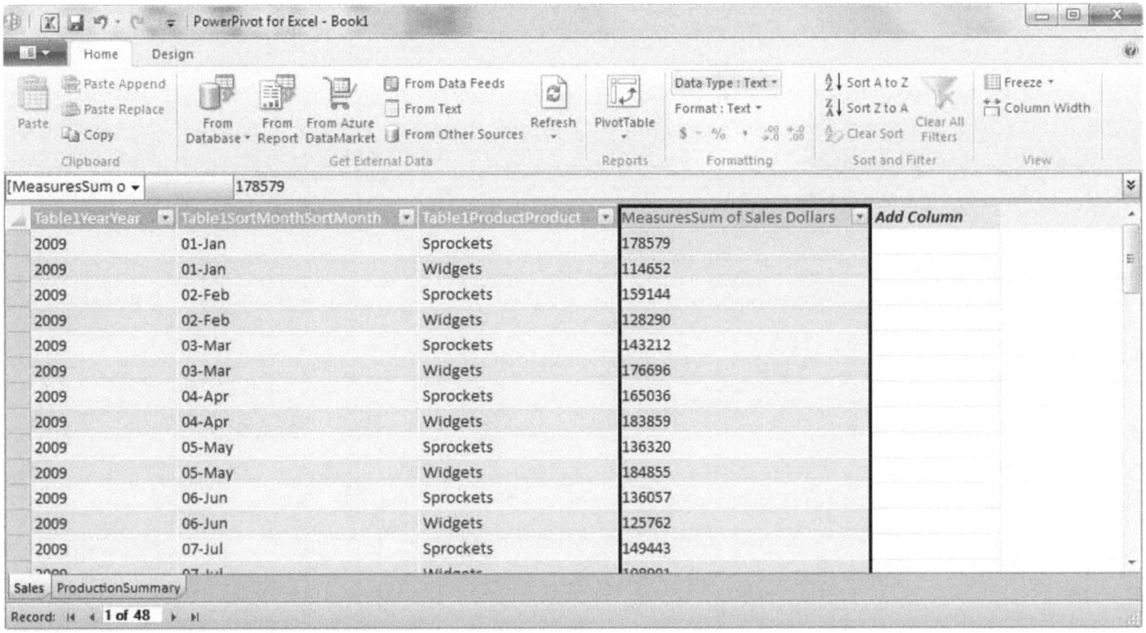

Figure 8-9. *Production Operations PowerPivot table*

A potential issue with using PowerPivot for SharePoint as a data source exists in how SSAS in SharePoint integrated mode unloads databases based on query usage by PowerPivot for SharePoint. If you recall from the PowerPivot Management Dashboard, in addition to loading databases into memory, PowerPivot will also free memory by unloading a database that is being under-utilized. The issue will be manifested by the desired database not being available in the Table Import Wizard pulldown. As an example, my development environment has unloaded the Production solution used as a primary source in this chapter. Illustrated in Figure 8-10, the pulldown list of databases is missing the Production solution and instead is showing both versions of the NCAA Dashboard and the PowerPivot Management Data solution. In order for the Production solution to reappear in the Database name pulldown, PowerPivot for SharePoint must reload the database into the SSAS instance running in SharePoint integrated mode.

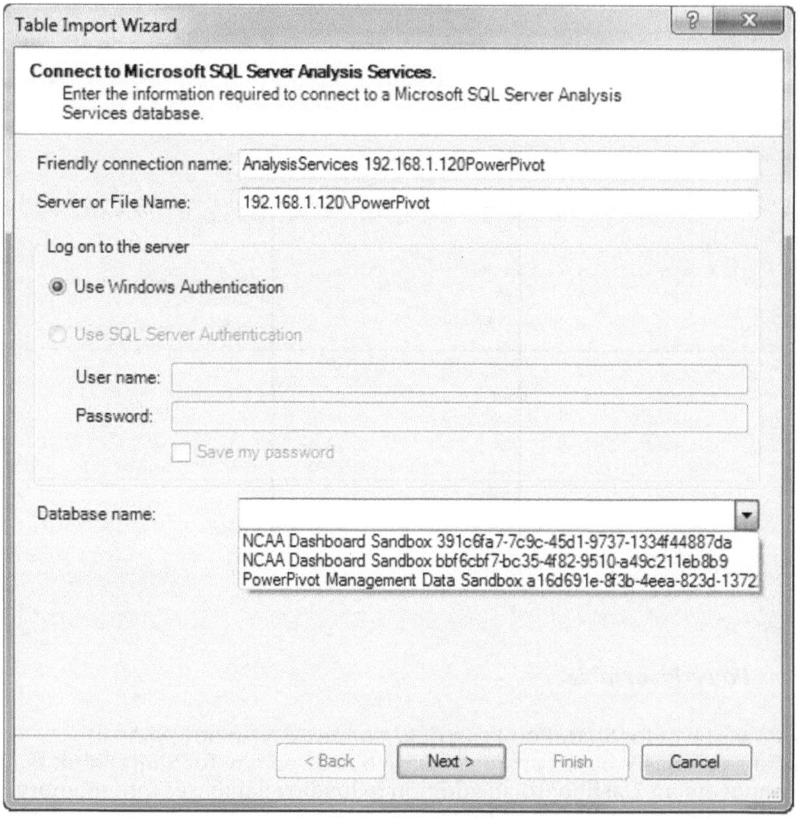

Figure 8-10. *Missing Production database name*

Loading a solution into SSAS is as simple as executing a query that requires the SSAS database for fulfillment. Opening the solution from within PowerPivot for SharePoint will not necessarily cause a database query operation. However, opening the solution and interacting with one of the slicers or expanding a drill-down will generate a query. PowerPivot for SharePoint will react to the slicer value change by dispatching a request to load the database for the current PowerPivot into the SSAS instance (\PowerPivot) servicing PowerPivot queries. The database will be loaded and the query results returned to PowerPivot for SharePoint, where the Excel Services user interface will be updated. As a practical example, changing the selected slicer values for Product in the Production solution causes the database to load. The database name would then be available in the Table Import Wizard dialog, as pictured in Figure 8-11.

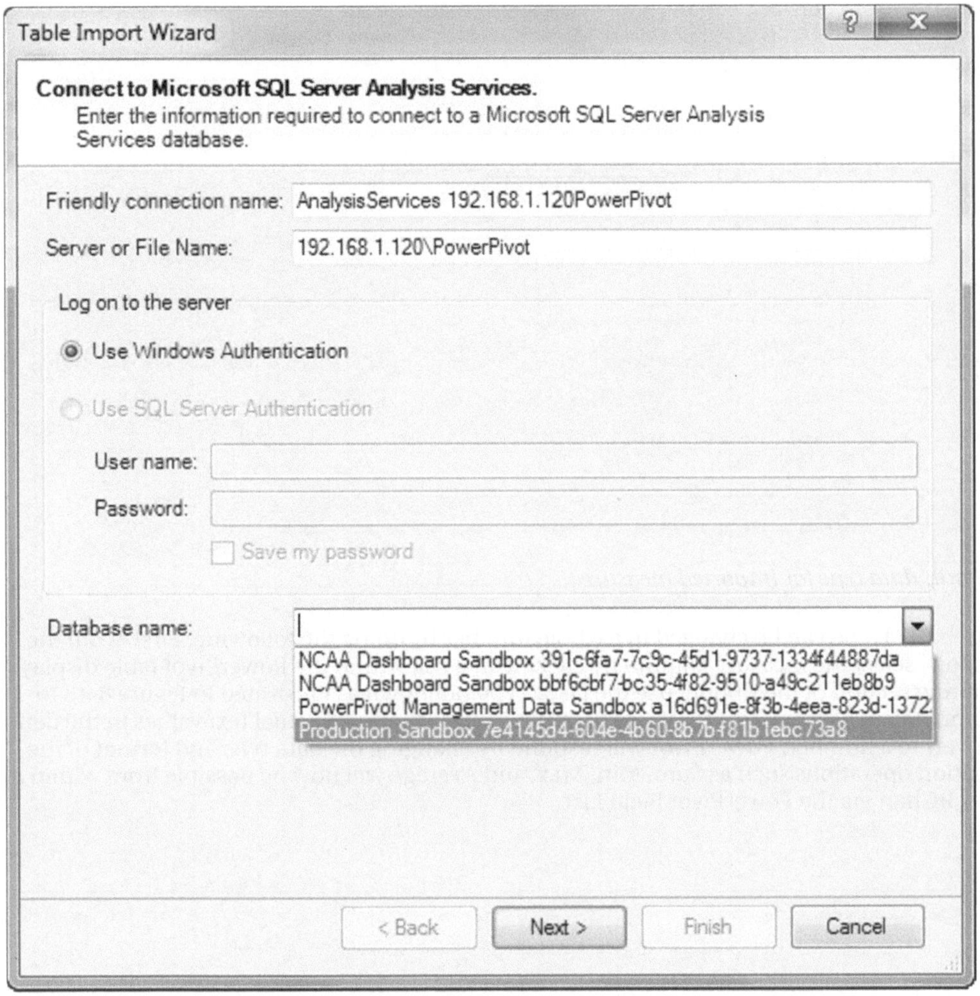

Figure 8-11. *Database name available in Table Import Wizard*

With data from both primary solutions, Sales and Production, available in our derived solution, PowerPivot reporting works the same as any other data source. There is a nuance to using PowerPivot as a data source that may not be readily apparent, however. The measures from the primary solutions (Sales and Production) are given a data type of text by the Table Import Wizard. This is in spite of the fact that each of the primary solutions defines the Sales Dollars, Production Units, and Production Cost measures as whole numbers. Figure 8-12 illustrates the default Table Import Wizard treatment of the Sales Dollars measurement as a text field.

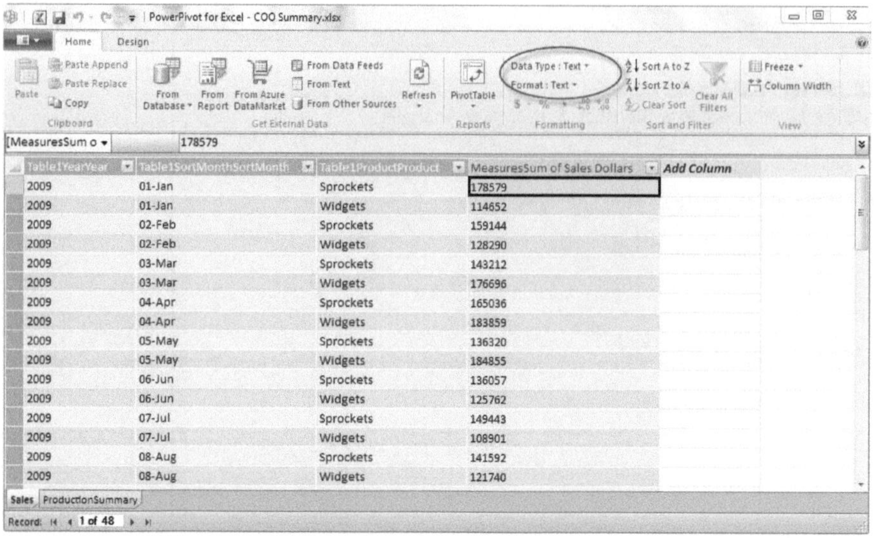

Figure 8-12. *Default data type for imported measure*

The measure's data type can be changed to a whole number by doing the following. First, from the PowerPivot window, select the measure column by clicking in a cell within the PowerPivot table display. From the Formatting section of the ribbon, use the Data Type pulldown as illustrated in Figure 8-13 to change the column data type from Text to Whole Number. Unless there are actual text values in the data that will not convert to a number, PowerPivot will respond by changing the data type and format of the column. Aggregation operations such as Sum, Min, Max, and Average will now be possible from within a PivotTable or PivotChart via the PowerPivot Field List.

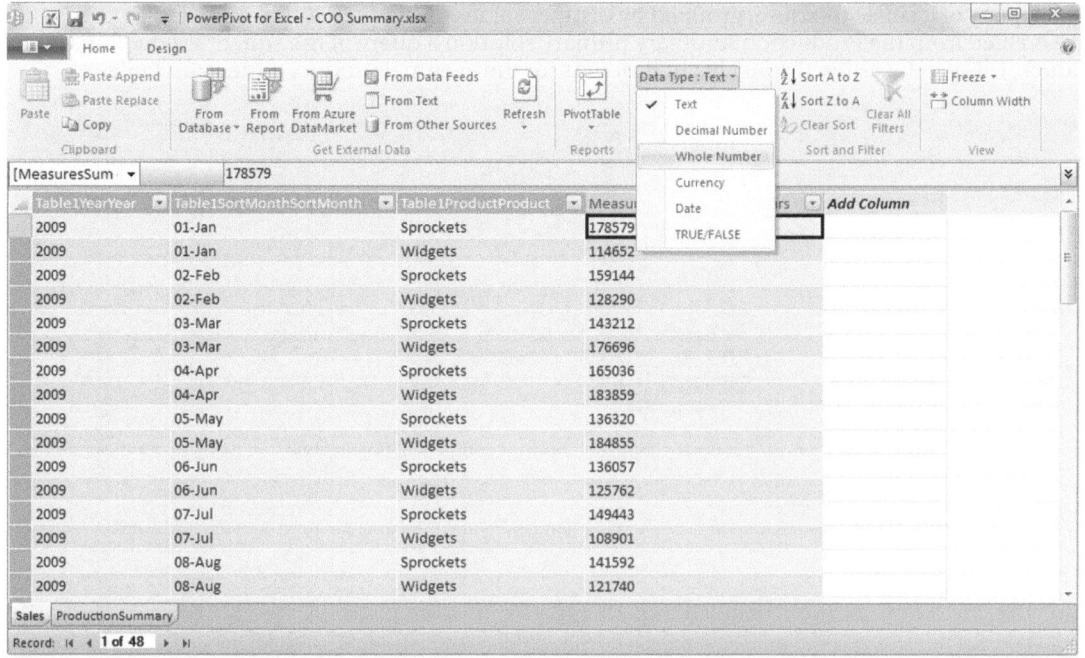

Figure 8-13. *Changing a column data type*

One final dataset needs to be incorporated into the summary solution, in order to have meaningful slicers. Recall from Figure 8-1 that we are combining two separate yet related fact sets to create a third, derived solution. Because each of the fact sets contains a Product identifier, we may be tempted to relate the Sales and ProductionSummary tables via the Product column. This approach would not be desirable based on the limitations, described in Chapter 4, that this places on our ability to report on both fact sets. However, because each primary solution contains many rows for each Product, relating the two tables (Sales and ProductionSummary) via Product is not possible. The many-to-many relationship this would attempt to create is not available in the initial release of PowerPivot.

Instead, we need to create a PowerPivot table containing the distinct master list of products. The "master" product list can become an additional PowerPivot table and a relationship with both measure sets (Sales and ProductionSummary) established. A slicer can then be based on the new Product table, and reporting for both Sales and ProductionSummary data can be modified using a consistent domain of products.

The trick in creating the master product list is dealing with limitations in the Table Import Wizard Query Designer. This feature was designed to produce datasets consisting of measures, described by columns containing dimension values, identical to how the Table Import Wizard was used to create the Sales and ProductionSummary PowerPivot tables. However, when used to create a dimension table, as we need for the master product list, the Query Designer has a few problems. Because we are using an SSAS data source (our PowerPivot for SharePoint primary solutions), there is a prescribed syntax for MDX to which the master product list query must conform. One of the syntax limitations is the inability to create a result set consisting of a single dimensional value column, without measures. We could, in straightforward MDX, create a set of columns for each distinct product, but the result would not be well suited for PowerPivot. Instead, the most expeditious means to create our master product list is by creating a query of a single measure, grouped by distinct values of Product. As illustrated in Figure 8-14, we have created from the ProductionSummary primary solution a query of the sum of Production Cost, by Product. This produces the distinct list of Products for the eventual product dimension table.

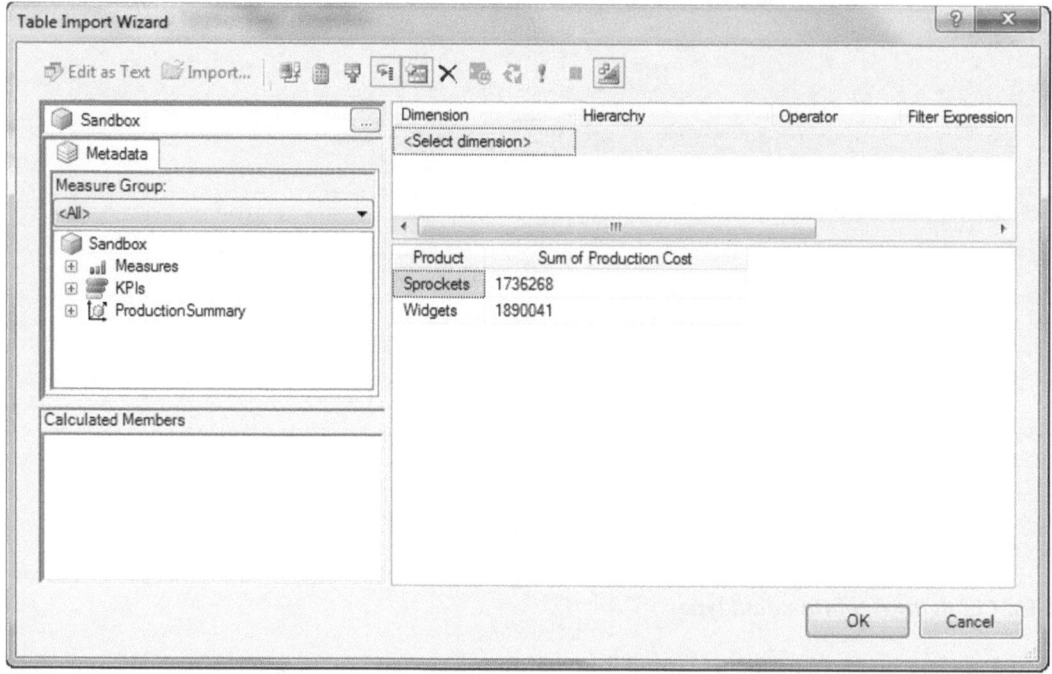

Figure 8-14. *Product Dimension Query Designer*

It is important for me to say here that the only reason for including the Sum of Production Cost column is to create a dataset with one row per Product. As you apply this technique in your own solution designs, ensure that you choose as a dimension source the dataset representing the more complete list of dimension members. Completing the Table Import Wizard for the new Product table will result in a table similar to Figure 8-15. The first column in the table has been renamed to "Product" for clarity.

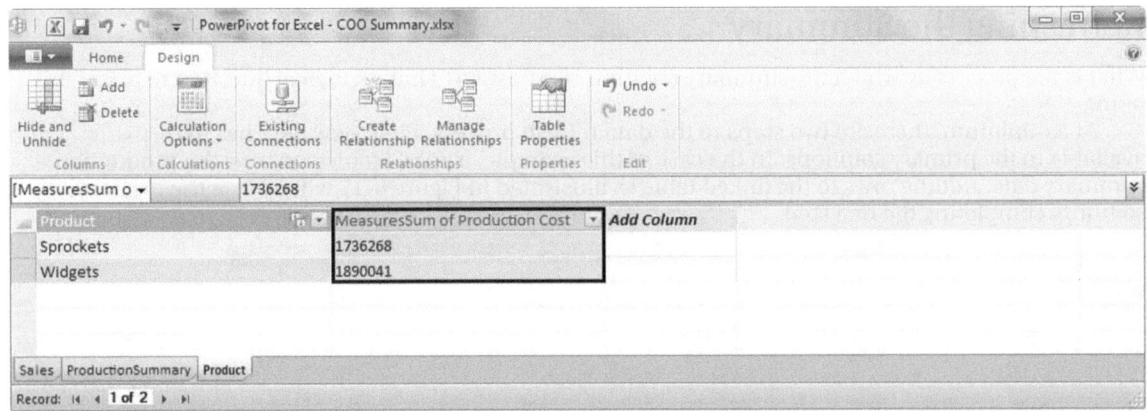

Figure 8-15. *Product table*

With the creation of the Product table, relationships from each of the Sales and ProductionSummary tables can be established. Figure 8-16 illustrates the final result of the example summary solution. A Product slicer has been added, sourced from the Product column of the Product table. Each of the PivotCharts detailing Sales or ProductionSummary measures are influenced by changes in the Product slicer. This allows for interactive use of the report by the consumer.

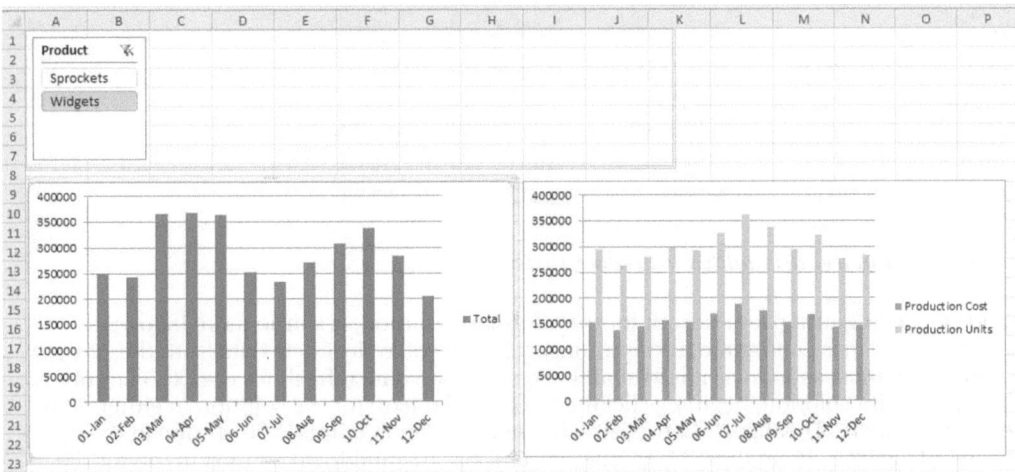

Figure 8-16. *Final summary solution*

One of the benefits of the technique just illustrated in this section is ensuring the data in the summary solution is in agreement with the source solutions. Another benefit is eliminating some of the details and complexity that exist in the primary solutions that may be of little or no interest to the summary solution audience.

Refreshing the Summary

What is the process by which the summary solution is refreshed? That's a logical question to ask at this point.

At a minimum, there are two steps to the data refresh process. First, new data has to be made available to the primary solutions. In the case of this example, a linked table contains the production summary data. Adding rows to the linked table as illustrated in Figure 8-17 will update the primary solution, completing the first step.

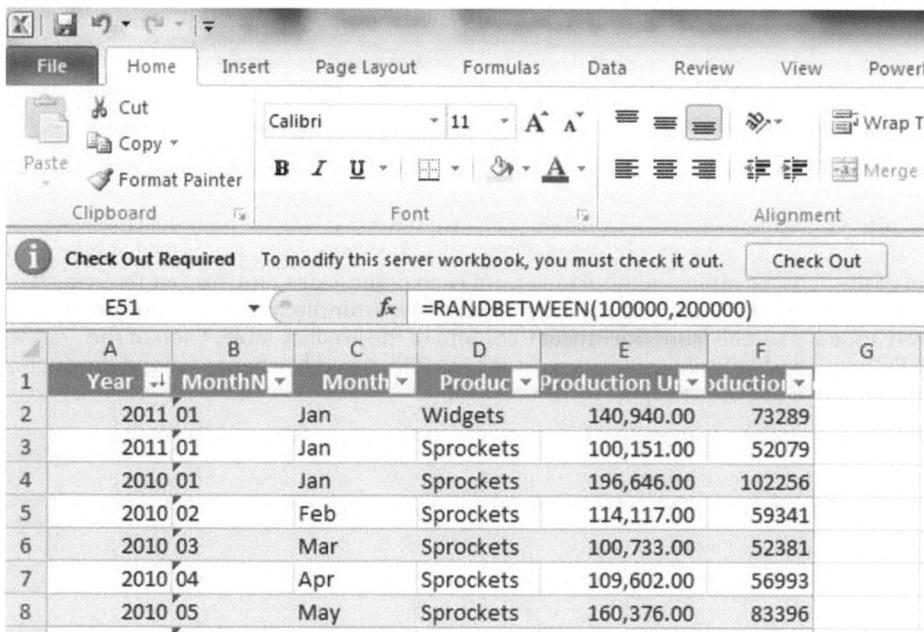

Figure 8-17. *Data for January, 2011 added to* ProductionSummary

The second step, configuring data refresh for the summary solution, is a little more involved. However, once data refresh is configured, the summary solution will reflect new data from the component solutions almost as soon as it is available. To configure data refresh for the COO Summary PowerPivot for SharePoint solution, begin by clicking the calendar icon for the solution in either of the visual Gallery views (Gallery, Theater, or Carousel). The Gallery version of this is illustrated in the upper right-hand corner of Figure 8-18. In the All Documents view, use the pulldown context menu for the document to access the Manage PowerPivot Data Refresh option.

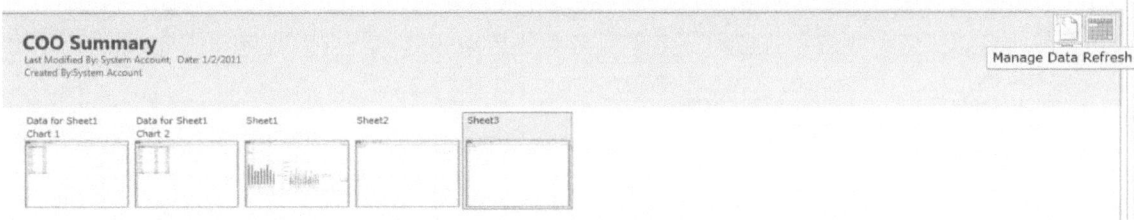

Figure 8-18. *Manage Data Refresh*

Regardless of the exact access method, each will result in the one of two dialogs being displayed. For a PowerPivot solution with no data refresh schedule currently configured, a dialog such as Figure 8-19 will be displayed. This Manage Data Refresh dialog will allow for activation of data refresh features, establish a schedule, set e-mail notification addresses, and configure the security credentials for the data refresh process.

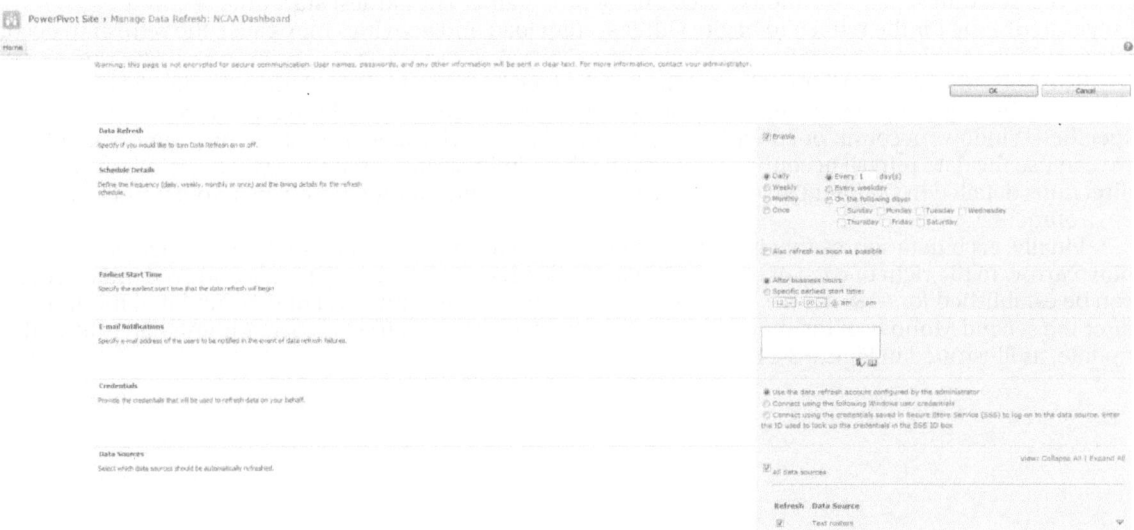

Figure 8-19. *Manage Data Refresh configuration*

However, if the workbook for which data refresh features are being accessed is currently configured to use data refresh, a different dialog is presented. As illustrated in Figure 8-20, a summary of the refresh operations and a detailed history of the success or failure of each data refresh are listed for the selected workbook. Clicking the "Configure Schedule..." link will present the detailed settings for this workbook, as detailed in Figure 8-19.

Name	COO Summary.xlsx		
Last Updated By	DEMOVM\Barry		
Last Updated	1/2/2011 3:18:33 PM		
Current Status	Succeeded		
Last Successful Refresh	1/2/2011 3:20:38 PM		
Next Scheduled Refresh	1/3/2011 12:00:00 AM	Configure Schedule ...	

Started	Completed	Time	Status	Comments
⊞ 01/02/2011 15:20:18	01/02/2011 15:20:38	00:00:20	Succeeded	

Figure 8-20. *Data refresh history*

Configuring data refresh is for the most part self-evident. Working from top to bottom from the Manage Data Refresh dialog (Figure 8-19), make the following decisions. First, checking the Enable check box actually makes the schedule active, making it possible to configure and pause or resume data refresh. Establish the schedule as Daily, Weekly, Monthly, or Once (one-time refresh). Each radio button will reveal relevant schedule options based on the time frame. The earliest start time is only a "suggested" time for the refresh to begin. Other system load and activities may cause the refresh to occur later.

The only other configuration option commonly questioned is the Data Source Credentials section. There are three options: use the data refresh account configured by the administrator, connect using a specified Windows account, or connect using Secure Store Service credentials. For our demo purposes, we can use the data refresh account configured by the administrator, assuming you have followed directions detailed in Chapter 6 to establish a development and training PowerPivot for SharePoint environment.

Finally, each data source that is part of a solution can have a separate schedule. By clicking the down arrow to the right of each of the solution's data sources, a separate schedule and credential setting can be established for each source. If we know Sales.xlsx, for example, will only be updated monthly after the second Monday of the month, we can set the data source refresh to occur immediately after the update, as illustrated in Figure 8-21.

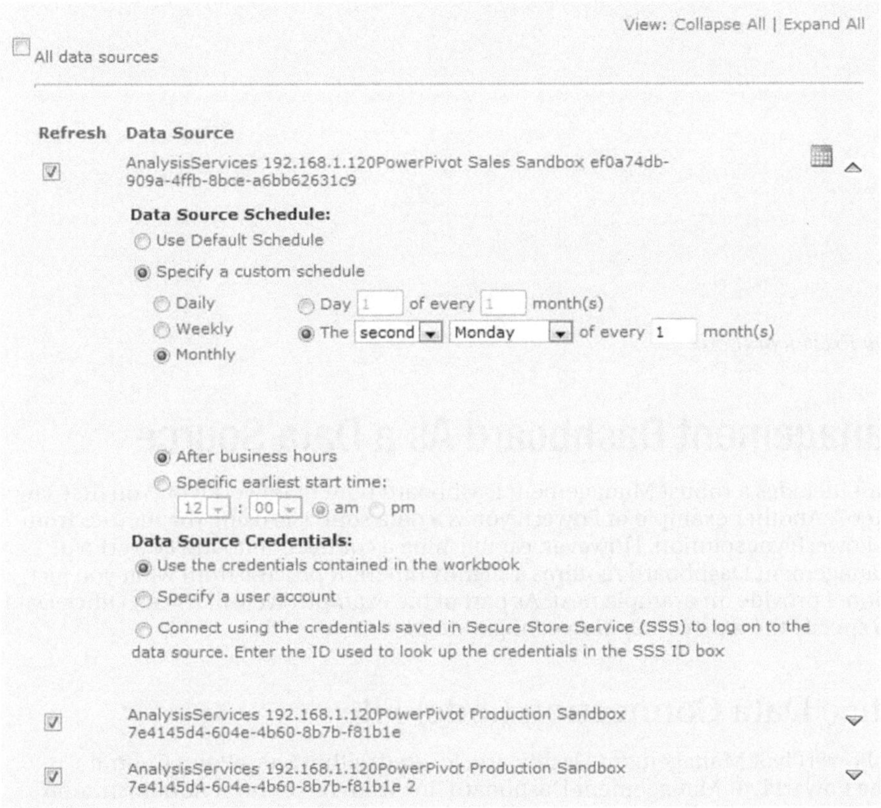

Figure 8-21. *Data Source Schedule*

While the PowerPivot data refresh schedule options are robust, the intent is to provide a facility to ensure the correct, fresh data is available in PowerPivot solutions. For example, in this initial release, features to attempt a failed refresh are not immediately available. Instead an e-mail notification of a failure is sent, based on the schedule configuration.

It is also possible to create an Excel report from a PowerPivot for SharePoint solution, using Office Data Connection (.odc) files. Strictly speaking, this technique does use PowerPivot as a data source, but does not leverage PowerPivot for display and user interaction as we have just detailed. Simply clicking the new report icon, as illustrated in Figure 8-22, to open an Excel workbook using the selected PowerPivot for SharePoint solution will prompt for file save or open dialog and result in an Excel spreadsheet PivotTable based on the PowerPivot source. None of the features of PowerPivot will be available in the user interface using this solution technique, as PowerPivot will only be a data source.

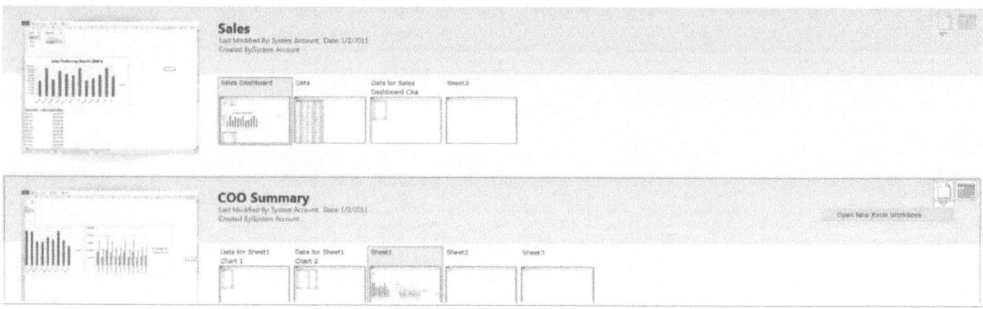

Figure 8-22. *Open in new Excel workbook*

PowerPivot Management Dashboard As a Data Source

PowerPivot for SharePoint includes a robust Management Dashboard built in PowerPivot. You first saw that dashboard in Chapter 7. Another example of PowerPivot as a data source is using the metrics from that dashboard within a PowerPivot solution. However, establishing a connection to the PowerPivot workbook behind the Management Dashboard requires a slightly different process from what you just saw in the previous section. I provide an example next. As part of the example, we will use an Office Data Connection (.odc) file to specify the data connection configuration.

Creating the Office Data Connection (.odc) File

Begin with access to the PowerPivot Management Dashboard, located within SharePoint Central Administration. Select the PowerPivot Management Dashboard link from the Central Administration page. That page is http://powerpivotbook:55555 in the case of the demonstration environment for these examples. At the bottom right of the resulting Management Dashboard page, right-click the PowerPivot Management Data report item illustrated in Figure 8-23.

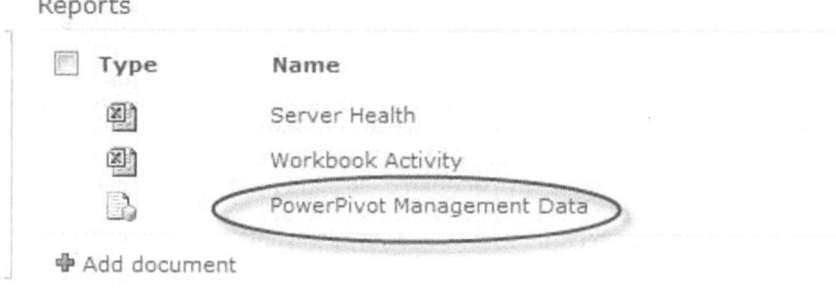

Figure 8-23. *PowerPivot Management Data report*

Save the file, a version of the `.odc` file that we will modify, to a location on your workstation. Open the local copy of the `.odc` file; it should be named `PowerPivot Management Data.odc` in a text editor. Locate the `<odc:ConnectionString>` tag within this element of the file illustrated in Figure 8-24.

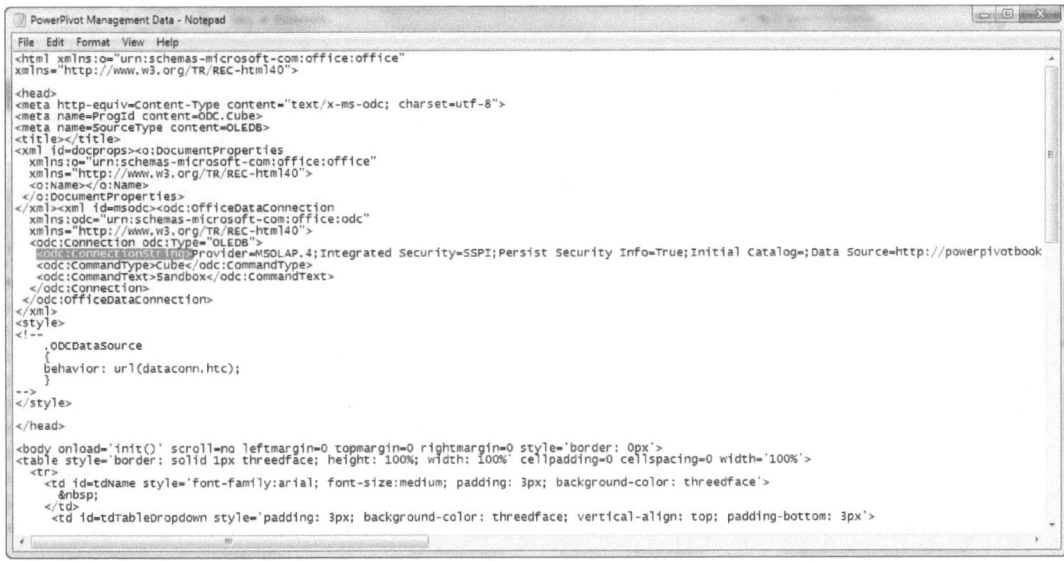

Figure 8-24. *odc:ConnectionString element*

Alter the section of the `<odc:ConnectionString>` element to remove the string `Embedded Data=False`. Additionally, ensure the string `Edit Mode=0` is removed from the `<odc:ConnectionString>` element. Finally, ensure there is no semicolon between the final character of the connection string and the closing `</odc:ConnectionString>` tag. Save the file to commit your edits.

To use the newly edited `.odc` file, open Microsoft Excel. From the PowerPivot window, select the Existing Connections item from the Design ribbon, as illustrated in Figure 8-25.

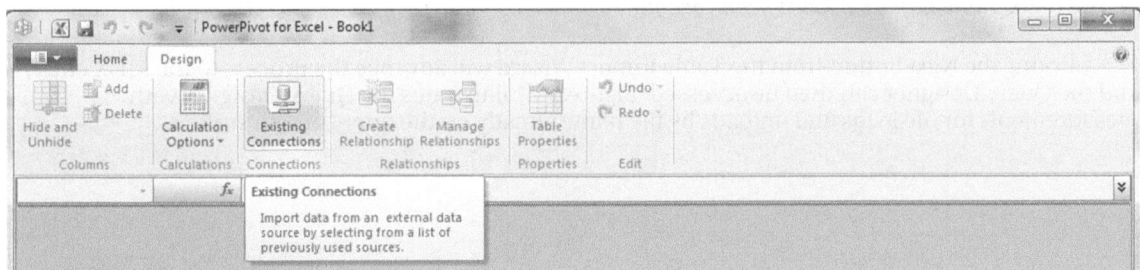

Figure 8-25. *Existing Connections in PowerPivot*

Click the Browse for More button to reveal the `.odc` files currently on your workstation. Open the newly created file, `PowerPivot Management Data.odc`. The new connection should now appear in the Existing Connections dialog. Highlight the `PowerPivot Management Data.odc` connection and click the Open button. This will begin the Table Import Wizard using the connection configuration from the `.odc` file, as in Figure 8-26. Press the Test Connection button to verify the ability to use the data connection. At this point, a friendly name for the connection should be entered as well.

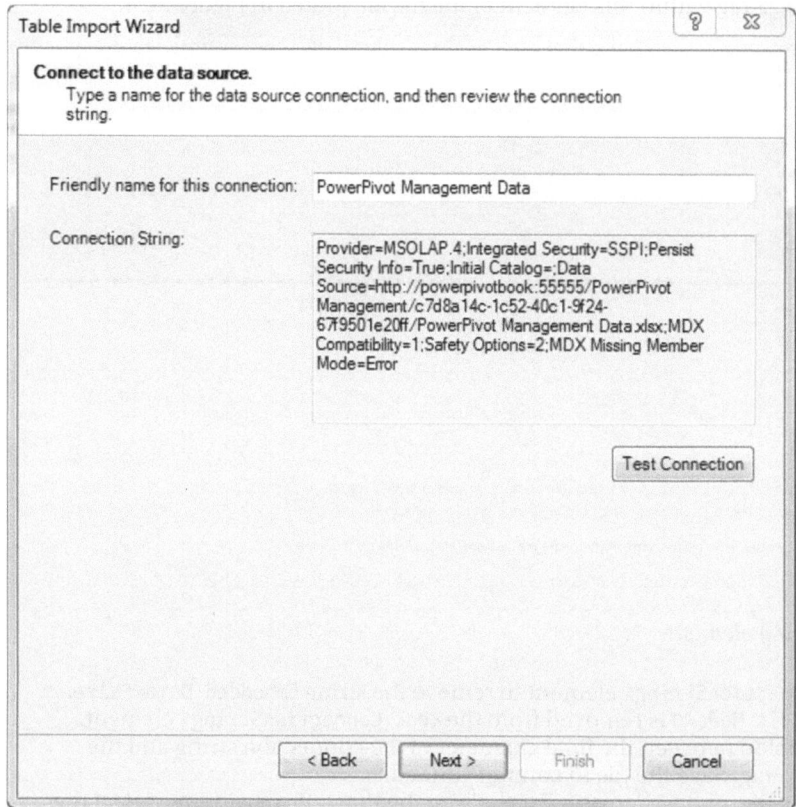

Figure 8-26. *Table Import Wizard from* `.odc` *file*

Clicking the Next button from the Table Import Wizard will advance the process to the MDX entry, and the Query Designer can then be accessed. Figure 8-27 illustrates the Query Designer with measurements for file loads and unloads by file name already on the query design surface.

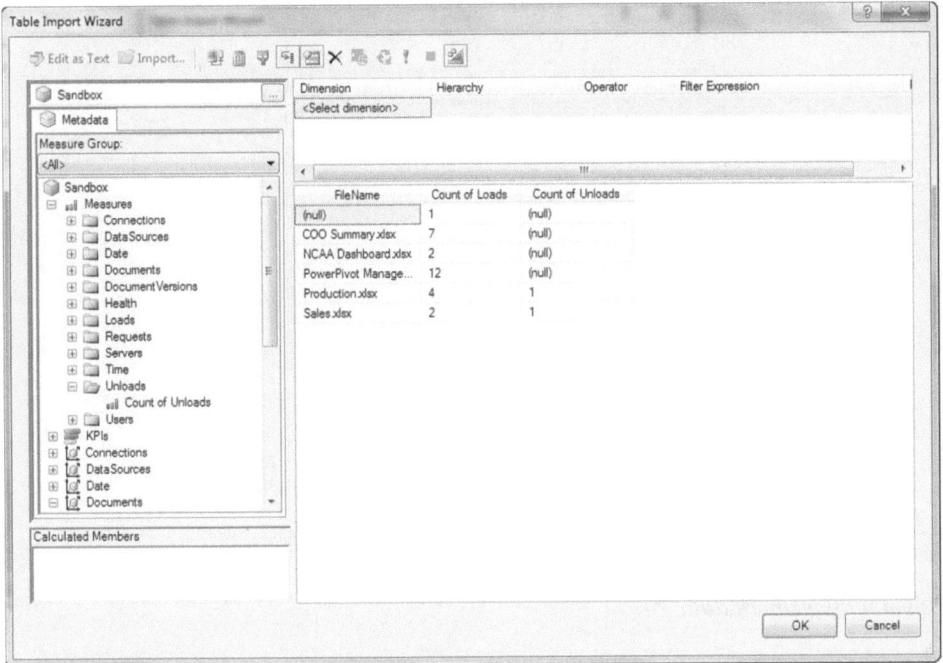

Figure 8-27. *Query design for PowerPivot management data*

Completing the query design, I have renamed this example query "LoadUnload" to have a friendly PowerPivot table name from which to surface the data in a report. Similar to other uses of SSAS as a data source, measures in the PowerPivot tables will be imported by default as Text data types. The final step before using the PowerPivot data in a report is changing the measures from text to numeric data types.

Writing a Report Using PowerPivot Management Data

Surfacing the data is a typical PowerPivot report-writing task. Place the load and unload measures available from the new PowerPivot table in the Values area for a new PivotChart. Place the DocumentsFileName in the Axis Fields area resulting in the PowerPivot workbook in Figure 8-28.

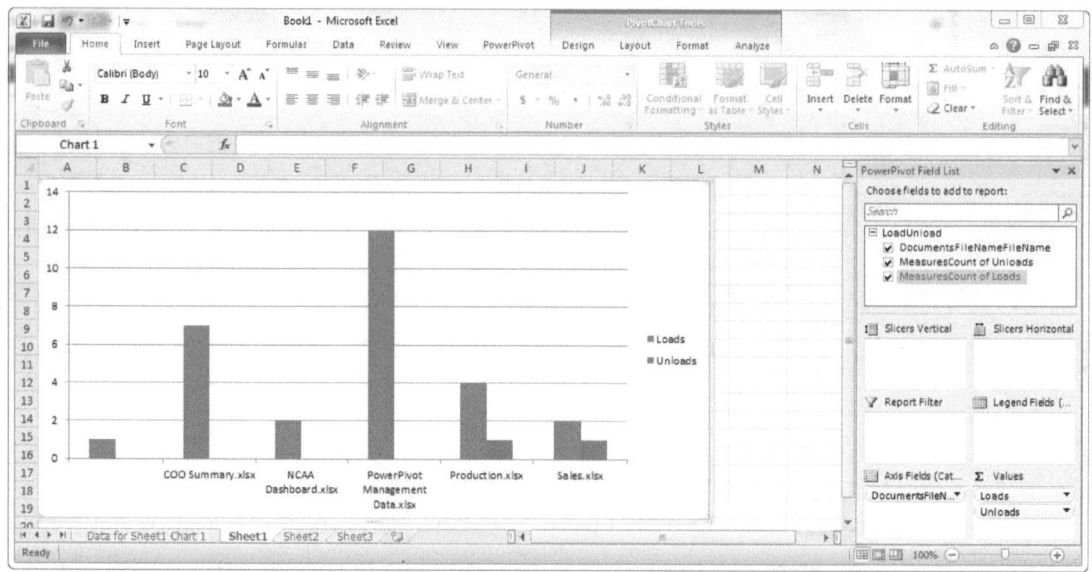

Figure 8-28. *PowerPivot management data*

The technique I've just described is limited only by the ability to access SharePoint Central Administration. Because the source .odc file refers to a location within Central Administration, users without farm administration privileges will not be able to develop PowerPivot solutions using the PowerPivot Management Dashboard as a data source.

PowerPivot and PerformancePoint Dashboards

PerformancePoint Services is a dashboard and scorecard development platform that is part of SharePoint Server 2010. Like PowerPivot, PerformancePoint can consume data from different data sources, including SSAS, Excel Services, SharePoint lists, and SQL Server relational database tables. PerformancePoint's more interesting analytic features, including interactive reports known as analytic grids and analytic charts, require a SQL Server Analysis Services database as their data source.

Installation and configuration of PerformancePoint Services is well beyond our scope. However, if you were able to create a development environment as described in Chapter 6, you have all the software required to install and configure PerformancePoint Services. The example to follow will assume a working PerformancePoint Services deployment. It further assumes the presence of an unattended service account, and that you have permissions to access the "\PowerPivot" SSAS instance.

SQL Server Management Studio (SMSS) can be used to verify the ability of a domain account to access the PowerPivot for SharePoint database. While logged on as the candidate unattended service account user, open SSMS from the Start Programs menu, under Microsoft SQL Server 2008 R2 and then SQL Server Management Studio. This will create a window similar to Figure 8-29.

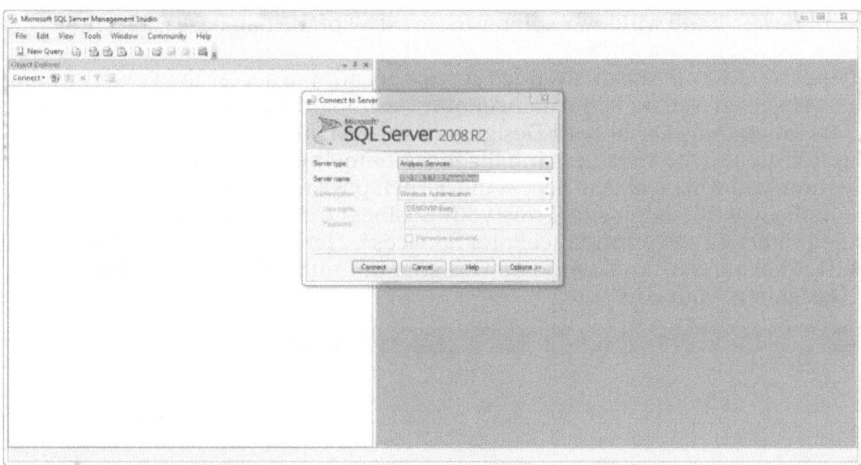

Figure 8-29. *SQL Management Studio login*

Ensure the Server type is set to Analysis Services. The Server name should be the name or IP address of your PowerPivot for SharePoint server followed by "\PowerPivot", just as the connection string was created earlier in the chapter for a connection to the PowerPivot for SharePoint database from a PowerPivot workbook. The final element of the connection dialog, the Authentication, should already be set to Windows Authentication, the only means of authenticating users for SSAS. Press the Connect button, and a window similar to Figure 8-30 should be generated.

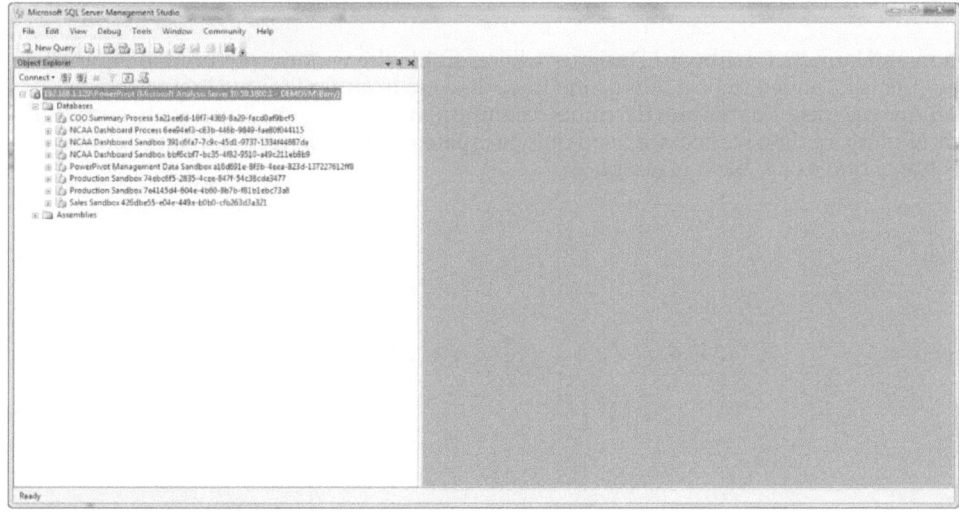

Figure 8-30. *Successful SSMS login*

If a login error occurs, the candidate account may not have access to the PowerPivot for SharePoint database server. Verify the permissions on the \PowerPivot instance. Otherwise, you should be able to expand the database listing in the left-hand window explorer to reveal all of the databases currently stored on the server.

After successfully verifying the ability of the unattended service account to access the PowerPivot for SharePoint database, the next step is to use the PerformancePoint Dashboard Designer to create a data connection. The exact address for opening Dashboard Designer in your environment will vary. However, if your SharePoint administrator utilizes the "Business Intelligence Center" site template to create your PerformancePoint site collection, you will be able to access the launch page for Dashboard Designer illustrated in Figure 8-31 from the new BI Center site. From your Business Intelligence Center site, choose any of the links labeled "Start using PerformancePoint Services". The result will be the launch page illustrated in Figure 8-31. Clicking the Run Dashboard Designer button will launch the ClickOnce deployment of Dashboard Designer to your computer.

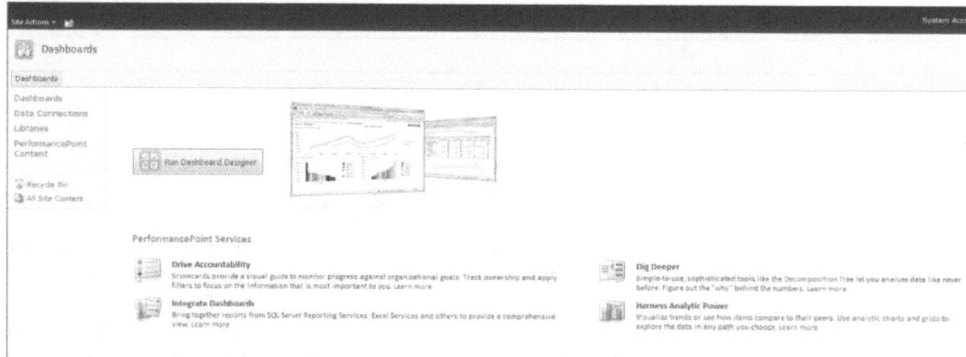

Figure 8-31. *Run Dashboard Designer*

After installation and launch, Dashboard Designer will resemble the window pictured in Figure 8-32. Dashboard Designer is intended to be a Microsoft Office–like environment for business users to create, publish, and manage dashboards and dashboard components. In order to illustrate basic use of PowerPivot for SharePoint as a data source, we need only to create a PerformancePoint data connection and then use that connection as the basis of a report.

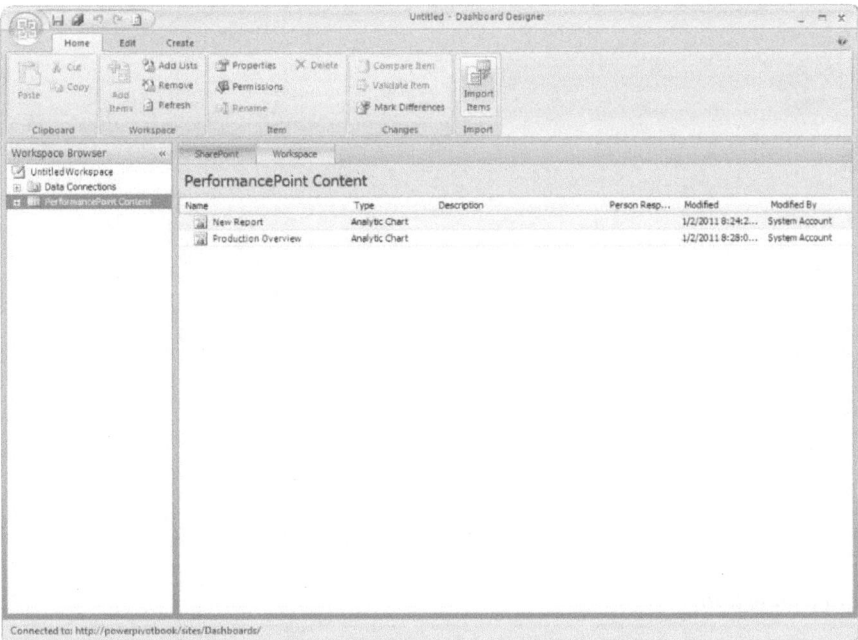

Figure 8-32. *Dashboard Designer*

Creating the Data Connection

To configure the data connection from PerformancePoint Services to the PowerPivot for SharePoint database, first select the Data Connections library from the left-hand explorer. Then choose Data Source from the Create ribbon menu. Alternatively right-click the Data Connection library in the left-hand explorer window and choose New Data Source from the context menu. Either method will generate a window similar to Figure 8-33, in which the data connection configuration can be entered.

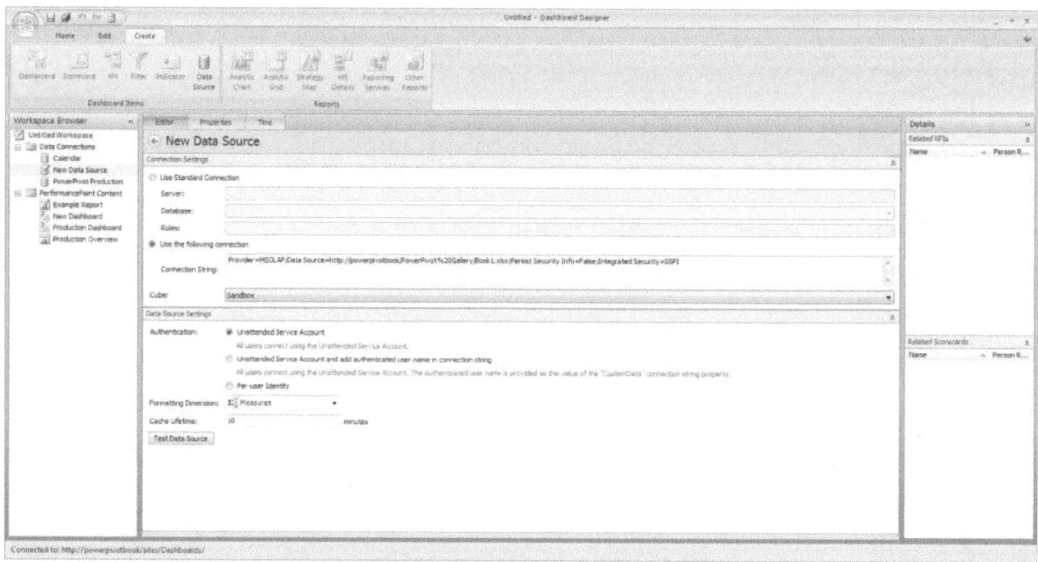

Figure 8-33. *PowerPivot data connection*

You can complete your connection configuration with the server name or IP address of the PowerPivot for SharePoint server, followed by "\PowerPivot" to indicate a connection to the database instance dedicated for PowerPivot operations. After entering the server, the Database pulldown can be used to list all of the currently loaded databases in the PowerPivot instance. The Cube pulldown for PowerPivot solutions will in this release be Sandbox, though the pulldown will ensure the correct value. Ensure the Authentication section's Unattended Service Account radio button is selected. Finally, pressing the Test Data Source button will verify the connection can be made. Upon a successful connection test, I recommend changing the name of the data connection, which will default to "New Data Source" to something more useful like "PowerPivot Sales" or "PowerPivot ProductionOps."

However, instead we will use the MSOLAP provider and a connection string in the form illustrated in Figure 8-33. Pressing the Test Data Source button will verify access to the PowerPivot data specified in the connection string.

If at this point an error occurs, repeat verification of the unattended service account for PerformancePoint and the ability of the unattended service account to access the "\PowerPivot" instance of SSAS via SQL Management Studio. If the unattended service account has access to the "\PowerPivot" instance, verify the PerformancePoint Services installation and that the PerformancePoint service is actually running on the SharePoint farm.

Creating the Analytic Chart

With the PerformancePoint data connection configured and verified, creation of the report to surface the PowerPivot data is a matter of drag and drop. To begin, from the Create ribbon menu, select the PerformancePoint Content library from the left-hand content explorer. Then choose Analytic Chart from the Create ribbon menu. Similar to the data connection creation, you may also right-click the PerformancePoint Contact library, choose New Report from the context menu, and then choose Analytic

Chart from the Report Template selector. Either method will generate the PerformancePoint data connection selection dialog illustrated in Figure 8-34.

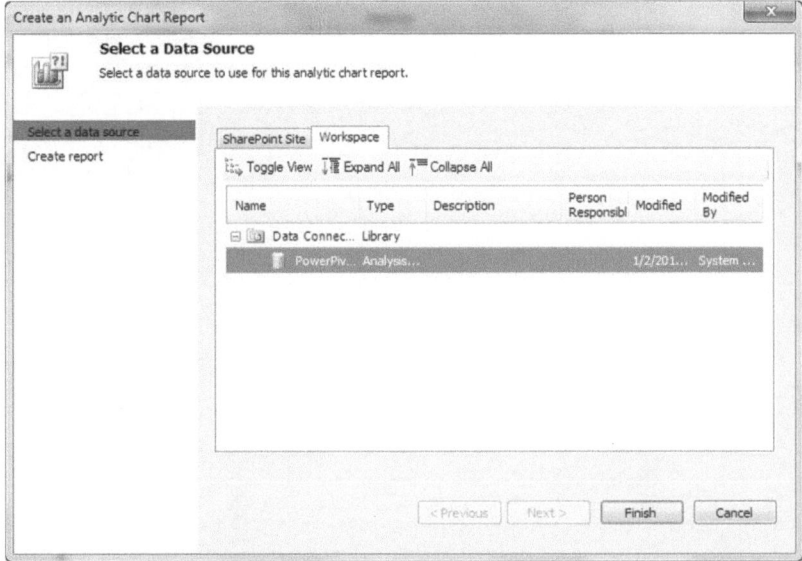

Figure 8-34. *Selecting PerformancePoint data source*

Choose the PowerPivot source created earlier and press the Finish button. This will launch the PerformancePoint report authoring environment illustrated in Figure 8-35. For convenience, the report has already been renamed to "Example Report" and the right-hand listing of the data source content has been expanded.

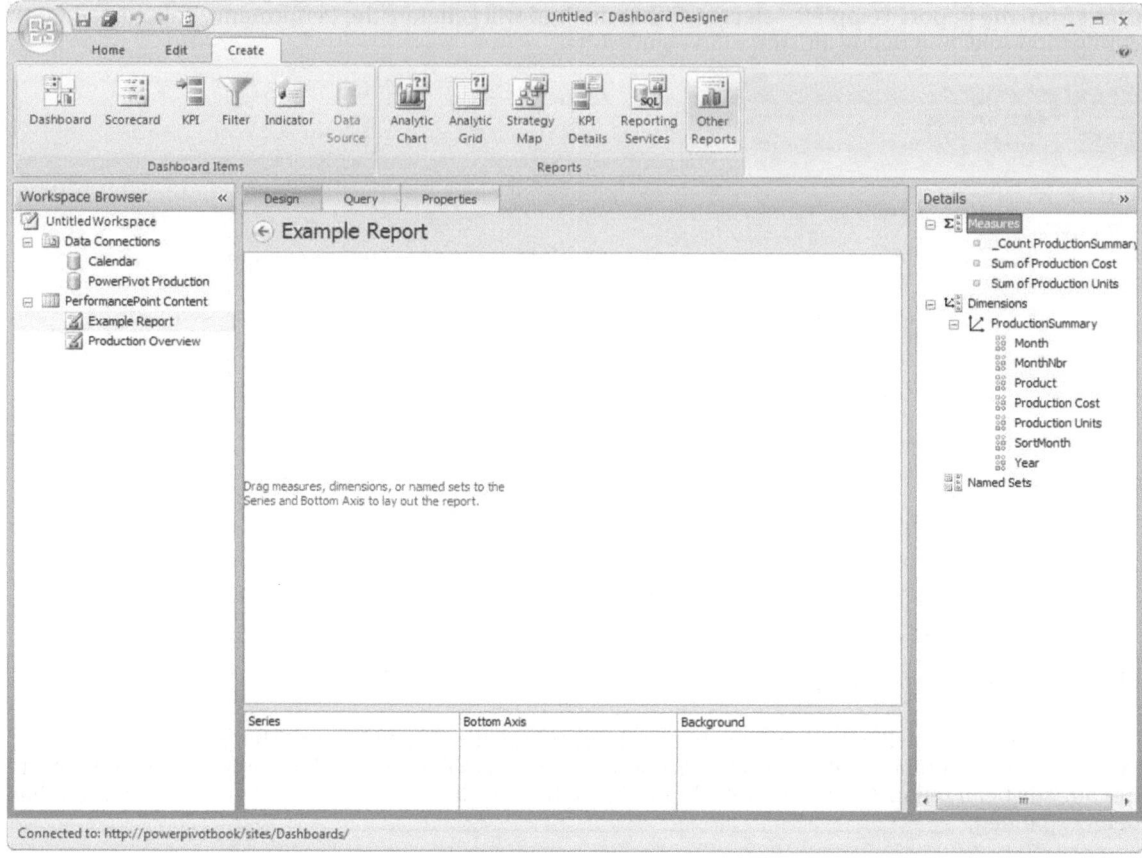

Figure 8-35. *PerformancePoint report development environment*

There are many variations and techniques possible via PerformancePoint analytic charts; however, the intent of this example is just to show the surfacing of information from PowerPivot by PerformancePoint. In order to chart both production cost and units, drag both of the measures from the right-hand explorer to the Series area in the bottom left portion of the report development environment. Drag the SortMonth from the right-hand explorer to the Bottom Axis area of the report designer. After adding the SortMonth, the report designer will create a preview of the chart, essentially a bar graph of both Production Cost and Production Units, for each of the 12 values of SortMonth.

Finally, drag the Year from the right-hand explorer to the Background area of the report designer. The purpose of the Background items requires a bit of explanation. Prior to your configuring a background selection, the analytic report reflects all data for all years in the PowerPivot for SharePoint database for the ProductionSummary.xlsx solution. Clicking the down arrow to the right of a background area element will produce a dialog to filter by that dimension, similar to what you see in Figure 8-36. As the dashboard is currently configured, only data for year 2010 is being reflected in the report. An additional benefit of adding a background element to an analytic chart is the automatic creation of a filter endpoint for connecting to a PerformancePoint dashboard filter, in order to interactively filter for values of Year.

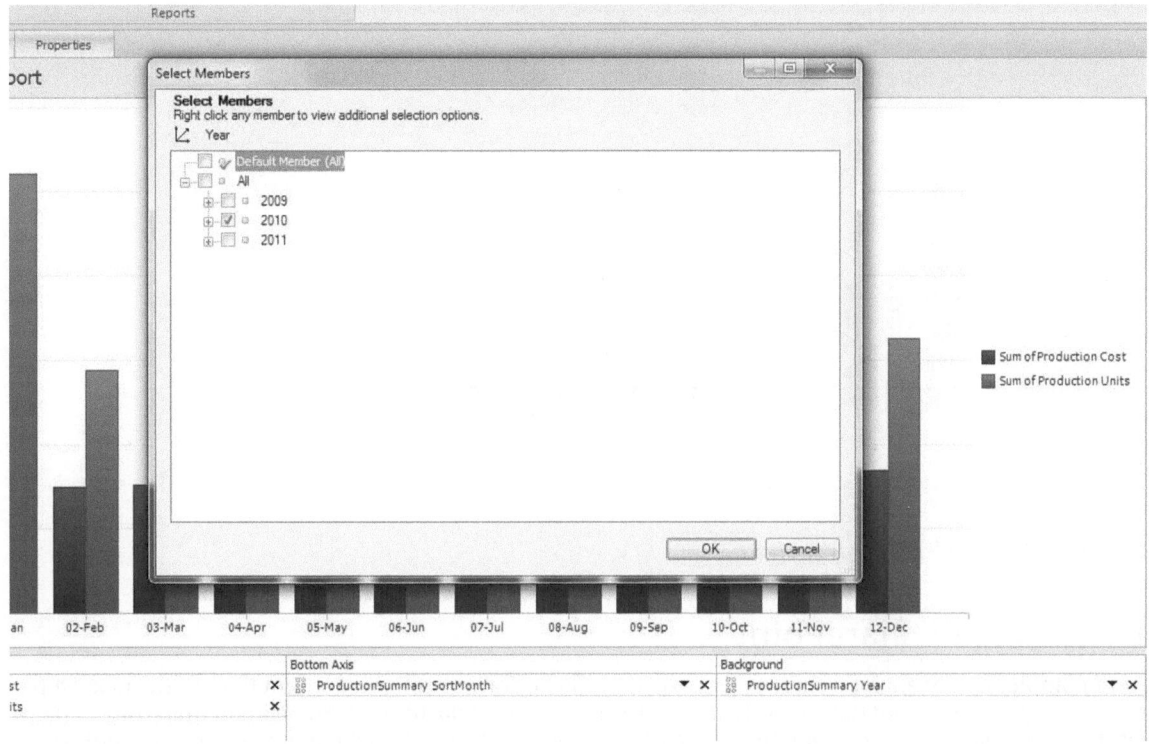

Figure 8-36. *Configuring background selection*

Finishing the background selection, the PerformancePoint analytic chart should resemble Figure 8-37. The chart can be saved to the PerformancePoint content library by clicking the disk icon in the upper left-hand corner of Dashboard Designer, just to the right of the ribbon menu button.

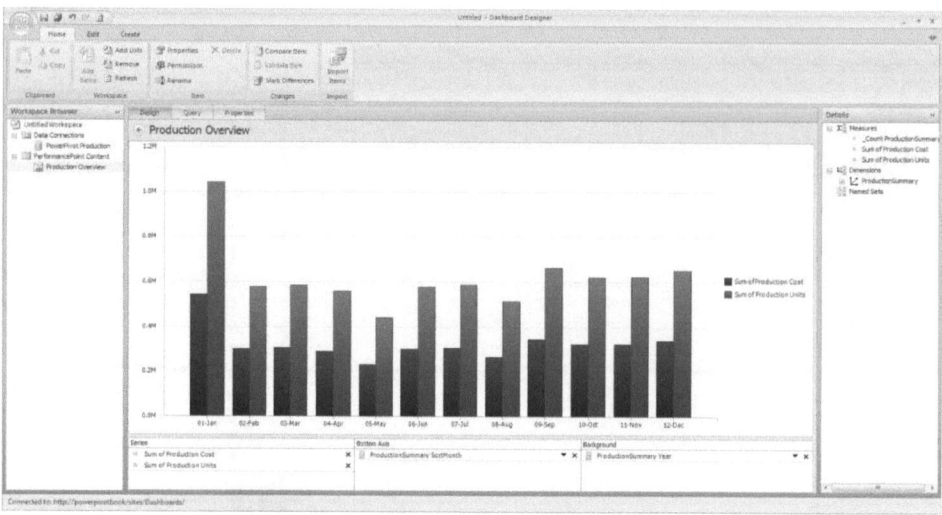

Figure 8-37. *Completed analytic chart*

Deploying to SharePoint

After completing the analytic chart and saving it to the PerformancePoint content library, the next step to surface the PowerPivot data is to create a PerformancePoint dashboard. You can do that from Dashboard Designer, either from the Create ribbon menu or by right-clicking the PerformancePoint content library. Either method will result in a Dashboard Page Template selection similar to that in Figure 8-38. Select the 1 Zone template, as highlighted in the figure.

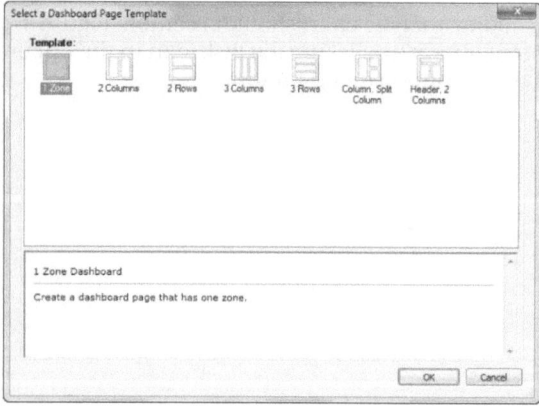

Figure 8-38. *Dashboard page template selection*

After selecting the page template, a dashboard design environment similar to Figure 8-39 will be presented. You can optionally rename the dashboard to something meaningful to replace the default

"New Dashboard" name. In the single zone of the dashboard, drag and drop the desired analytic report from the right-hand explorer view. The results should be similar to Figure 8-39.

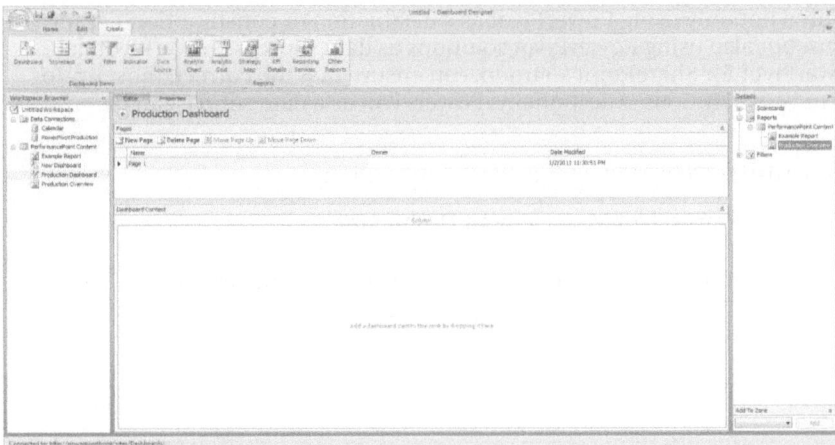

Figure 8-39. *Selection of dashboard content*

Finally, right-click the name of the dashboard in the left-hand explorer and choose Deploy to SharePoint from the context menu. Accept the defaults for the deployment dialog, and the PerformancePoint dashboard, with the sole content consisting of the PowerPivot-sourced analytic report, should open in Internet Explorer (or your default browser). Your results should be similar to Figure 8-40.

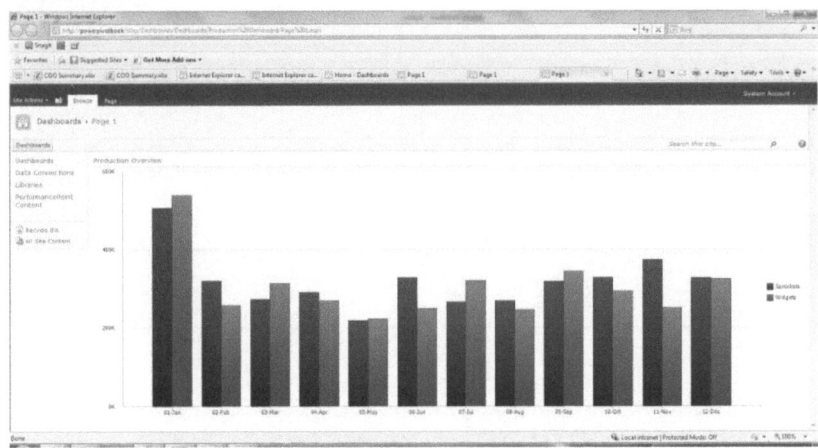

Figure 8-40. *PerformancePoint dashboard complete*

Summary

In this chapter, we have explored not only using PowerPivot as a destination or consumption tier for business intelligence solutions, but also using PowerPivot solutions as data sources. PowerPivot data refresh, combined with a PowerPivot for SharePoint solution, can ensure that the correct, most up-to-date information is reflected in your solutions. Additionally, PowerPivot as a data source can be leveraged for the following:

- Reporting based on existing PowerPivot for SharePoint solutions

- Accessing the data in the PowerPivot Management Dashboard

Using PowerPivot for SharePoint solutions as a data source for PerformancePoint Services

CHAPTER 9

∎∎∎

PowerPivot and SQL Server Reporting Services

Don't let what you cannot do interfere with what you can do.

—John Wooden

SQL Server Reporting Services is a set of features included with Microsoft's SQL Server product for the creation, management, and execution of predefined reports. PowerPivot for Excel and SharePoint can use SSRS reports as a data source for solutions developed in either mode of PowerPivot. Reversing the roles of PowerPivot and SQL Server Reporting Services is also possible—that is, SQL Server Reporting Services can utilize PowerPivot for SharePoint databases as a data source for SSRS reports. In this chapter, we will examine the case for using SQL Server Reporting Services and PowerPivot together in order to deliver analytics and predefined reporting from a common dataset.

Consider one of the potential uses of this architecture: organizations that already utilize SQL Server Reporting Services can reuse the datasets underlying existing reports as data tables for PowerPivot solutions. Logic and relationships established in the existing SQL Server Reporting Services report definition are available for ad hoc analytics using PowerPivot. When changes in data relations, business rules, or other logic are made to the SQL Server Reporting Services report, the changes "flow through" to the PowerPivot solution via the SSRS dataset.

Alternatively the flow of data from SQL Server Reporting Services to PowerPivot can be reversed. A PowerPivot for SharePoint solution can form the data source for a standard SQL Server Reporting Services report definition. A candidate scenario for this use of PowerPivot as a data source would be similar to the solutions outlined in Chapter 8 that show PerformancePoint services surfacing data from a PowerPivot pivot solution. The key difference to consider is the various rendering modes available in SQL Server Reporting Services to schedule reports as well as deliver the information in Adobe portable document format, word documents, HTML, and alternative file formats. From a data architecture perspective, connecting SQL Server Reporting Services to PowerPivot for SharePoint is very similar to the connection used with PerformancePoint services.

Certainly the purpose of this book is not to exhaustively cover SQL Server Reporting Services. Instead it is my intention to explain the tasks and operations necessary to create, store, and execute SQL Server Reporting Services definitions as they relate to PowerPivot as a data source and PowerPivot as a reporting front end. There are two example programs that form development environments you may use to create or alter SQL Server Reporting Services definitions files. The first is Report Designer, contained within both Visual Studio and Business Intelligence Developer Studio (BIDS). BIDS is available as part of SQL Server's installation. The second, Report Builder, is a click-once application available to SharePoint Server users. Report Designer provides report definition editing and management features without the complete software development environment of Visual Studio or BIDS.

Finally, there are two principal configuration modes for SQL Server Reporting Services. In *native mode*, SQL Server Reporting Services executes requests to save, edit, and execute report definitions without any special integration with SharePoint Server 2010. Configured with SharePoint *integrated mode*, SQL Server Reporting Services features for editing report definitions are enabled within SharePoint. These SSRS features enable users to edit SSRS reports just as any other document stored by SharePoint.

Consuming SSRS As a PowerPivot Data Source

In order to use SQL Server Reporting Services as a data source for PowerPivot, the first thing we need is a SQL Server Reporting Services report. For the example to follow, I'm using the SQL Server 2008 sample databases available from www.codeplex.com. We're going to use a very simple report from the AdventureWorks database. The report stored as a report definition language file or RDL file is available in the book's example download file.

Verifying Report Access

First we need to verify that we can actually access SQL Server Reporting Services. Troubleshooting connections among business intelligence products can be troublesome. It'll save time to verify access and connectivity up front. For this chapter's examples, I will be using a SQL Server Reporting Services instance named BlueMountain in native mode. The URL for the reporting server report management home page is in the form HTTP://BlueMountain/reports. Opening the URL for the Reporting Services report page from a browser should yield a result similar to Figure 9-1.

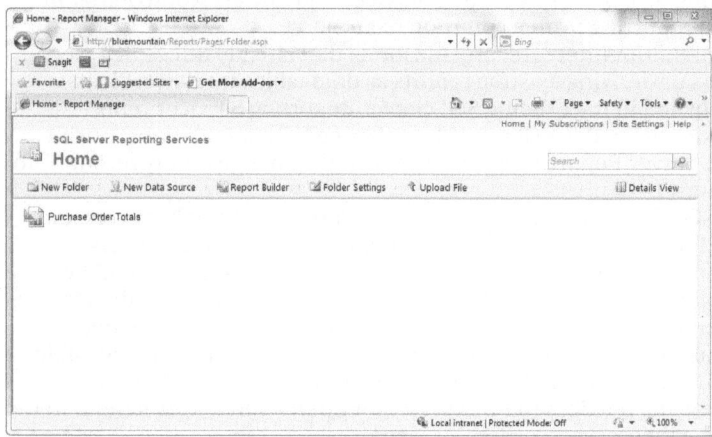

Figure 9-1. *Reporting Services report page*

It is probably worth taking some time to understand the features available from this page as SQL Server Reporting Services is integral to the examples. At the top of the page, the highlighted menu bar contains icons representing many of the key operations that can be performed from this location. Immediately below the menu bar is the listing of reports available. Finally in the upper right-hand corner of the page are links to return to the home page, manage report subscriptions, go to site settings options, and go to online help.

Clicking the Purchase Order Totals report link will execute the report and render the results in the browser. The Purchase Order Totals report will produce a result similar to Figure 9-2. Additionally, if the current user did not have the required privileges to execute the report, a prompt for credentials will occur. Executing this report in this manner ensures our ability to use the report from within PowerPivot for Excel.

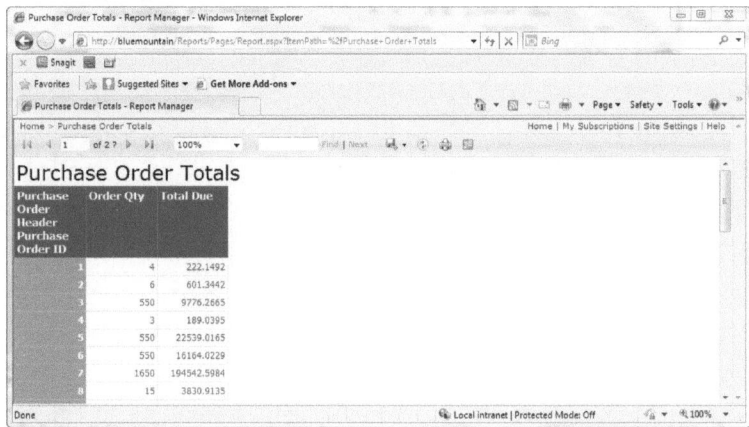

Figure 9-2. *SSRS report execution*

Note all that has happened here is the simple report, without parameters, executed its query to the database and has rendered the results in the browser. However, this test execution of the report will be valuable as we use the SSRS report as a data source for PowerPivot. Clicking the Advance to Final Page arrow, just to the left of the zoom level (set to 100%), will display the final page of the report, including grand totals, as pictured in Figure 9-3.

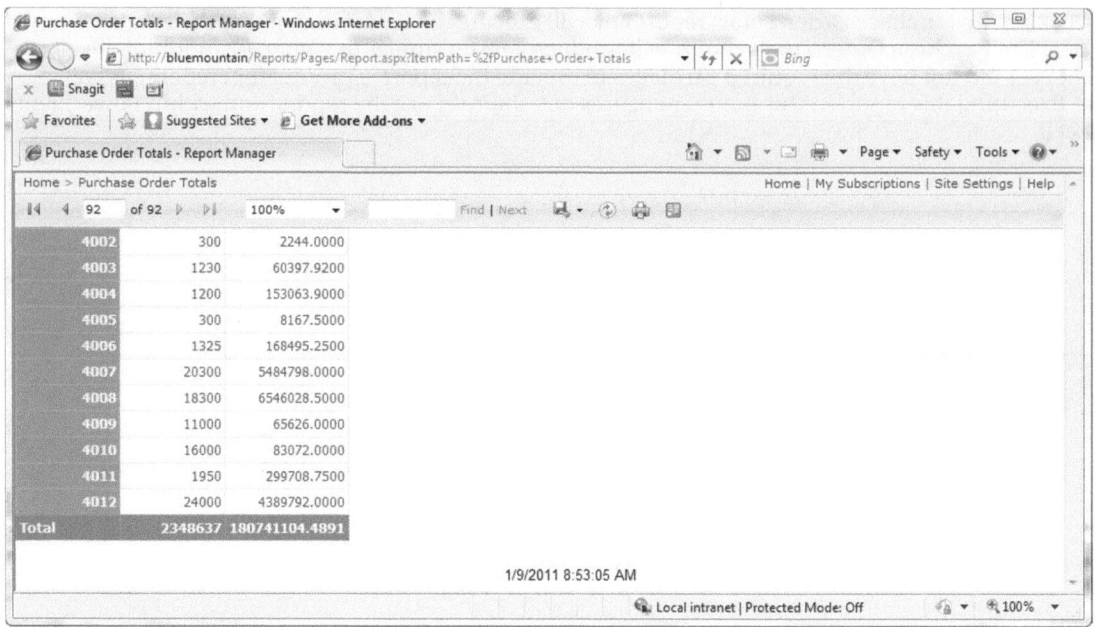

Figure 9-3. *Report grand totals*

Configuring the Connection

To set up a connection between the Purchase Order Totals report and a PowerPivot solution, begin in the PowerPivot window of a new, blank Excel worksheet. From the Get External Data section of the Home ribbon, use the From Report option, as illustrated in Figure 9-4.

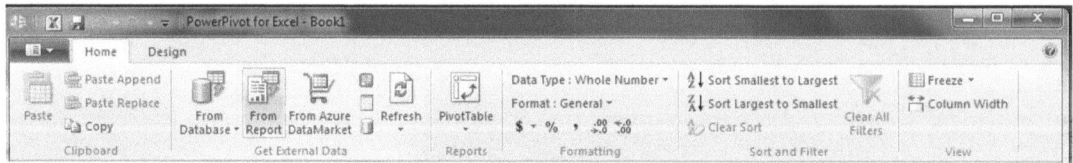

Figure 9-4. *PowerPivot Get External Data From Report menu*

Clicking the From Report menu item will begin the Table Import Wizard. The dialog will prompt for a friendly connection name. Choose a name that will allow you to easily reuse the connection definition within PowerPivot. Additionally, the path to the SSRS report definition file (`.rdl`) will be required. The URL for the sample report will be a little different from the Report Manager page used to execute and view the report. Instead of the Report Manager (`http://reportserver/reports`), the URL for the SSRS web service must be used. For our example, the URL for the SSRS web service is `http://bluemountain/reportserver`. In order to enter the URL, press the Browse button, which will result in a dialog similar to Figure 9-5.

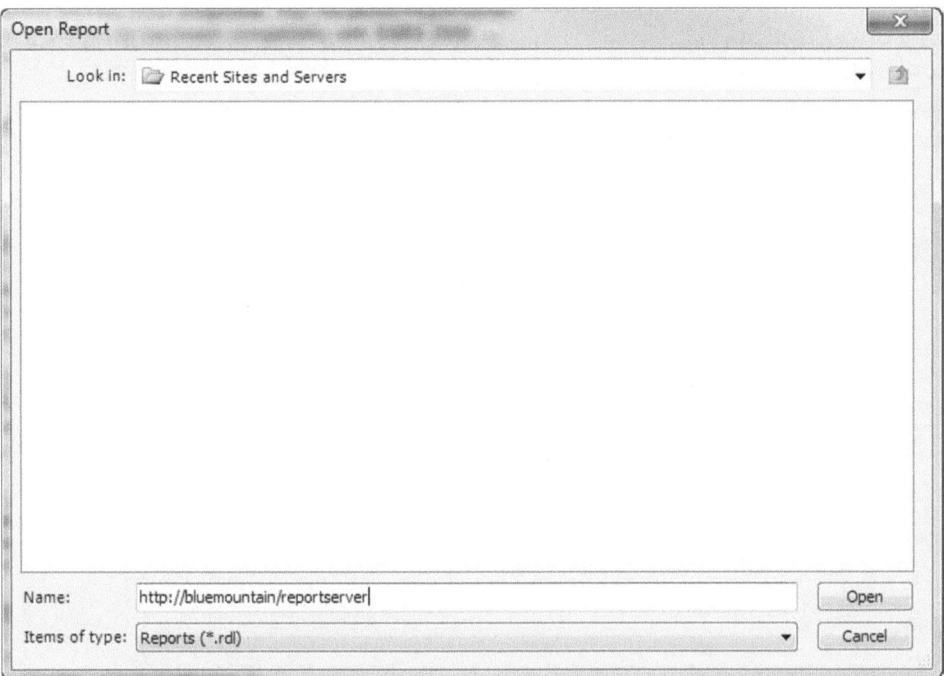

Figure 9-5. *Reporting Services web service URL entry*

After entering the reporting service URL, pressing the Open button will open a list of the reports, for the current user, from the SSRS server. The list from our example server contains the single report we are using, the Purchase Order Totals report. In a dialog similar to Figure 9-6, double-click the desired report in order to advance to the next step of the Table Import Wizard.

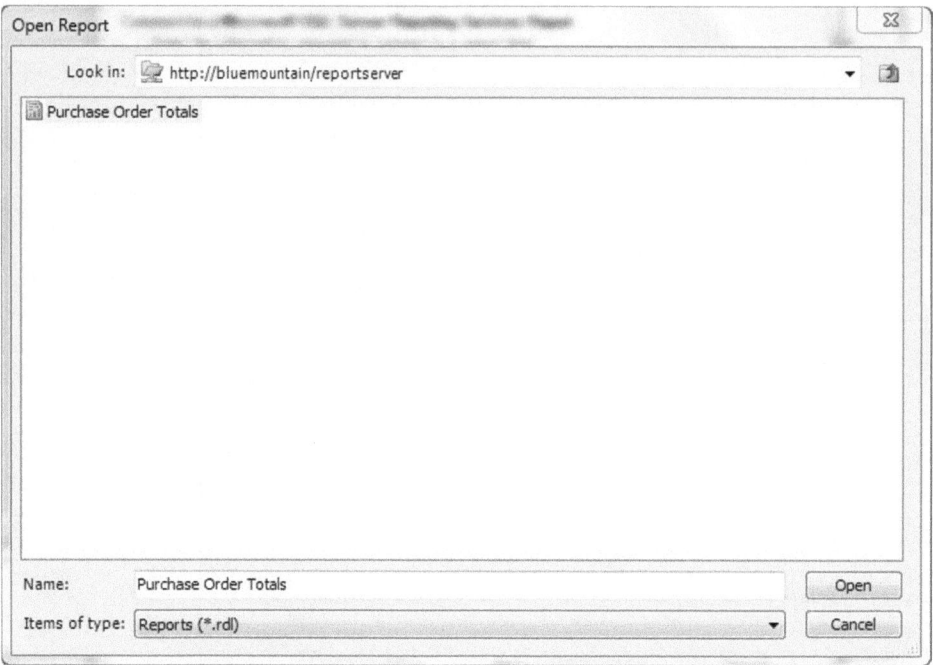

Figure 9-6. *Browsing SSRS reports*

The Table Import Wizard will trigger execution of the report, and the contents will be available for browsing in the central pane of the dialog, similar to Figure 9-7.

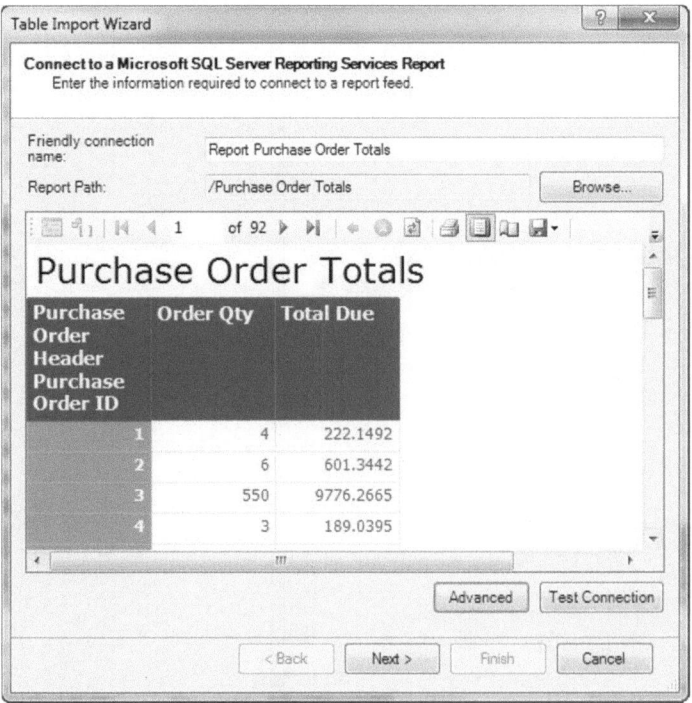

Figure 9-7. *Report execution in Table Import Wizard*

Pressing the Next button from the report preview will render the list of all tables within the report available for import, as shown in Figure 9-8. Our example report contains a single table, already named PurchaseOrders within the SSRS report definition language. PowerPivot's table import process has already used the source table name as the friendly name. As illustrated in Figure 9-7, the value of the friendly name can be changed by clicking in the text box and entering a new name.

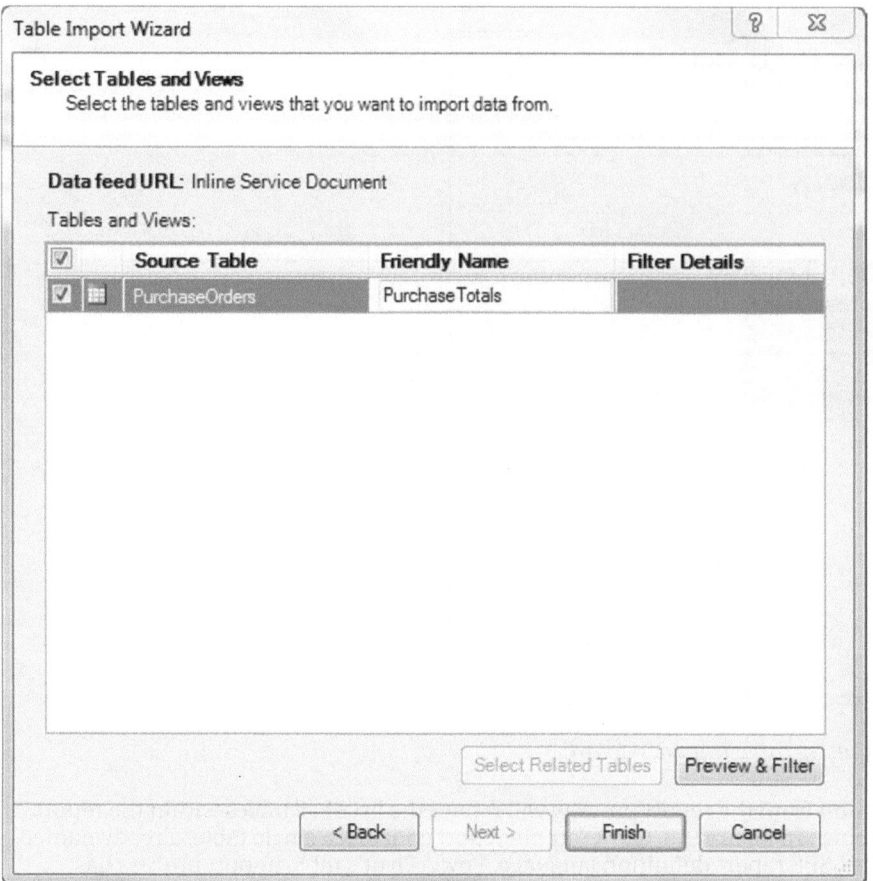

Figure 9-8. *Entering a friendly table name*

Clicking the Finish button will import all of the rows in the report. Alternatively, the Preview & Filter button can be used to access the data to be imported and optionally create filters. For this initial example, we will use all of the rows in the source report. The final dialog of the table import process will reveal the total rows imported. Clicking the Close button will reveal the new table, sourced from the SSRS report, within the PowerPivot environment, similar to Figure 9-9.

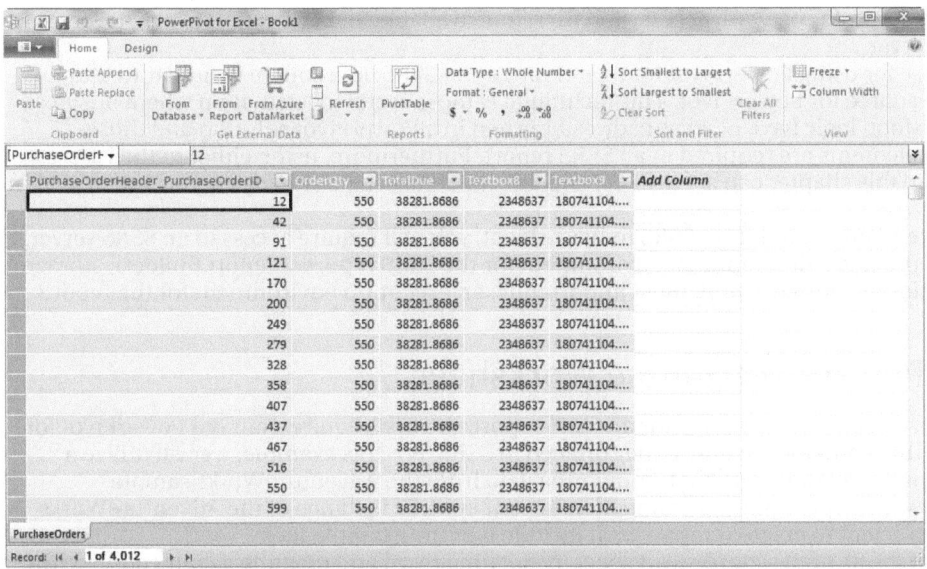

Figure 9-9. *Completed SSRS import*

Note there are two additional columns that were not immediately apparent in the original report. PowerPivot has named the columns Textbox8 and Textbox9, adding them as the final two columns in the PurchaseTotals table. These columns have been sourced from the grand totals for the OrderQty and TotalDue columns in the original report. The values in the Textbox8 and Textbox9 columns match with the grand totals from Figure 9-3. The first three columns in the PurchaseTotals table map directly to the three columns in the body of the original SSRS report: purchase order ID, order quantity, and total due.

The new table, from the SSRS report data, can now be related to data from other sources supported by PowerPivot. Just as any other PowerPivot table, the data in the PurchaseTotals table can be surfaced in PivotTables and PivotCharts as well as generate slicer values.

The real value in the technique I've just described can be realized in organizations with a robust library of Reporting Services reports. In addition to ensuring a consistent application of the business rules within the report logic, an organization's PowerPivot development is assured of using data that is synchronized with the existing SSRS reports. Furthermore, because the data source (SQL Server Reporting Services) is available online, when the PowerPivot for Excel solution is deployed to a SharePoint PowerPivot Gallery, the data refresh schedule can be managed as outlined in Chapter 7.

Using PowerPivot As an SSRS Data Source

The flow of data from SSRS to PowerPivot can almost be reversed completely, by using PowerPivot as a data source for an SSRS report. PowerPivot for Excel solutions can be stored in locations that may be only occasionally attached to a network, and therefore would have unpredictable availability. Examples of these occasionally connected locations include external USB hard disks, flash "keychain" drives, and even local disk drives. In these cases, PowerPivot for Excel solutions are not supported as a data source for SSRS. This is not the case in a PowerPivot for SharePoint solution. Deployment to SharePoint ensures the data is online, available for network access, and therefore available for connection to a SQL Server Reporting Services server.

The business case for using PowerPivot for SharePoint as an SSRS data source is similar to that for using SSRS as a data source for PowerPivot. This technique is most useful in a situation where business rules and data acquisition logic have been already established in a PowerPivot solution and those PowerPivot solution elements are required in an SSRS report. Furthermore, using either of the techniques covered in this chapter can serve to consolidate and reuse logic already created and tested in a new manner.

In order to create a connection from SSRS to PowerPivot, you will require access to an SSRS server. The SSRS server will provide a development environment for the SSRS reports (Report Builder), storage of the reports definitions (.rdl files), and, most importantly, an execution environment for the report.

Creating the PowerPivot Source Worksheet

In order to use PowerPivot as a data source for an SSRS report, the first requirement is a PowerPivot for SharePoint solution that contains the data to be surfaced in SSRS. For this example, we will utilize a simple PowerPivot for SharePoint workbook containing data from the AdventureWorks sample database. Since this worksheet requires a connection to your specific instance of the AdventureWorks database, it is more efficient to create it rather than include it in the example files.

Begin creation of the example source worksheet by opening Excel and creating a connection to the AdventureWorks sample database. As illustrated in Figure 9-10, select the From Database selection of the external data section of the Home ribbon. From the resulting drop-down menu, select the From SQL Server option in order to establish a connection with the SQL Server example database.

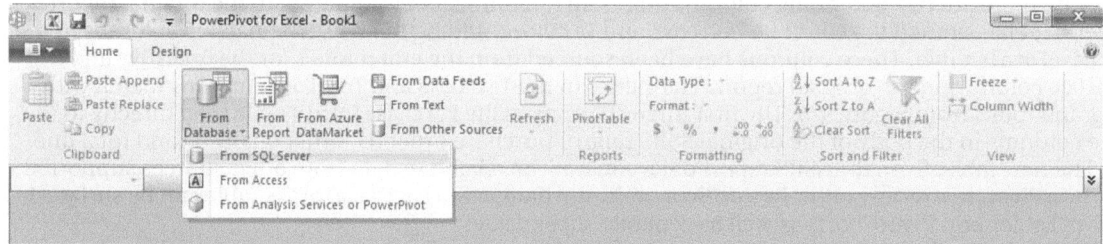

Figure 9-10. *Configuring a SQL Server database connection*

After clicking the From SQL Server option, PowerPivot will begin the Table Import Wizard. The first step of the wizard is a dialog similar to Figure 9-11. Complete the "Server name" text box with the location of your AdventureWorks sample databases. Additionally, the "Database name" pulldown should read "AdventureWorks". Press the Next button to advance the Table Import Wizard to the next step, defining the tables or query containing the required data.

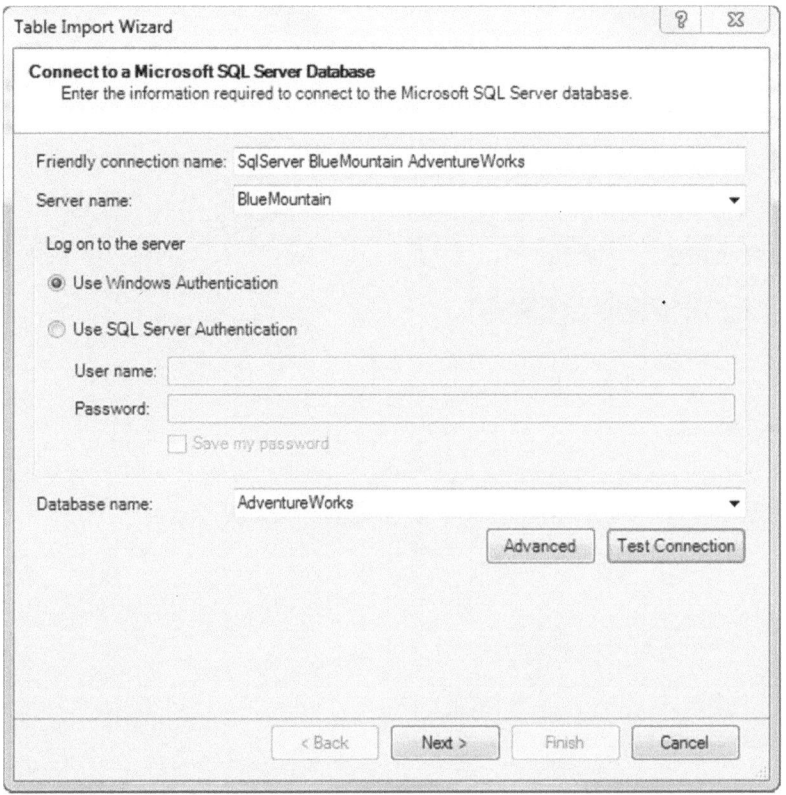

Figure 9-11. *Table Import Wizard, data connection*

For this example, we are using all of the data from three tables in the AdventureWorks database. Therefore, select the radio button option labeled "Select from a list of tables and views to choose the data to import", and press the Next button to advance to the next step in the Table Import Wizard.

The subsequent task of the Table Import Wizard is to gather the tables that will be imported into PowerPivot. A dialog similar to Figure 9-12 is presented for this operation. Select the Product, ProductCategory, and ProductInventory tables, as illustrated in Figure 9-12. Pressing the Finish button will end the Table Import Wizard by importing the data from the selected tables into PowerPivot.

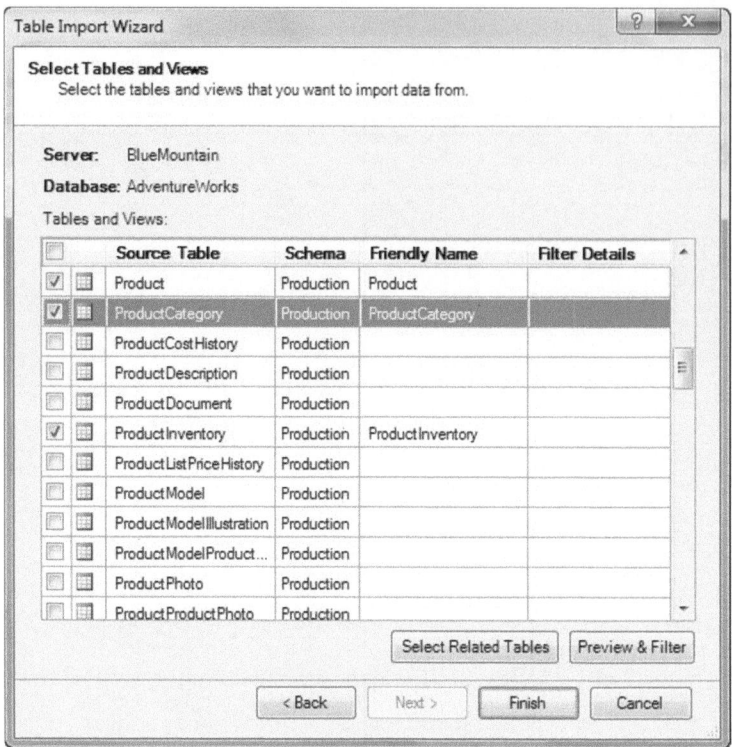

Figure 9-12. *Table import selection*

The final Table Import Wizard dialog consists of a list of the tables imported, and the row counts from each table. The final import success or failure dialog will be similar to Figure 9-13. Press the Close button to exit the Table Import Wizard and begin working with the data in PowerPivot for Excel.

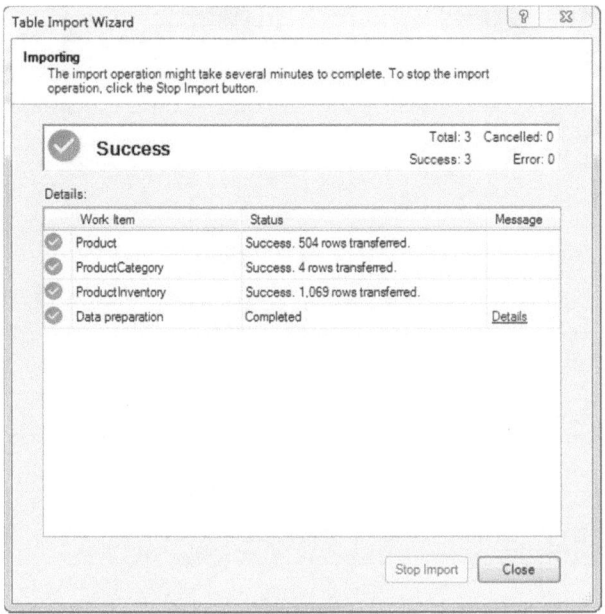

Figure 9-13. *Import row counts*

At the conclusion of the Table Import Wizard, the data has been imported into the local, in-memory instance of SSAS specifically for usage by PowerPivot for Excel. From this point, creating a PowerPivot report is the same, irrespective of the data source. For our PowerPivot as a data source example, we need only create a PowerPivot report and deploy the Excel worksheet to a PowerPivot for SharePoint Gallery.

To complete the first task, creating a PowerPivot report, first ensure you are in an Excel window and not PowerPivot. From the PowerPivot ribbon, select PivotTable to add a new PivotTable to the worksheet. Select the Product Name column from the Product table as the row labels by dragging the column to the Row Labels area of the PowerPivot Field List. Similarly, add the Quantity column from the ProductInventory table as the sole column in the Values area of the PowerPivot Field List. When finished, your report and worksheet should resemble Figure 9-14.

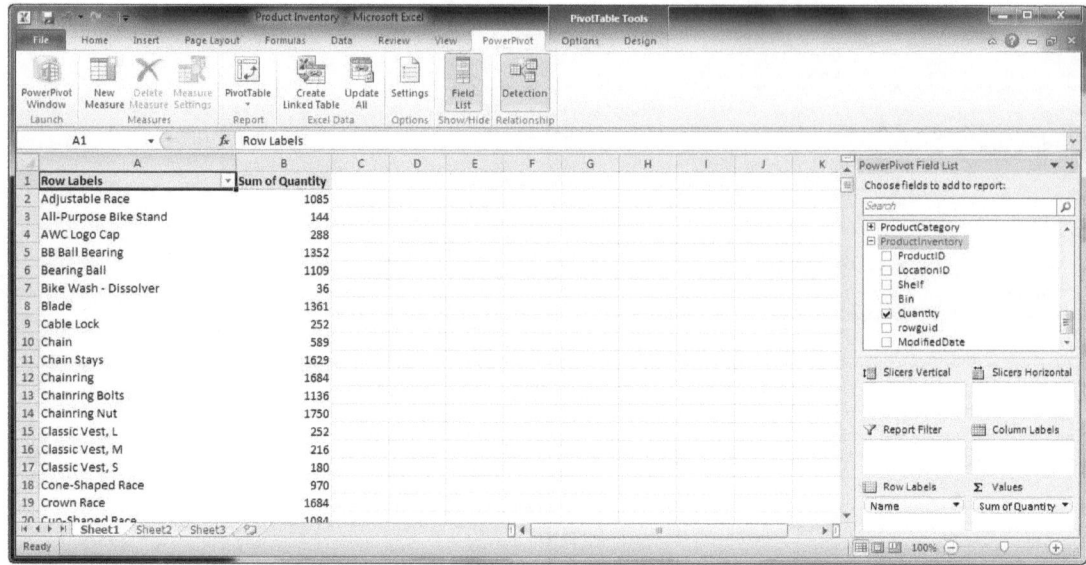

Figure 9-14. *PowerPivot report*

The final task before configuring the new PowerPivot solution as an SSRS data source is deploying the solution to a PowerPivot for SharePoint Gallery. From the File ribbon menu from within Excel, use the Save & Send selection to browse for and select a PowerPivot for SharePoint Gallery destination and file name. When the upload of the file to SharePoint is complete, ensure the .xlsx file is checked in and available for others to utilize. When finished with this step, you should be able to browse the PowerPivot Gallery and both see the new file and open the file via the browser. Figure 9-15 illustrates the new Product Inventory.xlsx file in the PowerPivot Gallery on the server named "powerpivotbook".

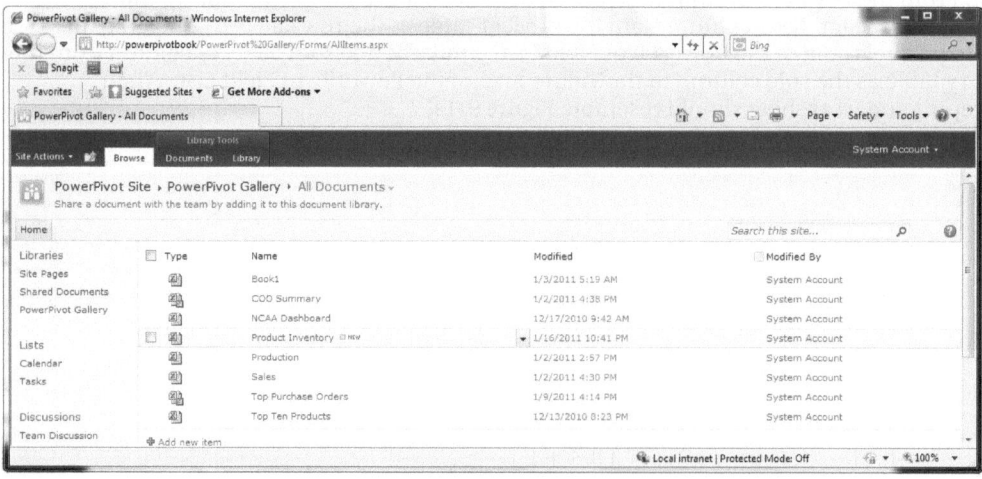

Figure 9-15. *PowerPivot Gallery with new Product Inventory file*

Opening Report Manager

Report Manager is a web application that is installed as a component of SSRS. While configurations vary, the usual URL for Report Manager is in the form http://<reportserver>/reports, where your server name is substituted for <reportserver>. In the case of this example, the SSRS server is located on a server named BlueMountain, and we are using the default port (80); therefore the URL for Report Manager is http://bluemountain/reports. Opening the URL in Internet Explorer will render a window similar to Figure 9-16.

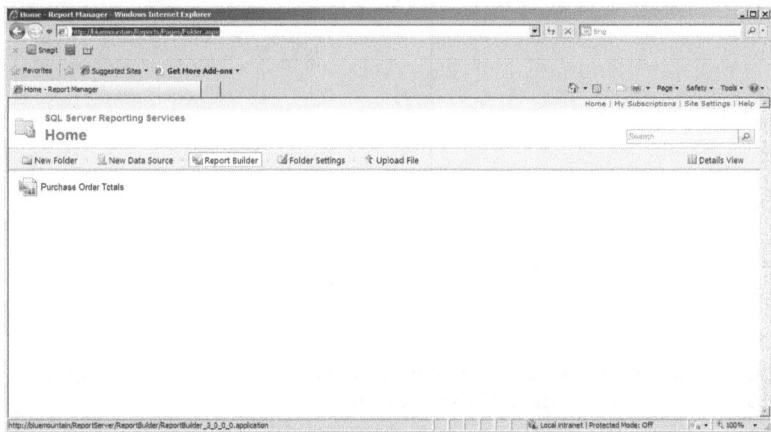

Figure 9-16. *Report Manager window*

Developing the Example SSRS Report

In order to launch the Report Builder application, click the Report Builder icon shown in Report Manager in Figure 9-16. The click-once deployment will then start the process of downloading the Report Builder application to your workstation. After the rapid download and quick installation process completes, you should see a dialog on top of the Report Builder main window similar to Figure 9-17, containing a number of menu selections for creating reports and data sources.

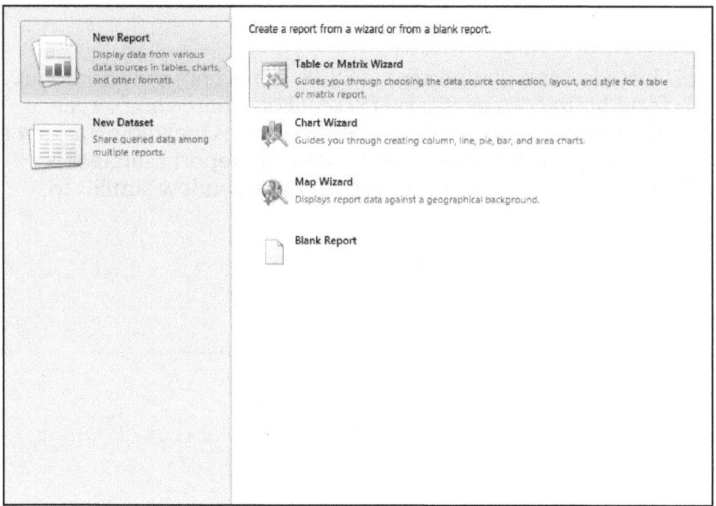

Figure 9-17. *Report Builder 3.0*

The default, highlighted selection, New Report, is our desired item. We could also, starting with the left-hand navigation and working down, select one of the following options:

- *New Dataset*: Creates a source data definition to be used by perhaps multiple reports

- *Open*: Opens an existing report that has been saved previously

- *Recent*: Acting as a most recently used file list, allows for the reopening of a previous file

We are concerned with developing a new SSRS report using a PowerPivot solution as the source. Selecting the New Report option will allow us to choose between several report options. In order to continue creating the report, choose the "Table or Matrix Wizard" selection by single-clicking the sub-menu selection.

Report Builder will respond with the next step in the Report Wizard, creating or choosing a dataset, represented by a dialog similar to Figure 9-18. As we have no existing datasets, this is a fresh Reporting Services server installation; choose the option to "Create a dataset" near the bottom of the screen, and press the Next button.

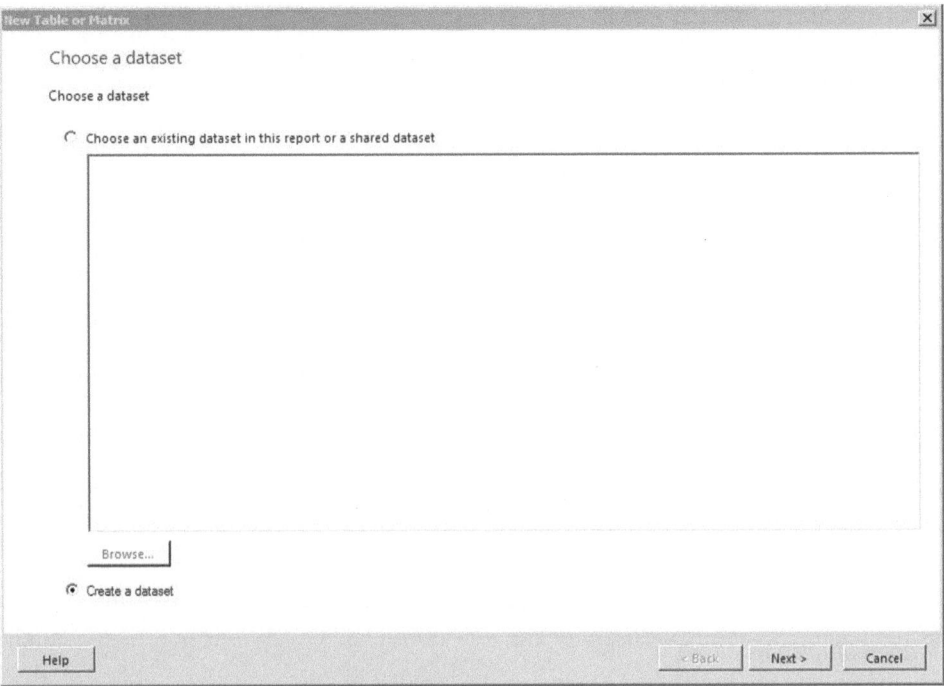

Figure 9-18. *Report Builder dataset selection*

The first step in creating a dataset is establishing a connection to the data source. Report Builder responds to the "Create a dataset" selection by rendering a dialog similar to Figure 9-19. Again, in the event of a fresh Reporting Services installation, no data source connections will exist. However, even if connections were available, this is the point at which we will define the connection to PowerPivot for SharePoint.

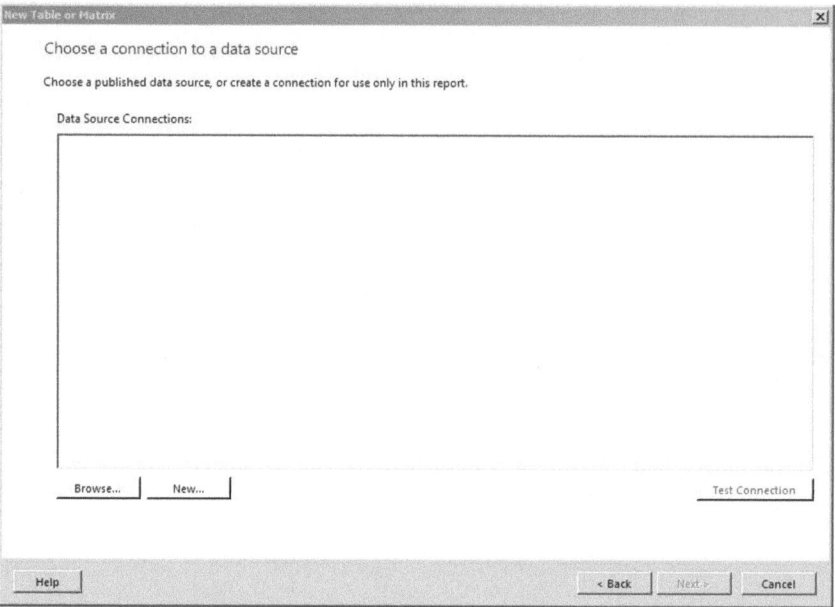

Figure 9-19. *Data source connection*

Select "New…" from the lower portion of the dialog in Figure 9-19 to create a connection to PowerPivot for SharePoint. The first step of the data connection is to identify a name for use in the ensuing dialog illustrated in Figure 9-20. The default name of "DataSource1" is fine for our purposes, but I am renaming the data source to "PowerPivot_ProductInventory". Be aware SSRS data source names must not contain spaces. Also, the data source name may contain numbers and the underscore character, but the first character must be a letter.

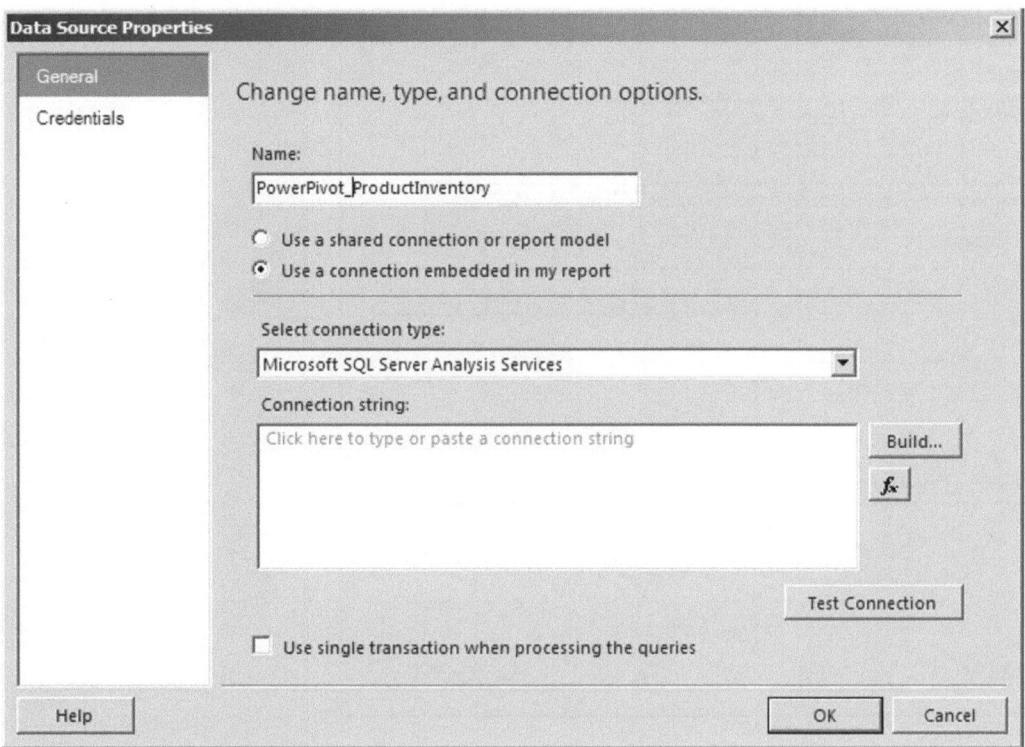

Figure 9-20. *Data source connection definition*

After establishing the name of the data source, the next set of radio buttons determine if this data source will reuse an existing, shared connection or use a connection that is embedded in the report. Choose the "Use a connection embedded in my report" option, as illustrated in Figure 9-20. Because we are using PowerPivot for SharePoint, the next element of the configuration, the connection type, should be set to Microsoft SQL Server Analysis Services. Finally, click the "Build…" button to create the connection string to PowerPivot for SharePoint. This will render a dialog similar to Figure 9-21.

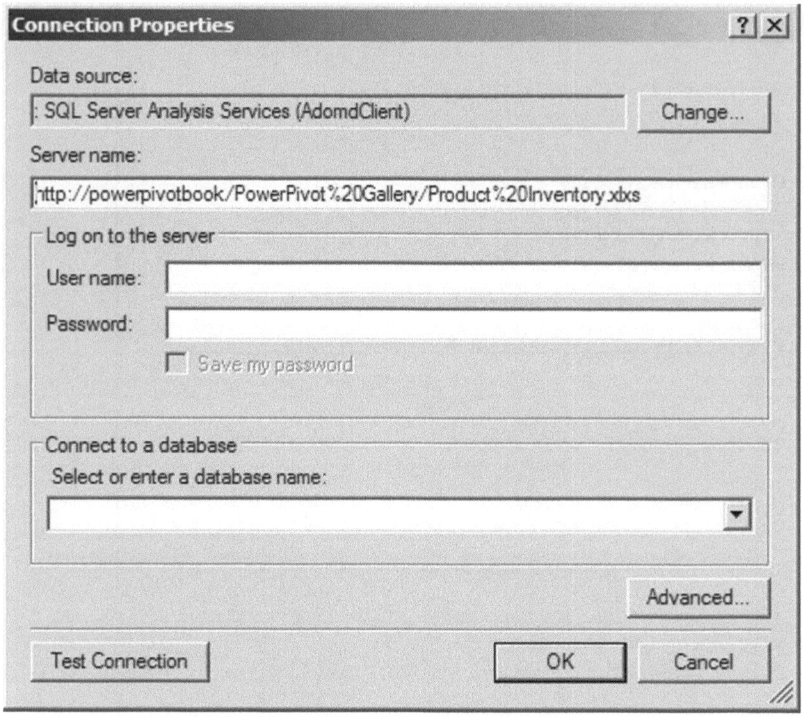

Figure 9-21. *Connection properties server name*

Notice that the server name text box in Figure 9-21 contains a URL for the source PowerPivot workbook. Instead of connecting to the underlying SSAS instance for PowerPivot, we are using the PowerPivot web service to load the requested workbook, if necessary. By using the PowerPivot web service, we also let the PowerPivot service application for SharePoint execute any necessary load balancing, finding a server either by health or round-robin assignment, by which our request will be serviced. Finally, the web service access also impacts user credential configuration. Press OK to complete the connection properties; this should return the Data Source Properties dialog, Figure 9-22, to the focus.

Within the Data Source Properties dialog, select the Credentials panel by clicking the label in the left-hand navigation list. This will render a dialog similar to Figure 9-22. This panel of the data source configuration allows for customization of the user credentials that authenticate access to the underlying data. For our example, it is sufficient to use the "Prompt for credentials" selection, ensuring the "Use as Windows credentials" check box is in a checked state, similar to Figure 9-22. Activating the "Use as Windows credentials" check box will cause SSRS to prompt for a user ID and password at each execution of the report, and in turn utilize the user-entered information as a Windows login to the data source.

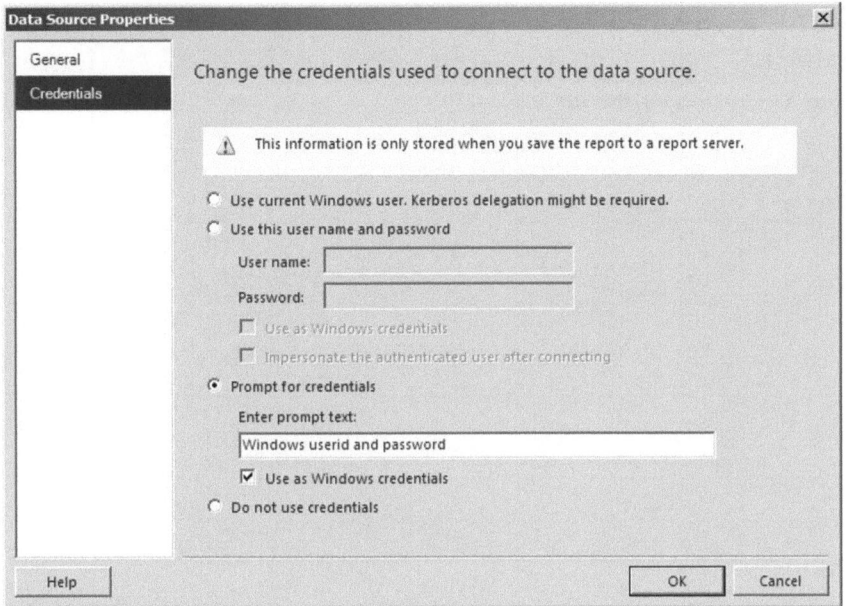

Figure 9-22. *Data source credential options*

At this point, we can now test the data source connection to verify the ability for SSRS to access the data in our PowerPivot for SharePoint solution. Select the General item from the left-hand navigation to return to the connection options panel illustrated in Figure 9-22. Press the Test Connection button. This will cause Reporting Services to respond with a prompt for Windows credentials. Entering credentials with access to the PowerPivot for SharePoint solution file will result in a successful connection message. If a connection error is generated, verify the connection properties and user credential privileges. Otherwise, press the OK button to save the data source. This will cause the next step in the Report Wizard, a window similar to Figure 9-23, to be rendered.

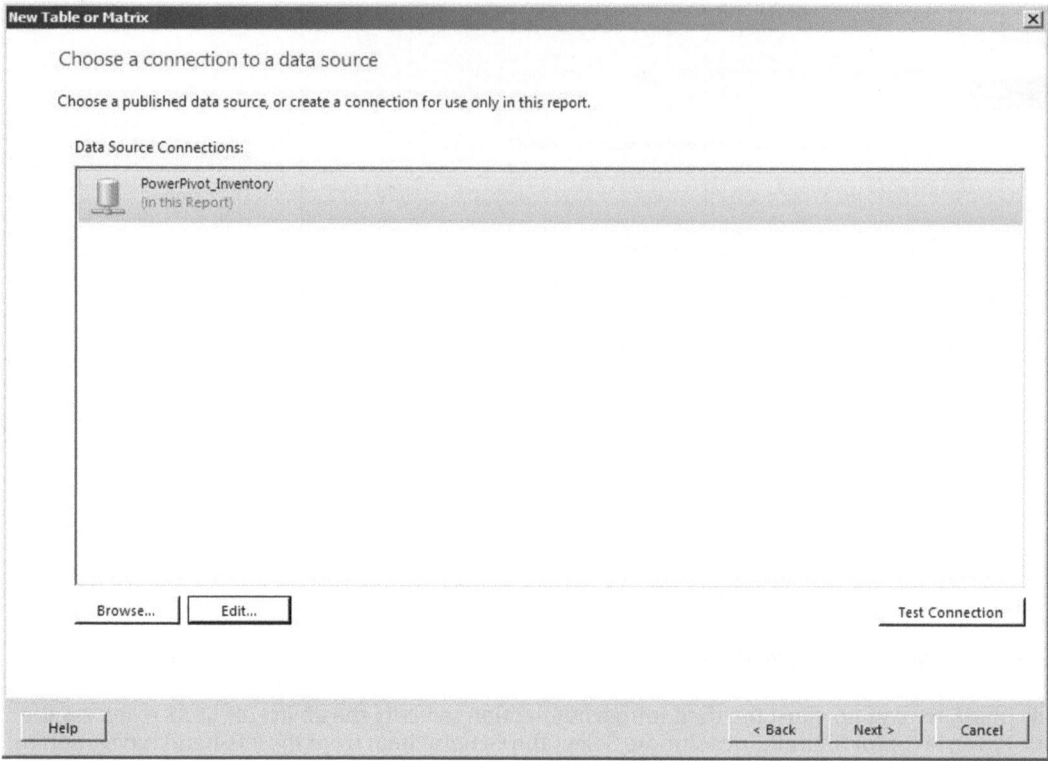

Figure 9-23. *Data source complete*

With a data source configured and saved, the next step in SSRS report development is creating the dataset containing information to be surfaced in the report. Pressing the Next button on the Report Wizard screen illustrated in Figure 9-23 will continue the dataset specification process. If you are prompted for Windows credentials, simply enter the user ID and password of an account used to test the data source configuration. Upon successful authentication, a Query Designer window similar to Figure 9-24 will be produced.

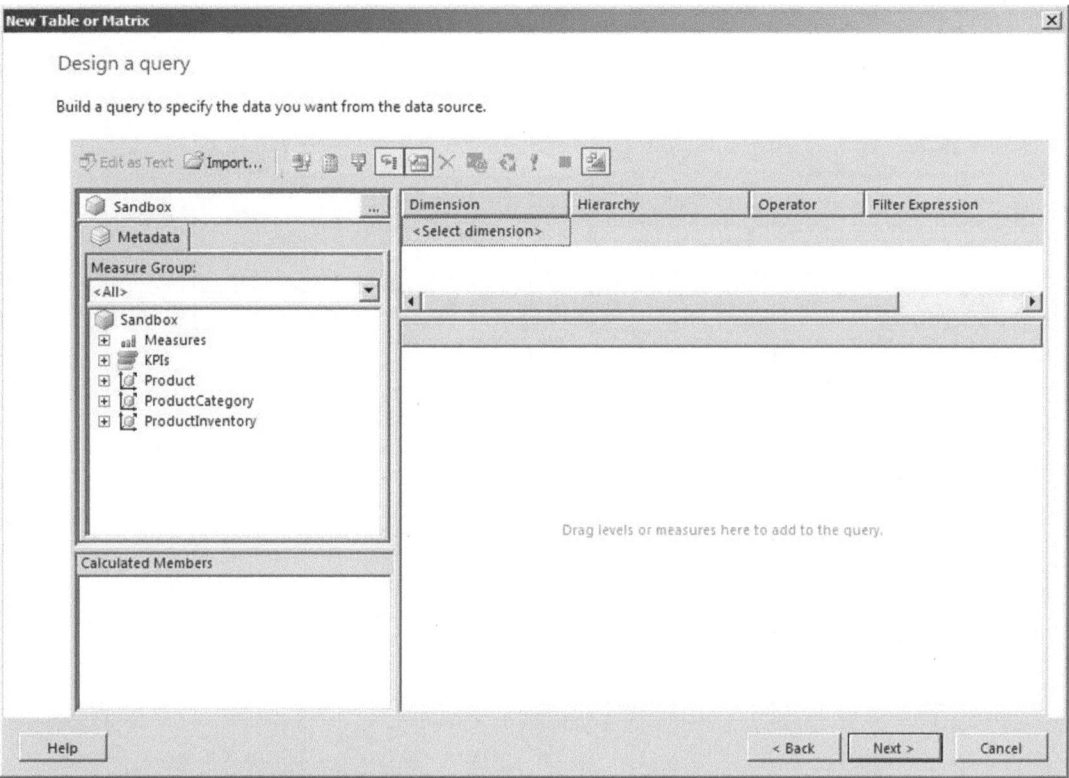

Figure 9-24. *Dataset Query Designer*

Similar to the Query Designer used in Chapter 8, this tool allows for creation of a dataset from the PowerPivot data source via a drag-and-drop interface. All of the tables contained in the Product Inventory.xlsx PowerPivot for SharePoint solution are enumerated in the left-hand navigation menu. Additionally, measures contained in the solution are listed under the Measures grouping in the metadata navigator. Dragging a dimension or measure to the central panel places that element in the dataset. Additionally, the dataset can be constrained or filtered based on attributes placed in the panel immediately above the dataset design surface. Drag the ProductID and Name attributes from the Product table onto the dataset design surface. Finally, drag the Sum of Quantity attribute from the ProductInventory measure group to the design surface. When finished, the Query Designer window should be similar to Figure 9-25.

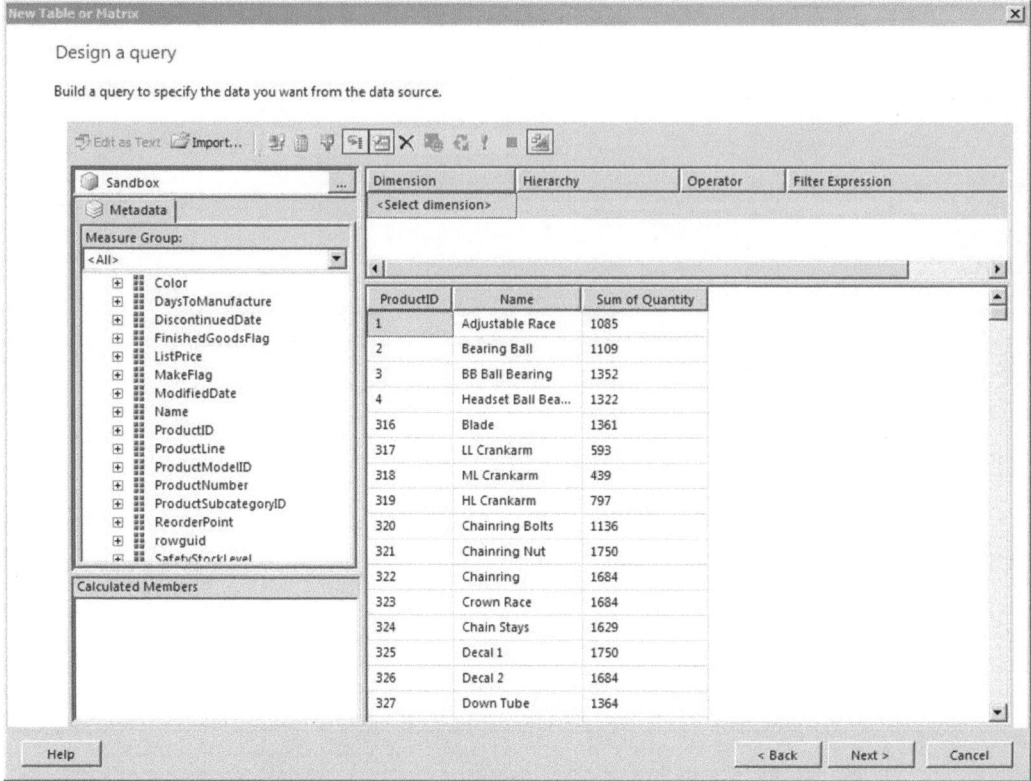

Figure 9-25. *Report Wizard Dataset Query Designer*

Press the Next button at the bottom of the Query Designer window to save the new dataset. This will also advance to the next step of the Report Wizard, laying out the report elements.

After completing query design, the Report Wizard will render a screen similar to Figure 9-20. This area of the wizard will allow for configuration of the report layout, specifying measure values and column and row groupings. The Values area of the layout form specifies the elements of the report that will be described by row and optionally column headers. This is very similar to the PowerPivot Field List in behavior. Measures that are typically aggregated are rendered in the Values section. Based on elements in the Row group and/or Column group areas, the Values are aggregated and grouped. For our example report, drag the three elements of our dataset to the Row and Values areas, as illustrated in Figure 9-26.

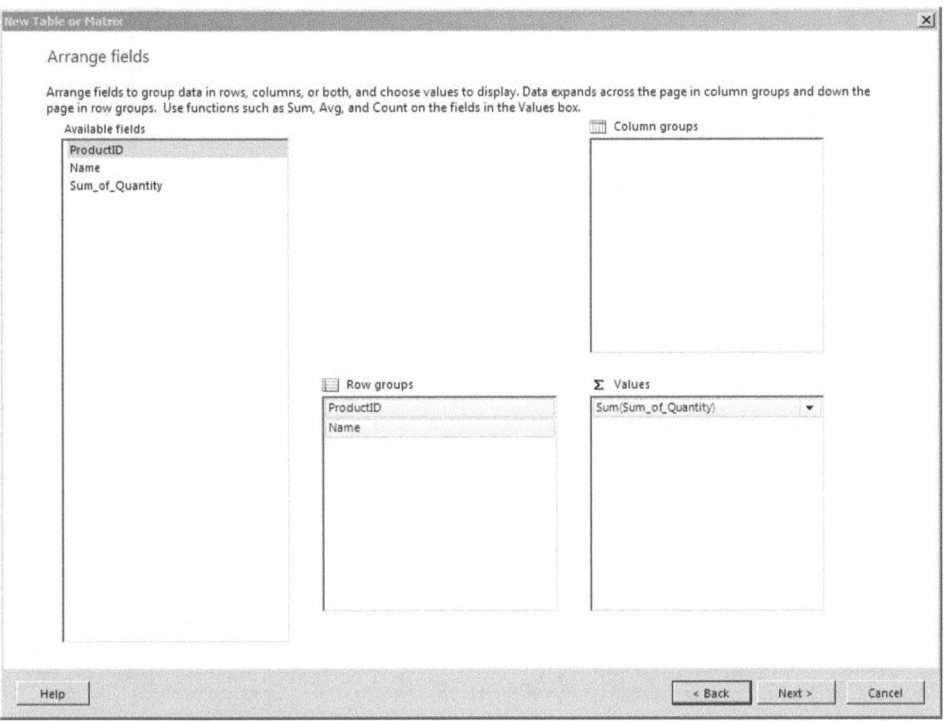

Figure 9-26. *Report layout*

Pressing the Next button from the field layout will advance the Report Wizard to the specification of the total and sub-total layout. The defaults are illustrated in Figure 9-27. For the purposes of our example, accept the defaults and press the Next button to advance the Report Wizard to the next step.

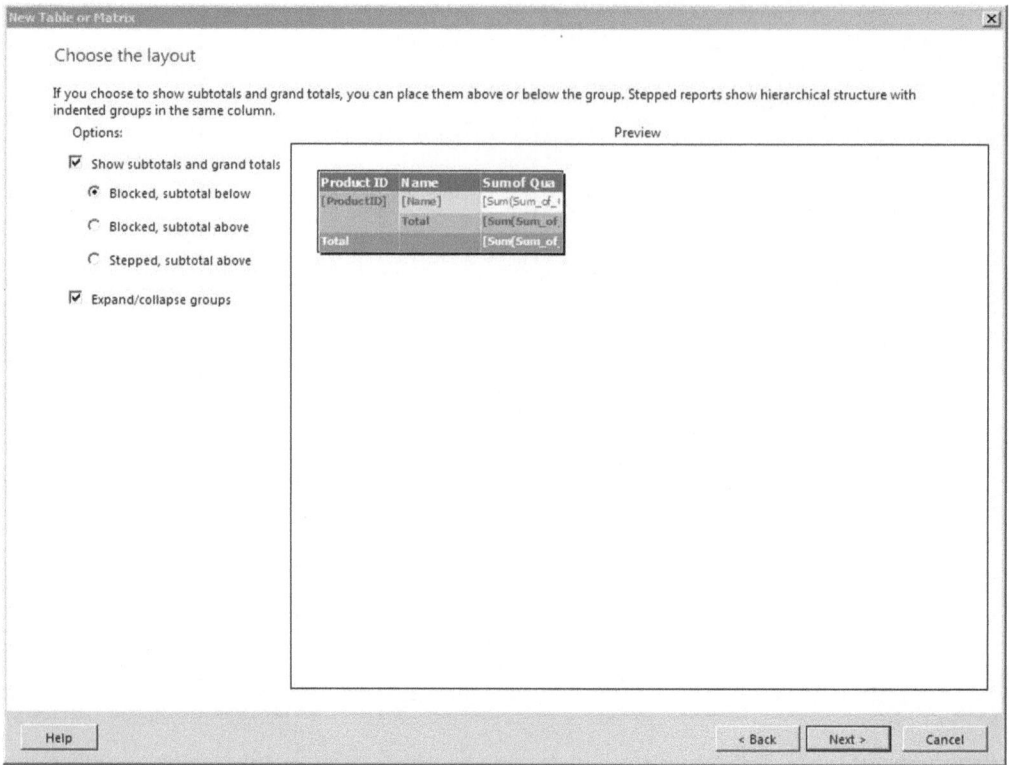

Figure 9-27. *Total and sub-total specification*

The next and final step in the Report Wizard will configure the settings for the report style. Pick any color scheme and click the Finish button to complete the report design. The Report Wizard will complete, leaving a fully configured SSRS report as the primary window of Report Builder, similar to Figure 9-28. In the example illustrated, the title of the report has been changed to "PowerPivot for SharePoint Example".

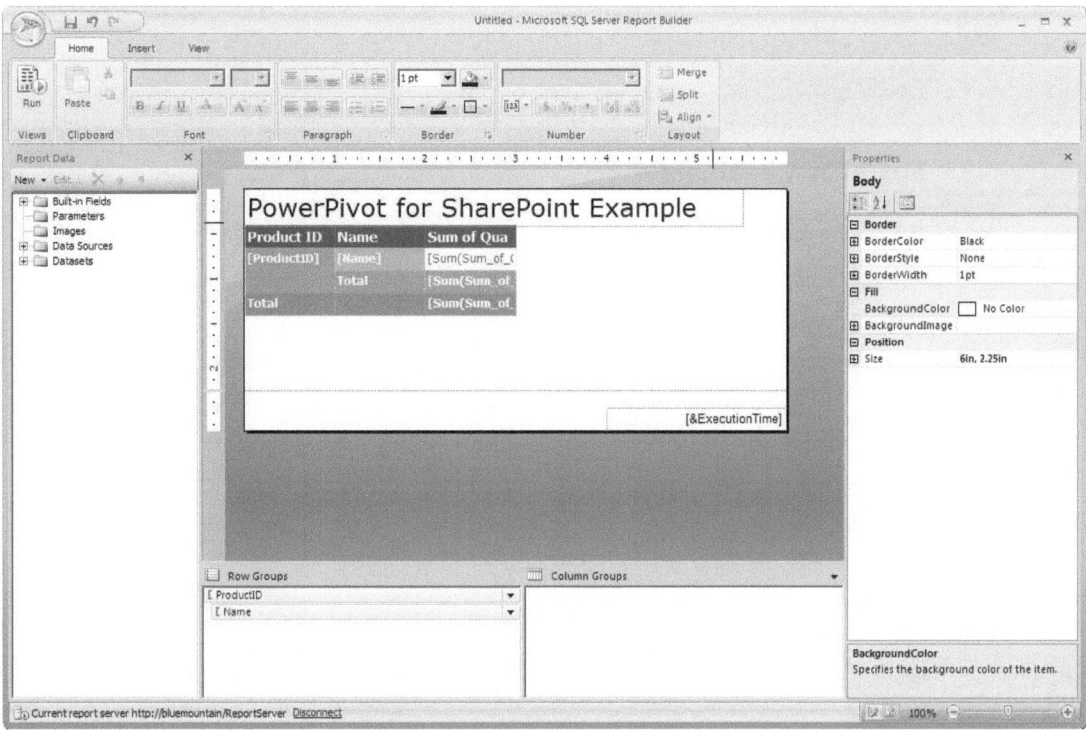

Figure 9-28. *Completed report definition*

At this point, the report is completely finished and ready for execution. Similar to most modern integrated development environments (IDE), Report Builder allows for execution from within the development tool. Pressing the F5 key or clicking the Run button in the upper left-hand corner will execute the new report. This should result in a window similar to Figure 9-29.

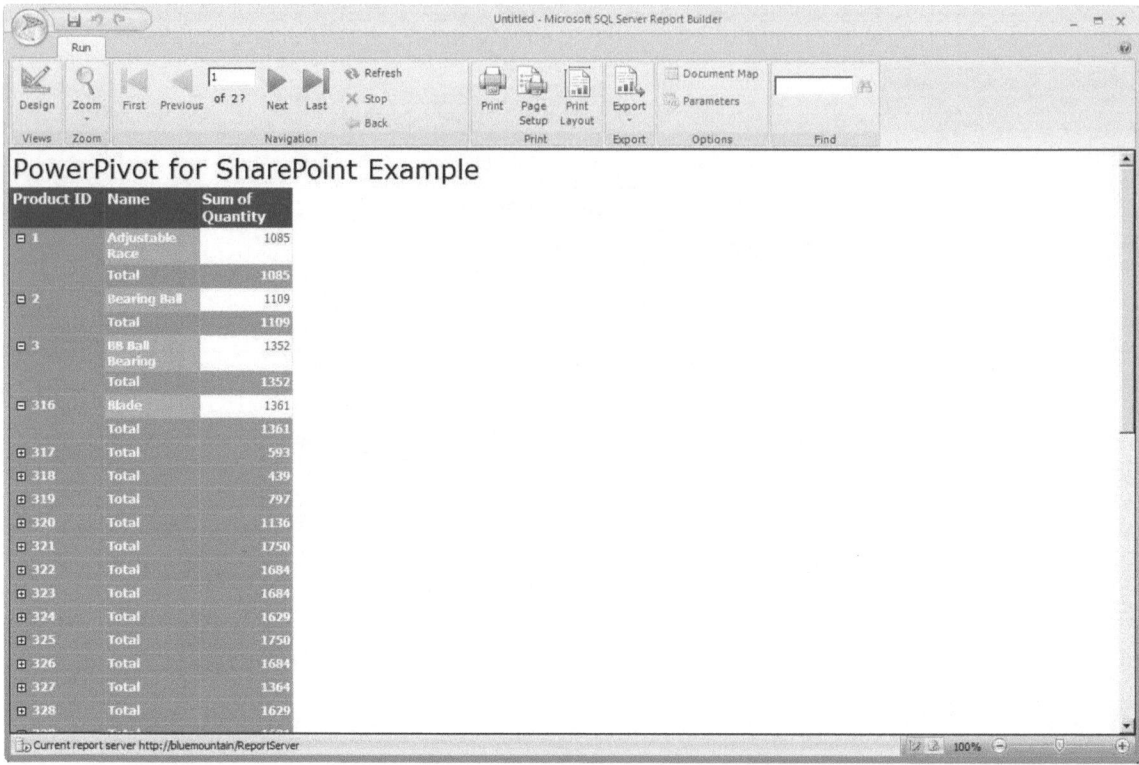

Figure 9-29. *Report execution within Report Builder*

After successfully executing the report, the definition in the form of a report definition language (.rdl) file can be saved to the SSRS server. Clicking either the disk icon, in the upper left-hand corner of the Report Builder title bar, or the ribbon "pearl" and selecting Save from the options will prompt for a name for the new report in a dialog similar to Figure 9-30. Note the location to which the report will be saved is the URL to the SSRS server. I have named the report "PowerPivot for SharePoint Example," but you can choose any name for the report.

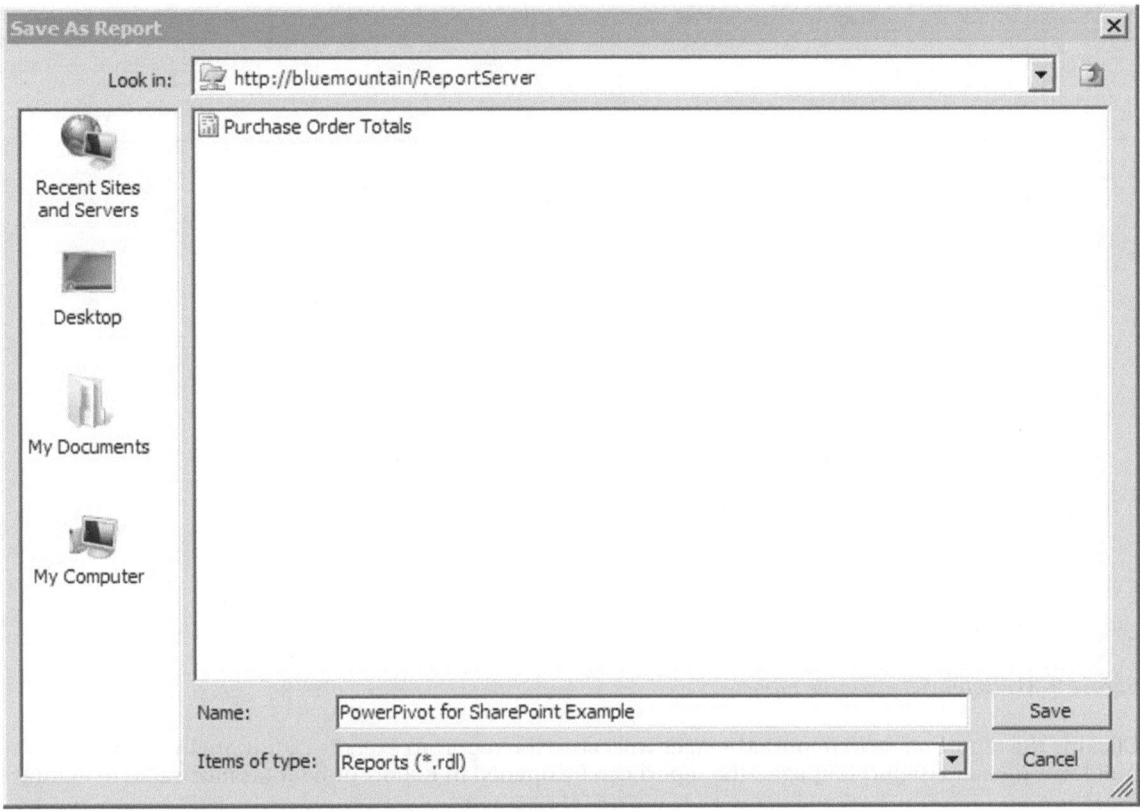

Figure 9-30. *Report Builder Save dialog*

Clicking the Save button will deploy the RDL to the SSRS server. Upon refreshing the Report Manager window, illustrated in Figure 9-16 earlier, you should see the new report listed, similar to Figure 9-31.

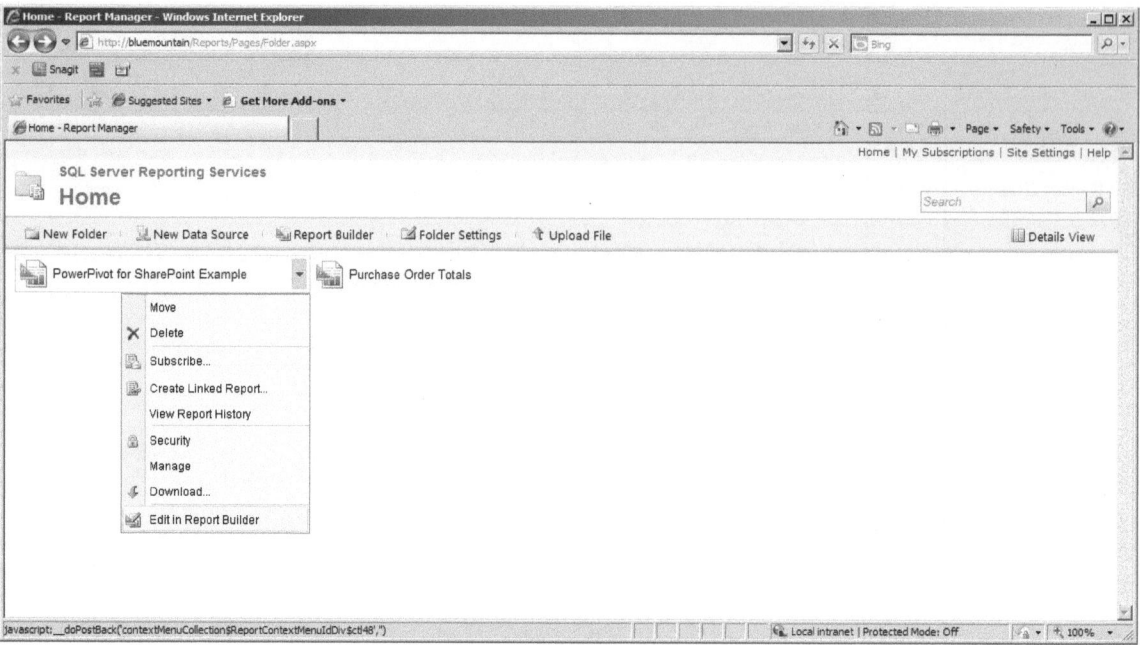

Figure 9-31. *Deployed example report*

Clicking the report name in Report Manager will cause the report to execute. Additionally, from the pulldown menu in Report Manager, the report can be opened in Report Builder (as illustrated in Figure 9-31).

Summary

PowerPivot for SharePoint can be a powerful tool for supplying data to a SQL Server Reporting Services report, as well as surfacing and analyzing data from existing SSRS reports. As components of the Microsoft Business Intelligence platform, both PowerPivot and SSRS can be integrated depending on the specific needs and information assets of the organization.

CHAPTER 10

∎∎∎

PowerPivot and Predictive Analytics

The only relevant test of the validity of a hypothesis is comparison of prediction with experience.

—Milton Friedman

Until this point, this book has been concerned with examples using data to look back at what has happened in the past—for example, determining which flights have been delayed in the past, for carriers and airports. Another example of historical reporting and analysis is the decomposition of sales by product and division. Both of these examples rely upon an historical record of activities that have already occurred.

PowerPivot is not limited to creating insight into the past, however. Imagine the level of perceptiveness that would be created by using PowerPivot to utilize the past and create a vision of what *could be* possible in the future. This sort of predictive analytics, also known as *data mining*, is no longer a field restricted to doctoral candidates in mathematics and statistics. You can readily create a data mining workstation by combining PowerPivot for Excel with add-in software already available from Microsoft and others.

Introducing the Data Mining Add-In for Excel

Originally introduced as a means of creating data mining solutions using Microsoft Excel, Table Analysis Tools for Excel 2007 (and later versions too) is available for download from the Microsoft web site. There are two primary limitations on using the tool to create predictive models. First, because the add-in was developed for Office 2007, it is available only in a 32-bit version. The second limitation is the requirement to access a SQL Server Analysis Services (SSAS) server. This is because Table Analysis Tools is intended to be an interface to SSAS for the creation of data mining models that are already integral to Microsoft's OLAP server. Look closely and you can see the similarity between PowerPivot for Excel as an interface for the creation of SSAS databases and Table Analysis Tools as a means for creating data mining models within SSAS. These limitations can combine to be quite tricky given the 64-bit–only nature of SQL Server 2008 R2 and the fact that Table Analysis Tools is available only for 32-bit Microsoft Office. The Table Analysis Tools example in this chapter was constructed using 32-bit Microsoft Office 2010 and a SQL Server 2008 R2 Analysis Services instance running on a separate physical machine.

Installing the Data Mining Add-In

The Data Mining Add-In is available from Microsoft via the Microsoft Download Center at
www.microsoft.com/downloads. Utilize the search text box at the top of the screen, and search for
Data Mining Add-In Office. Sort the result in order by date, picking the latest release. Opening the
location in a browser should yield a page similar to Figure 10-1. Download the file named
SQLServer2008_DMAddin.msi by clicking the Download button. Save the file to a location on your local
machine.

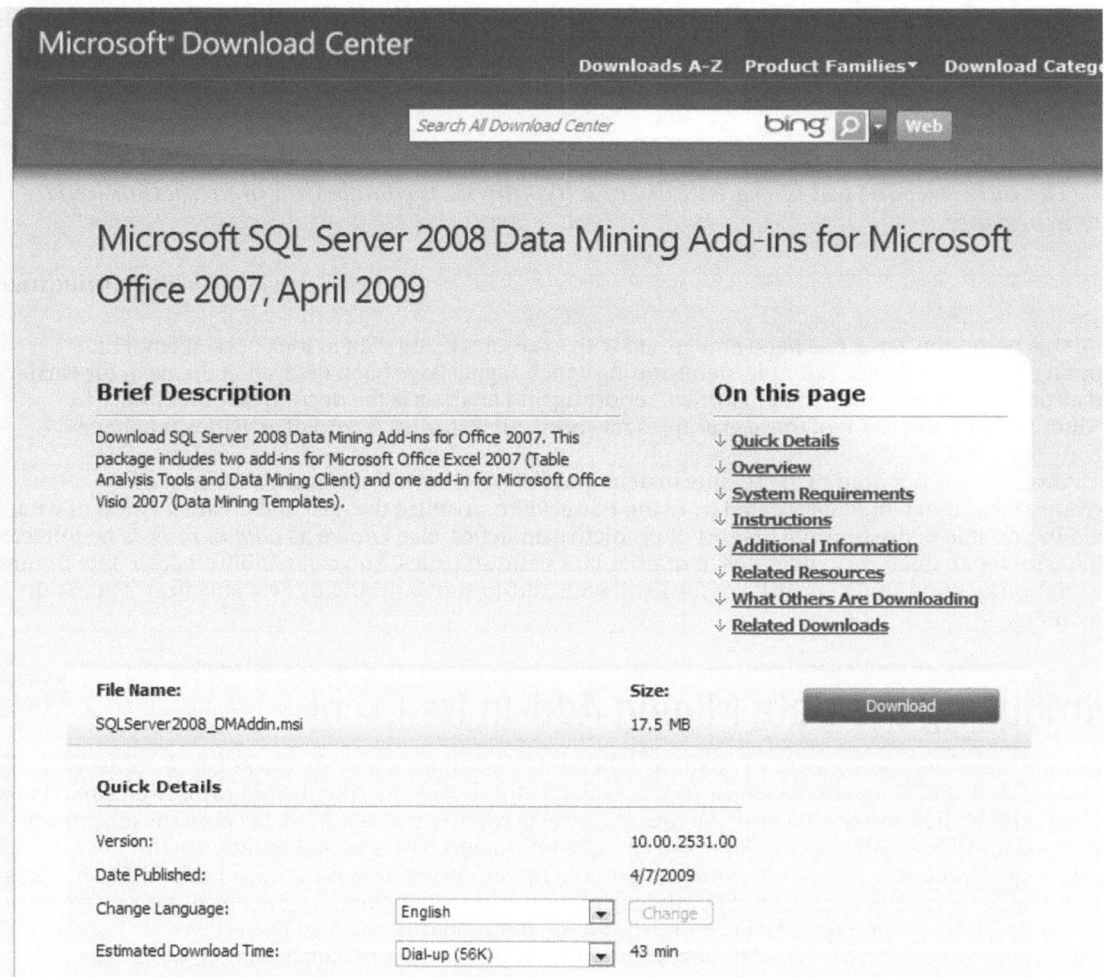

Figure 10-1. *Data Mining Add-In download page*

After the download completes, execute the installer. The first indication of the installation process
will be the welcome screen pictured in Figure 10-2.

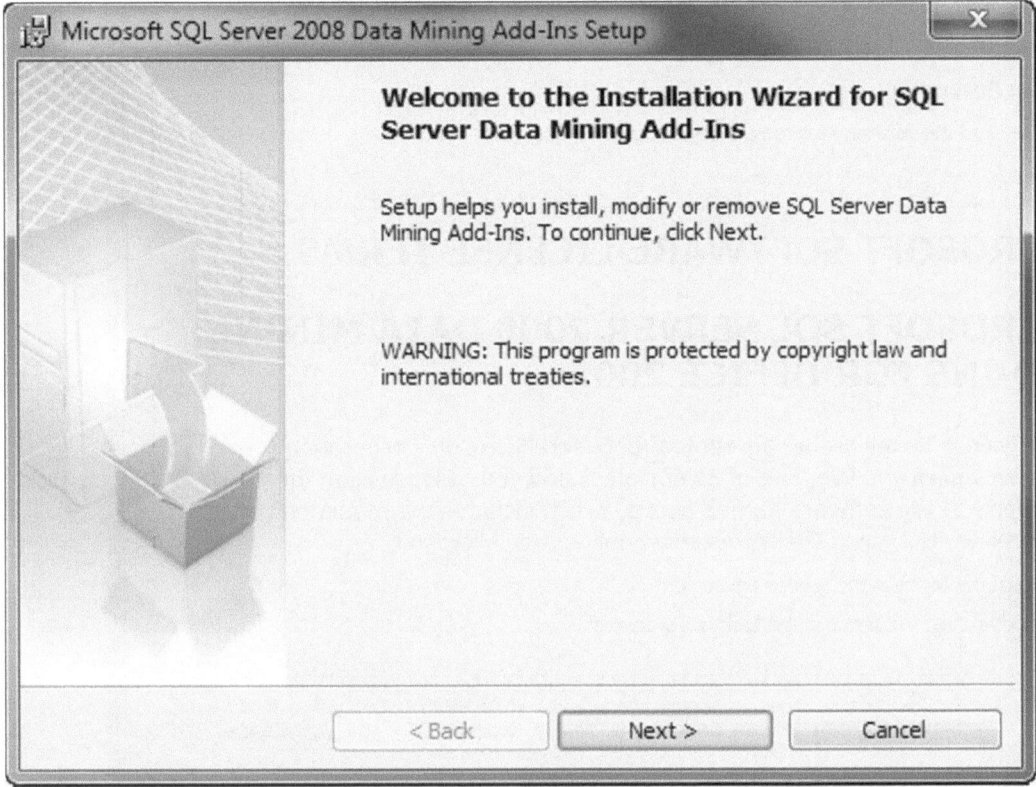

Figure 10-2. *Data Mining Add-In installer*

Click the Next button to advance the process to the license agreement, illustrated in Figure 10-3.

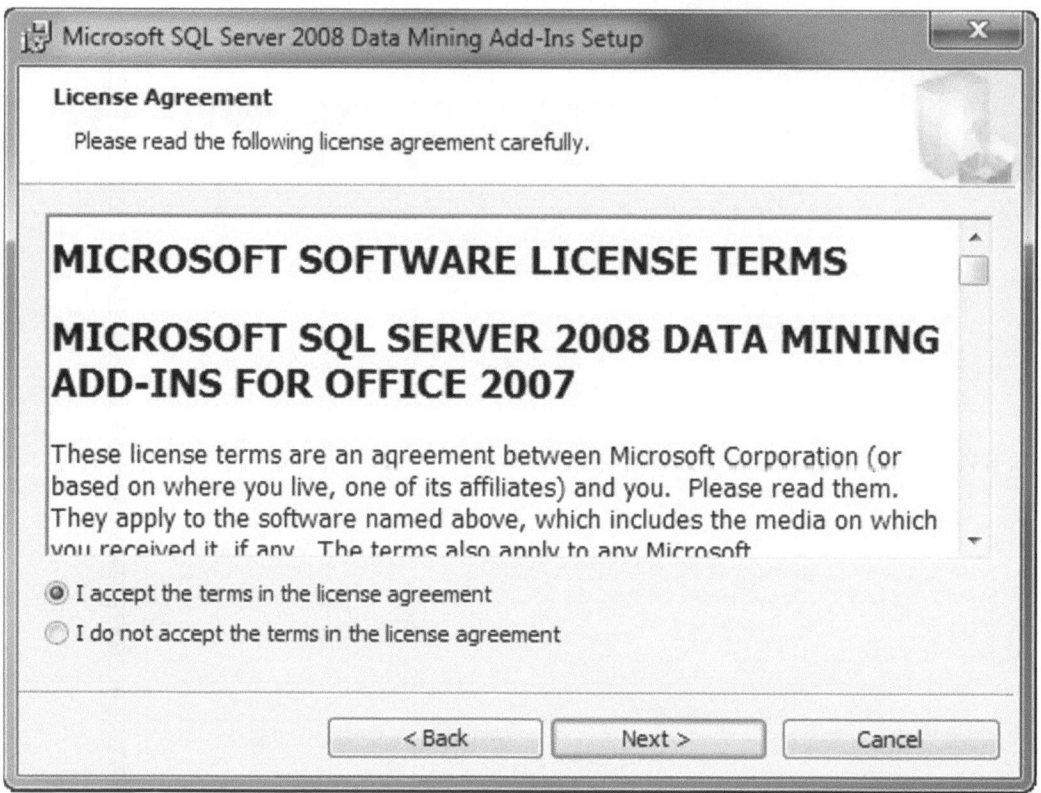

Figure 10-3. *Data Mining Add-In license acceptance*

Confirm that the radio button indicating acceptance of the license terms is selected, as illustrated in
Figure 10-3. Click the Next button to proceed to the Registration Information form, illustrated in Figure
10-4.

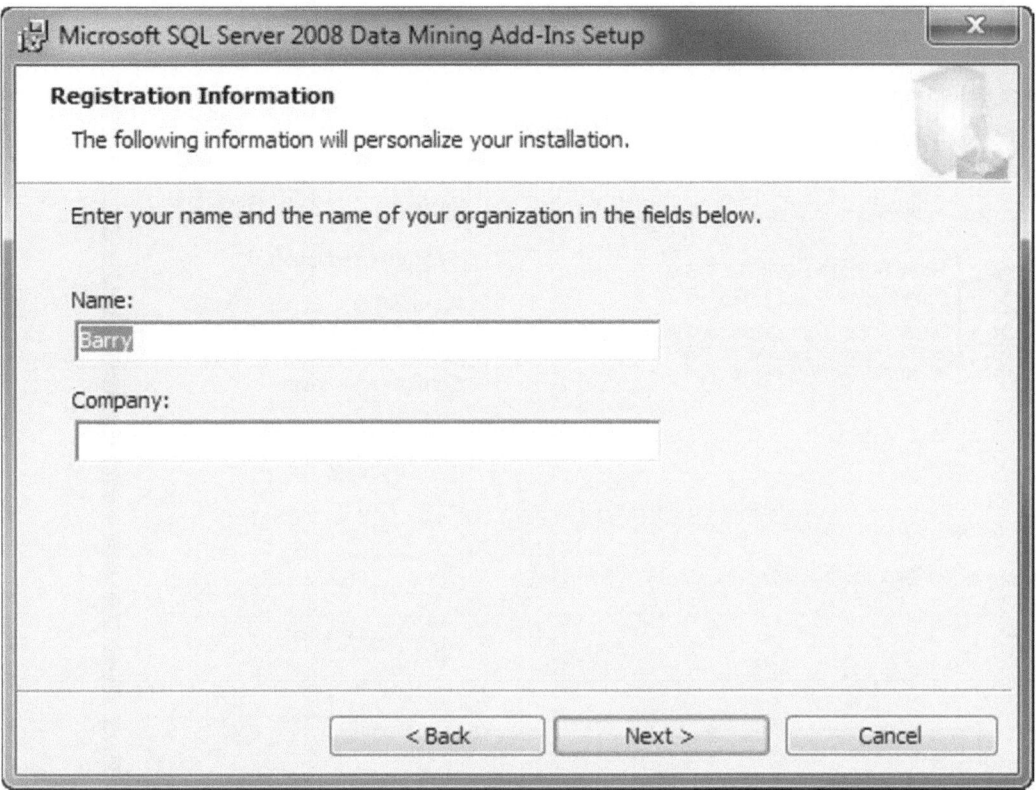

Figure 10-4. *Registration Information form*

Complete the form with your contact name and company, and press the Next button to continue the installation with the Feature Selection dialog, illustrated in Figure 10-5.

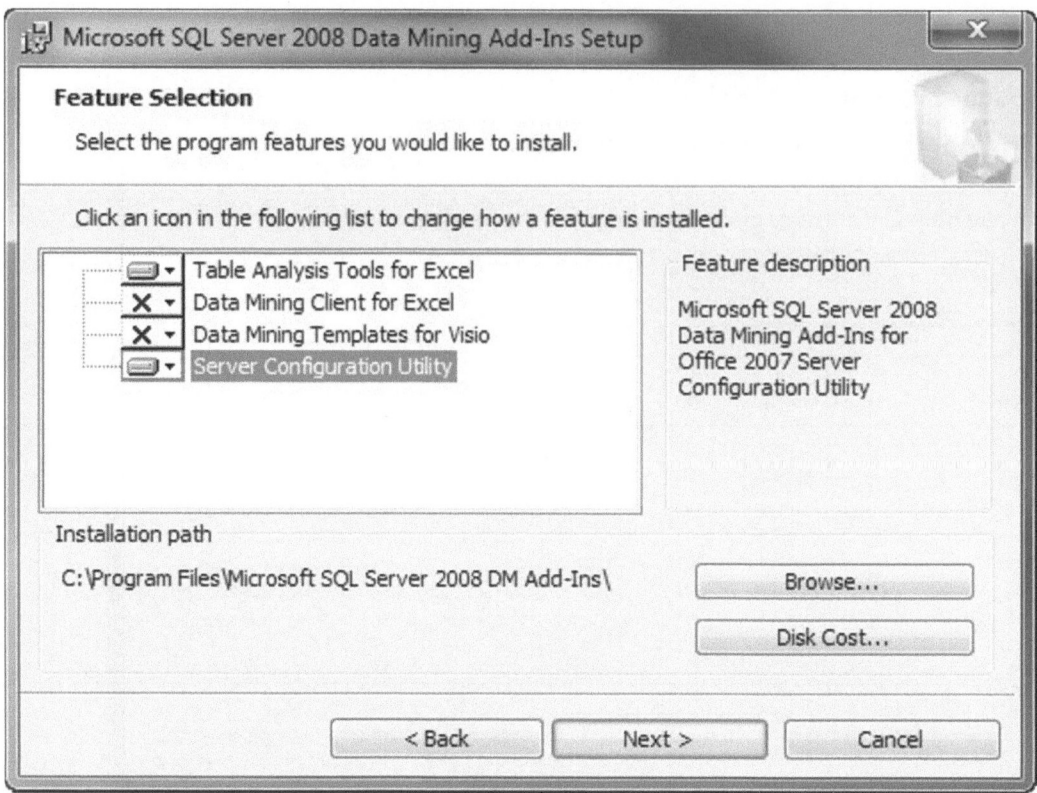

Figure 10-5. *Feature Selection dialog*

For this example, you will require only Table Analysis Tools for Excel and the Server Configuration Utility. You may optionally install the other features. Select a suitable location on your local machine, and press the Next button to advance to the final pre-installation review, illustrated in Figure 10-6.

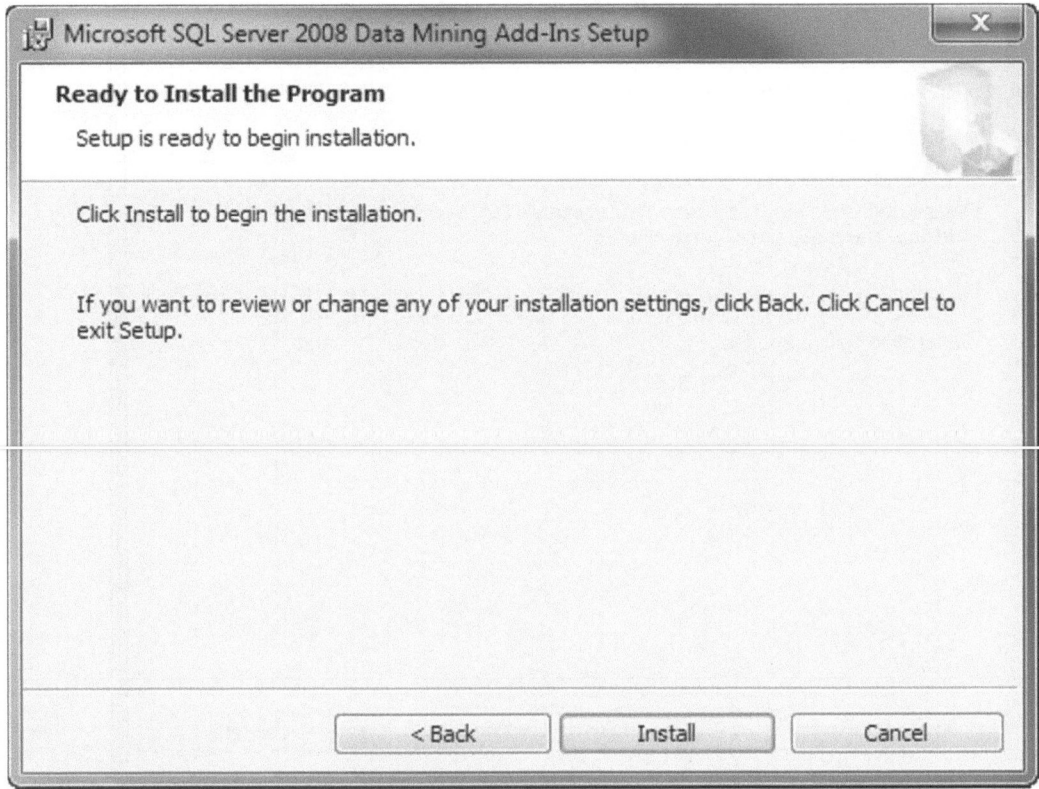

Figure 10-6. *Final pre-installation review*

The installation review dialog is the final checkpoint before the selected features are installed. If you are uncertain of any entries made in the preceding screens, use the Back button to verify your work. Otherwise, click the Install button to advance the installation process to the final step, putting the selected features on your local machine, illustrated in Figure 10-7.

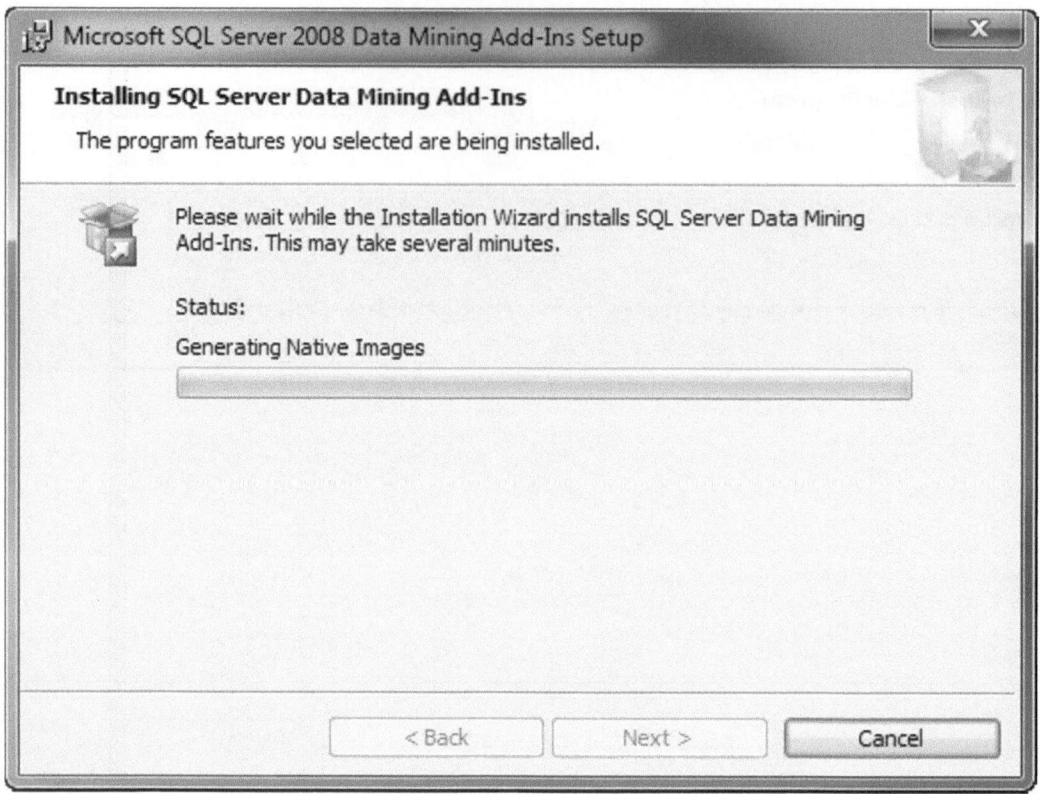

Figure 10-7. *Installation progress dialog*

The installation progress bar will advance from left to right, as the selected software components are installed. At the conclusion of the installation, the Next button will be made active. Click the Next button to advance to the final dialog of the Data Mining Add-In installation, illustrated in Figure 10-8.

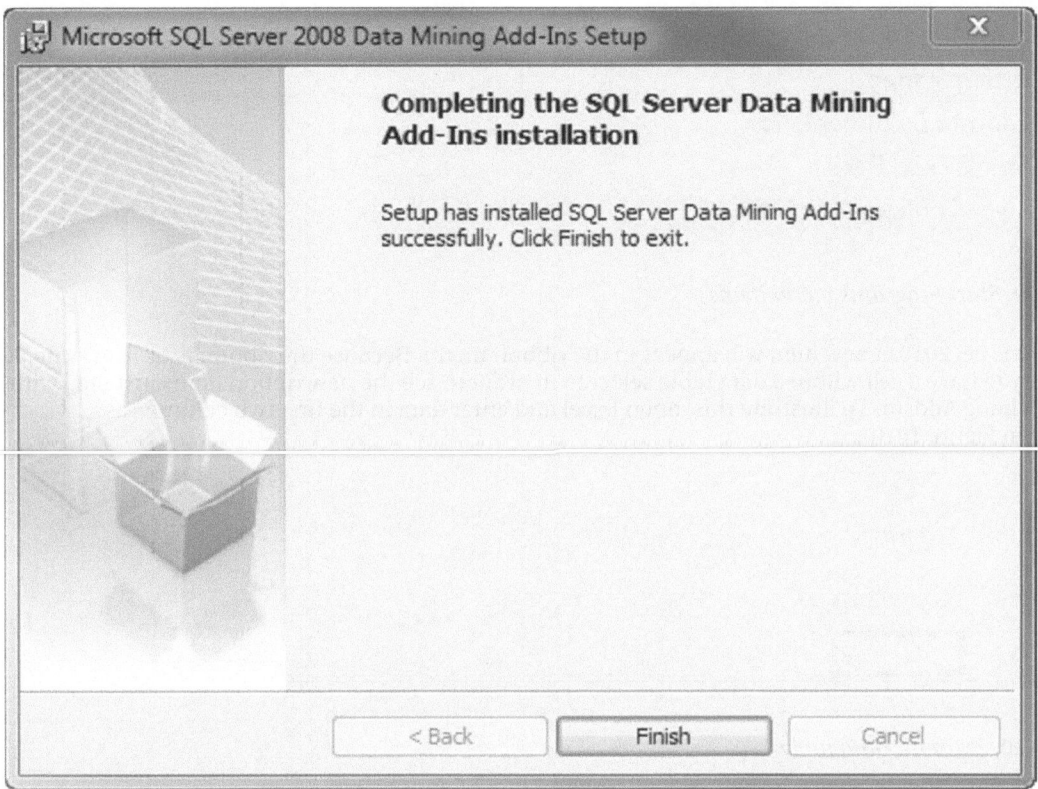

Figure 10-8. *Successful installation*

Click the Finish button within the final installation dialog to complete the installation.

Locating the Table Analysis Tools

Your main indication of the installation will be a new set of items within the Windows Start Programs menu. The new elements will appear in a group titled Microsoft SQL 2008 Data Mining Add-In. The new menu items should be similar to those illustrated in Figure 10-9.

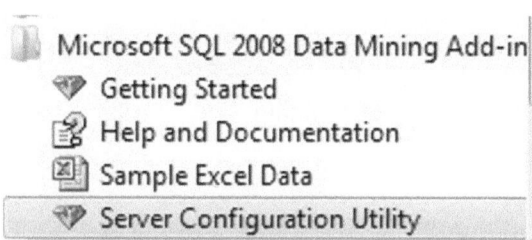

Figure 10-9. *Start Programs menu items*

Within Excel 2010, a new item will appear in the ribbon menu. Because the ribbon is task-specific, it is necessary to have a cell within a data table selected in order to see the new ribbon items installed with the Data Mining Add-In. To illustrate this, open Excel and enter data in the first two columns as illustrated in Figure 10-10.

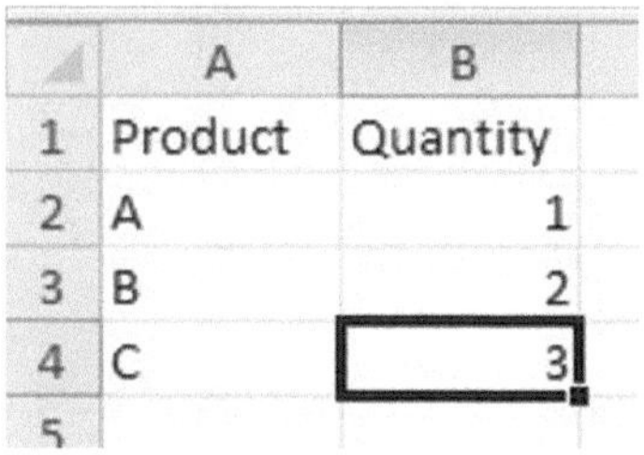

	A	B
1	Product	Quantity
2	A	1
3	B	2
4	C	3
5		

Figure 10-10. *Example data table*

Select any cell within the range of A1 to B4—that is, the column headings for Product and Quantity or any of the data rows. From the ribbon menu, select the Format As Table selection within the Styles group, as illustrated in Figure 10-11.

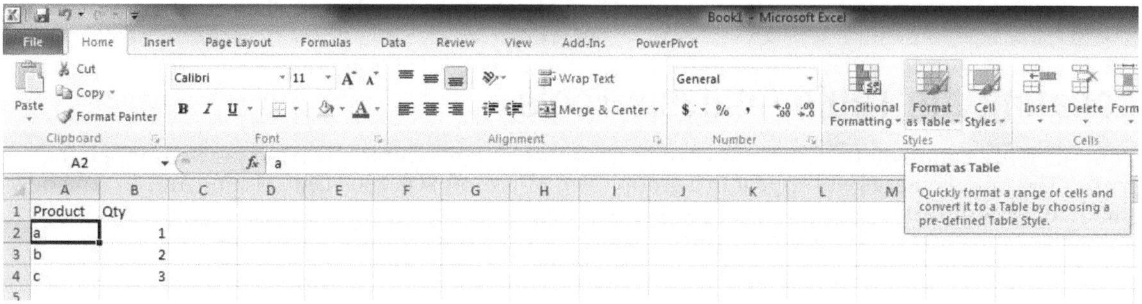

Figure 10-11. *Format As Table selection*

Select any graphical style in the list of table formats. Next, Microsoft Excel will calculate the table as the area of contiguous, non-empty cells, correctly guessing the range A1 to B4. Accept this area in the ensuing dialog, and check the box labeled "My table has headers," as illustrated in Figure 10-12.

Figure 10-12. *Format As Table range*

Clicking the OK button will format the trivial dataset as an Excel data table. The important reason for this is what we will then see in the ribbon. Keeping the Microsoft Excel cursor within the new table, the context-sensitive ribbon will reveal the items installed by the Data Mining Add-In. Illustrated in Figure 10-13 is the new Table Tools ribbon, containing Analyze and Design menus.

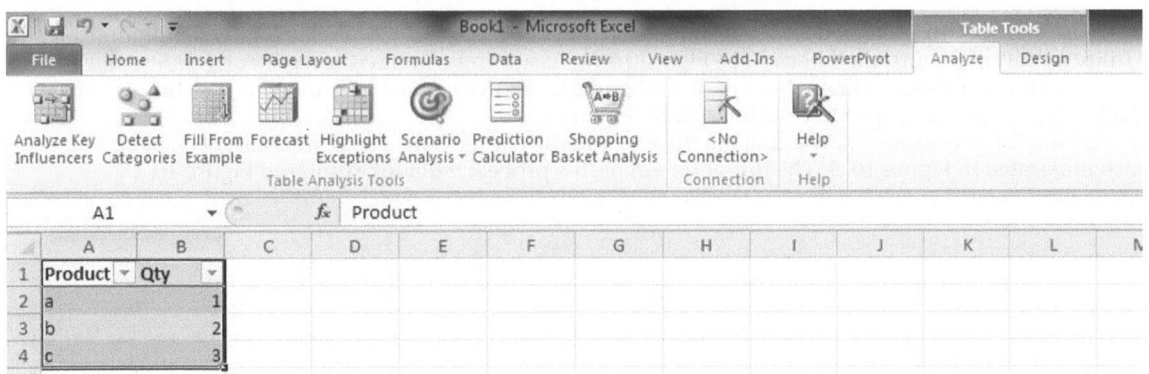

Figure 10-13. *Table Tools ribbon*

As you can see in Figure 10-13, the Analyze menu contains items for task-oriented data mining operations, within a group labeled Table Analysis Tools. While we have accomplished the installation of the Data Mining Add-In, we need to connect Excel to SSAS before we can create a data mining model.

Creating a SSAS Connection

Connecting the Data Mining Add-In to an SSAS instance involves two tasks. First, the SSAS server must be configured to work with the Data Mining Add-In. The second required task is adding the configured SSAS server connection within the Data Mining Add-In. In between those two tasks are some things that you can do to avoid common frustrations in making the connection to SSAS.

Configuring the SSAS Server

Within the Connection group of the Analyze menu, notice the No Connection label illustrated in Figure 10-14. This is an indication we have no SSAS server available to execute data mining operations. Therefore, our next step is configuring the connection between Microsoft Excel and SSAS.

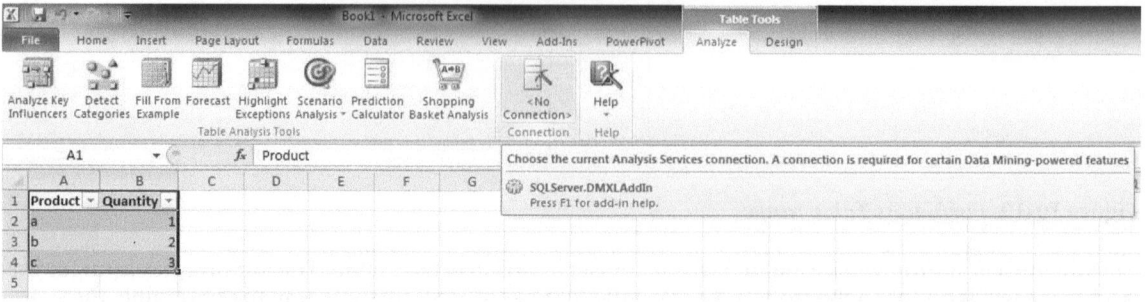

Figure 10-14. *Data Mining Add-In connection*

The installation process described earlier had you choose a feature labeled Server Configuration Utility as part of the installed items (see Figure 10-5). Assuming you have access to an SSAS server within your development environment, you may configure the SSAS instance to work with the Data Mining Add-In by following the process outlined in this section.

From the Windows, All Programs menu, execute the Server Configuration Utility. The program is also illustrated in Figure 10-9. The initial screen of this process will look similar to Figure 10-15.

Figure 10-15. *Data Mining Add-In Configuration Wizard*

Click the Next button to advance the wizard to the SSAS server selection, illustrated in Figure 10-16.

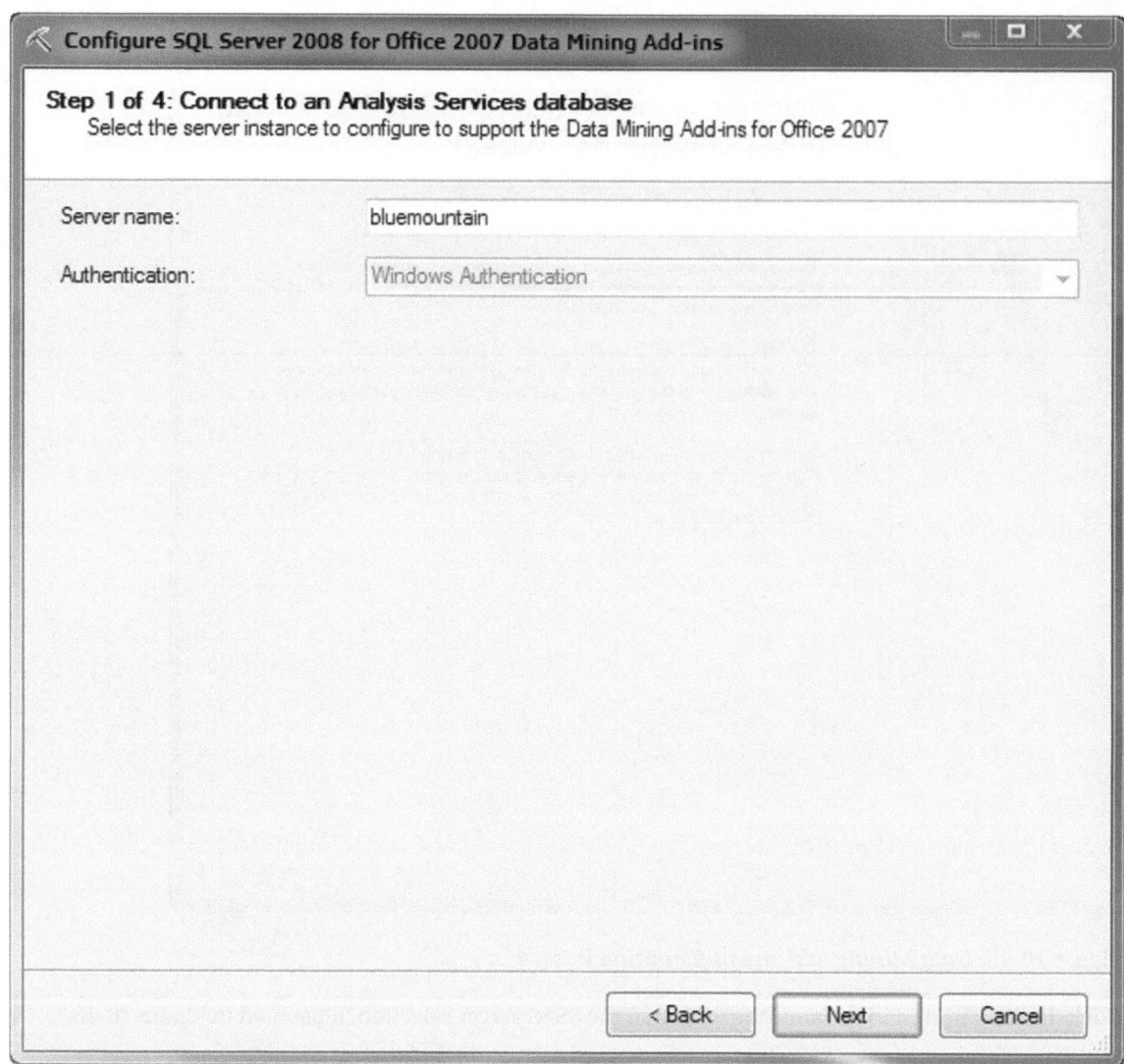

Figure 10-16. *SSAS server selection*

Because SSAS supports only Windows authentication, there is no mixed-mode authentication as it exists within the SQL Server relational database. Instead, the Authentication selection is already made for you.

Select an SSAS server to be configured to perform data mining operations for the Data Mining Add-In. If you have installed an instance of SSAS locally, then "localhost" is an acceptable value for this configuration item. If you wish to use a named instance, enter the name in the form of server\instance. Clicking the Next button will advance the wizard to the temporary mining model configuration settings, illustrated in Figure 10-17.

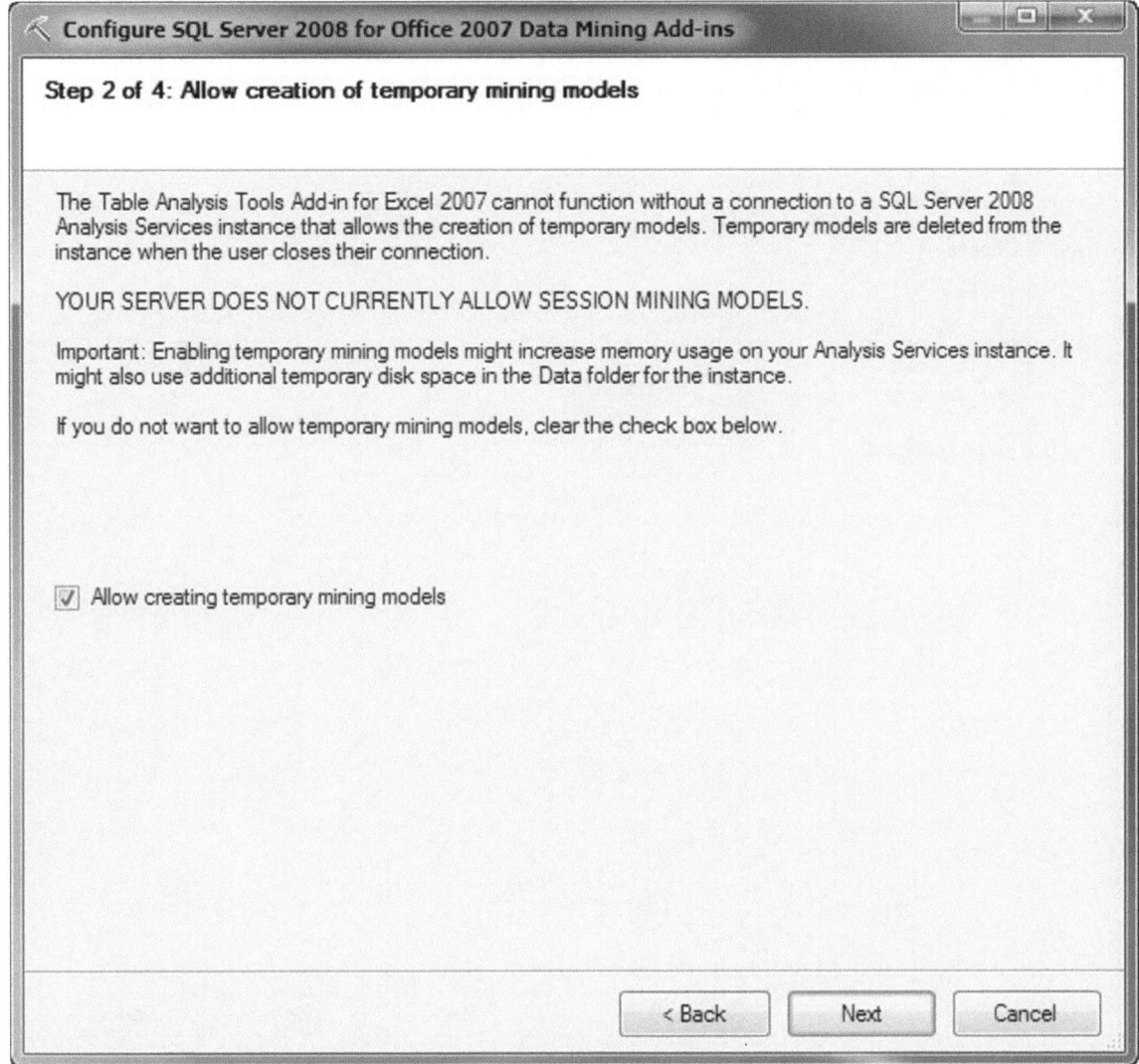

Figure 10-17. *Configuring session mining models*

In order to use the selected server with the Data Mining Add-In, verify that the check box labeled "Allow creating temporary mining models" is checked, as illustrated in Figure 10-17. Click the Next button to advance the configuration to the next step, database creation, illustrated in Figure 10-18.

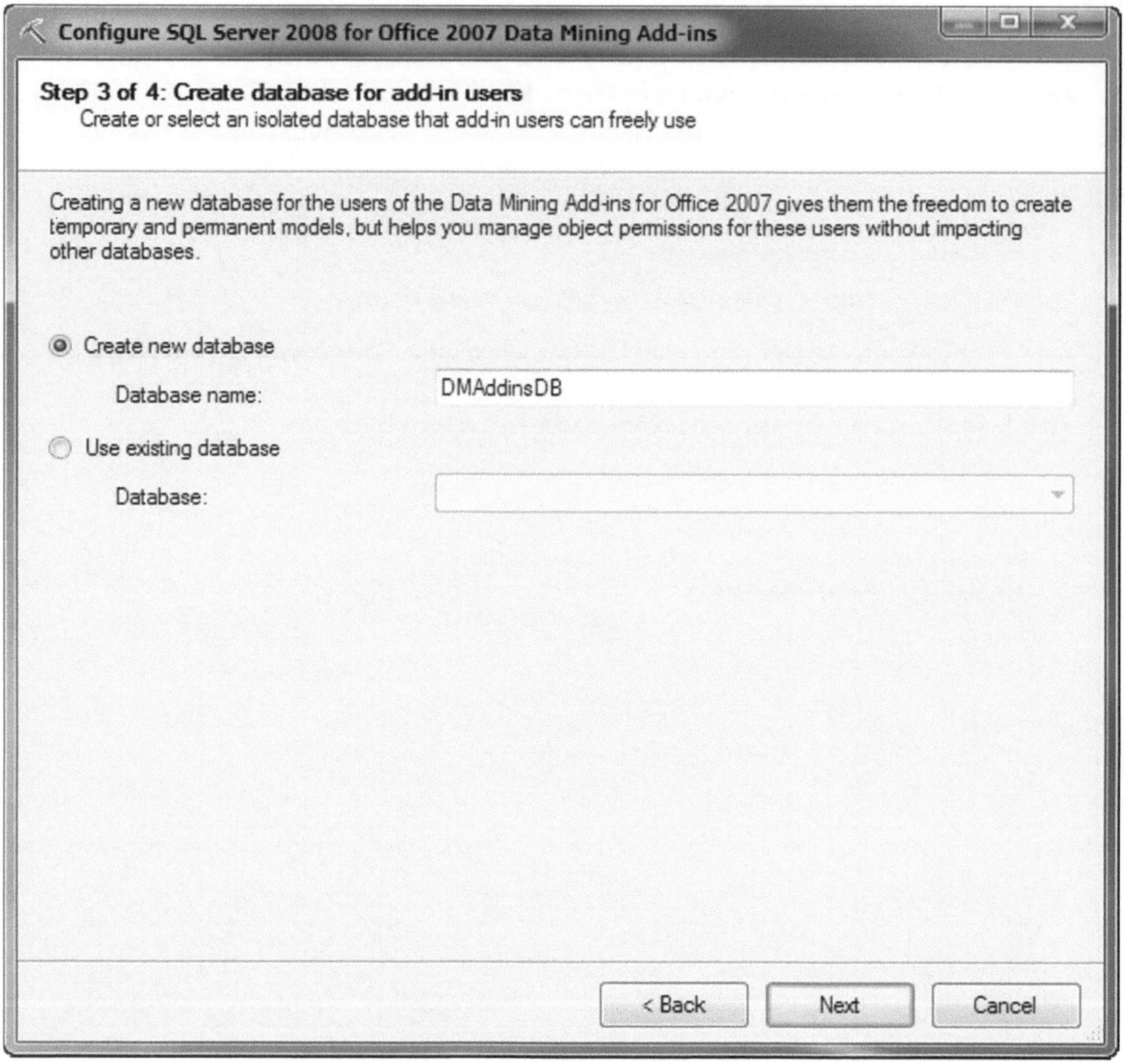

Figure 10-18. *Create database for add-in users*

The "Create database" dialog allows you to create a new database exclusively for data mining operations using Excel or to configure an existing database for use with the Data Mining Add-Ins. For our purposes, select the default database, DMAddInsDB. Your doing so will create a new SSAS database on the selected server, ensuring no conflicts with other SSAS database operations. Click the Next button to proceed to granting database administrator permissions, as illustrated in Figure 10-19.

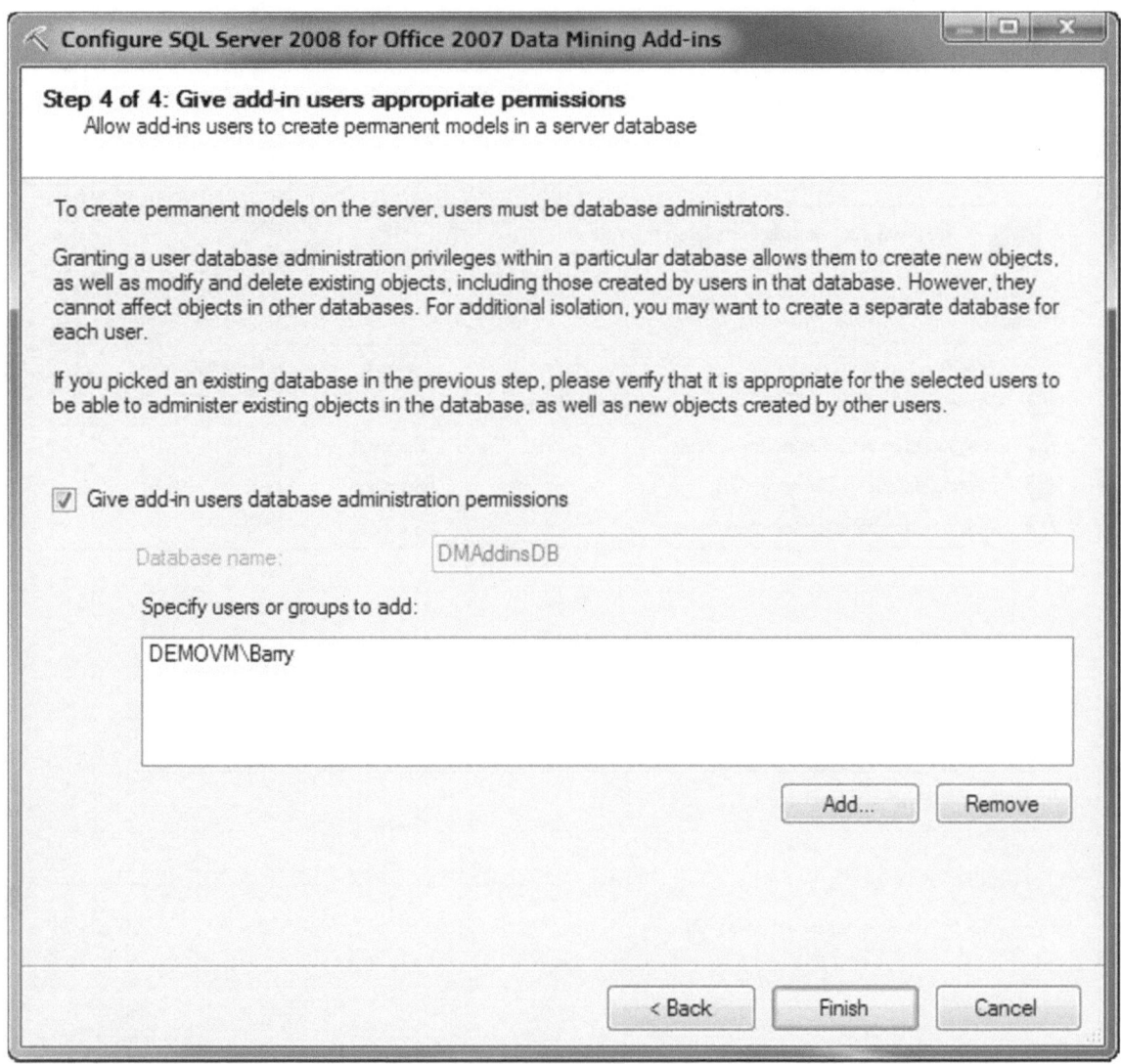

Figure 10-19. *Granting database administrator access*

For our example purposes, using the wizard defaults will be sufficient. Your own dialog should look similar, with the Windows username you are currently using pre-selected. Clicking the Finish button will advance the wizard to the final step, the Configuration Wizard status report, illustrated in Figure 10-20. Clicking the Close button will exit the Server Configuration Utility.

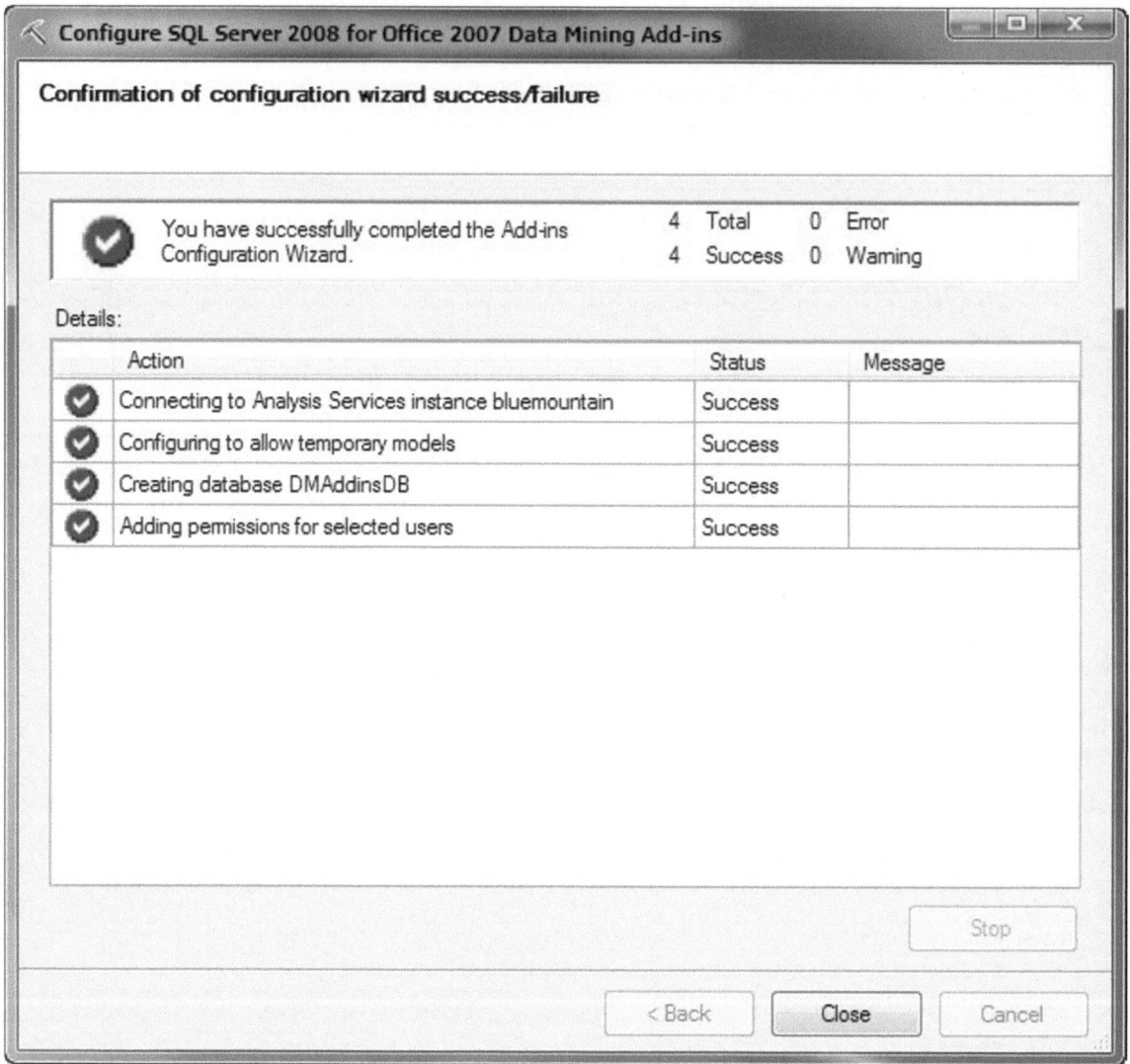

Figure 10-20. *Configuration Wizard status report*

Avoiding Connection Frustration

You may be tempted to utilize the Excel ribbon Connections item to define an SSAS connection via the dialog pictured in Figure 10-21. Unless the steps under Configuring the SSAS Server have been completed, defining a connection in this manner will fail in most cases. Follow the process I've outlined, and you'll save yourself some frustration.

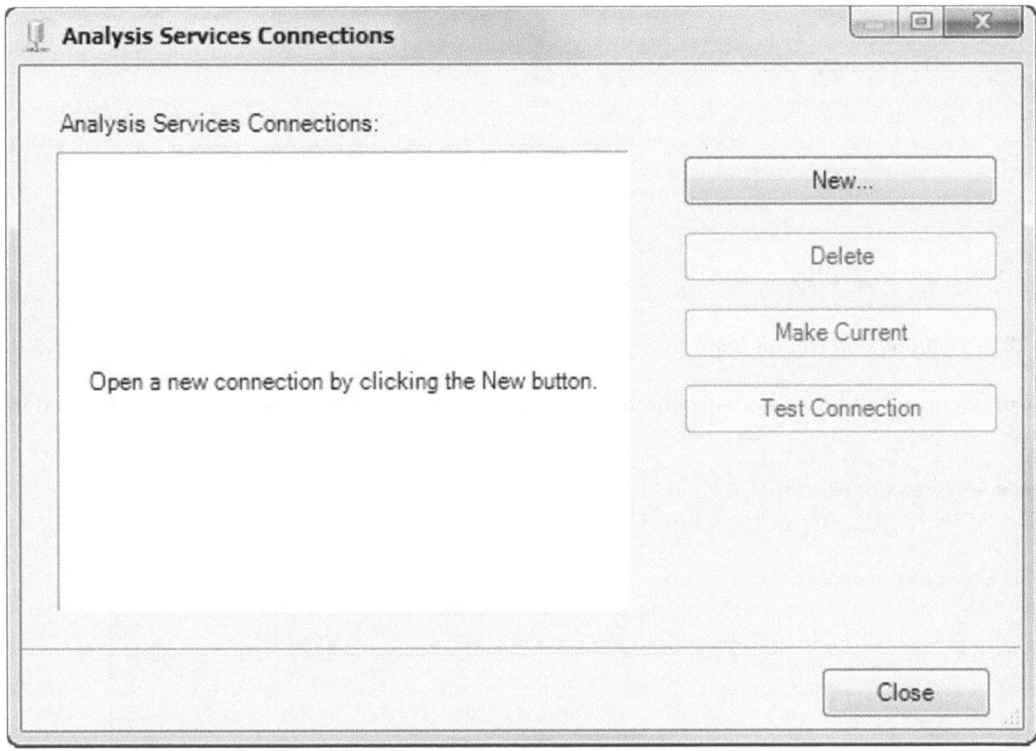

Figure 10-21. *Analysis Services Connections dialog*

Adding the SSAS Connection Within the Data Mining Add-In

The final task in establishing an SSAS connection is to add the connection within the Data Mining Add-In.

From within Excel, open the On Time Performance.xlsx file from the book's examples download file. From within a data table as created in the section "Locating the Table Analysis Tools," select the <No Connection> item from the ribbon, as illustrated in Figure 10-22.

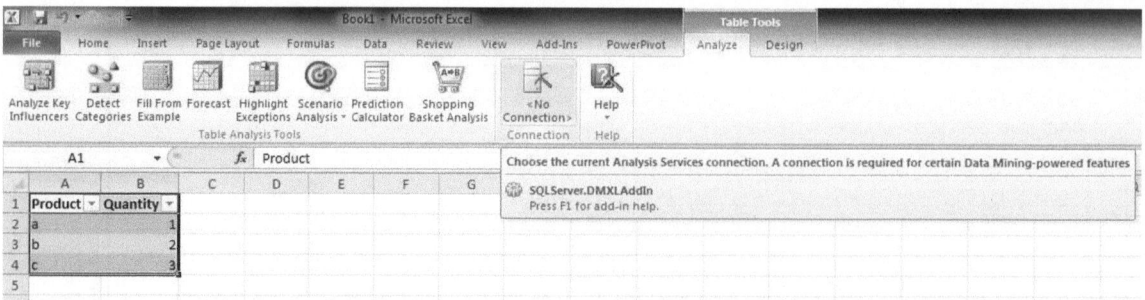

Figure 10-22. *No Connection ribbon item*

The "<No Connection>" ribbon item will generate the Analysis Services Connections dialog illustrated in Figure 10-23.

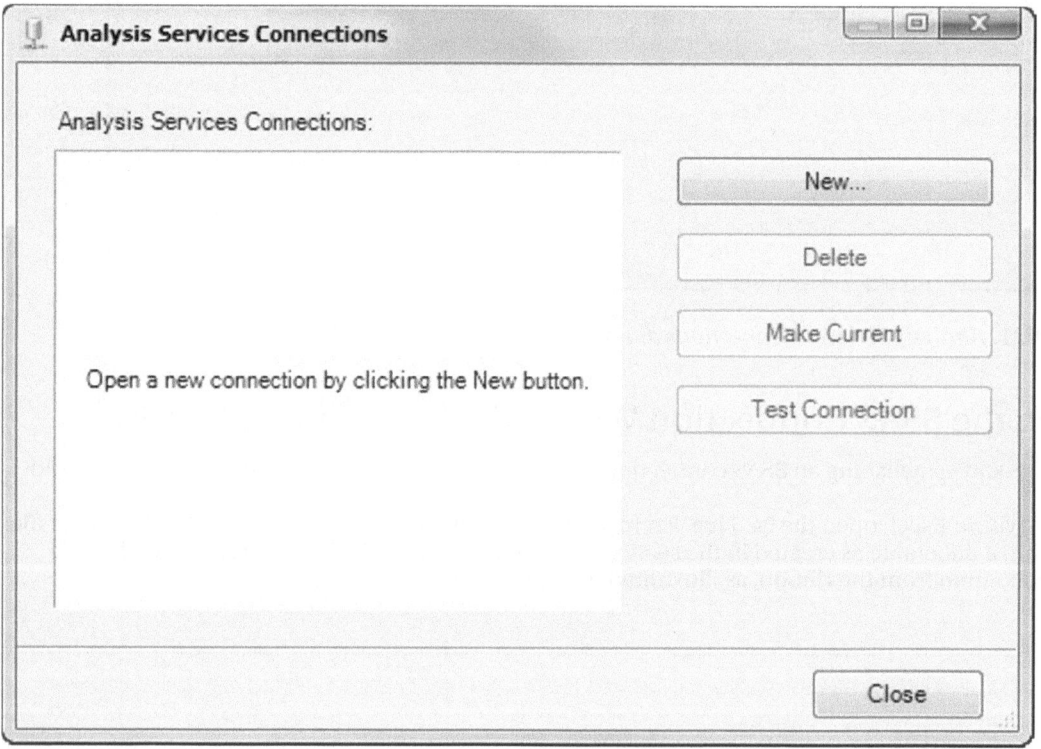

Figure 10-23. *Analysis Services Connections dialog*

Click the New button in order to define a connection for the SSAS server configured in the section of this chapter called "Configuring the SSAS Server." The configuration dialog, illustrated in Figure 10-24, will be presented.

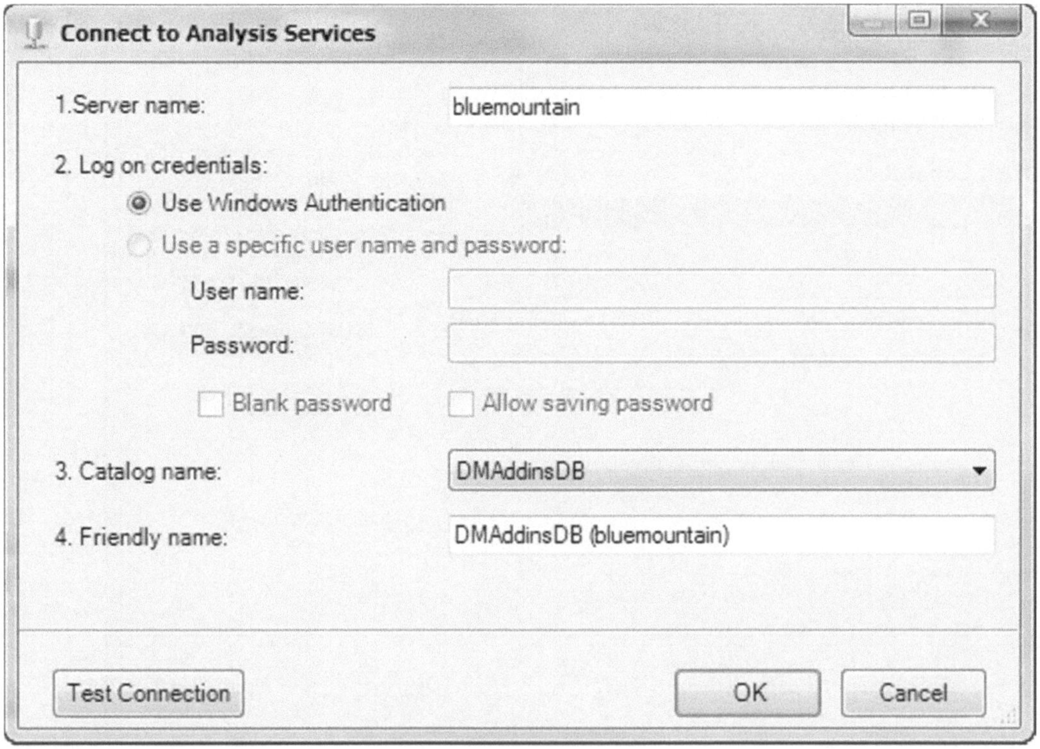

Figure 10-24. *Connect to Analysis Services dialog*

The "Server name" text box should contain the same name as the SSAS server established in the "Configuring the SSAS Server" section. In my specific case, this is the default instance on the server named Bluemountain. Logon credentials will be preset to "Use Windows Authentication". The catalog name should be set to the database created specifically for the Data Mining Add-In, DMAddInsDB. The friendly name will be calculated by the Data Mining Add-In in the form "database name + (servername)". While this can be edited to any name you would like to appear within the Data Mining Add-In connection manager, the default is sufficient for our example. Click the Test Connection button to verify the settings will establish communications with the SSAS instance. Upon a successful test, click the OK button to save the new connection. The new connection should now appear in the Analysis Services Connections dialog, as illustrated in Figure 10-25.

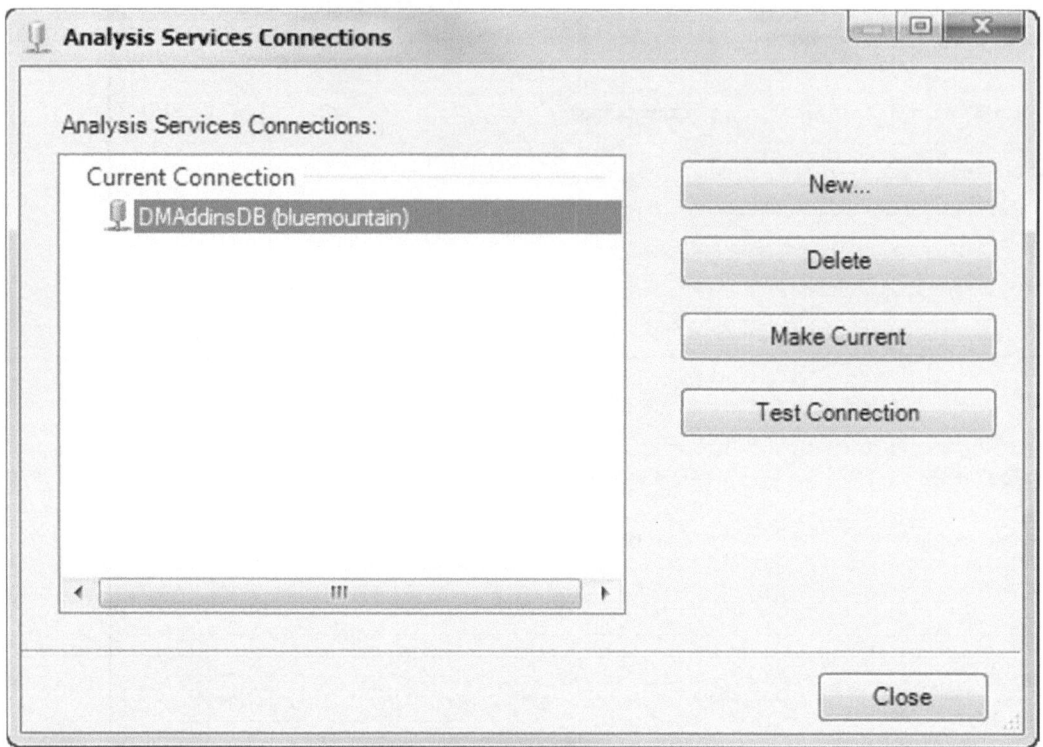

Figure 10-25. *Analysis Services Connections dialog*

Select the new connection, as illustrated in Figure 10-25, and click the Make Current button. This will establish the new SSAS server as the provider of data mining model services for the Data Mining Add-In. Click the Close button to see that the <No Connection> item in the ribbon has been replaced with the name of the new connection, as illustrated in Figure 10-26.

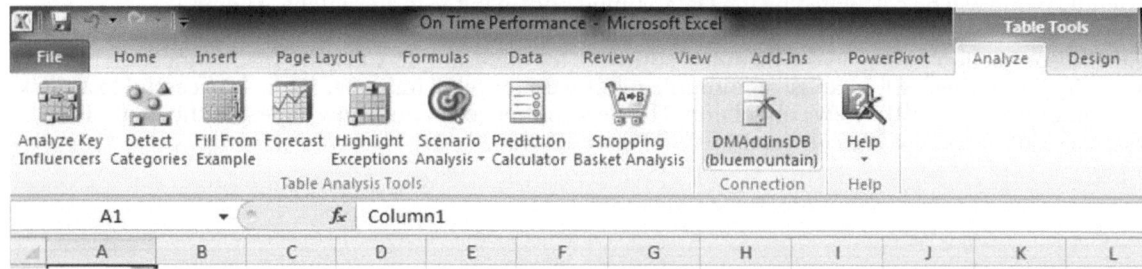

Figure 10-26. *Connection established*

Preparing Data with PowerPivot

With the Data Mining Add-In installed, and the SSAS server configured and connected to Excel, the next task is to prepare your data for data mining. PowerPivot for Excel is well suited for the assembly of the data.

Within the On Time Performance.xlsx file already used in the section titled "Adding the SSAS Connection Within the Data Mining Add-In," create a new flattened PivotTable from the PowerPivot ribbon menu. Use a new worksheet as the destination for the flattened PivotTable. Use Month, DayofWeek, Carrier, Origin, Dest, and DistanceGroup as row labels. Drag WeatherDelay to the Values area of the PowerPivot Field List. When finished, your PivotTable should resemble Figure 10-27.

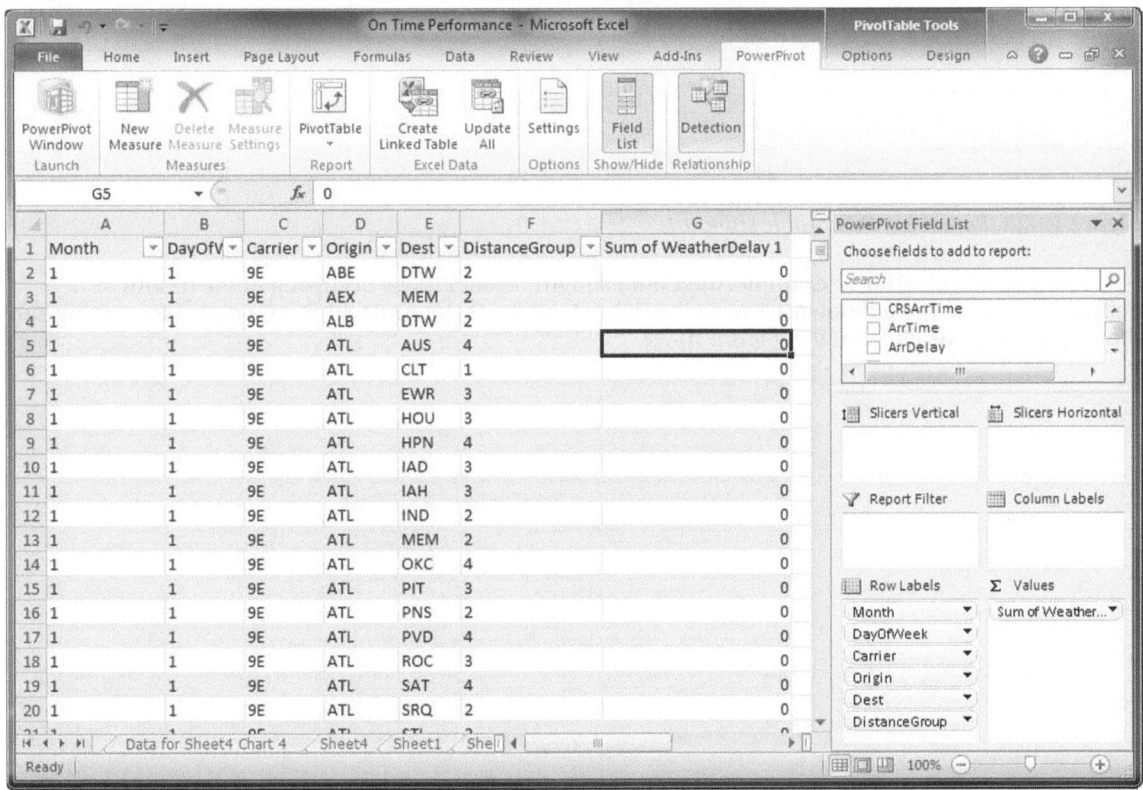

Figure 10-27. *Flattened PivotTable*

The reason for the flattened version of a PivotTable is the Data Mining Add-In's inability to consume data from a PivotTable. Because the add-in was created for use in Excel 2007, it understands only data tables. We can effectively work around this limitation by converting our flattened PivotTable into an ordinary Excel data table.

The first step in converting the PivotTable to an ordinary Excel data table is to remove any sub-totaling that may have been introduced by PowerPivot. From the PivotTable Tools ribbon, select Design and then Subtotals. From the Subtotals pulldown, select Do Not Show Subtotals, as illustrated in Figure 10-28.

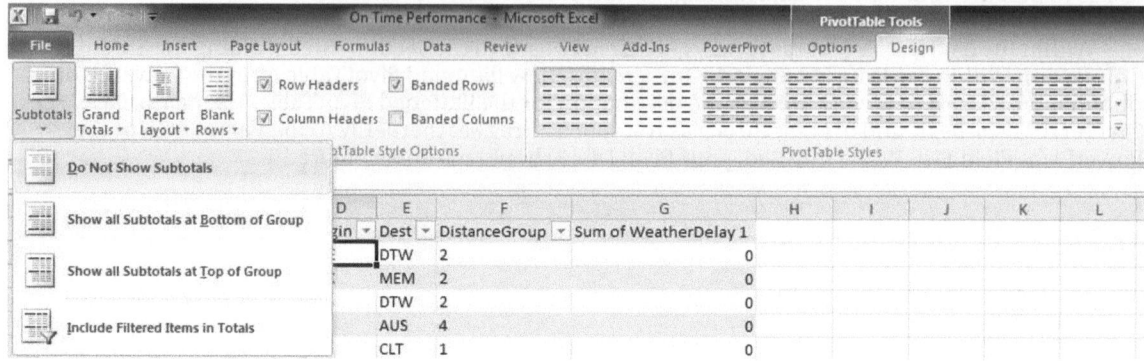

Figure 10-28. *Removing PivotTable subtotals*

To ensure an illustrative example, filter out all flights except those occurring in the month of February. Clicking the pulldown arrow to the right of the Month column will show a dialog for sorting and filtering the data, as illustrated in Figure 10-29.

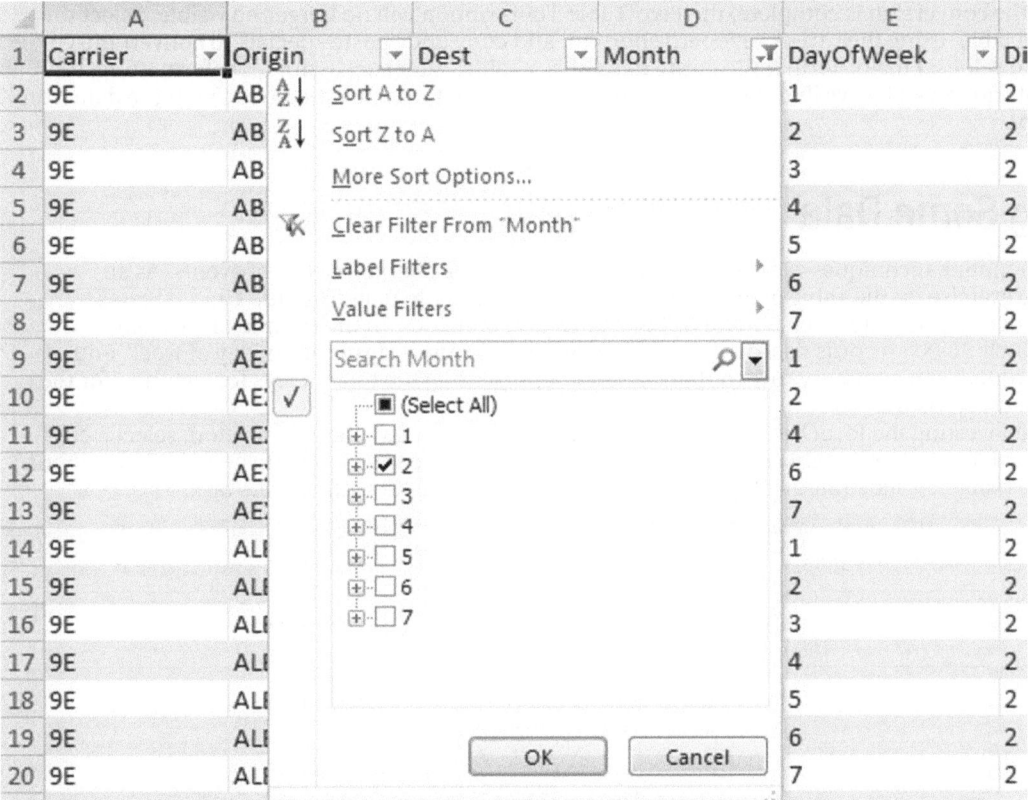

Figure 10-29. *Filtering the month*

After removing the sub-totaling rows, we need to convert the flattened PivotTable into a data table usable by the Data Mining Add-In. Begin the conversion by selecting any cell within the flattened PivotTable. Then select the OLAP Tools from the Options sub-menu of the PivotTable Tools ribbon, as illustrated in Figure 10-30. Finally, from the OLAP Tools pulldown, select the Convert to Formulas option.

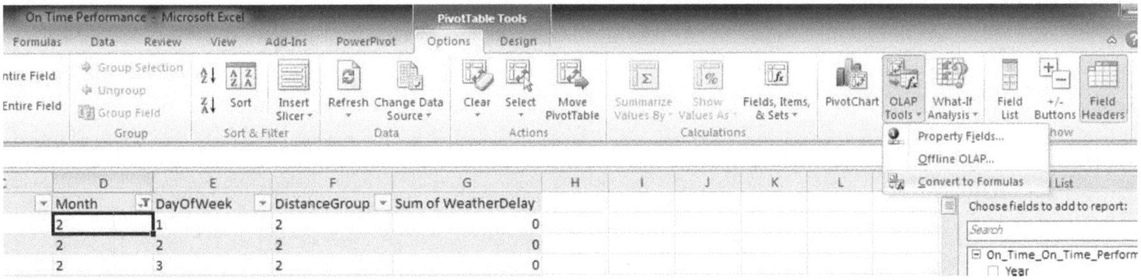

Figure 10-30. *Convert to Formulas selection*

After the conversion is complete, the PivotTable Tools ribbon will no longer be visible. Select the entire data table, using the Ctrl+A keyboard shortcut, and copy and "paste special" to convert the OLAP formulas to values. Finally, format the entire dataset as a table. After successful table formatting, the Table Tools ribbon will be visible. Now we can then begin to make some predictions with the data from PowerPivot.

Mining Some Data

Often data mining techniques are used to better understand the characteristics of events. As an illustrative exercise on the value of data mining, we are going to use data from the United States Department of Transportation's Bureau of Transportation Statistics. In the sample file, we have approximately 30,000 records summarizing flights by carrier, origin, destination, day of week, and distance group. Each summary row contains a value representing the total delays for weather, for the group of characteristics.

After converting the PivotTable to an Excel table as detailed in the previous section, select a cell within the table. Selecting a table cell is necessary in order for the context-sensitive Table Tools ribbon to become visible. As illustrated in Figure 10-31, select the Analyze Key Influencers task.

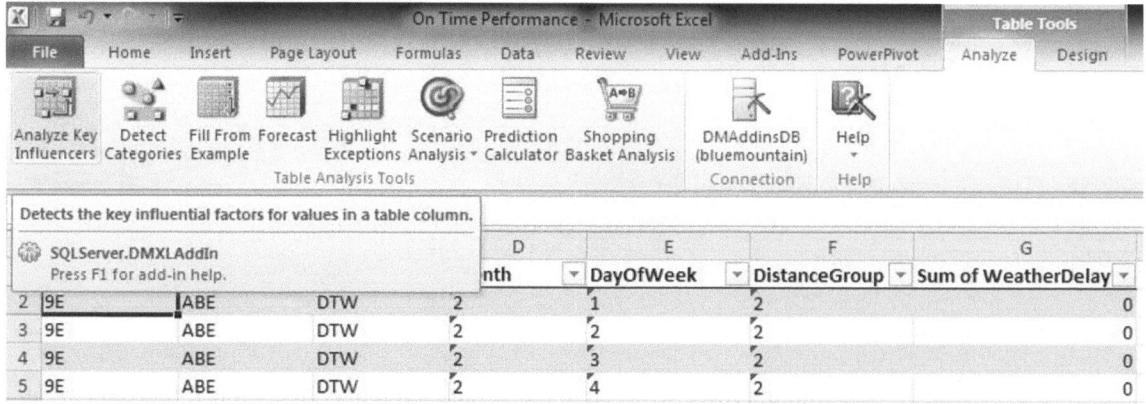

Figure 10-31. *Analyze Key Influencers task*

The Data Mining Add-In will begin the analysis process by prompting for a target column. See Figure 10-32.

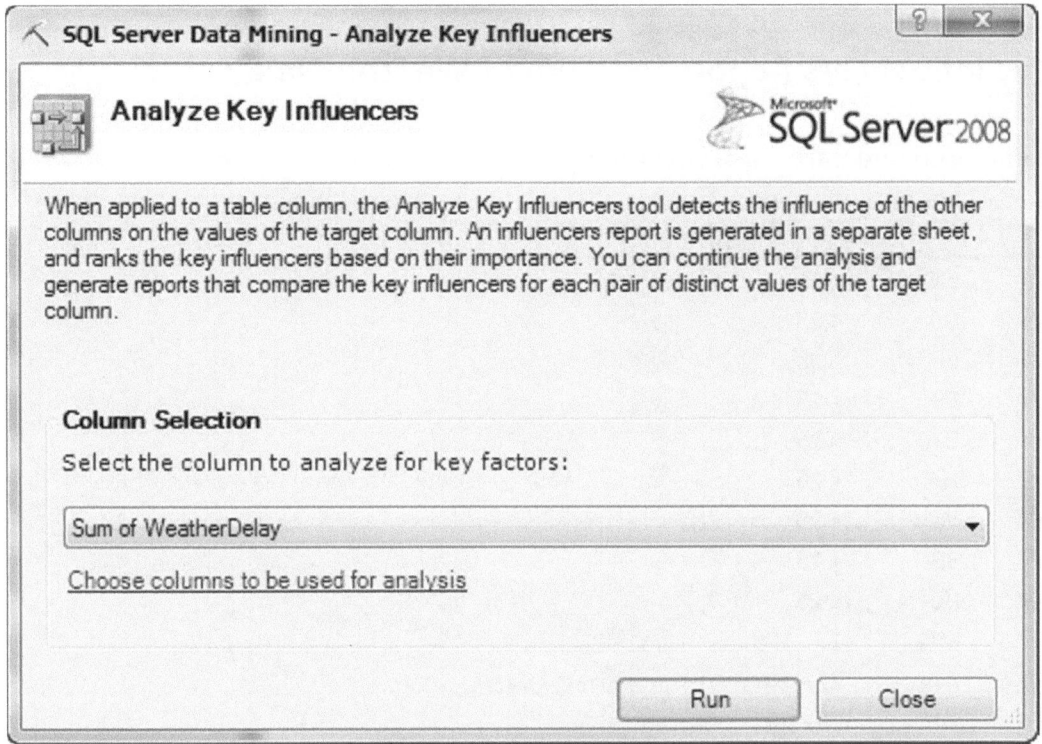

Figure 10-32. *Choosing a target column*

When analyzing key influencers, the target column represents the data values for which key predictors (or influencers) are being sought. Our target is the Sum of WeatherDelay column. We could optionally use the "Choose columns to be used for analysis" option to exclude columns from the remaining, non-target data. However, for this example, we have reduced the existing on-time arrival data to a few discriminating columns of data so that we can use the Carrier through DistanceGroup columns from the Excel table. Clicking the Run button at this point performs the actual data mining model creation, training, and processing. The end result of the process is a Key Influencers report similar to Figure 10-33.

	Column	Value	Favors	Relative Impact
	Key Influencers Report for 'Sum of WeatherDelay'			
	Key Influencers and their impact over the values of 'Sum of WeatherDelay'			
	Filter by 'Column' or 'Favors' to see how various columns influence 'Sum of WeatherDelay'			
5	Column ▼	Value ▼	Favors ▼	Relative Impact ⊽
6	Carrier	OO	< 25	▇▇▇▇▇▇
7	Carrier	US	< 25	▇
8	Carrier	FL	< 25	▇
9	Carrier	F9	< 25	▇
10	Carrier	UA	< 25	▌
11	Carrier	HA	< 25	▌
12	Carrier	WN	< 25	▌
13	Carrier	9E	< 25	▏
14	Carrier	B6	< 25	▏
15	Carrier	MQ	25 - 109	▇▇▇▇
16	Carrier	AA	25 - 109	▇▇▇▇
17	Carrier	OH	25 - 109	▇▇▇▇▇
18	Carrier	CO	25 - 109	▏
19	Carrier	OH	109 - 281	▇▇▇
20	Carrier	MQ	109 - 281	▇
21	Carrier	AA	109 - 281	▌
22	Carrier	DL	109 - 281	▏
23	Carrier	EV	109 - 281	▏
24	Carrier	EV	281 - 654	▇▇▇
25	Carrier	OH	281 - 654	▇▇
26	Carrier	DL	281 - 654	▇
27	Carrier	B6	>= 654	▇▇▇
28	Carrier	AA	>= 654	▏

Figure 10-33. *Key Influencers report*

Because of the small set of data columns and the use of only February data, the Carrier column has been determined as the primary influencer for all groups of Sum of WeatherDelay. The Key Influencers report has grouped statistically similar values of Sum of WeatherDelay into five classifications. Each value set has a color code associated with the bar graph in the Relative Impact column. The Key Influencers report is telling the reader, for example, that carrier code B6 (JetBlue) had a large relative impact on values of Sum of WeatherDelay greater than 654 minutes. In fact, there was a blizzard during February 10–11, 2010 affecting Boston and New York, causing massive weather delays.

Taking Data Mining to the Cloud with Predixion Software

In the previous section, we learned that the SQL Server Data Mining Add-In for Excel, in the simplest terms, is an interface for creating data mining models in SSAS, transporting the data to the SSAS model, and finally viewing the results of the processed model. At least one company, Predixion Software, is taking this architecture to the next logical step. If you can mine data using a server that is on your network, why not use a server or group of servers, anywhere available via the Internet, in a secure manner? Their products, Insight Analytics and Insight Now, are Microsoft Excel add-ins to deliver data mining as a service.

The benefits of the Predixion products include the ability to consume PowerPivot data directly. There is no need to define a PivotTable only to convert it for consumption by the Data Mining Add-In. This approach means larger data volumes can be used, because PivotTable to OLAP formula conversion time is avoided completely. Finally, Predixion has already created a 64-bit version of their tools. There is no need to install 32-bit Excel in order to use the Data Mining Add-In.

The best way to contrast data mining with Predixion and the Data Mining Add-In for Excel is to tackle the identical example, using the Predixion data mining as a service.

Setting Up the Predixion Add-In

In order to be a fair comparison, the steps to set up the Predixion software will be covered in this section. To begin, you will first need to create an account with Predixion Software at www.predixionsoftware.com. This example utilized the free service evaluation account.

After registering, follow the link to download Predixion Insight, available in the Predixion Products area, as illustrated in Figure 10-34.

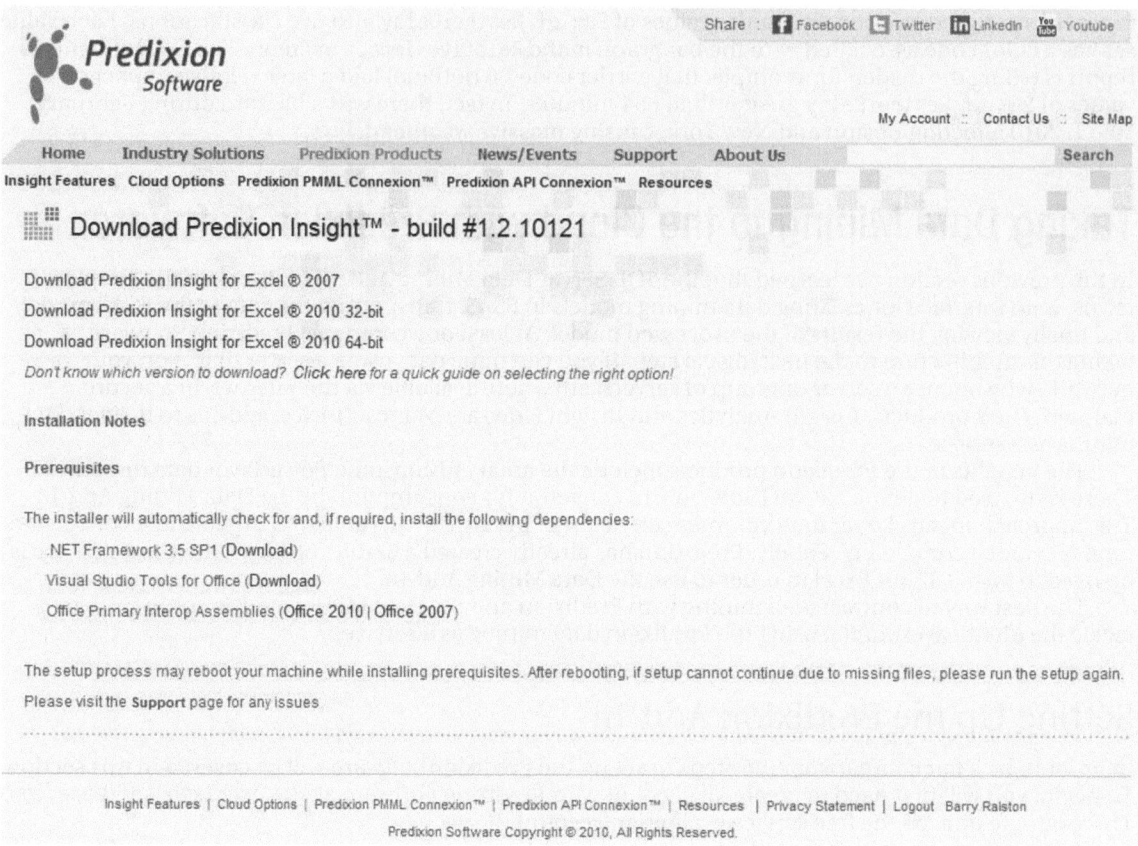

Figure 10-34. *Download page for Predixion Insight*

Notice another benefit of Predixion Insight from the download page. A download is available for Excel 2007. Just like PowerPivot for Excel, Predixion Insight has separate installers for the 32-bit and 64-bit versions of Microsoft Excel. As we are using the 64-bit version of Excel, the illustrations here are for the corresponding 64-bit version of Predixion Insight.

Executing the installer from within Internet Explorer, you may observe the security warning illustrated in Figure 10-35. Click the Run button to continue installation.

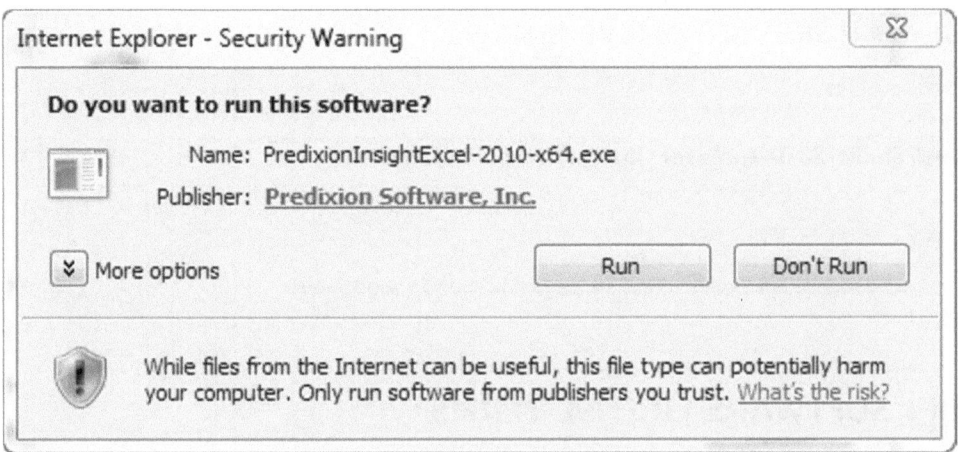

Figure 10-35. *Internet Explorer Security Warning dialog*

The Predixion Insight installer will proceed to elegantly check for and, if necessary, install required software components. Your specific installation path may vary, based on existing software installations. The next step in the installation is the verification and installation of the Visual Studio Tools for Office Runtime. Acknowledgment and agreement to the license terms will be required, as illustrated in Figure 10-36.

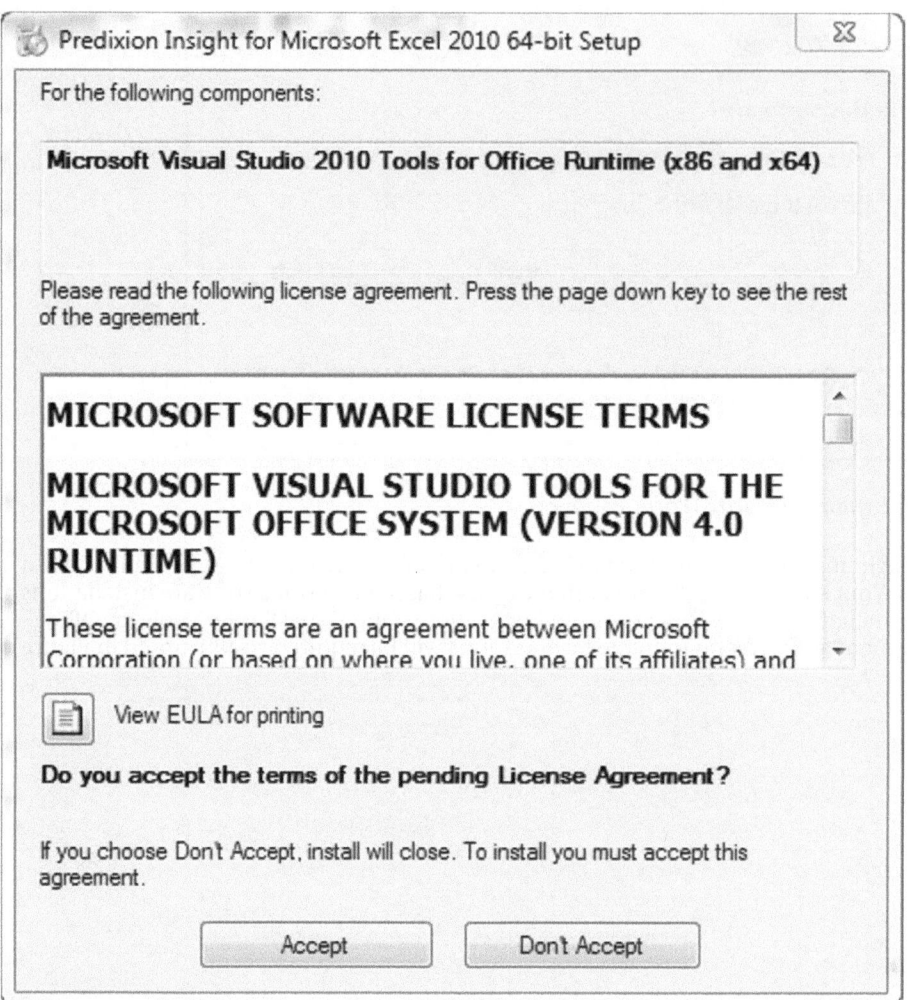

Figure 10-36. *Visual Studio Tools for Office Runtime license*

Clicking the Accept button will advance the installer to the next step, the Setup Wizard, as illustrated in Figure 10-37.

Figure 10-37. *Predixion Insight Setup Wizard dialog*

Clicking the Next button will continue the installation process. The next step is reading and accepting the Predixion Software license agreement, as illustrated in Figure 10-38.

Figure 10-38. *Predixion Insight subscription and license*

Verify that the I Agree radio button is selected, and click the Next button. This will continue the process at the installation location dialog, illustrated in Figure 10-39.

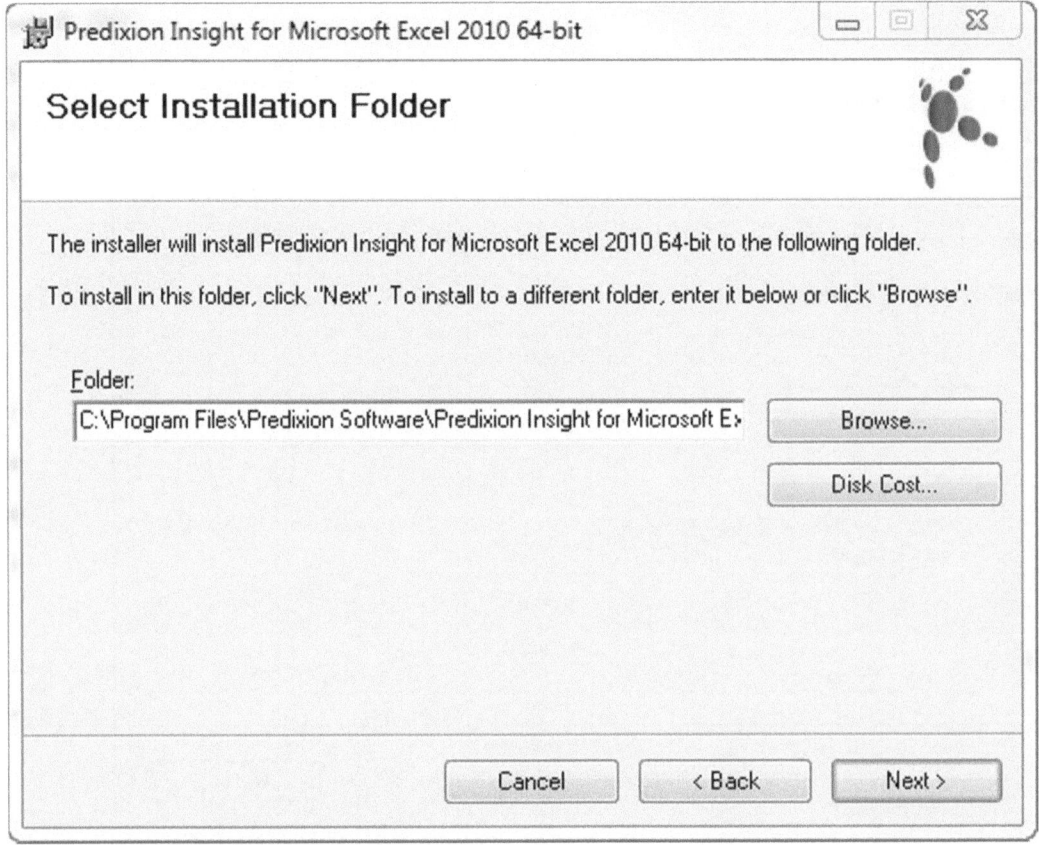

Figure 10-39. *Installation location*

Select a suitable location on your local machine for the installer to copy the Predixion Insight software. When you have selected the folder, click the Next button to continue to the next step, the installation confirmation illustrated in Figure 10-40.

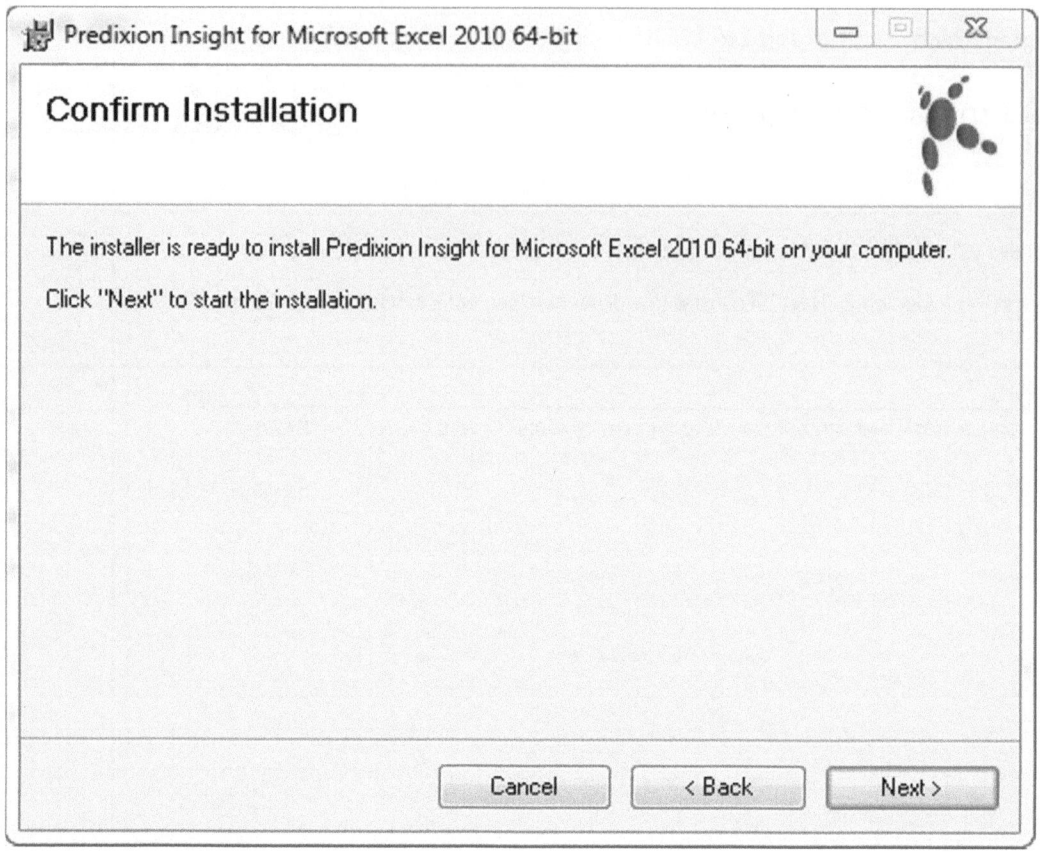

Figure 10-40. *Confirm Installation dialog*

This dialog is the final opportunity to change any of the installation values. Click the Next button if you need to verify or alter your installation settings. Otherwise, clicking the Next button will advance the process to the dependency check, illustrated in Figure 10-41.

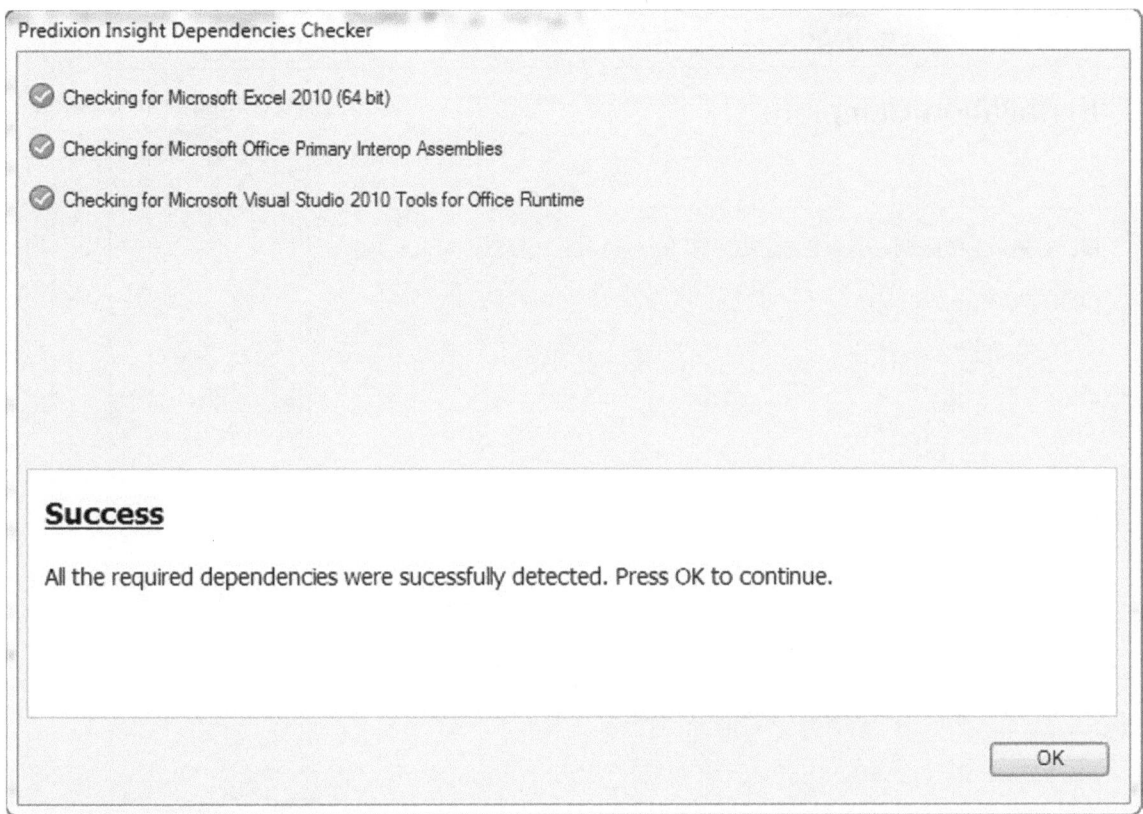

Figure 10-41. *Prerequisite check*

The dependencies check will verify the required software already exists on the target workstation. A failure at this step will likely require the installation of a software component to continue. Clicking the OK button will install the software, and the Installation Complete dialog, illustrated in Figure 10-42, will appear.

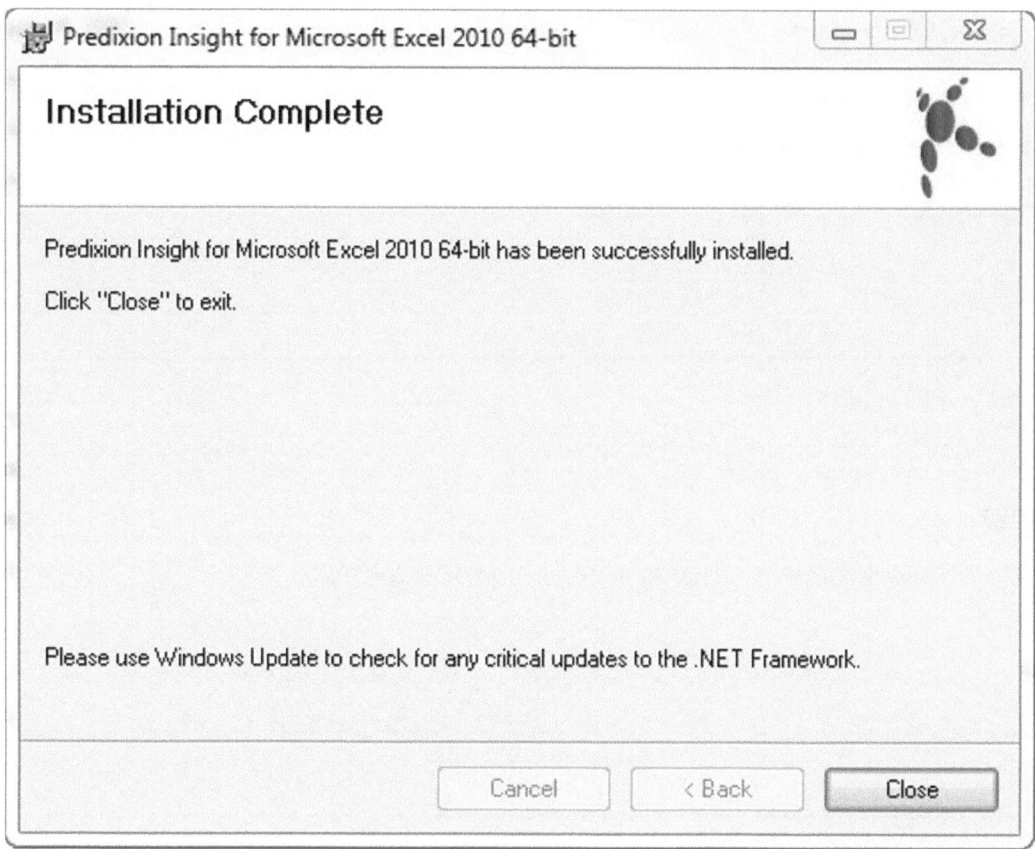

Figure 10-42. *Installation Complete dialog*

Click the Close button to complete the installation wizard.

When starting Microsoft Excel for the first time, after the Predixion Insight installation, you may receive a warning dialog similar to Figure 10-43. In order to use Predixion Insight, click the Install button.

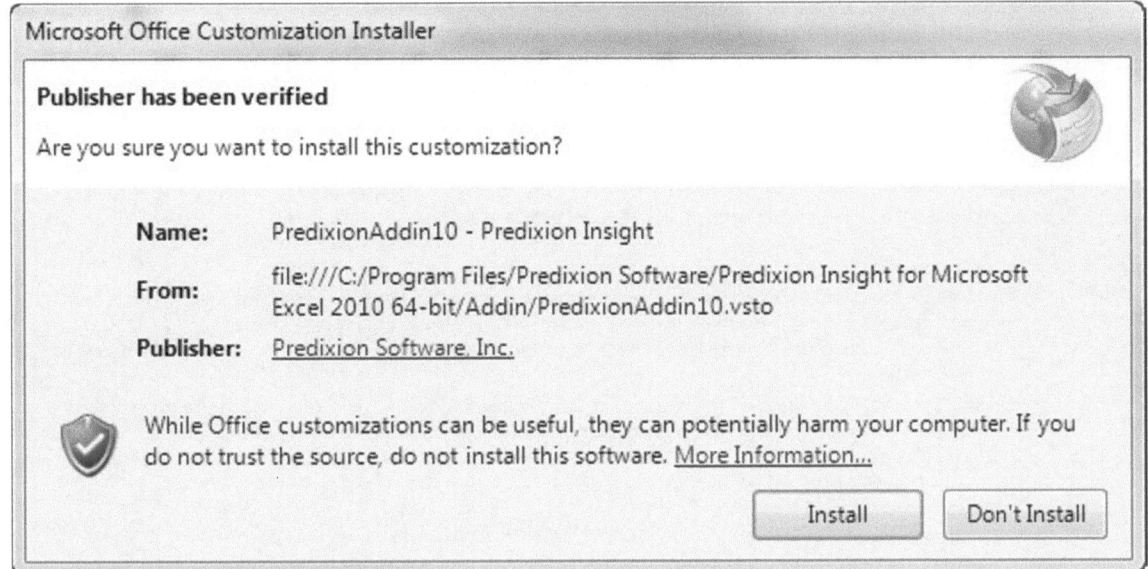

Figure 10-43. *Customization warning*

After advancing through the customization warning dialog, Predixion Insight will produce a banner similar to Figure 10-44, within the Excel window. The banner contains links to helpful tutorials, sample datasets, and support resources at Predixion Software. Close the banner in order to begin our example using Predixion Insight.

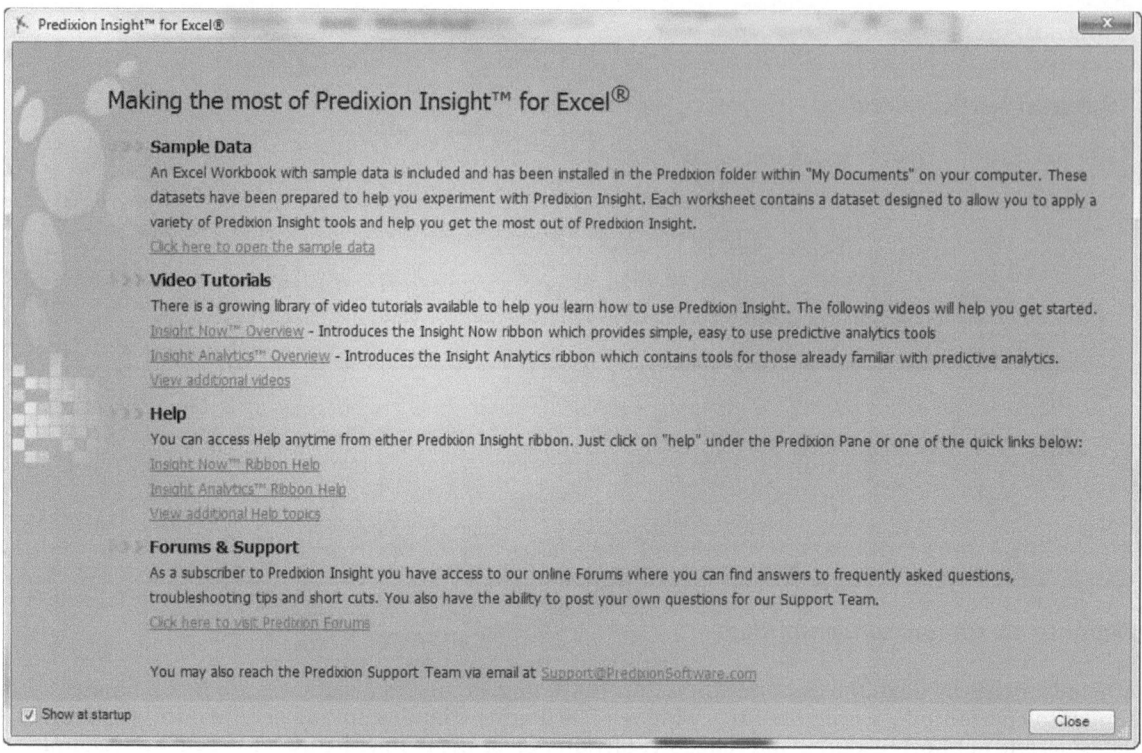

Figure 10-44. *Predixion Insight banner*

Predicting Airline Delays

To continue the airline delay example using Predixion Insight, it is necessary to understand a little about Insight Analytics and Insight Now. Much like the Data Mining Add-In for Excel, Insight Now is a task-oriented interface for creating and using data mining for prediction, forecasting, and classification. Additionally, Predixion Software includes Insight Analytics, which is less task-oriented and more closely related to an integrated development environment (IDE), hosted within Microsoft Excel. As Insight Now resembles the features and functions within the Data Mining Add-In for Excel, we will focus on re-creating our example with Insight Now. Both Insight Analytics and Insight Now are available from the Office Excel ribbon, at all times. Unlike the context-sensitive Data Mining Add-In for Excel, the Predixion Software add-ins are not context-sensitive. Figure 10-45 illustrates the menu items within Insight Now. Compare the selections available within the Insights group of the Insight Now ribbon with the Table Analysis Tools illustrated in Figure 10-31. The options are identical, but the interface is very different.

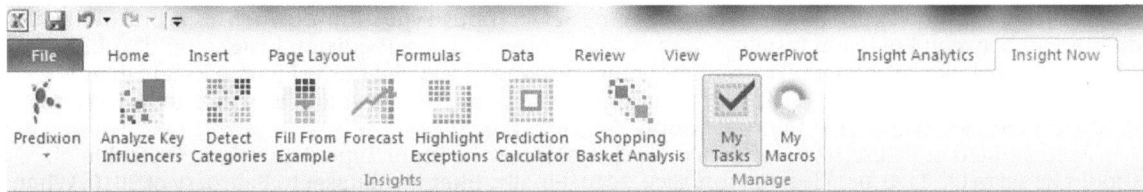

Figure 10-45. *Predixion Insight Now ribbon*

In order to see how different, we will have to create a model similar to the airline delay developed in the first half of this chapter. To begin, open the On Time Performance.xlsx worksheet from the example files. This should be the same file used in the first half of the chapter. Select the Insight Now ribbon, as illustrated in Figure 10-45, selecting the Analyze Key Influencers from the Insights group. The Analyze Key Influencers selection will generate a dialog similar to Figure 10-46.

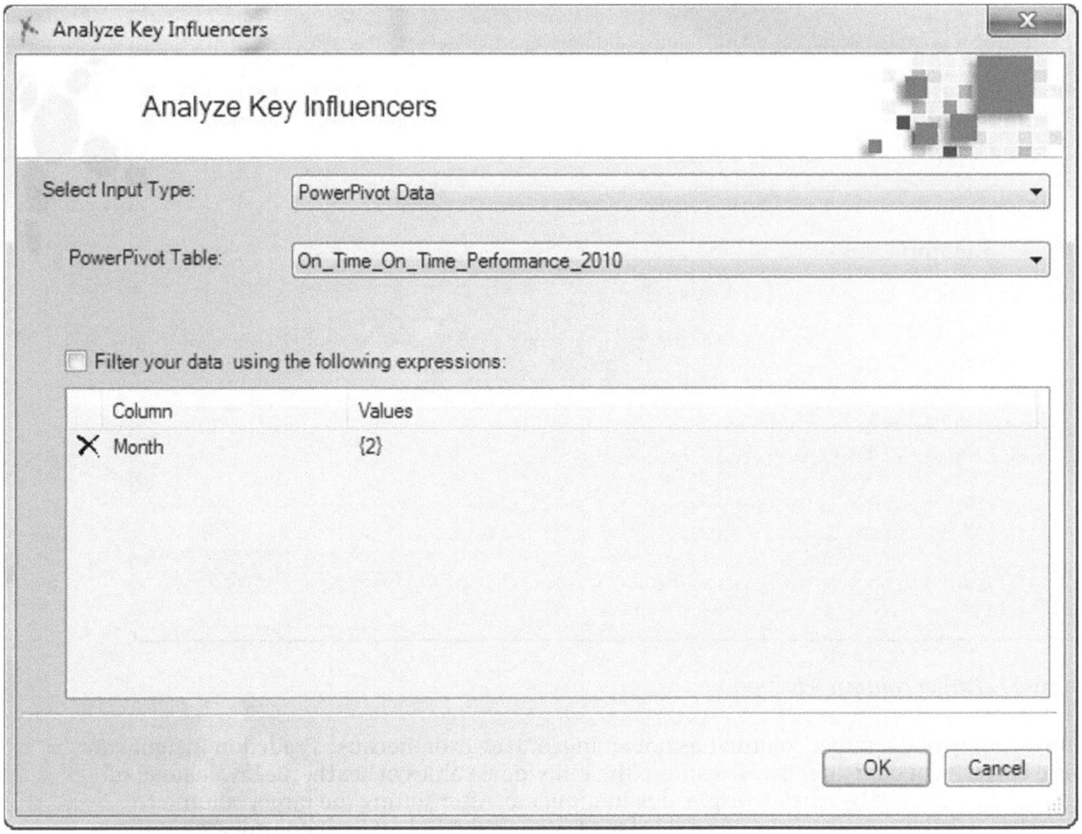

Figure 10-46. *Analyze Key Influencers Input Source dialog*

Notice the option to use PowerPivot data in the Select Input Type drop-down? This is one of the key differences between Predixion Insight and the Data Mining Add-Ins. Predixion Insight has the ability to natively utilize PowerPivot data. The manipulation required to go from PowerPivot to Excel tables is eliminated! Direct use of PowerPivot as a data source also permits large volumes of data to be fed into Predixion's SSAS servers in the Internet "cloud."

As illustrated in Figure 10-46, select PowerPivot Data as the Input Type. The PowerPivot table should be set to On_Time_On_Time_Performance_2010. Finally, filter the dataset to February of 2010. When finished, your settings should be identical to Figure 10-46. Click the OK button to continue to the target column selection, illustrated in Figure 10-47.

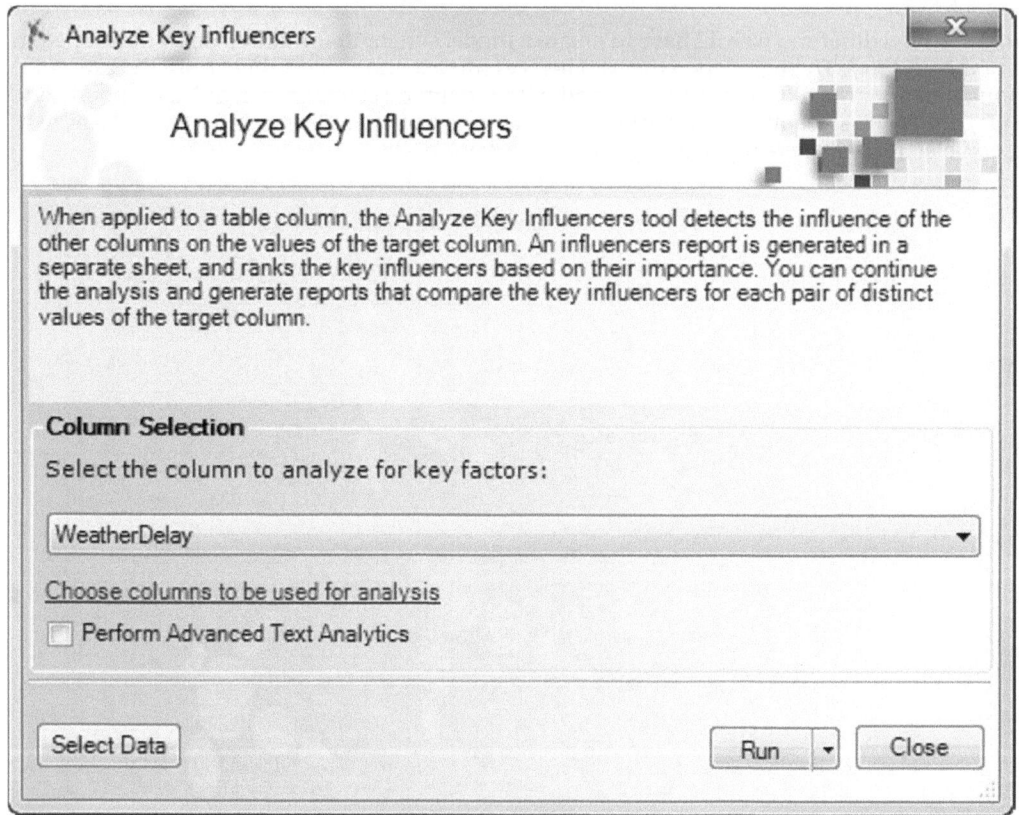

Figure 10-47. *Target column selection*

The meaning of the target column has not changed. However, because Predixion Insight can consume PowerPivot data directly, we can use the individual values of WeatherDelay, instead of aggregating the measure by carrier, origin, destination, etc. After setting the target column to WeatherDelay, use the "Choose columns to be used for analysis" link to filter columns from the PowerPivot table. Following the link will produce a dialog similar to the one illustrated in Figure 10-48.

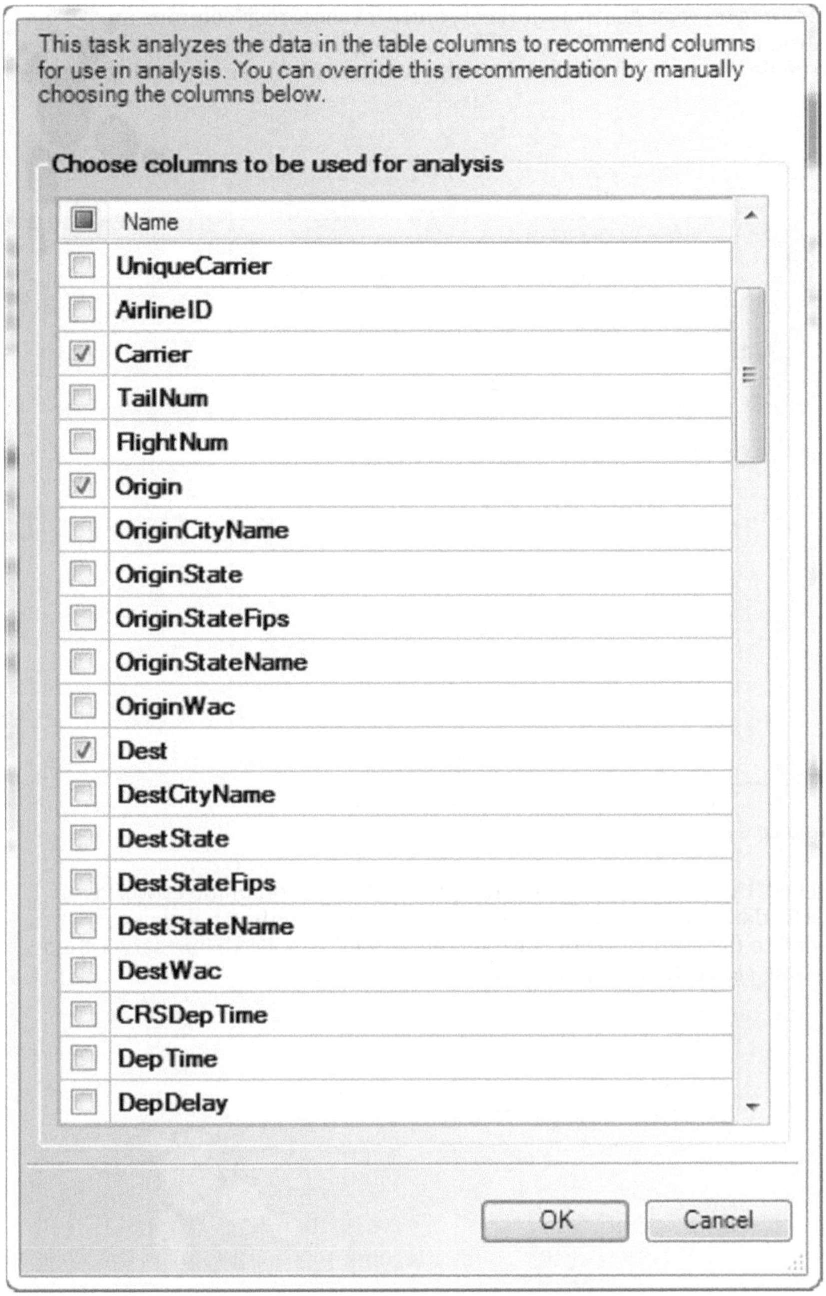

This task analyzes the data in the table columns to recommend columns for use in analysis. You can override this recommendation by manually choosing the columns below.

Choose columns to be used for analysis

☑	Name
☐	**UniqueCarrier**
☐	**AirlineID**
☑	**Carrier**
☐	**TailNum**
☐	**FlightNum**
☑	**Origin**
☐	**OriginCityName**
☐	**OriginState**
☐	**OriginStateFips**
☐	**OriginStateName**
☐	**OriginWac**
☑	**Dest**
☐	**DestCityName**
☐	**DestState**
☐	**DestStateFips**
☐	**DestStateName**
☐	**DestWac**
☐	**CRSDepTime**
☐	**DepTime**
☐	**DepDelay**

OK   Cancel

Figure 10-48. *Source column selection*

Verify that only the Carrier, Origin, Dest, Month, DayofWeek, and DistanceGroup columns are selected. Then click the OK button to return to the Target Column dialog. From the Target Column dialog, click the Run button to begin the analysis and produce the progress dialog similar to Figure 10-49.

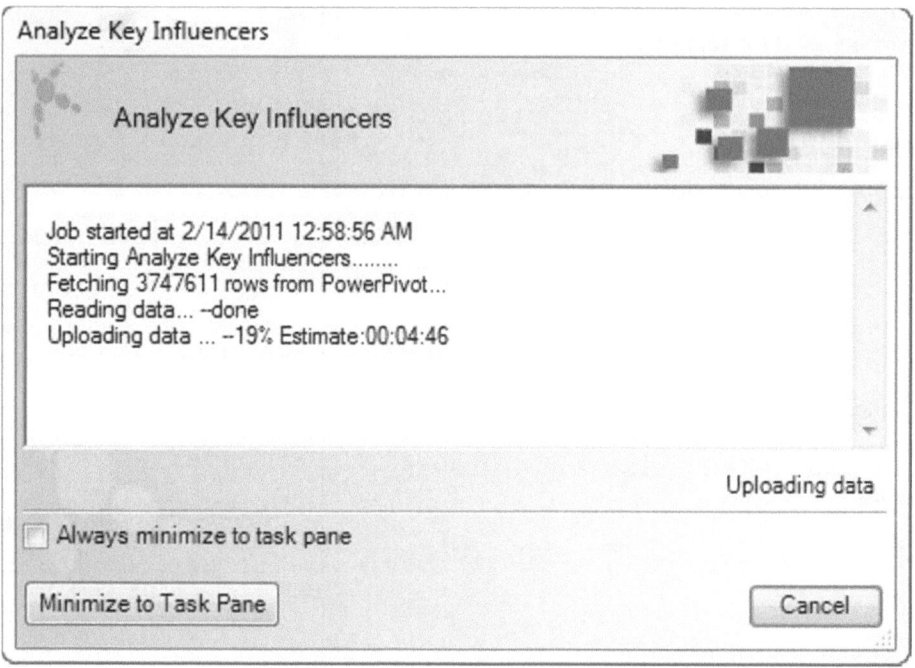

Figure 10-49. *Analyze Key Influencers progress*

After the Run button is clicked, the Insight Now software uploads the portion of the PowerPivot table selected to their servers. The data mining model, created by the dialogs of the Analyze Key Influencers selection, is uploaded to the Predixion Software servers as well. The Predixion server then executes the model, using the data, generating a report similar to Figure 10-50.

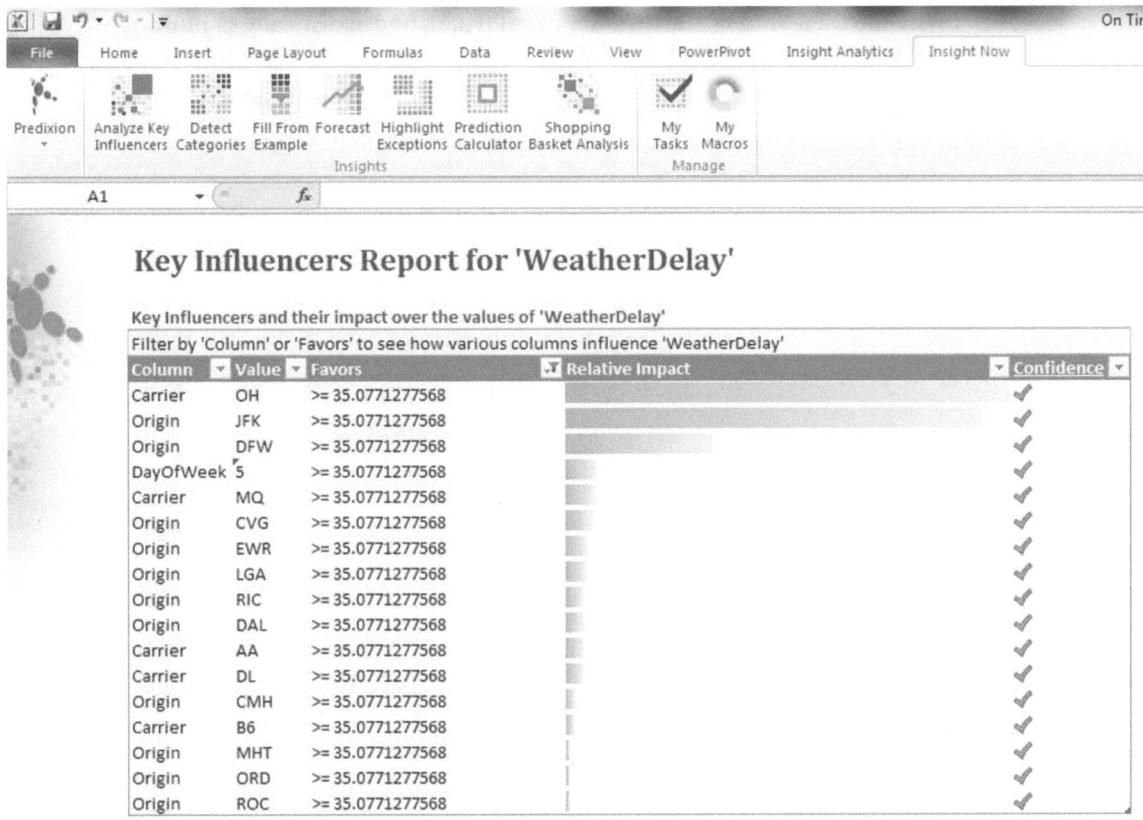

Figure 10-50. *Key Influencers report*

What a difference additional detailed data makes. The classification of WeatherDelay values were different, with the worst level being approximately 35 minutes. Evidently February 2010 was a bad month to be flying Comair (carrier code OH) or through New York's Kennedy Airport.

An additional observation is the speed at which the process was able to move, from software setup to final report. The Predixion Insight process has the additional advantage of being more flexible, should the data analyst want to include other data from the PowerPivot database in the model.

Summary

PowerPivot not only is a tool for evaluating history, but also can be used to model and predict what may happen in the future. Through Excel add-ins, SSAS servers can be used to execute native data-mining model algorithms. In this chapter we have covered the following:

- How to find and install the Data Mining Add-Ins for Excel 2007 into an Excel 2010 32-bit environment

- How to use the Data Mining Add-In and PowerPivot to find statistically significant influencers of measures within PowerPivot

- How to obtain and install Predixion Insight into a 64-bit Excel environment

- How to use Predixion Insight Now for task-oriented, predictive analytics

■ ■ ■

CHAPTER 11

Tips, Tricks, and Traps

Truth is what stands the test of experience.

—Albert Einstein

This chapter will be a departure from the organization of the previous chapters. The intent of this chapter is to organize a collection of experiences into a reference for some PowerPivot situations that don't necessarily apply to every solution developer. For example, you may have the occasional failure of the PowerPivot add-in for Excel. This chapter incorporates a set of tasks to troubleshoot the add-in, getting your PowerPivot for Excel environment back to work.

Also included is information on dealing with the quirks, nuances, dare we say features of PowerPivot that you may find. Finally there are some techniques for tuning your PowerPivot for Excel solutions. You'll learn about slicer overload to increase worksheet performance. You will also learn to trace the Multidimensional Expressions (MDX) query language by which PowerPivot makes requests to the in-memory database engine.

PowerPivot Annoyances

Sometimes they are referred to as features, sometimes "bugs," and other times by the harsher term "defect." By whatever name, PowerPivot for Excel contains the sometimes curious sort behaviors common to any complex software product in the initial release.

Disabled PowerPivot Add-In

Upon starting Microsoft Excel, you may find the PowerPivot ribbon item is missing, as illustrated in Figure 11-1. It is, of course, exceedingly difficult to do work in PowerPivot for Excel without the PowerPivot ribbon menu. The missing PowerPivot ribbon menu is the principal symptom of a disabled PowerPivot add-in.

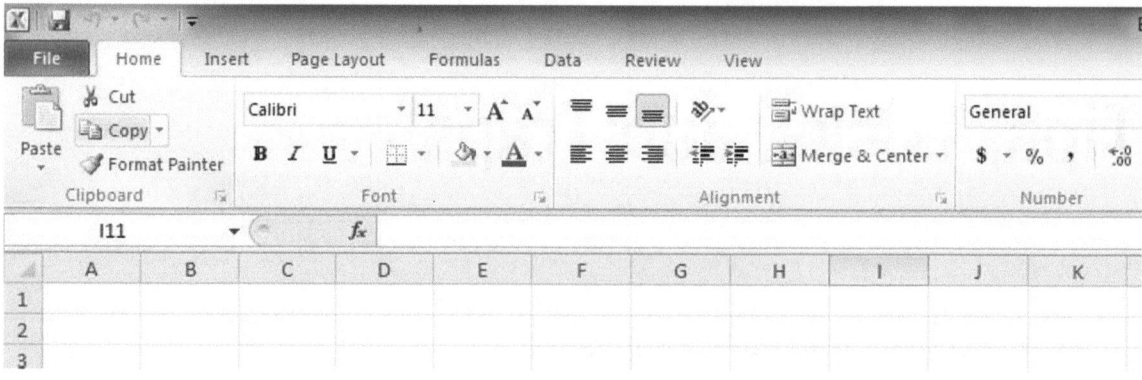

Figure 11-1. *Missing PowerPivot add-in*

In order to get your PowerPivot for Excel environment back up and running, perform the following steps. First, select the File ribbon item and then the Options sub-menu, as circled in Figure 11-2.

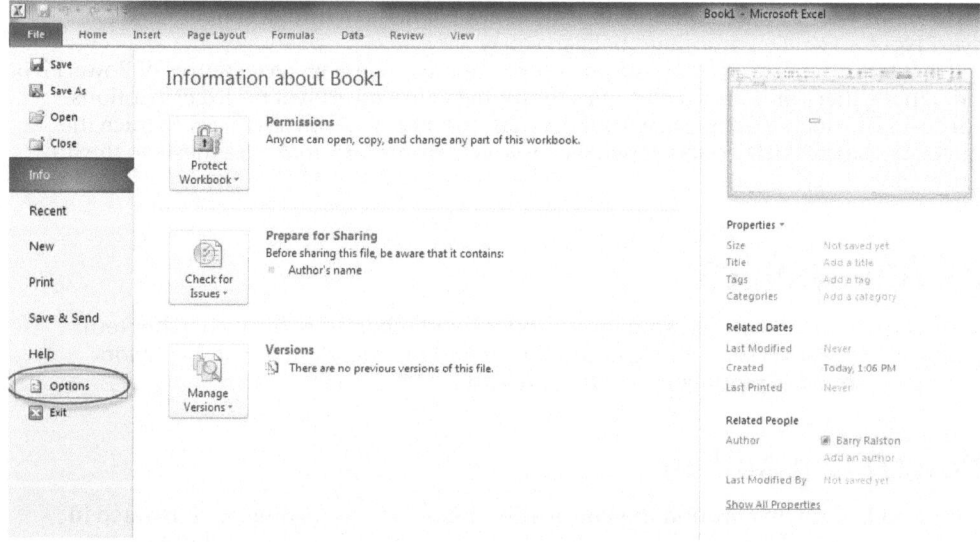

Figure 11-2. *File Options sub-menu*

Selecting the Options sub-menu will display the Excel Options panel, illustrated in Figure 11-3. Select the Add-Ins menu item, circled in Figure 11-3.

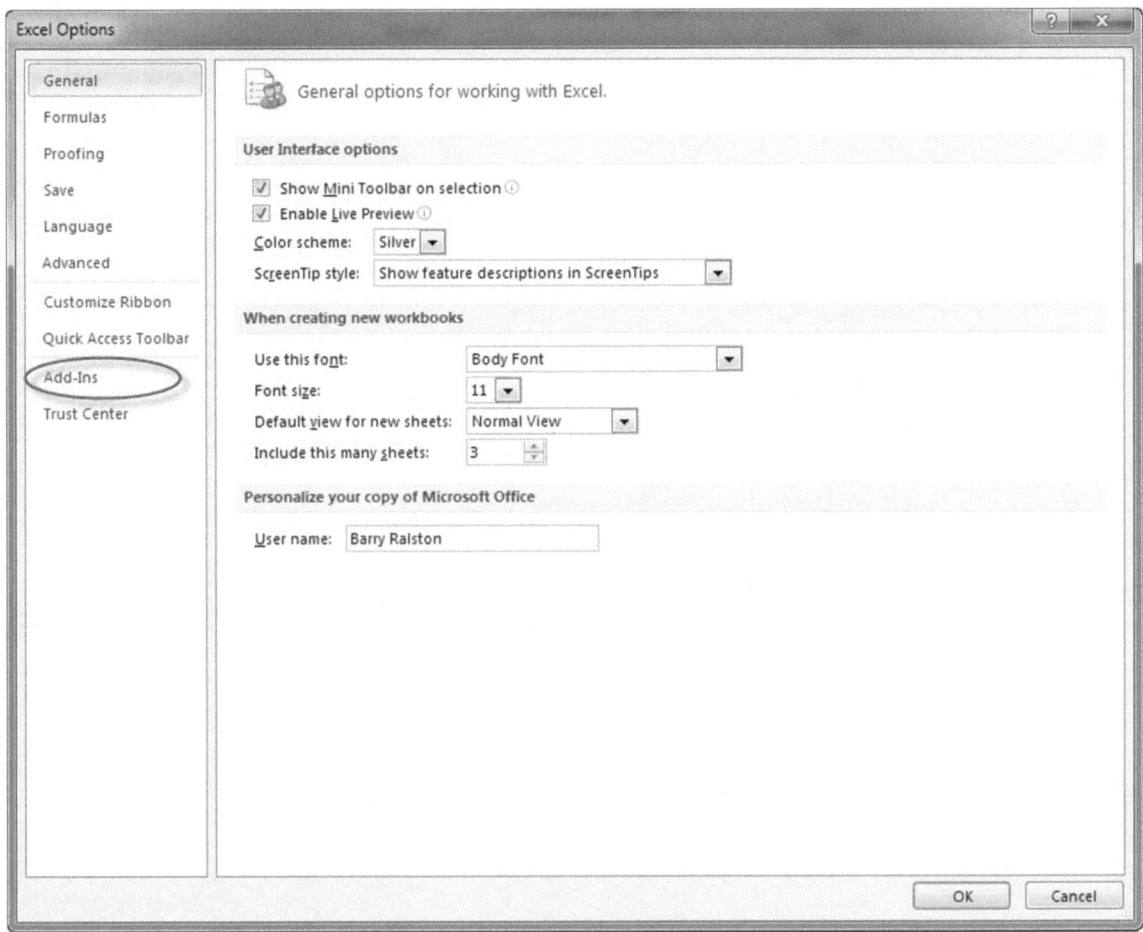

Figure 11-3. *Excel Options panel*

The Add-Ins panel, illustrated in Figure 11-4, will display all of the currently installed Excel extensions. Note the PowerPivot for Excel add-in is a COM-based (Component Object Model) add-in.

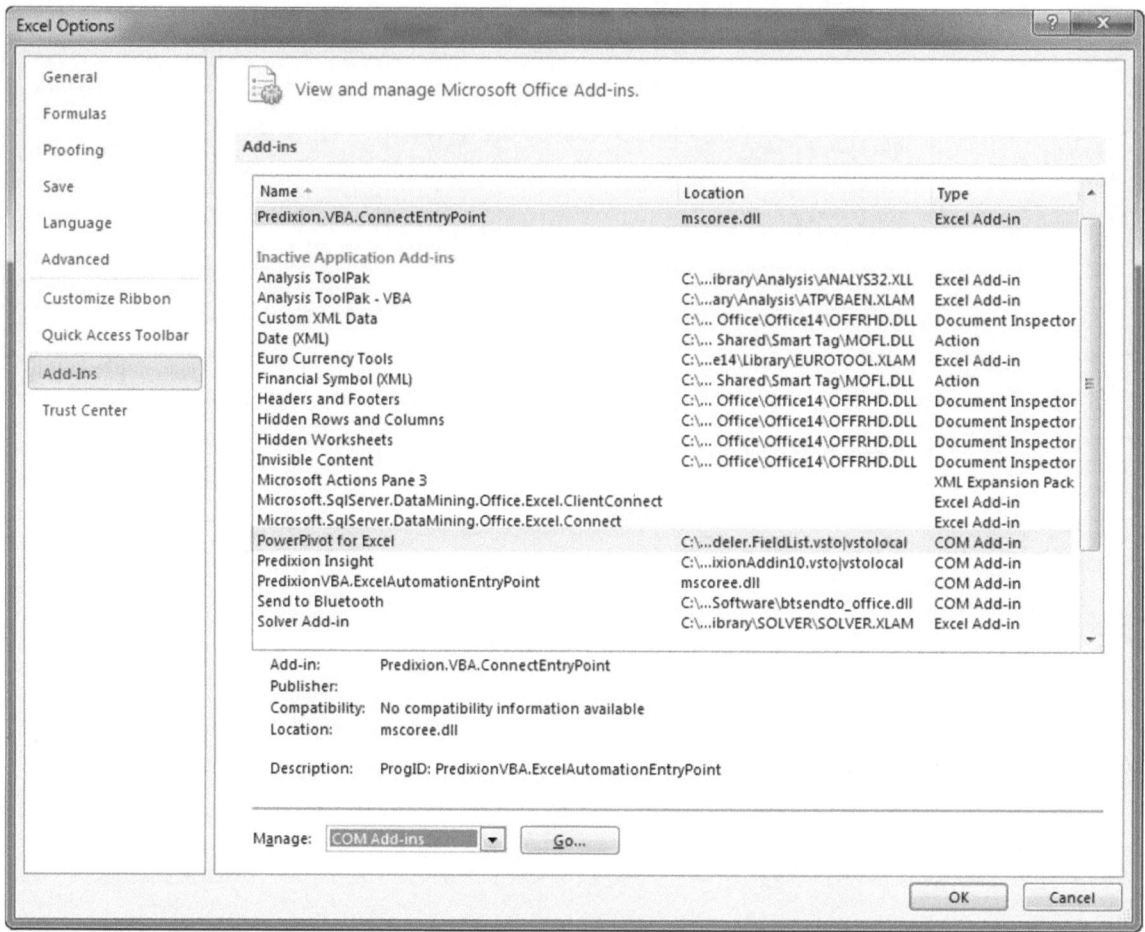

Figure 11-4. *Microsoft Office add-ins*

Also note the PowerPivot for Excel add-in is in the group of inactivated items. Following the next set of steps will re-enable the add-in, restoring the PowerPivot for Excel features. Using the Manage pulldown illustrated in Figure 11-5, select COM Add-Ins (recall PowerPivot for Excel is COM-based) and click the Go button.

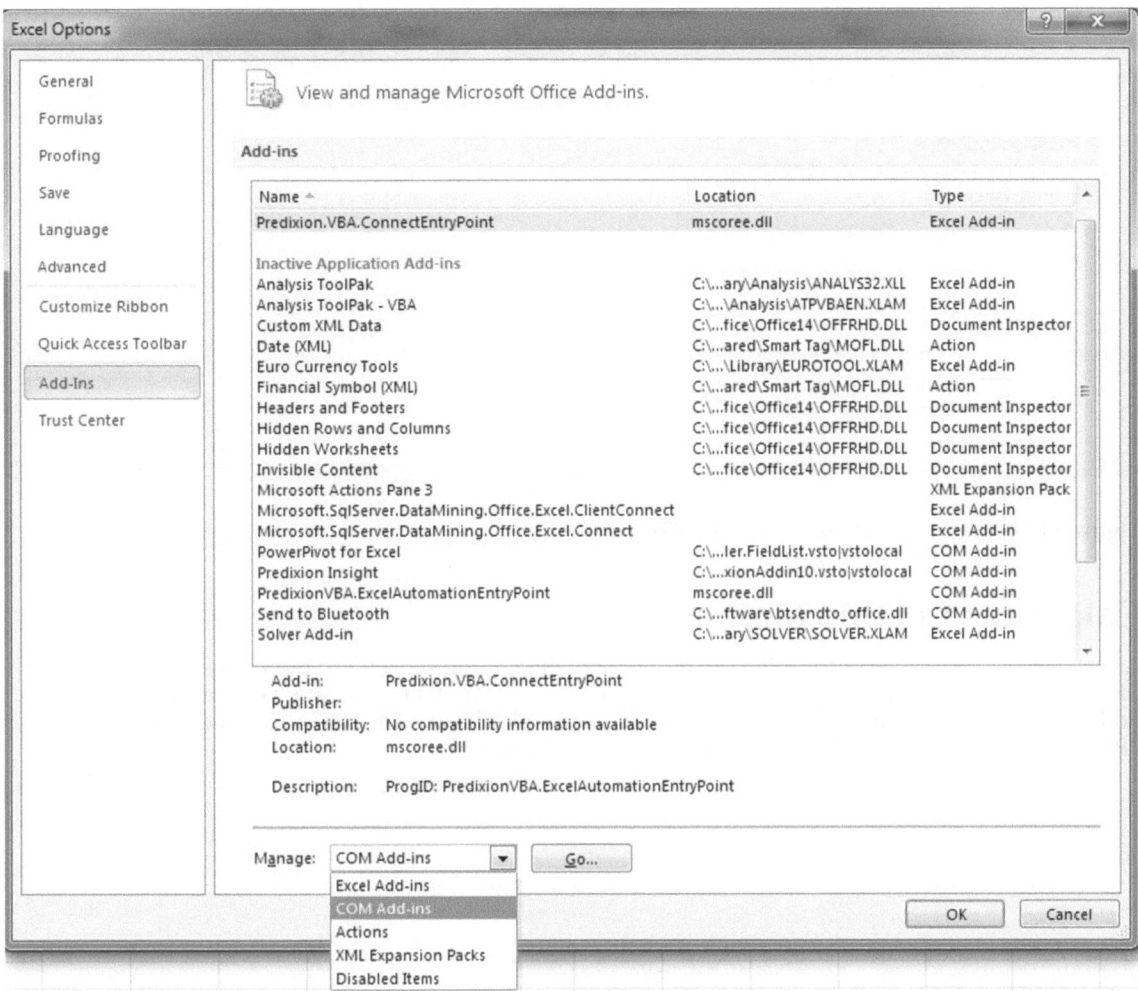

Figure 11-5. *Managing COM add-ins*

The dialog for managing available COM add-ins, illustrated in Figure 11-6, will be displayed. A disabled PowerPivot for Excel add-in will have an empty check box in the list of available add-ins. Click the check box corresponding to PowerPivot for Excel, ensuring it is in a "checked" state, and click the OK button. The PowerPivot for Excel add-in will be activated, and the PowerPivot menu will reappear on the ribbon.

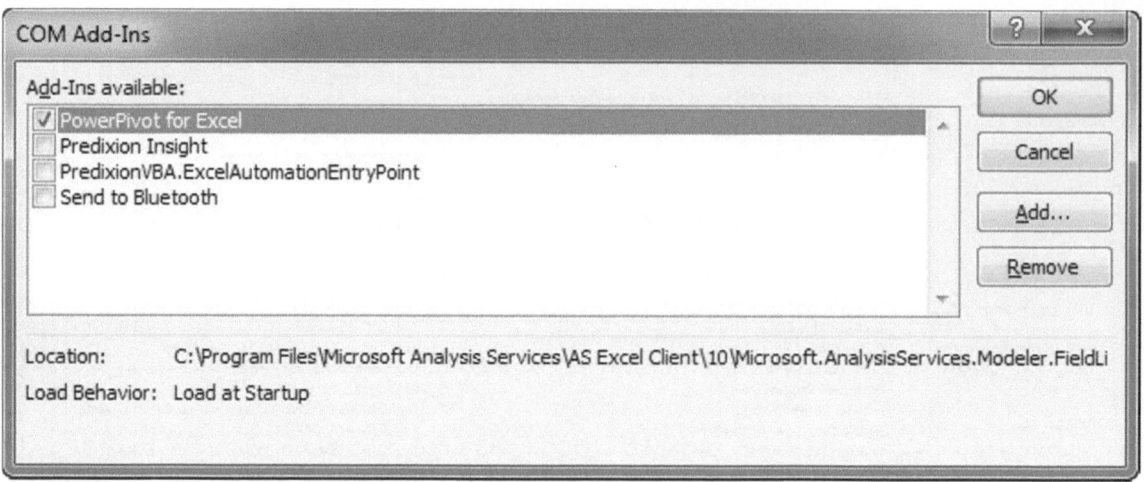

Figure 11-6. *Activating the PowerPivot for Excel add-in*

Calculated Column Missing

As you utilize calculated columns in your PowerPivot data, it is important to remember the PowerPivot Field List is not immediately synchronized with the PowerPivot data metadata. For example, after adding a calculated column to a PowerPivot table, the PowerPivot Field List in Excel will display the "PowerPivot data was modified" warning, as circled in Figure 11-7.

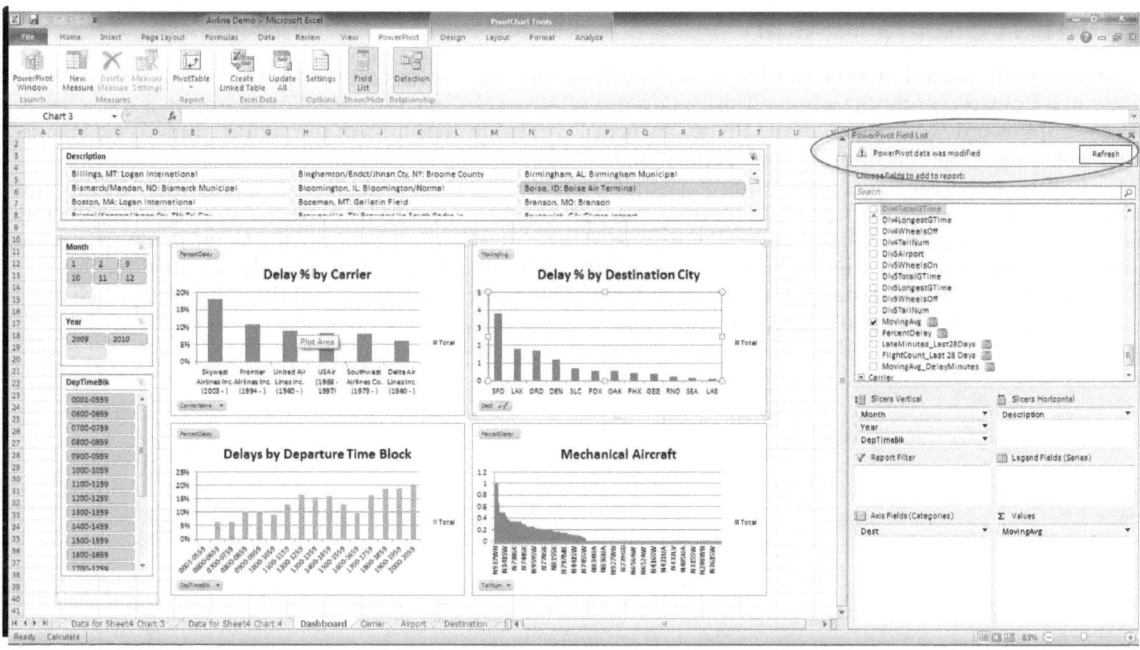

Figure 11-7. *"PowerPivot data was modified" warning*

However, it is important to remember that pressing the Refresh button does not refresh the PowerPivot Field List. In order for the new calculated column to appear in the field list, you must send a query to the underlying SSAS database. Simply interact with any of the slicer selections, even changing the selection illustrated in Figure 11-7 from Boise to any other value and back. Changing the selection will result in the new calculation appearing in the PowerPivot Field List.

User Experience for PowerPivot Solutions

PowerPivot for Excel provides an environment for rapid development of reports and dashboards from related yet potentially disparate data sources. However, the ease with which the data can be combined and reports created can cause the user experience to be overlooked.

■ **Note** I am at heart a database guy who geeks out over the data capabilities of PowerPivot. The intent of this section is to share a few tips on creating a pleasing user interface with PowerPivot. I am not a user experience professional, but have found my way to creating workable user interfaces.

Connect Slicers Visually

The ease with which PowerPivot slicers can be added can cause user confusion. This is especially the case in a PowerPivot report when all slicers do not relate to all charts/tables. For example, if a single slicer applies only to a subset of the PivotCharts or PivotTable elements of the report, there is no visual cue as to how a slicer is filtering each report element.

In this case, I use Excel formatting to visually link the elements that relate to each other. To illustrate the example, consider the reports in Figure 11-8. The Origin State and Departure Airport are connected in that they filter data for the Weather PivotChart. Those two fields affect only the Weather chart, and not others that you see in the figure. To make the relationship plain to the user, I've chosen to color the background cells blue to match the bars in the chart. You may need to explain that approach once or twice to your users, but you'll find that they quickly catch on.

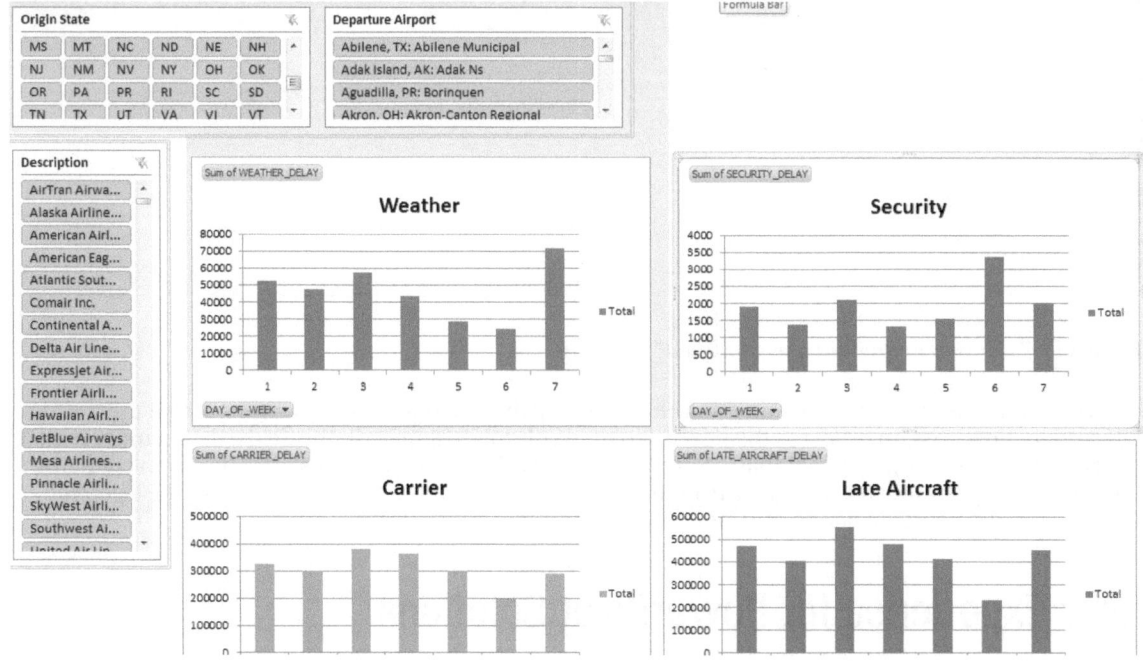

Figure 11-8. *Visual cue for slicer connection*

Lose the Grid

To reduce the number of steps, many of the examples in this book do not adhere to this very powerful tip to create a more pleasing user interface. However, it is widely held that PowerPivot tables and charts simply look more appealing to users without Excel's grid-lines. Combined with removing the row and column headers, a custom-application look and feel can be quickly created.

To hide the grid-lines, select Page Layout from the ribbon. Then uncheck the Gridlines View check box, as illustrated in Figure 11-9. Similarly, row and column headings can be removed by unchecking the adjacent Headings View check box.

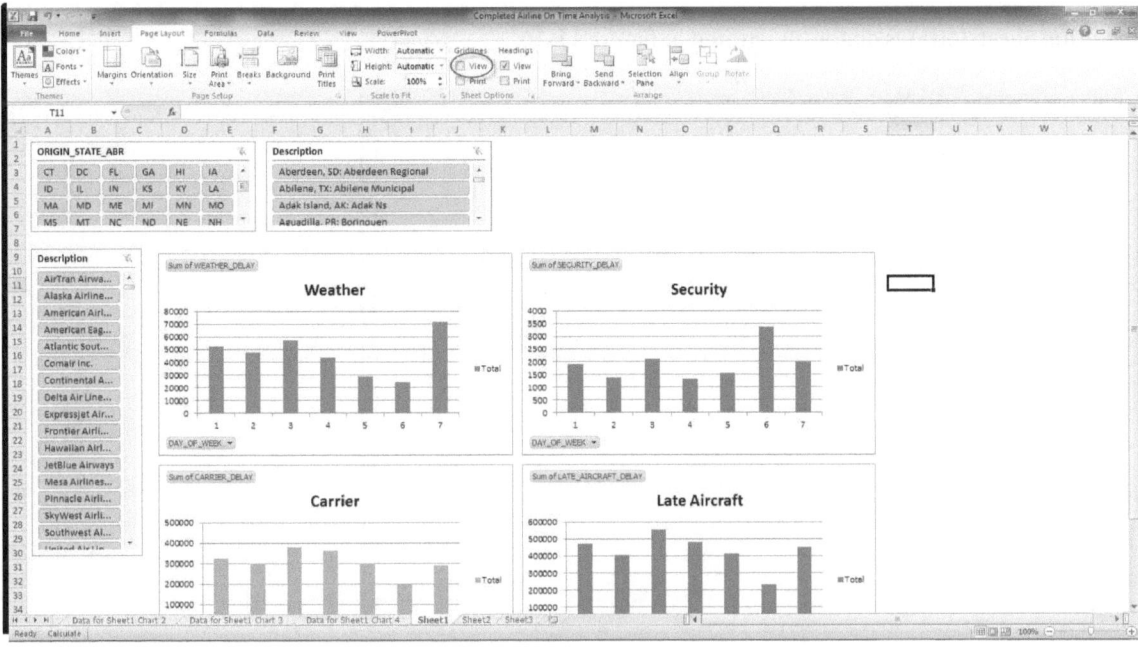

Figure 11-9. *Removing grid-lines*

Tuning PowerPivot Performance

PowerPivot for Excel's features for loading and combining data can be dazzling. In certain cases, these very data loading features can also lead to slow-performing PowerPivot for Excel solutions.

Slicers: Less Is More

In my opinion, slicers are the most visually unique element of PowerPivot. However, they can greatly impact the performance of report (PivotTable and PivotChart) updates. If you incur this type of performance issue in your PowerPivot solutions, here are a couple of suggestions for decreasing update runtimes.

First, endeavor to source slicers from dimension tables as opposed to fact tables in your solution. For example, consider an organization that works with a product set that contains 200 distinct products, and therefore only 200 distinct product names. The fact table for the same solution contains 500 million orders. The PowerPivot engine will more quickly update a slicer based on the 200-row product table as opposed to determining the distinct products using the 500-million–row fact table.

Second, consider eliminating the relationship between slicers. Recall how, by default, multiple slicers on the same PivotTable or PivotChart structure interrelate to visually indicate slicer tiles for which no fact data exists. While removing this feature is not applicable for all solutions, the reduction in workload for the PowerPivot engine is significant. Disabling this feature is a matter of right-clicking the

273

slicer, choosing Slicer Settings from the context menu, and then unchecking the items highlighted in the resulting Slicer Settings dialog, illustrated in Figure 11-10.

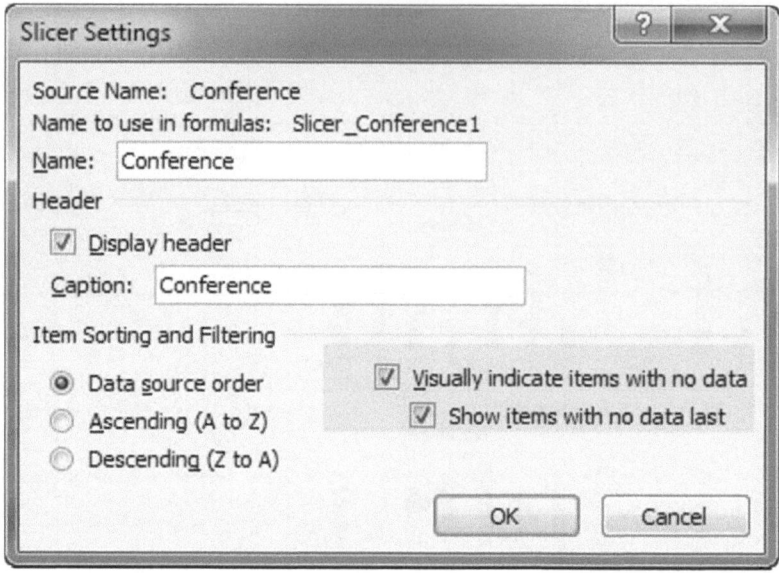

Figure 11-10. *Disabling slicer relationships*

PowerPivot and SSAS Interaction

PowerPivot for Excel is an environment for developing solutions using the SQL Server Analysis Services (SSAS) in-memory runtime. Because the language for querying SSAS databases is Multidimensional Expressions (MDX), you may find it useful in your PowerPivot tuning efforts to examine the queries being sent from PowerPivot for Excel to SSAS. This tactic requires SQL Server Profiler, in order to use the trace files that are generated from PowerPivot for Excel. To begin generating trace files, follow these steps.

First, open a PowerPivot solution from Microsoft Excel. Next, select the PowerPivot ribbon menu and then the Settings selection, as illustrated in Figure 11-11.

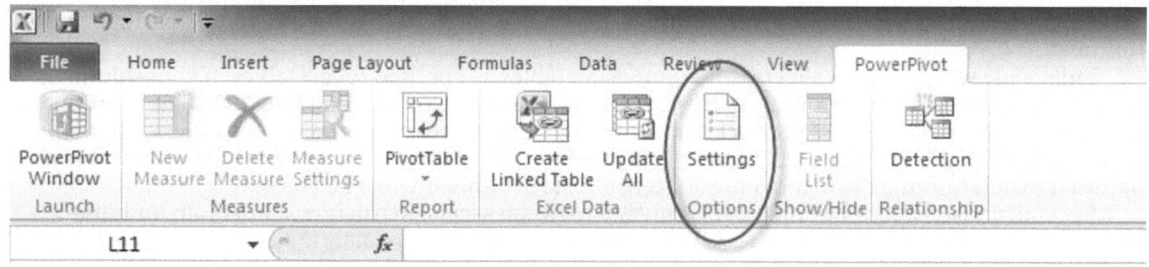

Figure 11-11. *PowerPivot Settings menu*

The Settings dialog illustrated in Figure 11-12 will be displayed. Check the "Client tracing is enabled" check box, and select a location for the resulting trace file. The default location for our purposes will be fine.

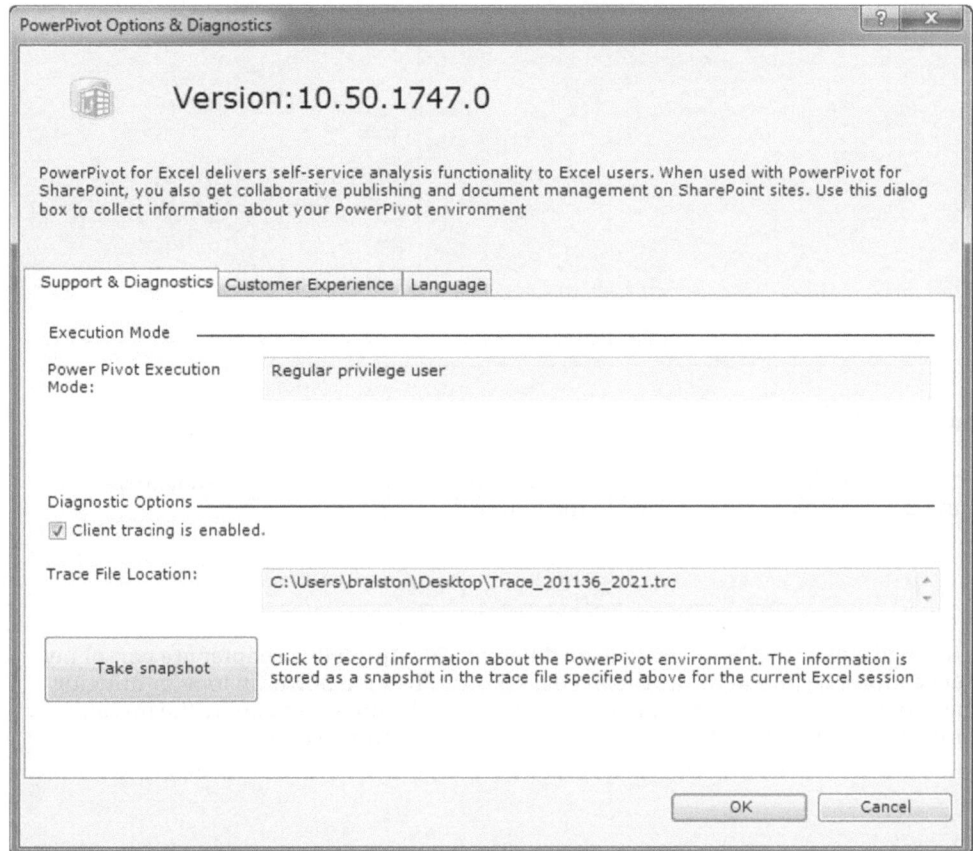

Figure 11-12. *PowerPivot settings*

Interact with the PowerPivot for Excel slicers or alter the composition of a PivotChart or PivotTable in your solution. By doing this, several queries are sent to the PowerPivot engine (SSAS). Return to the PowerPivot settings, and disable the client tracing feature by unchecking the check box illustrated in Figure 11-12. This is very important, as otherwise all PowerPivot activity will continue to be logged to the trace file.

The trace file created by PowerPivot requires SQL Server Profiler in order to actually open and view the contents. Figure 11-13 illustrates a portion of a trace file, highlighting the Query End event.

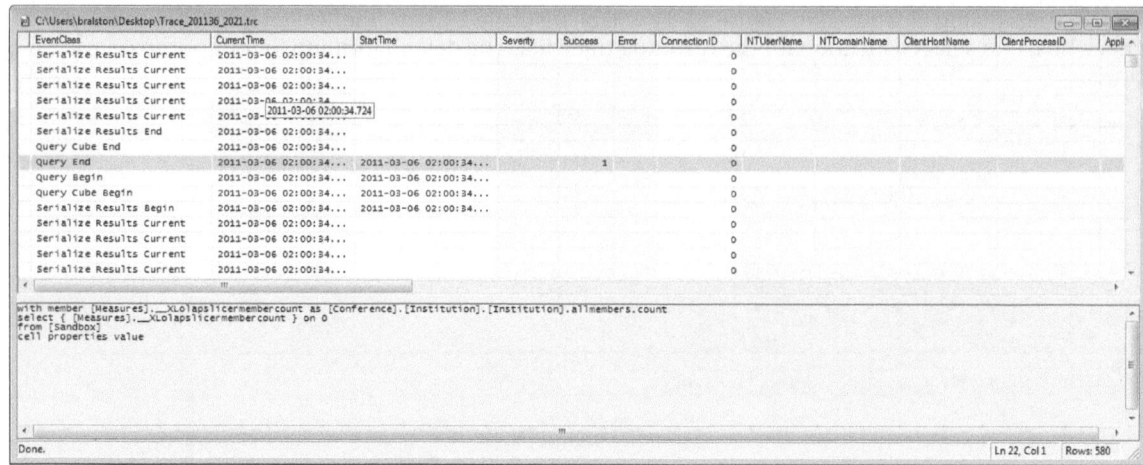

Figure 11-13. *Trace file in SQL Profiler*

Combined with SQL Profiler, the client trace files can be used to determine the actual query execution times and data volumes being utilized in the PowerPivot engine.

Summary

All tools have their rough edges, and PowerPivot is no different. The tips in this chapter are part of my hard-won experience. Don't be put off by the rough edges. PowerPivot is a powerful tool for bringing data mining to the end user. Take advantage of PowerPivot in your business, and apply the tips and techniques in this chapter and from earlier in the book, to make your work easier.

Index

Special Characters & Numbers

% Difference From option, 82
% of Column Total option, 78
% of grand total option, 78
% Of option, 78–79
% of Parent Column Total option, 80
% of Parent Row Total option, 79–80
% of Parent Total option, 80
% of row total option, 78
% Running Total In option, 83–84
=[Insitution ID]&, 53
=MONTH(A2) formula, 74
=MONTH(On_Time_On_Time_Performance_2
010[FlightDate]), 46
=RELATED(CalendarLookup[Quarter])
formula, 75
=RELATED(SortYear[SortYear]) formula entry,
61
=YEAR(DimDate[DateKey]) DAX formula, 75
100-million row dataset, 2
64-bit version, of Microsoft Excel, 3

A

.abf file, 23
Actions section, Management Dashboard, 144
Active Directory Domain Controller binaries
installation, 98
Activity report, in PowerPivot Management
Dashboard, 146

add-ins
installing, 3
requirements for using with Microsoft
Excel, 2–3
Add-Ins menu item, 266
Add-Ins panel, 267
Add PowerPivot for SharePoint to pulldown
menu, 121
Add Roles link, 98
Advance to Final Page arrow, 191
Adventure Works FactInternetSales table, 37
Adventure Works product key, 31
Adventure Works sales, 36
AdventureWorks database, 190, 198–199
AdventureWorksDW2008R2 database, 11–12,
14, 28, 32
airline delays example, using Predixion
Software, 258–264
All Documents view, 137, 140–141, 170
All Programs menu, 230
Alt+Tab keystroke, 7
Analysis Services backup, 23
Analysis Services Connections dialog, 230, 238,
240
Analysis Services, SharePoint, 98
Analytic Chart
Create ribbon menu, 182
for PerformancePoint Services dashboard,
182–185
Analyze Key Influencers, 244, 259, 262
Analyze menu, 229–230
annoyances, 265–271
calculated column missing, 270–271